DYNAMIC MONARCHIANISM

Dynamic Monarchianism

The Earliest Christology?

SECOND EDITION

THOMAS EDMUND GASTON

THEOPHILUS

NASHVILLE

Dynamic Monarchianism: The Earliest Christology?
Second Edition

© Thomas Edmund Gaston 2023

Theophilus Press
P.O. Box 1036
Nashville, TN 37188

www.theophilus-press.com

Edmund Gaston, Thomas (1984–20xx)

x + 395 pp.

ISBN 13: 978-1-7375783-1-4

Printed in the United States of America

CONTENTS

CONTENTS

Foreword

ACCORDING TO CATHOLIC ORTHODOXY, Jesus is a "godman," a single self who is in some sense truly human while also being fully divine. More exactly, he is supposed to be an eternal divine Person who "assumed" (entered into a mysterious relation of unity with) a "human nature" consisting of a human sort of body and a human sort of soul which do not, as in your or my case, constitute a human person. On the face of it, this Jesus is nowhere to be seen in the first three New Testament gospels or in Acts. Many readers have found a godman Jesus in the gospel according to John. If they're not just seeing things, this implies an evolution in Christology between the writing of the first three gospels and the writing of the fourth—on a commonly accepted timeline only around twenty-five years or so. But catholic traditions also insist that the earliest portions of the New Testament, the letters of Paul, also present a godman, although this is controversial.

Did early Christians preach Jesus the godman in the days of Paul (50s–early 60s), forget or hide this message when the first three gospels were (many assume) written (70s–80s), then rediscover it when (many assume) the fourth was written (90s)? Or was early Christianity just deeply divided on Christology, with some teaching a godman while others proclaimed "a man attested to you by God with deeds of power, wonders, and signs that God did through him"? (Acts 2:22, NRSVUE)

If God was really supernaturally delivering the greatest revelation of himself through the Messiah Jesus in the first century, both options seem unlikely.

Seeing this problem, some recent interpreters read Matthew, Mark, and Luke as if they were esoteric works, saying one thing out loud but quietly muttering their real main thesis. Thus, they plainly state that Jesus is "The Christ of God" (Luke 9:20), but they sneakily imply that he's actually God or a "Person" in God. But this is to mistake the genre of the synoptics; they proudly, clearly, and repeatedly proclaim their main thesis, and have no need to mutter. They are clearly not esoteric works.

In this book Dr. Thomas Gaston proposes a different solution. First, he doesn't put much weight on common assumptions about the dates when the gospels were written. Second, he knows that a sober interpreter of the New Testament must avoid anachronism, specifically, appealing to later ideas, particularly those propounded by the coalescing catholic orthodoxy of c. 325–787. First-century documents are to be understood in their first-century contexts, using first-century and earlier ideas. He is therefore willing to question traditional interpretations of John and Paul. Even in the fourth gospel the alleged godman refers to himself as "a man who has told you the truth that I heard from God" (John 8:40, NRSVUE). And like some other recent interpreters, he asks whether Paul's letters really teach any doctrine of Incarnation or a two-natured Christ. In short, what if we can actually see the New Testament writings to be fundamentally in agreement about Jesus?

Although I've first mentioned its theological and exegetical implications, *Dynamic Monarchianism: The Earliest Christology?* is fundamentally a work of historical scholarship. Dr. Gaston is proposing a new narrative of the history of Christian theologies and Christologies that better explains the known facts. Common catholic historical narratives are either that (1) the New Testament writings logically imply and/or assume all the conclusions of fully-developed catholic orthodoxy about God and Christ, or (2) they don't do that, but since the only way to make sense of it all is the eventual catholic scheme, it was inevitable that mainstream thinking developed in the direction of the so-called "ecumenical" councils. But we know that at least as early as the early third century some mainstream Christians claimed that a human (only) Jesus is the real star of the New Testament and had been taught by the apostles, only recently having been rivaled by the Logos of the logos theorists and the Son-Father of the Modalists. If they were correct then both catholic historical narratives are false, and in fact mainstream thinking has veered away from the New Testament teaching of the Father as "the only true God" (John 17:3) and Jesus as his unique human Son and Messiah (John 20:31, NRSVUE).

Dr. Gaston here builds a cumulative historical case that they were correct, that the earliest Christology was what historians have come to call "Dynamic Monarchianism," a teaching which stands opposed to later Adoptionist, Possessionist, or Incarnationist theories about Jesus. A key idea, Gaston argues, is that of Jesus' "virgin birth"—that his mother Mary became pregnant not in the usual way, but rather by a miraculous act of God. As the angel says, "therefore the child to be born will be holy; he will be called Son of God" (Luke 1:35, NRSVUE). Jesus' unique divine sonship, then, is from his miraculous origin, not from his possession of a divine nature, his adoption at his baptism, or his possession by or cooperation with a divine spirit. This sort of Christology has traditionally been pilloried as a "mere man" view, but Gaston's narrative fits this into all the New Testament books and has it as the original Christology from which all others deviated.

Our author argues carefully, as one well-trained in the history of theology. He starts with what we know about Dynamic Monarchian teachers from the late 100s and early 200s that were denounced by the catholic heresiologists and the then-new logos theorists inspired by the Christian philosopher-theologian Justin Martyr. While at a certain point the mainstream turned against Christian teachers of Jesus as a unique man, Gaston shows that earlier this sort of Christology was part of the catholic mainstream, co-existing with Logos speculations and Modalism. It was in fact a Modalist bishop of Rome who first expelled someone for teaching the human Jesus of the New Testament. Gaston then carefully reasons backwards from our sparse surviving evidence, tracing the history of speculations about Jesus' pre-human existence, early rival Christologies by

Gnostics and others, and what was probably a dossier of proof-texts assembled by some early Dynamic Monarchian teacher. He revisits the fourth gospel and the letters of Paul in light of the historical evidence, and as mentioned above, finds that they can be understood as teaching substantially what the first three gospels teach about Christ. Finally, he fends off recent claims that the earliest Christology was Adoptionism, and that belief in Jesus' miraculous conception arose only after the earliest New Testament writings.

This book is a game-changer. This new and more convincing narrative reveals that mainstream Christian teaching about Christ did evolve, but this was not simply an increase of clarity facilitated by more advanced terminology and concepts, as many catholic thinkers have suggested. Rather, it ultimately was a replacement of the human Jesus with an imagined godman, with many intermediate dead-ends explored, such as the various Christs of the Gnostics or the two-self Christ (the Logos plus the man) of Origen. Thus, today's Christian must choose between the human Jesus of the New Testament and the godman of later orthodoxy.

Dr. Dale Tuggy
WHITE HOUSE, TENNESSEE
AUGUST 31, 2023

Introduction

DYNAMIC MONARCHIANISM is a term that has since the 19th century been used in histories of Christian dogma to describe one view of the relationship between God and Jesus. This view is classed as being heretical, as it is in conflict with orthodox teaching regarding the Trinity, the view that God is three "Persons" (Father, Son and Spirit) existing in one "Substance." "Monarchianism," from the Greek *monarchia* (a single principle of authority), refers to the view that God is a single unified authority, in contrast to being three authorities as trinitarianism affirms. "Dynamic" is intended to distinguish this view from another form of Monarchianism, Modalism, which maintains the singularity of God by affirming that Father, Son and Spirit are three modes of God (either serially or eternally), as opposed to being three Persons.[1] The fact that these two views are both described as "Monarchian" should not be taken to mean that historically they were dependent or connected, though they are often paired by their critics.[2] "Dynamic" comes from the Greek *dunamis* meaning "power" or "force," and refers to the idea that these monarchians held Jesus' special status came from the divine power that filled him. As we shall see, this name does not adequately characterize their position.

---

[1] McGrath, *Christian Theology*, 254.

[2] Hippolytus, *Against Noetus*, 61 (3); Novatian, *The Trinity*, 104–7 (30.3–25); Kelly, *Early Christian Doctrines*, 115; Young, "Monotheism and Christology," 458.

Dynamic Monarchians held that Jesus was a man who, after his resurrection, ascended to heaven and to divine authority, as opposed to being an eternal divine Person who was incarnated. This view might be described as Jesus becoming divine, or even "becoming God," and indeed some of the reports about Dynamic Monarchians ascribe to them the view that Jesus "became God." However, we should be cautious as to our terminology. "God," for modern Christians, is usually used to describe that which is uncreated and eternal; on such a definition no one can *become* God. On the other hand, it is important to stress that the Dynamic Monarchians fully affirmed that Jesus ascended to heaven and acquired divine authority; they did not affirm that Jesus was just a good man. As we shall see, the term "god/God" (*theos*) did not necessarily carry the same implication for Christians in the second and third centuries, such that apparently "orthodox" writers might speak of there being two *theoi* or a second *theos*. By modern convention we capitalize "God" when speaking of the uncreated and eternal being and do not capitalize "god" when speaking of other purported divinities. Ancient Greek has no such conventions; the New Testament and other early Christian texts were written in all capital letters. Therefore, when encountering the word *theos* translators are forced to make a choice between "God" or "god." Imposing this dichotomy upon Christian texts of the second and third centuries is problematic. "God" (capitalized) suggests singularity, but many writers talk of Jesus as *theos* in a sense different from the way the Father is *theos*. This is one of the ambiguities we will need to be attuned to when addressing these ancient texts. In this book, I will be using "God" to refer to the Father; all other instances of "god" will be lower case and ambiguous uses will be noted.

"Dynamic Monarchianism" is usually associated with Theodotus of Byzantium (fl. 189–99), Artemon (fl. c. 230–50), and Paul of Samosata (fl. mid-third century), and with those who opposed them, such as Hippolytus (c. 170–236) and Origen (c. 185–c. 253). Thus, Dynamic Monarchianism is often only considered with regard to the late second and third centuries (though see Photinus, d. c. 376).

Dynamic Monarchianism has often been associated with a related view, known as "Adoptionism."[3] Adoptionism is the view that "Jesus was 'adopted' as the Son of God at some point during his ministry (usually his baptism), as opposed to the orthodox teaching that Jesus was Son of God by nature from the moment of his conception."[4] This view is most often associated with the Ebionites (2nd–3rd c.), as reported by Irenaeus (c. 130–202) and others.[5] There are obvious parallels between Dynamic Monarchianism and Adoptionism, which, no doubt, explain why these views have routinely been equated (or confused together) by scholars. For example, Stephen Hildebrand, describing Dynamic Monarchianism, states it is the view that "Jesus, who was a mere man but an exceptionally virtuous man, became God's (adopted) Son at his baptism."[6] Similarly Peter Phan writes of the view "attributed to Theodotus, Artemon, and Paul of Samosata . . . called *Dynamic Monarchianism* or *adoptionism,* and according to this Jesus is a human being whom God adopts as his son at his incarnation or baptism."[7] This confusion is unfortunate because it blends two views that should be treated as distinct. Adoptionism is the view that Jesus was adopted and therefore is principally a view about the Sonship of Jesus. It is misleading to describe Dynamic Monarchians as Adoptionists because they did not hold that Jesus became the Son of God by adoption; Dynamic Monarchians affirm the virgin birth. Equating Adoptionism with Dynamic Monarchianism perpetuates the idea of there being only two views as to the Sonship of Jesus, either Son-by-adoption or Son-from-eternity. The Dynamic Monarchians represent another view of the Sonship of Jesus, that is, Son-by-birth. Adoptionism is Monarchian in that the Father alone is God. Adoptionists like the Ebionites may have

[3] Kelly, *Early Christian Doctrines,* 115.

[4] McGrath, *Christian Theology,* 486.

[5] It is worth mentioning the proposal of Michael Goulder that the Ebionites are better classified as Possessionists, rather than Adoptionists, affirming the view that Jesus was possessed by the Spirit at his baptism. Goulder, *Tale of Two Missions,* 107–34; cf. Goulder, "Pre-Marcan Gospel," 456–57; Goulder, "Poor Man's Christology."

[6] Hildebrand, "Trinity," 100.

[7] Phan, "Developments of the Doctrine," 6.

been Dynamic Monarchians, inasmuch as Epiphanius (c. 315–403) reports that they affirmed the ascension of Jesus into heaven.[8] However, since Dynamic Monarchians did not believe that Jesus became the Son by adoption, it is unhelpful to call them "Adoptionists."

One other problem with conflating Adoptionism with Dynamic Monarchianism is the impact this has on our understanding of the two phenomena. Adoptionism is most often associated with the Ebionites, who, in addition to their Christology, were also condemned for keeping the Law of Moses and for rejecting what became the canonical New Testament texts. The Ebionites, therefore, represent a decidedly different starting point and approach to Christianity than those who condemned them. In contrast, the Dynamic Monarchians, despite moral charges variously made against them, were recognized to be "orthodox" (for want of a better term) with regard to doctrine and canon, excepting only their Christology. The dispute over Dynamic Monarchianism, both conceptually and practically, was a debate within the mainstream of second and third century Christianity. The issue was not that the Dynamic Monarchians were introducing different scriptures or different prophets but that they were interpreting the same scriptures differently than their critics. As I shall argue, the shared doctrine and practice of Dynamic Monarchians with other Christians presents a significant methodological problem regarding how to distinguish those holding Dynamic Monarchian beliefs from others prior to the time when they were formally distinguished as heretics by those who adopted a different Christology.

In this book we will run up against a familiar problem of how to use the terms "orthodox" and "heretical" without being either misleading or pejorative. For example, does "orthodox" refer to what is *now* regarded as right doctrine (and by whom), or to what was regarded as right doctrine in the second and third centuries (and by whom)? Is something "orthodox" because it represents a consensus or majority view, or because it is the view established by authority, and if so, which authority qualifies? Similarly, who determines who the heretics are? Is it modern scholars?

---

[8] Epiphanius, *Medicine Chest*, 1:133 (30.3.5).

Traditional creeds? The consensus of history? The problem is compounded by the fact that here we are primarily engaged in history, not theology; we are primarily describing the past rather than trying to determine religious truth. It is not the role of the historian to pass judgment on who is right and who is wrong. On the other hand, neither is it helpful to pretend that all are equally entitled to their opinions. Someone who creates a pseudonymous text for the purposes of deception is not entitled to the claims they make. Someone who makes claims about the historical Jesus on the basis of little or no historical information is not entitled to the claims they make. The fundamental disagreement between Dynamic Monarchians and their critics concerned which christology was truly in accord with apostolic tradition, which is a subject the historian can address.

One proposal to resolve the problem suggested by Bart Ehrman, among others, is to use the term "proto-orthodox," or "incipient orthodoxy," for those early Christians whose views were tending towards what eventually became orthodoxy. Yet, despite the intuitive appeal of this proposal, it assumes a historical schema which places early Christians on one of many trajectories. This may be a useful historical construct, but is unlikely to represent how those Christians understood themselves. What religious writer sees himself as holding half-formed doctrinal propositions that will later be superseded? Worse, it may fall into the trap of allowing later orthodoxy to define earlier periods, imposing categories and distinctions that may be simply inappropriate to the period in question. This is not to say the concept of conceptual trajectories is always unhelpful, but we should be cautious of reading historical inevitability into these constructs; history may have turned out differently. Lastly terms like "proto-orthodoxy" imply a degree of approximation; what doctrinal aspect was orthodox and to what degree? For example, for the present considerations, "proto-orthodoxy" might imply affirming the pre-existence of Jesus, as opposed to denying it. Yet such a binary choice has a danger of blinding one to the nuances at play. In this sense all labels can be limiting, regardless of their utility. Given the limitations of terminology, there is no alternative to using the terms "orthodox" and "heretical" with due nuance.

This book is about Dynamic Monarchianism, which I have described above as the view that God is the Father alone and that Jesus was born a man who later ascended to heaven and to special status. It will be helpful to add more clarity to this definition. I have already highlighted the current confusion between Dynamic Monarchianism and Adoptionism. To distinguish the former from the latter, I propose that one key criterion for distinguishing the Dynamic Monarchians is affirmation of the virgin birth, and the implied corollary that Jesus was Son of God by birth rather than by adoption. On the other side, it is not sufficient to distinguish the Dynamic Monarchians as those who denied the deity of Christ. Many Christians in the first three centuries denied that Christ is divine in the way that the Father is. Nor would it be sufficient to distinguish Dynamic Monarchians as the antithesis of trinitarians since, though there were triadic patterns in Christian thought, the idea of a (non-modalistic) tripersonal God would be anachronistic in discussing the theology of this period. Instead, I will focus on the person of Jesus and specifically the question of whether he existed prior to his birth. The Dynamic Monarchians denied the pre-existence of Jesus. Therefore, for the purposes of this book, the definition of a Dynamic Monarchian view is one on which (1) God is the Father alone, and (2) Jesus is a real human being, miraculously conceived and born to Mary, (3) who did not exist prior to that conception, and (4) who was later resurrected and exalted by God to a uniquely high position under him.

I have divided this study into three parts, which follow in reverse chronological order. Part One considers the late second and third centuries, when Dynamic Monarchians were clearly distinguishable from other Christians because they were declared heretical by some of those other Christians. Here the evidence for Dynamic Monarchianism is most explicit but this evidence is almost entirely negative in nature and the historian must be alive to the likelihood of bias. This part treats those figures usually associated with Dynamic Monarchianism, namely, Paul of Samosata, Artemon, and Theodotus of Byzantium, as well as some less noted examples, Beryllus of Bostra (fl. c. 222–35) and what I shall call the "other" Ebionites. I also consider other possible evidence of Dynamic Monarchianism from the synod over Heraclides (fl. mid-3rd c.), from the reports about the so-called "Alogi," and from textual variants of the New Testament. The geographic and chronological distribution of this evidence, and particularly the apparent independence of these examples, seems consistent with the view that Dynamic Monarchianism was more widespread than the number of examples alone might suggest. Furthermore, this distribution may support the claim, made by several of the Dynamic Monarchians reported, that Dynamic Monarchianism was not a recent invention but was an old and apostolic tradition. The remaining two parts of the book investigate this claim.

Part Two considers the period prior to the excommunication of Theodotus; that is, prior to the earliest recorded condemnation of Dynamic Monarchianism as heretical. The aim of this part is to explore whether there is evidence of Dynamic Monarchianism prior to Theodotus, what form this evidence takes, and whether there is evidence from this period of an older Dynamic Monarchian tradition. This part has to grapple with a number of methodological issues, such as how to distinguish Dynamic Monarchians from other Christians if they were not being distinguished as heretics, and generally how to form any significant conclusions given the paucity of the evidence from this period. I argue that Dynamic Monarchianism would not have been considered heretical around the mid-second century and that the excommunication of Theodotus was symptomatic of a changing doctrinal and ecclesiastical situation at Rome, as the Logos Christology of Justin Martyr (c. 100–65) took root.

Justin was not the first Christian to affirm the pre-existence of Jesus; this affirmation occurs in earlier texts. I explore examples of such texts from the late first and early second centuries and reveal the varied reasons why certain Christians were affirming the pre-existence of Jesus in this period. I argue that these reasons are neither those of later orthodoxy for affirming the pre-existence of Jesus, nor did they form part of the teaching of the earliest Christians. I then explore some potential evidence for

Dynamic Monarchianism in this period. A hypothesized proof-text dossier may be the product of Dynamic Monarchianism. I also attempt to project backwards from Gnostic (1st–3rd centuries) and other "heretical" Christologies to determine the form of Christology from which they deviated; I argue that in most cases the likely candidate is a Christology that affirmed the virgin birth and denied the pre-existence of Jesus. Lastly in this part I consider two Christian writers usually claimed for orthodoxy, namely Ignatius of Antioch (c. 35–107) and John the evangelist and ask whether they express any doctrinal commitments that are inconsistent with Dynamic Monarchianism.

Part Three completes the project by attempting to determine whether the Dynamic Monarchian tradition may date back to the earliest Christians. There is a lively debate within the New Testament scholarship between those who endorse an "Early High Christology" and those who do not. I side with those who do not, arguing that neither the synoptic gospels nor the Pauline epistles explicitly affirm or presuppose that Jesus existed before his human life. To this extent my thesis is consistent with a significant section of New Testament scholarship. Where I deviate is with regards to how the earliest Christians understood the Sonship of Jesus. One common proposal is that the earliest Christians were essentially Adoptionists, regarding Jesus as a good man picked out by God for special status because of his righteous acts. Were this the case it would be inconsistent with my thesis, since I have sought to distinguish Adoptionism from Dynamic Monarchianism. I argue that there is no strong evidence that the earliest Christians were Adoptionists. I then proceed to explore how the earliest Christians did understand the Sonship of Jesus, rejecting the proposal that they equated his Sonship with his role as Messiah and arguing instead that they had something distinct in mind. Finally, I explore whether the earliest Christians understood the Sonship of Jesus through the virgin birth by asking how early belief in the virgin birth was. I reject the idea that belief in the virgin birth post-dates Mark's gospel or the Pauline epistles. I argue that to explain the extant evidence belief in the virgin birth must be early and I speculate whether this belief may have been part of Jesus' own self-understanding and teaching. In so doing I endorse the proposal that Dynamic Monarchianism, far from being a phenomenon that appeared only in isolated cases in the third century, was instead a tradition that existed from the earliest days of Christianity and was part of the Christian mainstream until the emergence of newer Christologies led to it being regarded as heretical and thus led ultimately to its demise.

PART ONE
Dynamic Monarchianism

CHAPTER I

Ideas about the Logos in the Second and Third Centuries

BEFORE BEGINNING OUR EXAMINATION of Dynamic Monarchians in the second and third centuries, we need to lay a little groundwork. It is impossible to understand the accounts of the Dynamic Monarchians, and in particular the criticisms made against them, without understanding something of the doctrinal milieu in which they were operating. The modern doctrine of the Trinity is that God is three "Persons" in one "Substance" (though modern theologians still differ over exactly what those terms mean.) In the second and third centuries, such an idea hadn't yet emerged. While a number of Christian writers were speaking about Father, alongside Logos and Spirit, in triadic formulas, it is improbable that any yet regarded (what would become) the three "Persons" of the Trinity as a co-equal, co-eternal, unity.

For our purposes, it is particularly important to understand what Christians at this time might have thought about the pre-existence of the Son. A modern trinitarian believes that the Son was eternal, that he was always equal with the Father, that he was always a Person, and that there was no moment in time when the Son came into being. In the second and third centuries, none of those ideas were universally held nor widely agreed upon. As we shall see, Christians regarded as "orthodox" denied or equivocated over whether the Logos was eternal, regarded the Logos as secondary in greatness and in divinity to the Father, may have denied that the Logos was truly personal, and spoke about the emergence of the Logos at a moment in time. And I refer to "the Logos," rather than "the Son," because that is the key term for understanding this period.

When we examine the Dynamic Monarchians, we see this recurring theme: what did they think about the Logos, and what did their critics think? It is crucial to understand the ideas that began to emerge about the Logos in the second century and were developed further in the third. One way to understand the Dynamic Monarchians is as some of those Christians who resisted the emergence of these new theories about the Logos.[1]

GOSPEL OF JOHN

Before looking at how Christians in the second century thought about the Logos, it will be helpful to say something about the source passage for those discussions, John 1:1–18. The first verse of John's gospel introduces something called "the Word" (*logos*), of which it is said it "was with God" and it "was God [or, a god]." Modern readers will often take "Word" to be an alternate name for the Son, and so take this verse as proof-text for the Trinity: the Son was with God (multiplicity) and was God (unity). This is unlikely to have been John's meaning. There is no precedent in pre-Christian texts for a divine person called "Word."[2]

The most obvious allusion in John 1:1 is to Genesis 1:1 ("in the beginning") and the creative word of God that brought forth light out of darkness (cf. 1:1–5). So it is possible that when John refers to the Word, he may mean no more than the creative command of God.

However, many scholars have drawn parallels between the Word in John 1 and the Wisdom personified as a virtuous woman in Proverbs 8. In Proverbs, this character is not a real person, or goddess, alongside God; she

---

[1] Modalist Christians would also have rejected these emerging views about the Logos.

[2] Ancient Jewish writers do sometimes describe God's word as if this were a person (Ps. 147:15; Is. 55:11; Wis. 18:14–16), but personification is a literary device for describing what is not literally a person. Philo (c. 20 BCE–50 CE) comes closest, writing of a "power" of God called "Logos," though few scholars would now argue that John was aware of, or influenced by, the writings of Philo.

is a personification of God's own wisdom. Wisdom is a common theme in Jewish texts of the Second Temple period. Within these texts we find occasions where Wisdom is identified as "Word" (*logos*; Sirach 24:3; Wisdom 9:1–2). Assuming John is also referring to the same personification, it is reasonable to assume that he preferred the masculine noun *logos* ("Word") to the feminine noun *sophia* ("Wisdom"). John's description of the Word as the agent or catalyst of creation (1:2–3), as coming to men and being received by them (1:10–13), and even being called "God" (1:1), is not revolutionary or scandalous in the context of Second Temple Judaism (especially when compared with Philo). Before verse 14 John has not said anything that a first century Jew would not say "amen" to.[3] Elsewhere, when Jesus identifies himself as "the light of the world" (8:12; cf. 12:46), John retains the masculine pronoun, but in John 1:15 he identifies the Word as "the light of men" using the neuter pronoun. Therefore, when John says "the Word became flesh," he is not talking about a divine person taking on a human body; he is talking about God's wisdom finding expression and fulfilment in the person of Jesus Christ. This theme is not unique to John's gospel; it is widely acknowledged in modern New Testament scholarship that a similar theme is found in the writings of Paul (cf. Col. 2:3).

Thompson writes, "Wisdom is not an 'agent' of God in the same way that prophet or angels are," nor is it "a separate being and entity that must be 'related' to God but is in fact the expression of God's mind, will or ways." From this it follows that "to speak of Jesus as God's Wisdom incarnate is to say that he is God's self-expression."[4] John concludes that the Son has manifested the unseen God to us (John 1:18). It makes no sense to say that the Son *is* that unseen God; the Son reveals God because he is the expression of God's Wisdom/Word.

[3] Boyarin, *Border Lines*, 111; Boyarin, "Logos, a Jewish Word," 691.
[4] Thompson, *God of the Gospel*, 134–35.

JUSTIN MARTYR (C. 100–65)

By the mid-second century, the context has changed. Christianity is no longer a primarily Jewish phenomenon. Many Christians are now Gentiles and converts from pagan religions and philosophies. It would be too simplistic to say that Justin was solely responsible for changing the Christian theories about the Logos, just as it would be too simplistic to suppose that Justin knowingly "corrupted" Christianity by importing Platonic ideas.[5] Justin had a genuine conversion to Christianity which seemed in part to have been prompted by the deficiencies he perceived in Platonism. (Specifically, Justin was concerned by the impossibility of knowing God without revelation.) However it is evident that he attempts to understand many Christian concepts in Platonic ways; and, given Justin's undeniable influence on the direction on Christian thought, it is unsurprising that we see those Platonic concepts recur in later Christian writings.

Justin perceives two related problems deriving from the transcendence of God. If God is radically transcendent then (1) God cannot interact directly with the world, and (2) God cannot be known directly by humans. In this sense, Justin is grappling with a problem familiar to all philosophical schools: how to reconcile the transcendence and immanence of God.[6] This problem is, perhaps, more challenging for Justin because by his own account, his conversion was predicated on a rejection of the immortality of the soul and consequently the affinity of human souls with

---

[5] Plato (c. 429–347 BCE) is considered by many to be the founding father of the Western philosophical tradition, and in the early Christian centuries he was widely read and his ideas were commonly combined with those of other Greek philosophers. The Platonism of Justin's day is known as "Middle Platonism," though this is a modern grouping of a number of different philosophers and traditions whose views differ on many important topics. Suffice to say that the Platonism known to Justin would have differed both from that of Plato himself and from the Neoplatonism that emerged in the third century. Historians have proposed that Justin's views are most closely aligned to those of a Middle Platonic philosopher called Numenius of Apamea (fl. mid-2nd c.).

[6] Goodenough, *Theology of Justin*, 139.

God.[7] His solution to this problem, while including other powers like angels, centers on a power he calls "Logos."

For Justin, the Logos is not, as in John (or in Proverbs) a personification of God's wisdom. The Greek word *logos* can carry the sense of reason, rationality, or thought, particularly in a Platonic context, and it is these aspects of the word that are important for Justin. For Justin, the Logos is the rational power of God[8] through whom human beings get knowledge of Being (i.e. God).[9] The seed of the Logos (*logos spermatikos*)[10] is implanted in the whole human race, as human reason.[11] Through this seed, through human reason, each person is able to see "what is connatural to it" (i.e. the rational power of God). Justin explains that the seed of the Logos is not the same as the Logos, as an imitation of something is not the same as the thing imitated; but through the seed the Logos is in all humans.[12] Justin has forsaken the Platonic view that human souls have an innate affinity with God but seems to argue for something similar, i.e. that human reason has an innate affinity with divine reason (i.e. the Logos).

Here were see the influence of Platonic philosophers, like Numenius of Apamea, who says that knowledge is not only a gift of God, but that it

---

[7] Justin, *Dialogue*, 11 (5). Primacy sources are cited by the page number of the translation used followed by the original chapter or section number in parentheses.

[8] Justin, *Dialogue*, 93–95 (61).

[9] Justin, *Second Apology*, 83–84 (13).

[10] *Second Apology*, 79, 83–84 (8, 13). The same term was used in Stoicism in reference to the supposed gaseous element in sexual reproduction, and by extension to God as the active element in matter (Goodenough, *Theology of Justin*, 161). Justin does not use this concept. Similar spermatic language has been adduced in Philo in his *Questions,* 116 (2.68), and in Cicero (106–43 BCE), Arius Didymus (fl. 1st c. BCE), Apuleius (c. 124–70 CE) and others, enabling a plausible narrative of the evolution of this term from Stoicism to Justin via Platonism (Goodenough, *Theology of Justin*, 162; Barnard, *Justin,* 86, 98). However, it is possible that Justin uses the term in express defiance of the Stoics, insinuating that they have only partial knowledge of the whole spermatic logos (*Second Apology*, 79 (8); Edwards, "Justin's Logos," 277). In any case, it is unhelpful to merely match terms and not concepts; Justin's spermatic *logos* is not Stoic.

[11] *First Apology*, 45 (32); *Second Apology*, 79 (8).

[12] *Second Apology*, 83–84 (13).

has the same essence in both God and humans.[13] For Numenius, knowledge of God came through human souls, which he identifies as seeds from God.[14] Numenius held there were three gods. He seems to associate the First God with the seeds, and explains that in this way all things participate in the First God.[15] While Justin has abandoned the view that human souls have an affinity with God and so would reject the description of souls as divine, his association of human reason with the Logos could be viewed as a modification of this position. This would also explain how Justin came to adopt Numenius's analogy for the gift of knowledge (one lamp lit from another) to describe the procession of the Logos from God.[16] When one flame is lit from another, the first flame is not diminished, so God was not diminished when the Logos proceeded from God. By identifying the Logos as reason (both divine and human), Justin has taken a Platonic resolution to the problem of the transcendence and immanence of God and overwritten it with the terminology of John's gospel. In so doing, Justin has closely associated Jesus with the rational faculty of God. Justin is not clear about in what sense the Logos can be both God's reason and a being in addition to God; this is a question that will be engaged with by his successors.

For Justin, the Logos is the Son of God, not because he was born of a virgin, but because he proceeded from God.[17] Like Numenius, Justin is happy to use the language of fatherhood to describe the procession of the second god from the first.[18] This implies that the Logos is a personal being

---

[13] Numenius, *Fragments*, 337 (fr. 14).

[14] *Fragments*, 180 (fr. 13).

[15] For Platonists the people and things in this world "imitate" or "participate in" their transcendent "forms" or "ideas." A "form" is the true reality, which things in the material world "imitate." The highest form was the form of the Good. The form of a chair, for example, is imitated by and is therefore in all chairs. And this imitation can come in degrees; a good person more fully "participates in" the form of the Good than a bad person. As a Platonist of this era, Numenius thinks that God is the form of the Good, so to the extent that souls participate in or imitate God, they are good and divine to some degree.

[16] Justin, *Dialogue*, 94 (61.2).

[17] Justin, *Second Apology*, 77 (6).

[18] Numenius, Fragments, 182 (fr. 21); Guthrie, *Numenius*, 115–26.

from the moment he proceeds from God. For Justin, the Logos is "the First-Begotten of the Unbegotten God"[19]; he is begotten by an act of will of the Father.[20] Justin gives a couple of analogies to exclude some misunderstandings of his position. The Logos proceeds from God like a spoken word, which does not entail dividing the source, and like one flame lit from another, which does not entail reducing the source.

Since Justin says the Logos proceeds from God, it would be natural to read Justin as saying that the Logos was created at a point in time. Yet Justin seems reluctant to use that word. He quotes the Septuagint translation of Proverbs 8:21ff, which originally includes the word "created," but Justin "quietly ignores" this when interpreting the passage.[21] The most he will say is that the Logos is "the firstborn of all creatures"[22] and was begotten "before all creatures."[23] As Minns observes,

> While the logic of Justin's argument requires that the Logos cannot be, like God, *agen(n)ētos* (uncreated), it is not clear whether or in what sense being "begotten" of God differs from being created, except that it is said that God begot him from himself as a rational power before all the creatures (*ktismatōn*).[24]

This ambivalence may be explained by comparison with Numenius, who is also reluctant to equate procession with creation. For Numenius, the second god imitates the first, whereas created things in some sense exist because of their forms; the second god, as the intellect which contains the forms, could not come into being by the same process. Similarly, Justin, while making no use of the forms in his doctrine of creation, describes the

---

[19] *First Apology*, 60 (52).
[20] *Dialogue*, 93–94 (61.1).
[21] Goodenough, *Theology of Justin*, 147.
[22] Justin, *Dialogue*, 132 (85.2).
[23] *Dialogue*, 195 (129.3).
[24] Minns, "Justin Martyr," 264.

Logos as an *arche* (beginning)[25] begotten by God before all creatures.

Justin believes that Jesus can rightly be called "god,"[26] "second" after the Father,[27] and "another god."[28] Numenius had no reservations about positing a second god, but we might assume that Justin, who affirms the *Shema* and rebuked Marcion (d. c. 154),[29] had reservations about positing a second. But on the contrary, Justin is keen to argue in favor of another power called "god," because for Justin this answers the problem of the immanence of God. In those passages in the Old Testament where characters like Abraham or Moses are said to converse with "God," it cannot mean God because God is too transcendent to interact directly with the world. He writes:

> you should not imagine that the unbegotten God himself went down or went up from any place. For the ineffable Father and Lord of all neither comes to any place . . . but always remains in his place . . . Nor is he moved who cannot be contained in any place.[30]

For Justin, anyone who met or conversed with "God" actually met the Logos.

Justin argues that the Son "being the logos and First-begotten, is also God [or, a god]."[31] Yet one might suspect that analogical sonship does not necessarily entail divinity. The special function of the Logos, inasmuch as he imparts knowledge of God, might be seen as justification for ascribing deity to the Logos. But Justin's ontology seems to entail that only

---

[25] Justin, *Dialogue*, 94 (61.1). It is possible that Justin was aware of the well–attested Christian interpretation of Genesis 1:1 that reads "in the Son" for "in the beginning." (See Rutherford, "*Altercatio*," 143). Also see Philo, *On Confusion of Tongues*, 89–91 (146); Philo, *Allegorical Interpretation*, 175 (1.14); Goodenough, *Theology of Justin*, 169.

[26] *First Apology*, 68 (63).

[27] *First Apology*, 31 (13), 65 (60).

[28] *Dialogue*, 76 (50.1), 82 (55.1), 84 (56.4).

[29] *First Apology*, 33–34 (16), 41 (26).

[30] *Dialogue*, 191 (127.1–2).

[31] *First Apology*, 69 (63); Barnard, *Justin,* 88; Osborn, *Justin,* 30; Minns and Parvis, *Justin,* 61.

something that is unchanging is God[32], and there are reasons for thinking the Son does not qualify, as he is not unbegotten and Justin ascribes change to the Logos. One could infer from Numenius that to be a god is to be a transcendent mind; this definition would qualify the Logos for deity ("one endowed with reason").[33] But Justin's favored description for God—*agenneton* (unbegotten)—is not, and cannot be, given to the Son.[34] He explicitly rejects the idea that the Logos is "indivisible and inseparable" from the Father, like light from the sun, arguing that the Logos is "distinct in real number," i.e. numerically distinct (*heteros arithmo*).[35] Both Goodenough and Barnard claim that *heteros arithmo* means "different in person,"[36] but this phrase will not bear the trinitarian (or binitarian) weight these scholars place upon it. Justin explains that he considers the other god to be unified in will with the maker, in that he has never done anything that the maker did not wish him to do, but is a distinct power (distinct powerful being).[37] It is precisely because of their different natures that the Logos can speak to Moses from the burning bush and God (the Father) cannot. Justin is clear that the Logos is a separate substance from God, and it is in this way that Justin feels he can maintain one (unbegotten) God, even while positing a second (begotten) god.[38]

To summarize, for Justin the Logos was the rational faculty of God that proceeded from God thereby becoming a second god who was subordinate in nature and status. For Justin, it would have been

---

[32] "God is the Being who always has the same nature in the same manner, and is the cause of existence to all else." (Justin, *Dialogue*, 8 [3.5]).

[33] Justin, *Dialogue*, 95 (62.2).

[34] Osborn, *Justin*, 21.

[35] Justin, *Dialogue*, 194 (128.4). Goodenough seems to miss this point, when he supposes that Justin (like Philo) endorsed the analogy of light from the sun. Goodenough urges the Logos is "no sense independent of the Father", which seems the opposite of Justin's explicit statement (Goodenough, *Theology of Justin*, 148–50). As Minns responds, "when Justin says that the Logos was begotten from the Father by the Father's power and will, and not by abscission (*Dial* 128.4), this is to eliminate any suggestion that the divine substance (*ousia*) is divided or altered; it is not to make a claim of substantial unity of the Logos with God" (Minns, "Justin Martyr," 264).

[36] Goodenough, *Theology of Justin*, 146; Barnard, *Justin*, 89.

[37] *Dialogue*, 83, 85 (56.4, 56.11). Minns, "Justin Martyr," 264.

[38] Cf. Numenius, *Fragments*, 181 (fr. 16).

impossible for God to be incarnate; only a separate and secondary being could have descended and become incarnate.

TATIAN (D. C. 185)

Justin's influence on the course of Christian thought can be seen by his immediate successors. Tatian, author of the first known harmony of the gospels the *Diatessaron,* was a pupil of Justin. Even though Tatian is antagonistic to pagan influence, through Justin's influence there are clear Platonic undertones in his views about the Logos. He writes, "God 'was in the beginning,' and we have received the tradition that the beginning was the power of the Word" (cf. John 1:1–2; cf. Gen. 1:2).[39] This interpretation identifying the "beginning" of creation as the Logos also appears in Justin,[40] as well as in the Gnostic Ptolemy's (fl. mid-2nd c.) interpretation of John 1.[41] Tatian takes the description of the Word as Beginning (*arche*) to mean that Word is a cause of all created things. He writes, "the Word begotten in the beginning in turn begot our creation by fabricating matter for himself"[42]; the Logos also created humans and angels.[43] Since, according to Tatian, God does not pervade matter, the action of an intermediary is necessary for the ordering of matter.

Like Platonists of this period, Tatian refers to a two-stage creation. The potential creation was established by the Logos while it is still within God. Then the Logos is begotten, and in turn begets and then orders matter with the "shapes" from God;[44] just as in Plato's *Timaeus* the Craftsman looks to the realm of the forms and puts them into matter. The idea that the potential creation is formed by the Logos prior to the begetting of the Logos indicates that for Tatian the Logos was the rational power of God prior to proceeding from God as a separate substance.

---

[39] Tatian, *Address,* 11 (5.1).

[40] Justin, *Dialogue,* 93–94 (61.1).

[41] For Ptolemy the Beginning (= Son) is a different entity from the Word. See Irenaeus, *Against the Heresies (Book 1),* 44, 46 (1.8.5, 1.9.2).

[42] Tatian, *Address,* 11 (5.3).

[43] *Address,* 13 (7.1).

[44] Tatian, *Address,* 11 (5.3), 23 (12.1), 9 (4.2).

The Logos is described as springing forth from God and being begotten by him.[45] Tatian uses two analogies from Justin to describe this process: a lamp lit from another and spoken words. Both analogies are designed to show that in begetting the Logos, God is not diminished, and presumably retains his rational power.[46] Like Justin, Tatian seems ambiguous on whether the Logos is created. The Logos is described as the "firstborn work" of God and the "beginning of the universe."[47] This would imply that the Logos has a beginning and, by the same logic applied to matter, is not of equal power to God.[48]

ATHENAGORAS OF ATHENS (C. 133–C. 190)

While it is not explicitly recorded that Athenagoras was a pupil of Justin, this seems likely or at least he was influenced by Justin's writings. However, we also see in Athenagoras the influence of the Athenian Platonic tradition, particularly that represented by his close contemporary, the Platonist philosopher, Alcinous (fl. late 2nd c.). Athenagoras believes the Son is in some sense one with the Father. He writes,

> The Son of God is Word of the Father in thought and power. All things were made through Him and after His fashion. The Father and Son are one. The Son being in the Father and the Father in the Son by the powerful union of the Spirit, the Son of God is mind and Word of the Father.[49]

Athenagoras has inherited the tradition that the Son (as Logos) was instrumental to the creation of the world, and has reasoned that because the creator must be unbegotten, there can be only one creator. Although Athenagoras is keen to speak of only one creator,[50] we will see that he also

---

[45] *Address*, II (5.1, 5.3).
[46] *Address*, II (5.2).
[47] *Address*, II (5.1).
[48] *Address*, II (5.3).
[49] Athenagoras, *Embassy*, 40 (10).
[50] Athenagoras, *Embassy*, 33–39 (4–8).

wants to separate out God and the Logos. It is interesting to note the comparison with contemporary philosophers. The Platonist Numenius, for example, did not see a problem with distinguishing the first cause from the creator of the world, presumably because he was able to distinguish two separate acts or causations: the final and efficient causes of the world.[51] In this regard, Athenagoras is closer to Alcinous, for whom first cause and creator were the same.[52]

Having committed himself to two distinct personal beings (Father and Son), Athenagoras feels compelled to explain what "Son" means. His answer, in presentation, if not substance, is Platonic: "The Son of God is mind [*nous*] and Word [*logos*] of the Father."[53] During the Middle Platonic period we begin to the emergence of a triadic hierarchy, which will become the three hypostases of Neoplatonism. Emphasizing the transcendence of the first principle, God or the One, leads to creation being ascribed to a second principle, often called Nous, though the extent to which Nous is separate from God will vary with different Platonists. Middle Platonists will differ as to whether the forms/ideas, the intellectual realm, are the same as the Nous or exist independently. The utility of the Platonic Nous for Athenagoras is its quasi-independent status (cf. Plutarch [c. 45–120][54]). He can comfortably talk of Father and Nous separately even while equivocating about the way in which they are separate. This also allows Athenagoras to reconcile the Christian description of the Son as "first begotten" with his conclusion that the Son is necessarily uncreated. God is "eternal mind" and "eternally rational" and so had the Son "in himself" from the beginning; but the Son "proceeded" from God.[55] Here, we see the beginnings of the distinction

---

[51] ". . . as the farmer stands to the man who does the planting, in exactly the same way does the first god relate to the creator." (Numenius, *Fragments*, 180 [fr. 13]) See also Dillon, *Middle Platonists*, 366–72.

[52] Dillon, *Middle Platonists*, 282–84.

[53] Athenagoras, *Embassy*, 40 (10).

[54] Dillon, *Middle Platonism*, 200.

[55] Athenagoras, *Embassy*, 40 (10). Compare with Plutarch's statement that "This fable teaches by its legend that the mind [*nous*] and reason [*logos*] of the god, fixed amid the unseen and invisible, advanced [*proelthen*] to generation [*genesin*] by means of motion" (Plutarch, *Isis and Osiris*, 149 [376C]).

between begotten ("First-begotten") and created ("did not indeed come to be"). The most plausible interpretation of Athenagoras is that God had the faculty of reason (*logikos*) prior to the temporal generation of the personal Logos at the moment of creation.[56] Athenagoras believes he has scriptural support for the generation of the Son, though the passage he cites states explicitly that Wisdom was created (Prov. 8:22). This would seem to imply his concept of the "proceeding" of the Son owes more to philosophy than the Bible.

Athenagoras also describes the Son as the Idea (*idea*) for creation, the pattern after which all creation is made.[57] Athenagoras presupposed a distinction between Ideas (*idea*) and Forms (*eidos*)—terms used interchangeably by Plato. Athenagoras distinguishes the immanent Forms, "Forms-in-Matter" (*ta eide ta en te hule*) from the transcendent Idea (= the Son).[58] As Ruskin writes,

> It may in fact be that Athenagoras' employment of *eidos* rather than *idea* here may be a way of underlining that, for him, the philosophers did not actually know the true 'Idea' but merely those objects which are modelled in some way or other on that primary and sole 'Idea.'[59]

Here again we see Athenagoras engaging in a contemporary philosophical discussion, this time the relationship between the Ideas and God. He identifies the Nous with a singular Idea, which is the paradigm from which the Forms are copied. Yet the Idea is not passive but is also identified as the creative power (*energeia*): "for in his likeness and through him all things came into existence."[60]

---

[56] Barnard, "God, the Logos," 84.
[57] *Athenagoras, Embassy*, 40 (10).
[58] Rankin, *Athenagoras*, 58.
[59] Rankin, *Athenagoras*, 58.
[60] *Athenagoras, Embassy*, 40 (10).

THEOPHILUS OF ANTIOCH (D. C. 185)

Theophilus of Antioch is another Christian thinker who follows closely in the tradition started by Justin. Like Justin, Theophilus is convinced of the need for an intermediary between God and the world. For instance, it was the Logos, not God, who conversed with Adam in the garden. Like Tatian, Theophilus identifies the Logos as "the beginning."[61]

Theophilus says that God was originally alone, but the Logos was innate (*endiatheton*) in him as his mind. God formed a plan for creation and then generated the Logos as the firstborn of creation, making him external (*prophorikon*). This generation did not deprive God of the Logos (or of his reason) but made an external Logos with whom God converses.[62] This distinction between *logos endiathetos* (internal discourse) and *logos prophorikos* (uttered discourse), as applied to human speech, derives from Platonism,[63] and is also to be found in Philo. Here Theophilus is beginning to grapple with the problem of how the Logos can be both God's reason/mind and be something separate from God. Curry writes,

> Is it possible for the *Logos endiathetos* and the *Logos prophorikos* to exist in different places simultaneously? For Theophilus it is, as he envisions a continual line of communication existing between God and his Logos (2.22).[64]

Here Curry seems to ignore the distinction between the internal Logos, as God's mind, and the external Logos as separate person. Theophilus has now explicitly distinguished two different "stages" in the Logos.

---

[61] Theophilus, *To Autolycus*, 5 (1.3).
[62] *To Autolycus*, 63 (2.22).
[63] Plutarch, *Morals*, 35 (777b).
[64] Curry, "Theogony of Theophilus," 321.

The Logos has a creative function. Theophilus writes "God made everything through Logos and Sophia, for by his Logos the heavens were made firm and by his Spirit all their power" (cf. Ps. 32:6).[65]

IRENAEUS OF LYONS (C. 130–C. 202)

Irenaeus of Lyons, though not a philosopher, is significantly influenced by Justin and may have been another of his pupils.[66] Irenaeus also had a significant influence in the direction of Christian thought.

Irenaeus is often unclear and equivocates over terminology. For instance, Irenaeus says that "There is one God Almighty, who created all things through his Word,"[67] but also describes the Word as the "maker of all things" and the "Creator of the world."[68] Irenaeus writes, "His own Word is sufficient for the formation of all things."[69] By ascribing creative actions to both Father and Son, he is not saying they are the same. The Father is the ultimate source of creation, who creates through the Word. In contrast, the efficient cause of the world was, strictly speaking, the Word, not the Father.

Like those who preceded him, Irenaeus explains theophanies as involving the Logos. He says that it was the Word who walked in Eden with Adam, who spoke with Abraham, who was a wanderer with Jacob, who spoke with Moses, and who appeared to Balaam.[70] He writes, "for it was not the Father of all, who is not seen by the world . . . [it is not] this

[65] Theophilus, *To Autolycus*, 55 (17).

[66] Slusser, "Irenaeus Learn," 518–19.

[67] Irenaeus, *Against the Heresies (Book 1)*, 80 (1.22). For books 1–3 I will cite and quote from the three recent volumes translated by Unger and Dillon (books 1 and 2) and by Unger and Steenberg (book 3) in which this work is called *Against the Heresies*. For books 4–5 I shall have to cite the older translation by Roberts, Donaldson, and Coxe in the late 19th c. Volume 1 of *the Ante-Nicene Fathers* series, where this work is entitled *Against Heresies*.

[68] Irenaeus, *Against Heresies*, 539, (5.13.6), 547 (5.18.3). In another short work he refers to the Son as "the creative Word" (Irenaeus, *Demonstration*, 64 [38]).

[69] Irenaeus, *Against the Heresies (Book 2)*, 21 (2.2.5).

[70] Irenaeus, *Demonstration*, 47 (12), 69 (44), 66 (40), 70 (46); Irenaeus, *Fragments*, 577, 572 (fr. 53, 54, 23).

One who, standing in a very small space, talked with Abraham, but the word of God."[71] This is reminiscent of Justin's argument that God could not be confined to a spot on earth.[72] And yet Irenaeus is adamant that the prophets did not see a different god from the Father.[73] On the one hand Irenaeus seems to require some ontological distinction between the Father and the Word; on the other, Irenaeus will not allow for the existence of another god. There seems a disparity between what Irenaeus's arguments require and what he is prepared to say; this may be evidence of disquiet about the apparent polytheistic tendencies of these emerging theories about the Logos.

This dichotomy was resolved by Athenagoras by equating the Logos with the Platonic Nous (that is, the mind of God); the Logos could thus be closely associated with God but also treated as independent from God. Irenaeus seems to accept, or at least be cognizant of, this solution. (It is worth noting that Irenaeus discusses Nous as part of his rebuttal of Gnostic concepts of aeons proceeding from the Father, so it is not certain whether his comments are straw men or his own opinions). He identifies God's Logos as Nous.[74] However, Irenaeus is also critical of those who try to separate God and Nous; he primarily has the Gnostics in view, but his reasoning equally applies to the Platonists (and Athenagoras). If God's mind were something separate from himself then God would be a compound being and not simple; God cannot be separated from his mind.[75] He says "Mind [*Nous*] is the Father, and the Father is Mind."[76] Possibly inspired by the Greek philosopher Xenophanes (late 6th–early 5th centuries BCE) who says that a god "sees as a whole . . . thinks as a whole . . . hears as a whole,"[77] Irenaeus declares that God is "simple and not composite; with all members of similar nature, being entirely similar and

---

[71] *Demonstration*, 70 (45).

[72] Justin, *Dialogue*, 191–92 (127.1–5).

[73] Irenaeus, *Against Heresies*, 488–89 (4.20.5).

[74] Irenaeus, *Against the Heresies (Book 2)*, 58 (2.17.7); 90 (2.28.5); cf. Irenaeus, *Fragments*, 577 (fr. 54).

[75] *Against the Heresies (Book 2)*, 90 (2.28.5); 58 (2.17.7).

[76] *Against the Heresies (Book 2)*, 58 (2.17.7).

[77] Barnes, *Early Greek Philosophy*, 96.

equal to himself. He is all Mind, all Spirit, all Understanding, all Thought, and Word, all Hearing, all Eye, all Light."[78] By analogy to human understanding, he argues that mind cannot be separated or emitted from the person whose mind it is, though its "actions and passions are brought forth."[79] He argues that one mind could not send forth another, because that would entail that God's mind is divided or cut up (which is impossible).[80] He rejects the idea that something could be emitted and yet still remain within God (cf. Athenagoras), because it is meaningless to say that something is emitted if it remains within.[81] Neither Nous nor Logos can be produced because God is all Nous and all Logos from eternity; even those who say that the Nous is the Logos have an inadequate conception of the Father; God is the Logos.[82]

The logic of these arguments might take Irenaeus to a form of Modalism, as he seems to be denying any real distinction between God and the Logos beyond the manifestation of God in "actions and passions." And yet he is adamant, no doubt in accord with the tradition he has received, that the Son was *begotten of* God, which would entail he cannot be the same as the unbegotten Father. But he refuses to give any account of by what process the Son was begotten.[83] He rejects the analogy between the Logos and human speech, used by Justin and Tatian.[84] He cites Isaiah 53:8, "who shall describe his generation?" as proof that the generation of the Logos is beyond comprehension.[85] What he does say is that the Son existed before creation and co-existed eternally with the Father.[86] He believes that the Hebrew of Genesis 1:1 should be translated, "In the beginning the Son; then God established the heaven and the earth."[87] He

---

[78] Irenaeus, *Against the Heresies (Book 2)*, 43 (2.13.3); see also 45–46 (2.13.8).

[79] *Against the Heresies (Book 2)*, 43 (2.13.4).

[80] *Against the Heresies (Book 2)*, 44 (2.13.5).

[81] *Against the Heresies (Book 2)*, 44 (2.13.6).

[82] *Against the Heresies (Book 2)*, 46 2(2.13.8).

[83] *Against the Heresies (Book 2)*, 90 (2.28.6).

[84] *Against the Heresies (Book 2)*, 45 (2.13.8).

[85] *Against the Heresies (Book 2)*, 90 (2.28.5–6).

[86] Irenaeus, *Demonstration*, 60 (30); Irenaeus, *Against the Heresies (Book 2)*, 100 (2.30.9).

[87] *Demonstration*, 68 (43).

asserts that "before all creation, the Word glorified his Father, remaining in him,"[88] implying, perhaps, that at creation the Logos no longer "remained in him." It is possible, then, that his views were akin to Athenagoras; God was eternally rational, but the Logos came forth from God prior to creation. Wingren asserts that Irenaeus simply did not know how the Son proceeded from the Father and "limits himself to the facts."[89]

In one place Irenaeus asserts that "he who is born [or: begotten] of God is God [or: a god]"[90] to argue that the Son is God (or, a god). He gives no defense of that proposition in that book, but uses a similar argument elsewhere, saying that if one thing proceeds from another then both will be of the same substance. In the case of God, that which proceeds from God will also be Nous, perfect and impassible, which, for Irenaeus, amounts to saying it will be God.[91] Irenaeus draws out the conclusion:

> Therefore, the Father is Lord and the Son is Lord, the Father is God and the Son is God, since He who is born of God is God, and in this way, according to His being (*hypostasis*) and power <and> essence (*ousia*), one God is demonstrated; but according to the <economy> (*oikonomia*) of our salvation, there is both Father and Son.[92]

Here again Irenaeus verges on Modalism. And yet, Irenaeus also wants to say that the Logos can lose his impassibility, is dependent on God for his power, is lesser than God, and is subject to God.[93] He contrasts the omniscience of the Father with the limitations of the Son.[94] He seems to posit a hierarchy, saying that God "<made> man <in>the image of God, and the image of God is the Son, according to whose image was man

---

[88] Irenaeus, *Against Heresies*, 478 (4.14.1).

[89] Wingren, *Man and the Incarnation*, 101–2.

[90] Irenaeus, *Demonstration*, 71 (47), material in brackets added.

[91] Irenaeus, *Against the Heresies (Book 2)*, 58 (2.17.7).

[92] Irenaeus, *Demonstration*, 71 (47). The translator Behr uses <these> for corrections or additions he has made to the original language text.

[93] *Against the Heresies (Book 3)*, 82 (3.16.6); *Against Heresies*, 545 (5.17.3), *Against the Heresies (Book 2)*, 92 (2.28.8); *Demonstration*, 74 (51).

[94] *Against the Heresies (Book 2)*, 91–92 (2.28.7–8).

made."[95] Though some of his subordinationist language derives directly from Scripture, he also believes that such subordination is necessary to give us access to God: "since the Father of all is invisible and inaccessible to creatures, it is necessary for those who are going to approach God to have access . . . to the Father through the Son."[96]

Although he is clearly influenced by Justin and others, he avoids phrases like "second god" or "another god" (which would also be used by later thinkers like Origen.) Irenaeus seems to be struggling to reconcile the theories about the Logos he has inherited from Justin, which effectively result in a second god, with a strong affirmation of monotheism (particularly in rejection of Gnosticism), which will permit no second god.

ORIGEN OF ALEXANDRIA (C. 185–C. 253)

One of the most influential Christian theologians of the third century, and perhaps of the whole pre-Nicene period, was Origen. He was schooled in Platonic philosophy; his teacher Ammonius is often identified with the philosopher of the same name (c. 175–242) who taught the father of Neoplatonism, Plotinus (c. 204–70). Though Origen was the first Christian to speak of three "hypostases," he, like those before him, views these three as a hierarchy of three beings. The Father is the "only true God."[97] Origen refers to the Son as a "second god," though he is aware that this will sound controversial to some Christians.[98] The Logos is a god (not *the* God) inasmuch as he participates in God's divinity, just as humans can become "gods" by sharing (to a lesser degree) in that divinity,[99] and the Logos continues to be a god (only) by ceaseless

---

[95] *Demonstration*, 53–54 (22).

[96] *Demonstration*, 71 (47).

[97] Origen, *Commentary on John*, 98 (2.17). Elsewhere he describes "God, the Father of our Lord Jesus Christ . . . who is also the God of the Old and New Testaments" (*On First Principles*, 15 [Preface, 4]).

[98] Origen, *Against Celsus*, 296, 377 (5.39, 6.61); Origen, *Commentary on John*, 98 (2.16); Origen, *Dialogue*, 59 (2).

[99] Origen, *Commentary on John*, 98–99 (2.17).

contemplation of God.[100] While the Son transcends all creation, the Father transcends the Son.[101] The Son is worshipped in second place after the Father.[102]

Origen ascribes creative activity to the Logos. However, for Origen, the Logos terminology primarily refers to the relation of the divine Son to human creatures.[103] The Logos endows humans with the rational faculty and nurtures that rationality; humans only exercise rationality through their participation in the Logos. (Here we see echoes of Justin's ideas about the "seed of the Logos.")

Unlike his predecessors, Origen resists the conclusion that the Logos is to be identified with the Forms; he criticizes the pagan philosophers for these imaginary entities.[104] The Logos is not the paradigm for creation, or the potential creation. Origen also resists the identification of the Logos as speech, or the creative word, as this might be taken to mean the second god was merely an action of the first.[105] In relation to God (the Father), Origen prefers to talk about the Son as the Wisdom of God, rather than his mind. He argues it was inconceivable that there was ever a time when God was without his Wisdom. While identifying the Son as Wisdom in Proverbs 8:22, he rejects the implication of the word "created" that the Son had a beginning in time. Origen implies that the Son always existed.[106] The Father was eternally a father; the Son is begotten continuously from the Father[107] as an act of will proceeds from the intellect.[108] So, even though Origen describes the Logos as the rational power of God, he does not believe there was a time when the Son had not yet proceeded as a separate person from the Father.

---

[100] *Commentary on John*, 99 (2.18).
[101] *Commentary on John*, 224 (6.200).
[102] Origen, *Against Celsus*, 443 (8.57).
[103] Origen, *On First Principles*, 75–77 (1.3.6).
[104] Origen, *On First Principles*, 171 (2.3.6).
[105] Origen, *Commentary on John*, 38 (1.24)
[106] Origen, *On First Principles*, 41–43 (1.2.2).
[107] Origen, *Homilies on Jeremiah*, 92 (9.4.4).
[108] *On First Principles*, 563 (4.4.1).

SUMMARY

To repeat the point made at the beginning of the chapter, the doctrine of the Trinity did not exist in the second and third centuries. Those who criticized (and excommunicated) Dynamic and Modalistic Monarchians, often called "orthodox," believed in a divine hierarchy, with the Son in a second rank after the Father. The Son was called "God," but in a different sense than the way that the Father was called "God." Sometimes the Son was called "another god" or a "second god," and since God created *through* the Logos, the term "creator" was applied variously to either Father or Son. When the critics of Dynamic Monarchianism defended the divinity of Christ, they had some sort of secondary status in mind. For them, Christ being a god, or called "god," did not mean his being "fully God," in the post-Nicene sense.

We have seen there are broadly two ways of thinking about the Logos. Some thinkers held that the Logos was the mind of God which somehow proceeded from God as a separate person/god at a point in time before creation. Others held that the Son proceeded eternally from God; there was never a time when the Son did not exist as a person separate from God. When the critics of Dynamic Monarchianism talked about the pre-existence of Jesus (or of the divinity of Jesus), they had something like one of these two theories in mind.

Therefore, within this context, when Dynamic Monarchians claimed that Jesus was a "mere man" (if indeed that was their own claim, rather than a characterization by their critics), they were rejecting the view that Jesus was a second god. As we shall see, the Dynamic Monarchians accepted the Gospel of John and its close association of Jesus with the Logos. Within this context, the Dynamic Monarchians had to frame their understanding of what it meant to be the Logos in contrast with the Platonic-influenced view of the Logos as the mind of God and the source of human rationality.

CHAPTER 2

Paul of Samosata *(fl. mid-third century)*

P AUL OF SAMOSATA was bishop of the church at Antioch from c. 260, when he succeeded Demetrianus. In 268 he was condemned at the synod of Antioch but refused to surrender the church buildings until forced to do so by the Roman emperor Aurelian (214–75).[1] In the following centuries Paul gained the reputation of an arch-heretic; his name was used to

> blacken almost every theological opponent, so that he was associated in polemical literature with figures as diverse as Artemon (or Artemas), Sabellius, Mani, Origen, Arius, Marcellus, Photinus, Diodore of Tarsus, Theodore of Mopsuestia, and Nestorius.[2]

The polemical way in which his name was used makes many testimonies about Paul suspect and as such we have little reliable source material with which to reconstruct his life and teachings.

---

[1] Kelly, *Early Christian Doctrines,* 117.

[2] Behr, *Way to Nicaea,* 207. Approximate dates for the newly introduced people: Sabellius (fl. early 3rd c.), Mani (c. 216–76), Arius (c. 250–336), Marcellus (c. 280–374), Diodore of Tarsus (d. c. 390), Theodore of Mopsuestia (350–428), and Nestorius (c. 381–452).

Javier Teixidor writes "Samosata was an Eastern city where Syriac Aramaic was spoken even though the inscriptions were written in Greek."[3] It is likely that Paul was born and raised in Samosata and spoke Aramaic.[4] However in Antioch he would have engaged with Greek speakers from the West. As bishop of Antioch, Paul is sometimes seen in the context of other Antiochene Christianity. Paul is reported to have received no wealth from his family and to have been destitute before becoming bishop,[5] although this testimony has been doubted as largely rhetorical (see below).

SOURCES

There are three known sources for Paul of Samosata that have received varying assessments of their authenticity.[6] The first is the synodal letter preserved by Eusebius (c. 260–340)[7] and his other remarks, which are presumably either based on this letter or on other primary source material. The letter was issued by the synod that excommunicated Paul, and "is the earliest such document known."[8] It is generally considered this letter is authentic, although it includes the least information about Paul's Christology.

The second known source is the *Letter of Six Bishops*. The authenticity of this letter has sometimes been questioned but its theology seems appropriate for the period ("it represents a period that still holds in tension a curious mixture of subordinationism and ditheism"[9]) and does not give the impression of a later polemic. However, Norris questions its utility as a source about Paul's teachings since the positive confessions of its authors "could have been developed against various claims which are quite

---

[3] Teixidor, "Palmyra," 214.

[4] Teixidor, "Palmyra," 214.

[5] Eusebius, *Ecclesiastical History*, 277 (7.30).

[6] Ehrman, *Orthodox Corruption*, 62. For a useful summary of the scholarship on these sources see Norris, "Paul of Samosata," 50–58.

[7] Eusebius, *Ecclesiastical History*, 276–78 (7.30).

[8] Behr, *Way to Nicaea*, 209.

[9] Sample, "Christology," 22.

contradictory."[10] Therefore it would be difficult to reconstruct Paul's own thought from the statements made by the bishops to refute it.

The third known source is the *Acta,* no longer extant but seemingly preserved in quotations by later writers. The *Acta* purports to be a record of the synod, and Eusebius refers to the existence of a stenographic record taken at the synod.[11] The authenticity of the *Acta* has often been questioned because they are not quoted earlier than the fifth century and because of the apparently late theology of some of the fragments. Behr argues that it is possible that the *Acta* were not quoted earlier because it was not common practice to quote such precedents before this and because Paul's case probably wasn't relevant for earlier writers.[12] Nevertheless Behr concedes that the collection of testimonies undoubtedly include "Apollinarian forgeries"[13] and that even authentic testimonies were likely subject to some "editing" when deployed for polemical purposes.[14] Since the period of the Apollinarian dispute (362–81) produced several spurious texts (e.g. *Symbol of Antioch; Letter of St. Felix to Maximus*), it is plausible that the *Acta* were also composed during this period.[15] Further, Sample has noted contradictions between the position of Paul's adversaries in the *Acta* and that in the *Letter of Six Bishops,* which adds to the doubts regarding the *Acta.*[16]

More recently, Lang has argued for the authenticity of the *Acta,* addressing several of the common objections.[17] In favor of their authenticity, Lang points particularly to the type of synod represented in the *Acta,* which was known in the mid-third century but later fell out of use. Given that most of what is claimed about the Christology of Paul comes from the *Acta,* the doubts over the reliability of these testimonies makes reconstructing Paul's views very difficult.

[10] Compare: Norris, "Paul of Samosata," 53–54.
[11] Eusebius, *Ecclesiastical History,* 275 (7.29).
[12] Behr, *Way to Nicaea,* 227.
[13] *Way to Nicaea,* 226.
[14] *Way to Nicaea,* 227.
[15] Sample, "Christology," 19.
[16] "Christology," 20.
[17] Lang, "Christological Controversy," 54–80.

SYNOD

The synodal letter recounts the circumstances of the synod of Antioch (during which Paul was excommunicated), to which Eusebius adds some details. It is not clear who originally complained about Paul or who instigated the gathering of the synod (Eusebius seems to skip over this part of the letter). The letter says "We invited even the more distant bishops to come and cure this deadly teaching," and the letter is addressed from a number of clergy, apparently local to Antioch.[18] Presumably it was these local clergy who invited other bishops to intervene. Their initial approach was to invite two eminent bishops from neighboring regions: Dionysius of Alexandria (d. 264) and Firmilian of Cappadocia (d. c. 269). The letter says Dionysius considered "the leader of the heresy . . . unworthy of personal correspondence," so he sent a letter to the entire parish;[19] Eusebius states that it was age and infirmity that prevented Dionysius attending.[20] According to the letter, Firmilian came twice, apparently both times at gatherings of the local clergy. On both occasions Paul "promised to change" and Firmilian was "duped."[21] Eusebius reports that many eminent churchmen gathered to Antioch, assembled at different times and frequently discussed the matters; he accuses Paul of trying "to hide or disguise his heterodoxy."[22] Paul was not excommunicated at any of these meetings, indicating that those gathered were unable to convict him of anything meriting disciplinary action.

Clearly someone (presumably the local clergy) was not satisfied with the outcomes of these earlier meetings. Another synod was called and Firmilian was summoned, but he died in Tarsus on his way to Antioch.[23] This synod was composed of many bishops, but it was the Antiochene presbyter and rhetor Malchion (fl. mid-3rd c.) who conducted the

---

[18] Eusebius, *Ecclesiastical History*, 276 (7.30).
[19] *Ecclesiastical History*, 276 (7.30).
[20] *Ecclesiastical History*, 275 (7.27).
[21] *Ecclesiastical History*, 276 (7.30).
[22] *Ecclesiastical History*, 275 (7.28).
[23] *Ecclesiastical History*, 276 (7.30).

discussion. This approach is the same adopted in the cases of Beryllus (see Chapter Four) and Heraclides (see Chapter Seven), where the main discussion is conducted by Origen, a presbyter, and the gathered bishops were largely observers.[24] Lang characterizes this synod, as those regarding Beryllus and Heraclides, as "a doctrinal disputation with the *didaskalos* [teacher] of the church."[25] The purpose of such synods was to demonstrate the heresy and bring the offender to retraction. In this regard, the synod of Antioch was unsuccessful.

According to Eusebius, Malchion "alone was able to expose that crafty deceiver."[26] The synod excommunicated Paul and appointed Domnus (fl. mid-3rd c.), the son of the previous bishop Demetrianus (fl. mid-3rd c.), as bishop of Antioch.[27]

Paul refused to surrender the church building. Eusebius records that the Emperor Aurelian was petitioned, presumably by the clergy of Antioch who had sought to excommunicate him. Aurelian ordered that the building be given to those deemed appropriate by the bishops of Italy and of Rome; thus Paul was finally driven from the church.[28] This cannot have happened sooner than 272, when Aurelian captured the region from Zenobia (c. 240–c. 274), and it is not clear what happened in the intervening period. It is possible that a congregation loyal to Paul continued to meet in the church at Antioch and Domnus headed a separate congregation.

POLITICS

There is more than a whiff of politics in the circumstances surrounding Paul's excommunication. Bart Ehrman writes, "the fact that the council deposed him in favor of Domnus, the son of the previous bishop, Demetrianus, makes one suspect that the proceedings had as much to do

---

[24] Behr, *Way to Nicaea,* 210–11.
[25] Lang, "Christological Controversy," 61.
[26] Eusebius, *Ecclesiastical History*, 275 (7.29).
[27] Eusebius, *Ecclesiastical History*, 278 (7.30).
[28] *Ecclesiastical History*, 278–79 (7.30).

with rivalry and personal loyalty as with Christology."[29] Similarly Behr writes, "the sheer effort expended in condemning Paul suggests that his doctrinal errors were not at all self-evident, and the overall impression given by Eusebius is that other issues were at least as important, casting a shadow over the appointment of the previous bishop's son to the episcopacy in Paul's stead."[30]

Whatever excuses are made on behalf of Dionysius of Alexandria, he neither travels to Antioch nor sends a delegation to the synod; the synodal letter is addressed to his successor, Maximus of Alexandria (d. 282), who evidently did not attend either. Firmilian twice visits Antioch and twice leaves satisfied; presumably no stable testimony of Paul's misconduct or of his heresy could be produced. The letter says Paul promised to change his opinions, whereas Eusebius gives the impression that Paul concealed his true views, and these were later only exposed by the rhetorical skill of Malchion (fl. mid-3rd c.). These two statements appear to be inconsistent, one saying Paul acknowledged his heterodoxy and repented, and the other saying Paul hid his heterodoxy. A skeptical reader might consider these as excuses for the failure of repeated synods to establish any guilt. The persistence of the meetings at Antioch, which presumably lasted several years, implies a serious determination to oust Paul. Ultimately it was not a foreign bishop that deposed Paul, but Malchion, a local presbyter who was trained in rhetoric.

The local tension between Paul and the other clergy may be explained by class division. For instance, Paul was a native of Samosata whereas the clergy of Antioch may have been Greek in tongue and outlook; Paul may have been considered inferior. Also, if it is true that Paul was a self-made man, then he may have clashed with the established elite like Malchion and other bishops.[31] We can well imagine that with such class divisions in play the appointment of Paul as bishop may have ruffled feathers and caused

---

[29] Ehrman, *Orthodox Corruption*, 62.
[30] Behr, *Way to Nicaea*, 212.
[31] Burrus, "Rhetorical Stereotypes," 222.

resentment. Perhaps the local clergy were only too keen to find any excuse to be rid of him—though this is speculation.

Secular politics may have motivated some of the antagonism against Paul. The synodal letter accuses Paul of assuming "worldly honors and wants to be called *ducenarius*."[32] It was previously argued that Paul was given the role of *procurator ducenarius* (the chief financial officer of the district) by Zenobia, queen of the short-lived Palmyrene Empire that occupied Antioch for a time. On this presentation, the synod was a power struggle between pro-Roman and pro-Syrian parties in Antioch.[33] Teixidor suggests "it would have been skilful of Zenobia to make such an independent bishop the instrument of her policy in Antioch."[34] However it is now considered doubtful that Antioch was under Palmyrene control before 270,[35] that is, after Paul's deposition in 268. The claims of later writers, like Athanasius, that Zenobia was a supporter of Paul are likely ahistorical and polemical in nature. It is possible that Paul lent his support to the Palmyrene soldiers when they occupied the city in 270; this might explain why Aurelian chose to unseat him but has no relevance to the synod of 268.

Yet there seems to no reason to doubt that Paul was a *procurator ducenarius*.[36] This would explain many of the accusations made against him in the synodal letter. For example, there seems no reason for a religious leader to become involved in lawsuits over property,[37] and even if he had his decisions would not have been binding, but this would be explained if he held an administrative position. Similarly, it is unsurprising that a *procurator ducenarius* would have been accompanied by a bodyguard when walking in public, or that he should dictate letters and conduct other business during these journeys, as is claimed. The letter also claims that Paul introduced a tribunal, a lofty throne and a *secretum* (a

---

[32] Eusebius, *Ecclesiastical History*, 277 (7.30).
[33] See Bardy, *Paul de Samosate*, 239–62.
[34] Teixidor, "Palmyra," 215.
[35] Millar, "Samosata, Zenobia and Aurelian," 1–17.
[36] Norris, "Paul of Samosata," 62–67.
[37] Eusebius, *Ecclesiastical History*, 277 (7.30).

smaller chamber for private discussions) into the church assembly.[38] This is the furniture of the chambers of a Roman administrative official. Strip away the rhetoric and the synodal letter claims that Paul had dual occupation as both bishop of the church and as a secular official. Ironically, the main antagonist at the synod was Malchion, who was the head of a school of rhetoric in Antioch in addition to being a presbyter.[39] Norris observes that

> in his post, Malchion would have been called upon to argue cases in public disputes as well as give public orations. He might even have been hired by the city and have been given a place on the city council.[40]

It is also worth noting the role of Rome in these proceedings. Though the local clergy do not initially involve the bishop of Rome, the Roman bishop Dionysius (fl. mid-3rd c.) is named co-recipient (alongside Maximus of Alexandria) of the synodal letter.[41] When Emperor Aurelian removes the church building from Paul, he states that it is for the bishop of Rome to determine to whom it should be given.[42] It may have been convenient for Aurelian to "tie Antioch more closely to Roman institutions."[43] It may also be that it was the Roman church that petitioned Aurelian for his intervention. The bishops of important cities (Alexandria, Jerusalem, Rome) were beginning in this period to consider that they should have more authority.

CONDUCT

The synodal letter makes many accusations against Paul's conduct, despite saying that there is no need to recount them. This is also the main part of the letter that Eusebius preserves, omitting whatever details the letter gave

---

[38] *Ecclesiastical History*, 277 (7.30).
[39] *Ecclesiastical History*, 275 (7.29).
[40] Norris, "Paul of Samosata," 65.
[41] Eusebius, *Ecclesiastical History*, 276 (7.30).
[42] *Ecclesiastical History*, 278 (7.30).
[43] Norris, "Paul of Samosata," 66.

about Paul's teaching. The charges against Paul include gaining great wealth by "robbing churches, and blackmailing his fellow Christians," being ambitious and arrogant, conducting services in a vulgar fashion and living with a number of "spiritual brides." [44] The letter implies that this conduct is a consequence of his heresy and needs no other explanation.

There are reasons for doubting the accusations made against him.[45] Firstly, had there been credible charges of significant immorality against Paul then his excommunication could have been accomplished much more swiftly. As it was it took many years and several meetings for Paul to be deposed and, it is implied, this was only achieved when Malchion could catch Paul confessing to some heresy. Instead the accusations in this synodal letter read more like a "parting shot," rather than a list of proven charges.

Secondly, as Virginia Burrus has demonstrated, the portrayal of Paul in the letter is "a commonplace stereotype in the rhetoric of the Second Sophistic movement."[46] We know that Malchion was the head of a school of rhetoric and we should not be surprised to see these techniques deployed in this letter.

Burrus compares the portrayal of Paul with Lucian's description of the bad rhetorician. For example, the bad rhetorician is portrayed as having worked his way up from lowly beginnings and as having been immoral in the pursuit of wealth. The claims that Paul started life penniless and acquired his wealth through blackmail may have no more substance than this pagan rhetoric. Similarly, the descriptions of Paul's vulgar services may also be rhetorical; Lucian parodies the bad rhetorician as slapping his thigh to please the crowed and as having a "well-attuned chorus."[47] We have already seen that it is likely that Paul had some civil office that was the reason for some of the conduct his accusers find unpalatable, yet even here the accusations may be exaggerated for rhetorical purpose. While it would

[44] "These were women who lived among the bishops, priests and deacons. Their behavior was not faulty; in actual fact they were the 'sons (or daughters) of the Covenant.' " (Teixidor, "Palmyra," 215).

[45] Ehrman, *Orthodox Corruption,* 61.

[46] Burrus, "Rhetorical Stereotypes," 215.

[47] Lucian, *Public Speaking,* 161, 163 (19, 21).

be natural for a busy *procurator ducenarius* to dictate letters to his attendants while on the move, Lucian describes the bad rhetorician as having "many attendants, and always a book in hand."[48] Even the insinuation of sexual immorality is paralleled in Lucian's text. Therefore, the passage of the synodal letter about Paul's conduct reads like an example of ancient rhetoric. This does not mean it has no basis in fact. Burrus writes "it is likely . . . Paul was trained as a rhetorician, acted as an advocate in legal disputes (whether civil or ecclesial), and was theatrical and charismatic in his style of preaching and leadership."[49] However it does seem likely that Paul's accusers have exaggerated his conduct for rhetorical effect so as to present him as worldly, arrogant, and immoral.

CHRISTOLOGY

As Kelly states, "Paul's thought is notoriously difficult to evaluate."[50] Much depends on whether one accepts all the testimonies attributed to him as authentic or just the testimony of Eusebius and the synodal letter. Even those accepting the same source material can reach differing conclusions, based upon different analogues to systematize Paul's thought.[51] I will examine what can be known from each of our sources.

SYNODAL LETTER

The major claim of the synodal letter is that Paul "will not confess that the Son of God descended from heaven." [52] It is interesting that the synod seems to anticipate that this claim might be doubted because they add "which will be documented shortly in many of the attached notes, especially where he says that Jesus Christ is 'from below.'"[53] Presumably, they considered this to be his most damning admission (else why not

[48] Lucian, *Public Speaking*, 155 (15).
[49] Burrus, "Rhetorical Stereotypes," 221.
[50] Kelly, *Early Christian Doctrines*, 118.
[51] Pollard, *Johannine Christology*, 114.
[52] Eusebius, *Ecclesiastical History*, 277 (7.30).
[53] *Ecclesiastical History*, 277 (7.30).

include a more damning one). Yet one may doubt the objectivity of his accusers. Eusebius writes that Malchion "unmasked" Paul and only Malchion was able to expose Paul's heresy through his rhetorical skill.[54] Anyone predisposed to be skeptical might suspect Malchion's intention was to catch Paul in words; as Ehrman judges, "on such terms, one wonders who would have been safe."[55]

The synodal letter also claims that Paul prevented the singing of hymns to Jesus because they were modern compositions.[56] Behr concludes that these hymns were "probably Paschal as it is further alleged that Paul had women sing songs to him on the great day of Pascha."[57] While singing hymns to Jesus is sometimes taken has recognition of his divinity, it is by no means obvious this is how they were interpreted in this context or that this was Paul's objection to them. Indeed, at one point in his career, Origen taught that prayer should be offered through Jesus but not to Jesus.[58] The fact that Paul objected to the hymns as modern compositions may be variously interpreted. It may indicate that he denied the deity of Christ and held that the doctrine was a later addition to the apostolic doctrine (cf. Artemon). Alternatively, he may have been a traditionalist and disliked new liturgies.

Eusebius had access to the full synodal letter and, presumably, the notes that accompanied it. As such, Eusebius can be taken as a witness to its contents. Eusebius states that Paul held "a low view of Christ . . . regarding him as an ordinary man."[59] In using this terminology Eusebius may be trying to associate Paul with Artemon, as he does elsewhere,[60] and as does the synodal letter.[61] In his *Ecclesiastical Theology* Eusebius takes the view that Jesus could not have had a human soul, but that the Logos took the place of his soul, else he would have been a "mere man."[62] There is a

---

[54] *Ecclesiastical History*, 275 (7.29).
[55] Ehrman, *Orthodox Corruption,* 62.
[56] Eusebius, *Ecclesiastical History*, 277 (7.30).
[57] Behr, *Way to Nicaea,* 213.
[58] Origen, *Dialogue,* 60 (4); Origen, *On Prayer*, 269–71 (15).
[59] Eusebius, *Ecclesiastical History*, 274–75 (7.27).
[60] *Ecclesiastical History*, 201 (5.28).
[61] *Ecclesiastical History*, 278 (7.30).
[62] Eusebius, *Ecclesiastical Theology*, 203 (1.20).

significant question whether this means that Paul taught that Jesus had a human soul or whether Eusebius is trying to associate Marcellus of Ancyra with Paul.[63] He certainly does not mention this as an issue for Paul in earlier works.[64] Eusebius distinguishes Paul from the Ebionites. He also writes:

> although he [i.e. Paul] teaches that Jesus is the Christ of God, and, like Marcellus, confesses one God of all, the Church fathers declared that the Samosatene was alien to the Church of God because he does not confess that Christ is the Son of God and God before his generation in the flesh.[65]

Here Eusebius is summarizing the charges against Paul and the basis on which he was excommunicated. We do not know how closely Eusebius is following the synodal letter and notes. Presumably, the first charge means something other than denying any kind of sonship to Jesus, since even the Ebionites recognized Jesus was in some sense the son of God. It may mean that Paul denied the virgin birth, however since Eusebius distinguishes Paul from the Ebionites this seems unlikely. Even in the later reports about Paul, his belief in the virgin birth is affirmed. It seems more probable that Eusebius means Paul denied *Eusebius's* concept of Son of God, that is, as pre-existent Son and so having a divine nature before his human career. (It is worth noting that Eusebius probably understood the Son as a different and lesser being than God; he was not trinitarian in the modern sense.) The second charge is the familiar charge made against Dynamic Monarchians.[66] The clear implication is that Paul denied the pre-existence of Jesus, as Eusebius states elsewhere.[67] This would be consistent with the claims of the synodal letter that Paul denied that Jesus

---

[63] Behr, *Way to Nicaea*, 214; Norris, "Paul of Samosata," 51.
[64] Sample, "Christology," 21.
[65] Eusebius, *Ecclesiastical Theology*, 182–83 (1.14).
[66] Norris, "Articulating Identity," 205.
[67] Eusebius, *Prophetic Extracts*, 3.19.

came from heaven and with the association made between Paul and Artemon.[68]

It is worth commenting briefly on the account given by Theodoret (c. 393–460), as it is sometimes thought to be based on independent information. He describes Paul as a follower of the heresy of Artemon and was motivated to reconcile Christianity with certain Jewish beliefs. Theodoret includes a description of the actions taken against Paul, which is largely consistent with Eusebius's. Regarding Christology, Theodoret writes that Paul said "Christ [was] a man, eminently privileged by divine grace."[69] I do not see any particular reason to believe Theodoret does not simply re-hash Eusebius, though it is possible he had access to other sources as well. The statement about Christ being "privileged by divine grace" is presumably a summary of Paul's explanation for Christ's power and authority, not as a result of incarnation but as directly given him by God.

LETTER OF SIX BISHOPS

Our other source for Paul's Christology is the *Letter of Six Bishops.* While this does not include descriptions of Paul's views, the positive affirmations made by the bishops are likely to react to specific teachings of Paul. These affirmations can be summarized in three main points. Firstly, Christ is "eternally with the Father,"[70] a clear denial of any suggestion that Christ did not pre-exist. The bishops describe the Son as "existing before the ages, not as to foreknowledge,"[71] which would imply that this is something that Paul asserted (i.e. that the Son pre-existed only in the foreknowledge of God). Secondly, Christ was "sent by the Father" and "became a man,"[72] an affirmation of Christ's personal pre-existence and of his incarnation.

---

[68] Also see Athanasius, *Ariminum and Seleucia*, 474 (45); Athanasius, *Against Apollinaris*, 119 (2.3).

[69] Theodoret, *Compendium*, 209 (2.8).

[70] Hymenaeus, *Letter of Six Bishops*, 367.

[71] *Letter of Six Bishops*, 366.

[72] *Letter of Six Bishops*, 369.

Thirdly, Christ is "as to being and nature God,"[73] a denial that Christ became divine. This third affirmation, taken with Theodoret's statement, may suggest that Paul taught that Christ did become in some sense "divine," perhaps at his baptism or, more probably, on his ascension. On the other hand, the statement could be meant to correct Paul's view that Christ was human by nature and not divine (at any time).

These sources tell us all we can say with confidence about Paul's theology.

ACTA

Eusebius says that the presbyter and rhetor Malchion "had his debates with Paul taken down in shorthand, which are extant to this day."[74] This work has not survived except for some alleged fragments quoted in other works, collectively dubbed by Lawlor the *Acta*.[75] Were these to be authentic, then they would allow for a much fuller treatment of Paul's ideas.[76]

Lawlor provides useful summary of Paul's teaching:

He insisted strongly on the unity of God . . . and this unipersonal God he identifies with the Father . . . But the Word or Wisdom was from eternity (*aei*) in God, in the same manner reason (*logos*) is in the heart of man, as an element of his personality . . . He accepts the Virgin Birth . . . the Logos or Wisdom went forth from God and was joined to him [i.e. Jesus] . . . It was not without precedent, for Wisdom was in the prophets, and still more in Moses . . . Christ was a distinct human person, who possessed the Logos as an attribute.[77]

---

[73] *Letter of Six Bishops*, 366.

[74] Eusebius, *Ecclesiastical History*, 275 (7.29).

[75] This is short for *Acta Disputationis*, that is, Acts of a Disputation, i.e. an account of a debate.

[76] Lawlor, "Sayings of Paul of Samosata," 20–21. For recent defence of the authenticity of the *Acta*, see Lang, "Christological controversy," 54–80.

[77] Lawlor, "Sayings of Paul of Samosata," 41–42.

Lang identifies two key points of contention in *Acta* between Paul and Malchion. The first issue is that of "substantial union."[78] Malchion holds that Jesus Christ was composed by the union of the Logos and the human body. Paul rejects this view, arguing that if the Logos was compounded with the body, then the Logos would abandon its dignity. Instead, Paul sees Jesus as cooperating with the Logos/Wisdom while being a separate entity.

The second issue is "the anthropological paradigm."[79] Malchion seems to hold the view that the Logos had the place of a soul in Jesus; whereas humans are composed of body and soul, Jesus was body and Logos. Paul rejects this view, arguing that the constitution of Jesus cannot be compared to that of other humans.

There is one issue worth further comment given the significance afforded it by later writers. It is attested that Paul used the term *homoousia* (same substance) and that the use of this term was condemned at the synod.[80] This is the term employed positively at the council of Nicaea to exclude the so-called "Arians" by stipulating that the Son is same substance with the Father. In contrast, at the synod of Antioch Paul's accusers argued that the Logos was a separate *ousia* (being) from God.[81] We can make sense of these claims if we reflect on the fact that Paul believed that Jesus had no existence prior to his birth and therefore the Logos, described in John 1, could not be a description of Christ in his pre-existent state as something separate from God. Indeed, as John says, "the Word was God [or, a god]" (John 1:1). On this basis, Paul would have agreed that the Logos pre-existed but disagreed that it was a separate *ousia* from God, thus denying any personal pre-existence to Jesus.

---

[78] Lang, "Christological Controversy," 66–72.

[79] Lang, "Christological Controversy," 72–79.

[80] Athanasius, *Ariminum and Seleucia*, 473 (45); Hilary (c. 315–67), *On the Councils*, 25 (81); Basil (330–79), *Letter 52*, 155 (1).

[81] cf. Epiphanius, *Medicine Chest*, 2:458 (73.12); Kelly, *Early Christian Doctrines*, 118.

As explored in Chapter One, from the second century onwards, Christian writers understood the Logos to be the rational faculties of God, and there were a variety of views about the extent to which the Logos could be separated from God. Justin describes the Logos as "a certain rational power" that proceeded from God before all creation.[82] Athenagoras called the Son the "mind (*nous*) and Word (*logos*) of the Father"; God is eternally rational, so always had the Son within him but the Son came forth from the Father.[83] Similarly, Theophilus says the Logos was innate within God as his mind; later God generated the Logos externally as the firstborn of creation.[84] Irenaeus equivocates, identifying the Logos as Nous but identifies Nous as the Father; Nous did not emanate from God but the Son was begotten.[85]

These views represent a tension between identifying the Logos as God's rational faculty and identifying the Logos as a separate power. Paul may have been at one end of this spectrum, asserting that in no sense was the Logos separate from God; towards the other end of the spectrum would be his accusers, represented by Malchion, asserting that the Logos proceeded from God and was thereafter a separate substance. For Malchion, the Logos was separate from God and was combined with a human body, in Mary's womb, to form Jesus Christ. For Paul, the Logos was not a separate power, and could not be compounded with a human body; Christ participated in the Logos.

Therefore, if these reports in the *Acta* are to be trusted, they place Paul within the thought world of third century discussions about the relation of the Logos to God.

It has often been commented that Paul's accusers are likely to have been schooled in Origen's theology; these include Dionysius of Alexandria and Firmilian of Caesarea. Behr writes "it is to be expected that the critics of Paul based themselves on Origen, and thus it is not surprising that

---

[82] Justin, *Dialogue*, 93–94 (61.1).

[83] Athenagoras, *Embassy*, 40 (10).

[84] Theophilus, *To Autolycus*, 63–65 (2.22).

[85] Irenaeus, *Against the Heresies (Book 2)*, 58, 43–45, 90 (2.17.7, 2.13.4–6, 2.28.5–6).

characteristic elements of Origen's theology are reflected in this letter."[86] Pollard goes further presenting the synod of Antioch as the first instance of "open conflict between the theological traditions of Antioch and Alexandria."[87] However, Sample urges caution, stating "although many of the attending prelates followed Origen and his school, there is no record of conscious appeal to the writings of the Alexandrian master."[88] Lang argues that the Christology of the Paul's accusers, primarily Malchion, as represented in the *Acta* are not Apollinarian (which would make the *Acta* late and inauthentic) but originates in the theology of Origen.[89] If correct, then that the Synod of Antioch is not so much addressing the beliefs of one particular individual as being symptomatic of conflict between two diverging Christological traditions.

SUMMARY

There are, broadly, two ways of assessing the evidence of the deposition against Paul. Given the suspicious whiff of politics, one might be tempted to conclude that Paul has been misrepresented. If his rivals were determined to oust Paul, then associating him with a known heretic like Artemon may have been a convenient smear. Once convicted his accusers would further blacken his name with rumors about his conduct, which would never be tested in synod, and so ensure that Paul was completely cut off from the Church. However, this picture doesn't quite fit the circumstances. If Paul was entirely orthodox then what hope did his rivals have that Malchion would be able to trap him in words? And which orthodox churchman would, when faced with losing his episcopacy no less, state openly "Jesus Christ is from below"?

The more probable option is that Paul did deny the pre-existence of Jesus, though, no doubt, this was not the only grievance of his accusers. There are two explanations for the difficulty in convicting Paul of heresy. Firstly, contrary to the suggestion of the synodal letter and Eusebius, it is

[86] Behr, *Way to Nicaea,* 221.
[87] Pollard, *Johannine Christology,* 113.
[88] Sample, "Christology," 18.
[89] Lang, "Christological Controversy," 79.

doubtful that Paul had any association with Artemon (see below) or any other known heretic. Secondly, at that time subordinationist language was common stock in Christology. In the absence of universally accepted creeds, a considerable amount of equivocation was possible about what one meant by certain terms. What was controversial about Paul's position was not that he considered Jesus to be inferior to God but that he denied the personal pre-existence of Jesus and even that may have been difficult to pin down had Paul spoken unclearly about the Logos.

ORIGINS

The synodal letter states that Artemon was the "father" of Paul's heresy; Eusebius writes that Paul was reviving the heresy of Artemon;[90] Theodoret describes Paul as a follower of Artemon's heresy. Yet it seems unlikely that Paul had had any contact with Artemon, or that he derived his Christological views from Artemon. The synodal letter ends by saying that Paul "had better write to Artemas, then Artemas and his gang can be in communion with him." This suggests that Paul had previously had no contact with Artemon. In any case, if Paul was in contact with someone excommunicated from the Church, like Artemon, it would surely have been easier to prove his heresy and depose him.

A second common explanation for Paul's views is purported contact with Judaism. Theodoret recorded that Paul was attempting to reconcile Christianity with certain Jewish beliefs.[91] A Syriac chronicler attributes Paul's heresy to Zenobia, writing "as Paul wanted to please her and she was interested in all things concerning the Jews, he was led into the heresy of Artemon."[92] This suggestion of a connection between Zenobia and Paul is also found in Athanasius, who writes "Zenobia was a Jewess, and a supporter of Paul of Samosata; but she did not give up the Churches to the Jews for [i.e. to be turned into] Synagogues."[93] Yet, as we have seen, it is unlikely that Antioch was under Palmyrene control before 270. Even if

[90] Eusebius, *Ecclesiastical History*, 201 (5.28).
[91] Theodoret, *Compendium*, 208 (2.8).
[92] Teixidor, "Palmyra," 217.
[93] Athanasius, *History*, 296 (71).

Paul did at some point form a relationship with Zenobia or the Palmyrene administration, this cannot have been the source of Christological views formed many years earlier. Given the existence of the Ebionites, Jewish Christians who denied the pre-existence of Jesus, there are some grounds to equate denial of the pre-existence of Jesus as a "Jewish" belief, even if this was not its source. In addition, as at various times Christians faced opposition from the Jews about such doctrines as the deity and incarnation of Christ, it is an understandable supposition that Judaism was the source of the rejection of these doctrines by Christians. However, nothing in the synodal letter, Eusebius, or the *Letter of Six Bishops* gives us reason to suppose that Paul was a Jewish Christian, sought to adopt elements of Judaism or was otherwise conversant with those holding Jewish beliefs.

A third sort of explanation might be in the theological history of Antioch, though the paucity of the evidence makes this difficult to assess. In the previous century Theophilus of Antioch wrote in his *To Autolycus* that the Logos was generated by God as the firstborn of creation and was external to God,[94] contrary to the purported claim of Paul that the Logos is not a separate substance.[95] Further Theophilus states that it was the Logos, not God, who conversed with Adam, indicating that Theophilus regarded the Logos as a pre-existent person.[96] It is difficult to argue that such ideas could prompt Paul's position, though his may have developed as a reaction against the Logos theorists. It may be that multiple views co-existed at Antioch until this period. If the Christology of Paul's accusers originates in the theology of Origen and of the Alexandrian tradition, as

---

[94] Theophilus, *To Autolycus*, 63 (2.22).

[95] Rick Rogers argues that Theophilus regarded the Logos as nothing more than a personification of God, but this seems difficult to square with Theophilus's statement that the Logos does what is impossible for God, that is, appear to men. See Rogers, *Theophilus of Antioch*, 74.

[96] The view that it was the Logos who appeared as God in Old Testament theophanies was common amongst the second century apologists, going back at least as far as Justin Martyr, i.e. mid-2nd c.

some scholars propose, then it may be that Paul's more closely represents the tradition of Antioch.

There are two other ways to explain the origins of Paul's views: (1) that he arrived at his views through his own contemplation of the scriptures, independent of any other tradition, or (2) that his views derived from a broader Dynamic Monarchian tradition extant in this period. Given the paucity of evidence about Paul's views, let alone his earlier life, it is impossible to judge either way whether he arrived at his views independently. However, I will be arguing that the geographic distribution of the Dynamic Monarchians, and their independence, is highly suggestive that Dynamic Monarchianism did not emerge from a clear sky, so to speak, but was a wide tradition with, I shall argue, an old pedigree.

CHAPTER 3

Artemon *(fl. c. 235–50)*

"VIRTUALLY NOTHING IS KNOWN about Artemon, especially his period of activity," J. T. Fitzgerald writes.[1] Eusebius quotes extracts from a polemic known as *The Little Labyrinth* which, he says, was targeted against Artemon's heresy.[2] However, most of what Eusebius quotes verbatim concerns Theodotus of Byzantium.[3] Later Eusebius quotes the letter of the bishops to Dionysius of Rome regarding Paul of Samosata, which mentions "Artemas" in places.[4] Our other source is Theodoret of Cyrus, whose account is so brief we may cite it in full:

> A certain Artemon, whom some name Artemas,[5] on the one hand held beliefs about the God of the universe very similar to ours, saying that he was the creator of everything. By contrast, he said that the Lord Jesus Christ was a mere man, born of a virgin, yet better than the prophets in virtue. He claimed that the apostles also proclaimed these things, misinterpreting the meaning of the divine Scriptures, [and] that it was those who [lived] after them [i.e. the apostles] who made Christ divine, although he was not God.[6]

---

[1] Fitzgerald, "Eusebius," 124 note 20.

[2] On the contents, authorship, and date of *The Little Labyrinth* see Chapter Five below, 67-68.

[3] Eusebius, *Ecclesiastical History*, 201 (5.28).

[4] Eusebius, *Ecclesiastical History*, 278 (7.30).

[5] "Artemas, which is itself a hypocoristic abbreviation of the name Artemidorus. Artemon . . . is in turn a variant of Artemas" (Fitzgerald, "Eusebius," 139).

[6] Theodoret, *Compendium*, 208 (2.4).

Other references to Artemon are based on these sources and do not provide any independent information.[7] Later I will address the question of whether Origen refers to Artemon anonymously in his *On Titus*.

Given the paucity of information, it is difficult to fix dates for Artemon with accuracy. Eusebius implies a long gap between Artemon and Paul of Samosata.[8] On this basis Fitzgerald proposes that Artemon's primary period of activity was no earlier than 235-40.[9]

Scholars have routinely associated Artemon with Rome, but neither Eusebius nor Theodoret mention any particular city either as his place of birth or as the location of his activity. One reason for associating Artemon with Rome is a connection made with Theodotus and his followers in *The Little Labyrinth*. However, as we shall see, this connection may be one drawn by Artemon's critics and may not imply anything about their locale. And if there is no connection between the followers of Artemon and the followers of Theodotus, how strange that these two communities should exist independently in Rome (this, of course, assumes the following of Theodotus lasted a generation). The other possible mention of a Roman connection is the line in *The Little Labyrinth:*

> They claim that all their predecessors and the apostles themselves taught what they do and that the true teaching was preserved until the time of Victor, the thirteenth Bishop of Rome after Peter, but that the truth has been perverted from the time of his successor Zephyrinus.[10]

---

[7] A letter by the bishop of Alexandria Alexander (d. 328) which is preserved by the historian Theodoret states that the teaching of Arius "is the same as that propagated by Ebion and Artemas, and rivals that of Paul of Samosata, bishop of Antioch, who was excommunicated by a council of all the bishops" (Theodoret, *Ecclesiastical History*, 38 [1.3]). Photius (c. 810–95) states that Gaius (fl. early 3rd c.) wrote "a work specially directed against the heresy of Artemon" (Migne, *Patrologia Graeca*, 103:85a), presumably thinking of *The Little Labyrinth*. Also see Nicephorus Callistus (c. 1256–c. 1335) (Migne, *Patrologia Graeca*, 145:1029c) and Epiphanius, *Medicine Chest*, 2:216 (65.1.4).

[8] Eusebius, *Ecclesiastical History*, 201 (5.28)

[9] Fitzgerald, "Eusebius and *The Little Labyrinth*," 141.

[10] *The Little Labyrinth*, quoted in Eusebius, *Ecclesiastical History*, 201 (5.28).

It might be argued that the naming of Roman bishops frames Artemon's teaching in a Roman context, however alternative interpretations are available. Firstly, it is possible that the Roman bishops were mentioned only as chronological markers (hence, "till the times of"), though it is seems unlikely that non-Roman Christian communities were yet dating according to the sequence of Roman bishops. Secondly, it may be that Artemon and/or his followers perceived Zephyrinus (d. 217) to have had an impact outside Rome. This may be why they did not consider the excommunication of Theodotus by Victor (d. 199) to be a deliberate perversion; this was a localized issue, not impacting the wider Christian community. Given the antagonism and ultimate schism of Hippolytus in reaction to Zephyrinus and his successor Callistus (d. 222), we can believe that Zephyrinus caused doctrinal upset both in Rome and in the wider Christian community. Given that Irenaeus wrote about the actions of Victor in the late second century, we should not be surprised that the actions of the Roman bishop should attract attention of those outside Rome.

There is no record of any action taken by the church in Rome (or anywhere else) against Artemon. However, the implication of the bishops' letter regarding Paul of Samosata is that Artemon and his followers are out of communion with the Roman church. It is impossible to judge how successful this alternative communion was, except that it was still active by the time of the *Letters of Six Bishops* (c. 268), so perhaps around 240–70.

BELIEFS

Eusebius records that Artemon claimed that "the Savior was merely human."[11] The bishops' letter to Dionysius associates the beliefs of Paul of Samosata with those of Artemon,[12] so they presumably bore some similarity, or were perceived to do so. Theodoret gives the most detailed account of Artemon's beliefs, presenting him as orthodox regarding the

---

[11] Eusebius, *Ecclesiastical History*, 201 (5.28).
[12] Eusebius, *Ecclesiastical History*, 278 (7.30).

doctrine of creation but divergent as to the nature of Christ.[13] It is not clear whether Artemon used the term "mere man" (*psilos anthropos*); it is more probably an expression invented by the opponents of Dynamic Monarchianism. Although he denied the deity of Christ, Artemon believed in the virgin birth, so for Artemon Jesus was not born in the ordinary human manner (i.e. two biological parents.)

One other possible source of information is Origen's list of heresies in his commentary on Titus (preserved by Pamphilus [c. 240–310]). Origen writes of those

> who deny that he is the "firstborn," the God "of all creation" [Col. 1:15] and "the Word" [John 1:1] and "the Wisdom," which is "the beginning of the ways of God" [Prov. 8:22], which "came into being before anything else" [cf. Col. 1:17], "founded before the ages" [Prov. 8:23] and "generated before all the hills" [Prov. 8:25], and who say instead that he was a mere man [*psilos anthropos*].[14]

The phrase "mere man" may indicate any Dynamic Monarchian, given the phrase is used against Paul of Samosata, as well as the followers of Theodotus or of Artemon. It is possible that Origen is only making a general statement, though his collation of scriptural phrases suggests he has in mind a specific refutation. If so then Artemon, as a contemporary of Origen, is probably the more likely option. Given the use of pre-prepared proof-texts, it is interesting to speculate whether Origen wrote a polemic against Artemon or engaged him in debate, though it is impossible to evidence either speculation. It is unlikely that Artemon rejected the canonicity of Proverbs, John, or Colossians; indeed, such attempted refutations would be stronger if Artemon accepted them. However, these proof-texts do indicate where the debate lay, at least as far as Origen was concerned. Artemon plainly denied the pre-existence of Christ and consequently must have had a different understanding of Word (Logos) and Wisdom (Sophia).

---

[13] Theodoret, *Compendium*, 208 (2.4).
[14] Pamphilus, *Apology for Origen*, 56–57 (33).

RELATION TO THEODOTUS

The Little Labyrinth gives the impression that Artemon was a successor of Theodotus, describing the latter as the one "who invented this heresy."[15] On the other hand, Theodoret presents Artemon as the leader of a different heresy from that of Theodotus.[16] As Fitzgerald suggests, it was "not the Artemonites who want to connect the two men, but rather the author of *The Little Labyrinth,* who wants thereby to apply the Shoemaker's [i.e. Theodotus's] condemnation to Artemon."[17] A number of statements within *The Little Labyrinth* support this conclusion. The author is attempting to contradict the claim of the followers of Artemon that their teaching was taught from the apostles until the time of Victor. He considers this claim to be a slander on Victor, since Victor excommunicated Theodotus. Now the author claims that the followers of Artemon know "perfectly well" about Victor's actions against Theodotus, which they might be expected to do if Artemon was the successor to Theodotus. Yet the followers of Artemon claim that "the true teaching was preserved till the time of Victor."[18] This presents us with two possibilities. Either Artemon and his followers were simply unaware of Theodotus and his excommunication, or Artemon and his followers did not consider Victor's actions against Theodotus to be a sign of Victor's rejection of Artemon's teaching. If either of these possibilities is correct, then Artemon cannot have been a successor of Theodotus.

If Artemon did not inherit his teaching from the followers of Theodotus, is there another available explanation for its origin? Both Theodoret and *The Little Labyrinth* agree that Artemon claimed that his teaching was also the teaching of the apostles, and Eusebius, no doubt based on *The Little Labyrinth,* claims that Artemon and his followers "tried to make it respectable by claiming it as ancient."[19] *The Little Labyrinth* states their claim as being that the "true" teaching was preserved

[15] *The Little Labyrinth,* quoted in Eusebius, *Ecclesiastical History,* 201 (5.28).

[16] Theodoret, *Compendium,* 2.5.

[17] Fitzgerald, "Eusebius and *The Little Labyrinth,*" 142.

[18] *The Little Labyrinth,* quoted in Eusebius, *Ecclesiastical History,* 201 (5.28).

[19] Eusebius, *Ecclesiastical History,* 201 (5.28)

until the time of Victor, whereas Theodoret states only that "it was those who [lived] after them [i.e. the apostles] who made Christ divine."[20] While it is possible that Theodoret has the same chronological claim in view, he gives the impression that the claim has a much shorter terminus. Further he seeks to explain Artemon's claim by stating that he misinterpreted Scripture. Based on Theodoret's testimony alone we might conclude that Artemon arrived at his views by his own reading of Scripture.

However, the claim attested in *The Little Labyrinth* seems too specific and too objectionable to the author to be fabricated, and so it seems likely that Artemon sincerely believed that his teaching was shared by the Christian community until the times of Victor. Artemon may have been mistaken in his views about Victor, but he may have known no more of Victor than that he was Zephyrinus's predecessor. The most straightforward explanation for Artemon's claim is that something happened at the time of Zephyrinus, and perhaps instigated by him, that impacted unfavorably on Dynamic Monarchians, as Neander suggests.[21] Zephyrinus's adoption of Patripassianism (Modalistic Monarchianism) would be a ready explanation.

Just as I see no reason to connect Paul of Samosata with Artemon, I see no reason to connect Artemon with Theodotus of Byzantium. Artemon seems independent of those both chronologically prior and subsequent. While we may speculate that Artemon arrived at his views independently, I am building the case that Dynamic Monarchianism was a wide and old tradition, as the followers of Artemon themselves claim.

---

[20] Theodoret, *Compendium*, 208 (2.4).
[21] Neander, *History of Christian Dogmas*, 1:160.

CHAPTER 4

Beryllus of Bostra *(fl. c. 222-35)*

USEBIUS'S FIRST MENTION of Beryllus, bishop of Bostra, in his *Ecclesiastical History* is part of a list of "learned churchmen" who wrote letters that were preserved in the library at Aelia.[1] Eusebius seems to date these writers to the episcopate of Zephyrinus (r. 199–217) and the reign of Emperor Caracalla (188–217); he explicitly lists Beryllus as a contemporary of Hippolytus. He records that Beryllus wrote, in addition to letters, other works, which, Eusebius judges, were "admirable compositions." Later Eusebius records how Beryllus "perverted church doctrine" and how his ideas were later "corrected" by Origen.[2] Eusebius seems to date these events to the reign of emperor Gordian III (r. 238–44) and the episcopate of Fabian (r. 236–50). Eusebius writes, "Records of Beryllus and the synod he occasioned still survive, which contain Origen's questions, the discussions at Bostra, and all that took place."[3] Unfortunately, these documents have not survived. Eusebius continues that "the most important information may be gathered from the *Defense of Origen*,"[4] which may imply that this work contained some information about Beryllus. This book is preserved by a translation of the first book by Rufinus of Aquileia and two digests in Photius's *The Library*,[5] but none of these sources mention Beryllus. However, the historian Socrates's (c.

[1] Eusebius, *Ecclesiastical History*, 223 (6.20).
[2] *Ecclesiastical History*, 230–31 (6.33).
[3] *Ecclesiastical History*, 231 (5.33)
[4] Also called the *Apology for Origen*.
[5] Photius, *Library*, 205–8 (chs. 117–18).

380–450) comment about Beryllus is probably based on the book, which he mentions.[6]

EVENTS

The sequence of events described by Eusebius is that initially Beryllus was orthodox, as demonstrated by his writings (c. 210?), and later brought in "opinions alien to the faith" (c. 240?). Initially a number of bishops disputed with him, and then Origen was sent for, who convinced Beryllus of his error. Eusebius mentions records of the synod, of the questions put to Beryllus by Origen, and of discussions held in Bostra as though these were separate events. This may suggest a more protracted sequence of events than initially indicated by Eusebius's brief summary.[7] Socrates mentions a letter sent to Beryllus by the synod convened on his account.[8] This may imply that Beryllus was not present at this initial synod.

It is also possible that Eusebius's description of these events anachronistically molds them into the formal process through which heretics were addressed in his own day. Brent writes,

> The one and only player in this debate is Origen, a lay catechist or a presbyter, depending on the date, who conducted examinations and discussions with a bishop of a See . . . there are no actions or contributions of any bishop mentioned other than Beryllus. It is more like a dispute in a philosophical school between two protagonists, one of whom wins the debate which the other concedes . . . Eusebius has in the case of Beryllus clearly imposed the model of a Synodical process upon proceedings which were more open–ended. The process of correction at this point in time was to educate rather than juridical.[9]

---

[6] Socrates, *Ecclesiastical History*, 81 (3.7); Van Nuffelen, "Two Fragments," 105–11; Pamphilus, *Apology*.

[7] Eusebius, *Ecclesiastical History*, 230–31 (6.33).

[8] Socrates, *Ecclesiastical History*, 81 (3.7).

[9] Brent, "Was Hippolytus a Schismatic?" 221–22.

This didactic approach seems to be the way Origen addressed several cases of divergent teaching, as Eusebius records, including refuting the Valentinianism of Ambrose and the views of certain Arabians regarding the mortality of the soul.[10] This is also the approach taken in Origen's recently discovered dialogue with the bishop Heraclides, which probably occurred around 244–49.[11]

BELIEFS

Eusebius records that Beryllus asserted that "our Savior and Lord did not preexist before residing among men and had no divinity of his own apart from the Father's indwelling."[12] Socrates records that the letter of the synod to Beryllus included the doctrine that "Christ in his incarnation was endowed with a soul [*empsychos*],"[13] which may suggest that Beryllus rejected this doctrine. The only other testimony we have about the beliefs for Beryllus is a fragment of Origen's *On Titus* preserved in Rufinus's translation of *Apology for Origen*. Origen is expounding what is meant by "heretic" (Tit. 3:10) and describes a number of different doctrinal positions which would be considered heretical. One of these closely resembles Eusebius's description of the beliefs of Beryllus:

> Moreover, not without danger may those be associated with the Church's membership who say that the Lord Jesus was a man, foreknown and predestined, who before his coming in the flesh had no substantial and proper existence, but that, because he was born human, he possessed only the deity of the Father within him.[14]

Beryllus's position was linked to that of the Patripassians by Schleiermacher and to that of Artemon by Baur.[15] However Origen has

---

[10] Eusebius, *Ecclesiastical History*, 220, 232 (6.18, 6.37).
[11] Behr, *Way of Nicaea*, 1:210–11; Origen, *Dialogue*.
[12] Eusebius, *Ecclesiastical History*, 230–31 (6.33).
[13] Socrates, *Ecclesiastical History*, 81 (3.7).
[14] Pamphilus, *Apology*, 57–58 (33).
[15] Dorner, *History*, 2:35–45. See also Schleiermacher, *Discrepancy*, section 5.

already mentioned those who say he was "a mere man" (*psilos anthropos*), and later mentions the Patripassians, so clearly he considered the position of Beryllus to be something different.

Dorner understood the claims of Beryllus as being that, prior to the Incarnation there existed only God (the Father), but at the Incarnation a circumscription of God became an independent existence in Christ. This seems to be based upon Eusebius's phrase "did not pre-exist in his own form of being," which Dorner takes to mean Christ pre-existed in the Father's being but not yet circumscribed. However, Origen connects Jesus having "no substantial and proper existence" with his having been "foreknown and predestined," that is, that Jesus pre-existed in the foreknowledge of God but not in being. It seems most likely that Eusebius is referring to the same doctrine.

The idea that the divinity of the Father dwelled within Jesus, as mentioned by Origen, seems to be taken from the conjunction of Col. 2:9 and John 14:10, which mention "divinity" (*theotetos*) and "Father," respectively, dwelling within Jesus. Perhaps, then, Beryllus tried to account for the specialness of Jesus by positing the indwelling of God within him, though this is speculation.

It is not mentioned whether Beryllus believed in the virgin birth, but two facts make it likely. Firstly, Origen distinguishes his doctrinal position from those who say Jesus was born of Joseph. Secondly, there is no mention of Beryllus rejecting any of the New Testament canon, which he would have had to if he had he rejected the virgin birth.

One intriguing question is: what relevance did the doctrine that Jesus was "endowed with a soul" [*empsychos*] have for the position of Beryllus? Since Beryllus believed Jesus was a man, we might expect him to believe that Jesus was endowed with a human soul; indeed, this might seem less problematic for Beryllus than for others, who had to reconcile this human soul with the pre-incarnate Son. It seems unlikely that Beryllus believed that Jesus had the divinity of the Father in the place of a soul. Perhaps instead, the synod mentions the *empsychos* doctrine in their letter, not because Beryllus rejected it, but to reassure him on some other point. For example, perhaps Beryllus felt that the doctrine of the pre-incarnate Son was too close to Carpocrates's (2nd c.) doctrine of the pre-existent soul of

Christ;[16] the letter might have sought to reassure Beryllus that the Son (i.e. the Logos) did *not* take the place of the soul in Jesus. Alternatively, Beryllus may have been convinced of the humanity (and mortality?) of both Jesus' body and soul[17] and may have been unable to reconcile this human soul with an incarnated divine Son; the letter may have sought to address this point.

It is interesting to note that Eusebius, in connection with Paul of Samosata, argues that the Logos took the place of the soul within Jesus.[18] The soul of Jesus is also raised at the synod to discuss the views of Heraclides; though there the issue is how to reconcile the resurrection of Jesus with his purported divinity.[19] The question of the soul of Jesus was evidently a live question in this period. The common anthropology of this period was that a human person was composed of body and soul. For the Logos theorists, Jesus was a body indwelt by a divine person (the Logos). This presented a dilemma regarding the human soul. If Jesus had a human soul, then this would imply two persons sharing the same body. The Dynamic Monarchians would not have had the same difficulty. Though Jesus was filled with God's power, they could assume that Jesus had the same composition as any other human person.

ORIGINS

Our sources give us no clue as to the origins of Beryllus's beliefs. He is not associated with Artemon or Theodotus by any writer and, geographically, it seems unlikely that they ever met. The sequence presented by Eusebius might seem to imply that Beryllus was orthodox in the 210s and only later changed his beliefs. However, it may be that Eusebius's only source for Beryllus's orthodoxy was the books of his that Eusebius had access to. It is by no means certain that Eusebius has dated them correctly. More importantly, unless the works of Beryllus that Eusebius read dealt with the

[16] Irenaeus, *Against the Heresies (Book 1)*, 87 (1.25.1).

[17] See Matt. 2:20, 20:28, 26:38; Mark 10:45, 14:34; John 10:11, 15, 17, 12:27, 15:13; Acts 2:31; 1 John 3:16.

[18] Eusebius, *On Ecclesiastical Theology*, 203–4 (1.20.6.40–43).

[19] Origen, *Dialogue*, 61–64 (5–8).

pre-existence of Jesus, they may well have appeared orthodox to Eusebius despite Beryllus's denial of the pre-existence of Jesus. Only if he wrote about that topic would his views appear heterodox.

If we dismiss the testimony of Eusebius as superficial then we have no reason to suppose that Beryllus came to his views independently. This raises the alternative possibility that Beryllus was part of that wider and older Dynamic Monarchian tradition, as witnessed in Antioch by Paul, and somewhere in the West by Artemon, and now in Bostra by Beryllus.

CHAPTER 5

Theodotus of Byzantium *(fl. 189-99)*

THE EARLIEST SOURCES for Theodotus of Byzantium, also known as Theodotus the Shoemaker, are those written by Hippolytus: a brief reference in *Against Noetus*[1] and a more detailed description in *Refutation of All Heresies* (also called *Philosophoumena*), which was previously attributed to Origen.[2] Hippolytus considers Theodotus orthodox, in part, because he acknowledges that all things were created by God, but associates his Christology with the Gnostics, Cerinthus (fl. end of the 1st c.), and the Ebionites.[3] Later, he describes the second "Theodotus," the banker, as introducing a new doctrine of Melchizedek as the greatest power.[4] In *Against Noetus,* Theodotus (the Shoemaker) is briefly mentioned as allegedly having a one-sided approach to Scripture to support his Christology.[5]

Slightly later than Hippolytus is *The Little Labyrinth,* a work known through several quotations by Eusebius.[6] Two common candidates for the author of *The Little Labyrinth* are Gaius, based on the testimony of Photius, and Hippolytus, since the tenth book of *Refutation* is called

---

[1] Hippolytus, *Against Noetus*, 61 (3).
[2] Many recent scholars deny that there is sufficient evidence to ascribe this book to Hippolytus. On this see the translator Litwa's comments in *Refutation*, xxxii–xl. Nonetheless, for convenience I shall refer to the author of this book as "Hippolytus."
[3] *Refutation of All Heresies*, 571 (7.35).
[4] *Refutation of All Heresies*, 573 (7.36).
[5] Hippolytus, *Against Noetus*, 61 (3).
[6] Eusebius, *Ecclesiastical History*, 201–2 (5.28).

"Labyrinth."[7] Both of these candidates seem unlikely. The testimony of the ninth-century Photius is at best uncertain, and the author of *The Little Labyrinth* alludes to the Gospel of John, which would be inconsistent with Gaius's rejection of it. Hippolytus differed with the author of *The Little Labyrinth* over the orthodoxy of Tatian and in his characterization of Zephyrinus. Following Fitzgerald, it is preferable to view *The Little Labyrinth* as anonymous;[8] I shall refer to its author as LLA. *The Little Labyrinth* is primarily a polemic against Artemon and his followers, and so may be reasonably dated to the 240s or 250s.[9] The writer recounts how Victor excommunicated Theodotus, the "father" of Artemon's following. LLA accuses the Theodotians of using pagan sources, of corrupting scriptures, and of repudiating some Old Testament books.

Three later sources are *Against All Heresies* (wrongly attributed to Tertullian), *Medicine Chest* by Epiphanius (374–76), and *The Book of Various Heresies* written by Philastrius (fl. late 4th c.) around 385. These three works are often considered to all be dependent on Hippolytus.[10] The author of *Against All Heresies* describes how Theodotus was arrested for being a Christian and denied Christ; after this he "ceased not to blaspheme against Christ."[11] Epiphanius expands the report.[12]

Epiphanius also seems to have access to an unnamed work by Theodotus which seems to be a series of proof-texts for his Christology. Epiphanius does not say where he got this work. Bertrand noted the parallels between these fragments and a similar selection of texts used by Tertullian in *On the Flesh of Christ*.[13] It is possible that both Theodotus and Tertullian were dependent on some earlier work on the humanity of Christ (see Chapter Ten below). There does not seem to be any plausible reason for assuming Epiphanius invented the work, though it is possible

---

[7] *Refutation of All Heresies,* 697 (10.5).

[8] Fitzgerald, "Eusebius," 126–36.

[9] Fitzgerald, "Eusebius," 136–44.

[10] Löhr, "Theodotus der Lederarbeiter," 101, note 1.

[11] *Against All Heresies,* 654 (8). This accusation of apostasy is absent from *Refutation of All Heresies,* 733 (10.23).

[12] Epiphanius, *Medicine Chest,* 2:73 (54.1.3–7).

[13] Bertrand, "L'argumentation," 161–63; cf. Löhr, "Theodotus der Lederarbeiter," 110.

he knows it only from an earlier source (e.g. *The Syntagma,* a lost work by Hippolytus).[14] I present an English translation of these fragments in an appendix and references to these fragments in this chapter will be cited simply by fragment number. Philastrius adds little to the other sources.[15]

BIOGRAPHY

Theodotus is described by Hippolytus as being a native of Byzantium,[16] but he was clearly active in Rome. LLA records that he was excommunicated under Victor, bishop of Rome (r. 189–99).[17] He is not mentioned by Irenaeus, which may suggest he was not active in the mid-170s, though it is possible he was not considered heretical at this time. Carrington suggests that Theodotus may have been a refugee from Byzantium following the destruction of its fortifications by order of Emperor Severus in 196,[18] but he may have come to Rome for other reasons at an earlier date. LLA describes him as a *skuteus* (leather worker or shoemaker).[19] Epiphanius, however, describes Theodotus as "a man of broad learning."[20]

Hippolytus implies that Theodotus had followers, but only names one, Theodotus the Banker, who, he says, introduced a new doctrine.[21] The later sources give the same picture, though they describe the followers of the second Theodotus as a separate sect; Epiphanius styles them "Melchizedekians."[22] LLA names an additional disciple of Theodotus as Asclepiodotus (fl. c. 199–217). He records an incident during the episcopacy of Zephyrinus when Asclepiodotus and Theodotus the Banker persuaded Natalius (fl. c. 199–217) to become bishop of the sect, who later

---

[14] Löhr, "Theodotus der Lederarbeiter," 112.

[15] Philastrius, *Book of Various Heresies,* 50.1–3.

[16] *Refutation of All Heresies,* 571 (7.35).

[17] Eusebius, *Ecclesiastical History,* 201 (5.28).

[18] Carrington, *The Early Christian Church,* 2:415.

[19] Lampe, *Christians at Rome,* 344.

[20] Epiphanius, *Medicine Chest,* 2:73 (54.1.3).

[21] *Refutation of All Heresies,* 573 (7.36).

[22] Epiphanius, *Medicine Chest,* 2:78 (55.1.1).

relented and was readmitted into communion by Zephyrinus. The implication of this is that the followers of Theodotus had a church of their own that was not in communion with the "orthodox" church. We do not know who separated from whom, though it is conceivable that Natalius was the first bishop of the "Theodotian" church and that his ordination was the moment of separation.

APOSTASY CHARGE

The author of *Against All Heresies*, Epiphanius, and Philastrius all report that Theodotus denied Christ under pressure of persecution, something not mentioned in our earlier sources. The first of these merely says that he was apprehended for being a Christian and apostatized;[23] Philastrius writes similarly.[24] Epiphanius greatly expands the report, saying that Theodotus was arrested along with others by the governor of Byzantium during a persecution of Christians. While others went to martyrdom, Theodotus denied Christ. Moved with shame at his denial he fled Byzantium and came to live in Rome. The Christians in Rome, recognizing him, charge him with losing his grip on the truth. In response he creates the excuse that he did not deny God, but denied a man.[25]

The story of Epiphanius is suspicious. Epiphanius is a much later source than our others and is known for being unreliable. He cannot identify the persecution during which Theodotus is meant to have been arrested or any of the particulars of the story. It seems probable that Epiphanius has imaginatively created this story out of a single line from an earlier source. While the author of *Against All Heresies* dates Theodotus's adoption of his Christology from after his apostasy, Epiphanius considers it to be the cause. The editor of a recent critical edition of *Medicine Chest* suspected the story was spun out of fragment 2 of Theodotus (see the appendix below), which is based on Matt. 12:31–32, where Jesus seems to make a distinction between blasphemy against him and blasphemy against

---

[23] *Against All Heresies*, 654 (8).
[24] Philastrius, *Book of Various Heresies*, 50.1.
[25] Epiphanius, *Medicine Chest*, 2:73 (54.1.4–7).

the Holy Spirit.[26] We can probably disregard most of the apostasy story. Since it is mentioned in three sources, we cannot rule out that Theodotus did deny Christ following his arrest by some authority. However, since it is not mentioned in *Refutation of All Heresies* or *The Little Labyrinth*, despite it being perfect fodder for their polemics, we must consider this story to be highly suspicious.

EXCOMMUNICATION

LLA states that Victor excommunicated Theodotus the shoemaker "when he first said that Christ was merely human."[27] He is responding to the claims of the followers of Artemon that their Christology was taught by the church until the times of Victor. His argument is that Victor cannot have agreed with the views of Theodotus since he excommunicated him. While our other sources do not mention the excommunication of Theodotus, there is no good reason for doubting that it occurred. The establishment of a separate church by his followers implies a break from communion with the rest of the church at Rome. The excommunication of Theodotus would explain the need for a separate church. Our other sources regard Theodotus as a heretic, which while not necessarily entailing formal excommunication would certainly suggest it.

The other recorded instance of excommunication enacted by Victor relates to the Quartodecimanism controversy. Eusebius records that following conferences on the issue, a rule was proposed by leading bishops that Easter should always be celebrated on Sunday regardless of the date of Passover.[28] The Asian bishops (i.e. those whose churches were in Asia Minor) responded with a letter from Polycrates (c. 130–96) to Victor stating their intention to continue with the tradition that had received. Victor reacts by attempting to excommunicate all the Asian dioceses on the ground of heterodoxy (or, perhaps, all Asian Christians dwelling in Rome). Several others, including Irenaeus, intervened on behalf of the

---

[26] Löhr, "Theodotus der Lederarbeiter," 110.

[27] Eusebius, *Ecclesiastical History*, 201 (5.28).

[28] Eusebius, *Ecclesiastical History*, 197 (5.23).

Asian churches, arguing that the churches should not be divided over this issue. Eusebius does not record the outcome of this intervention.[29] The order of events is, perhaps, illustrative. While the Asian churches had a different tradition, no action was taken until a rule was adopted and, significantly, until the Asian bishops made open declaration of their intention to excuse themselves from this ruling. It would appear that it was this open variance that prompted Victor's action. As Irenaeus, a determined combatant of heresy, notes, the date of Easter had never previously been a prerequisite for communion.

It is possible that Victor and the Roman church simply regarded the views of Theodotus to be beyond the pale, that he was excommunicated for something commonly regarded as heretical. The Quartodecimanism controversy suggests an alternative explanation: Theodotus was excommunicated not so much for his views but for his open disagreement with Victor and/or the Roman church.

SCRIPTURES

LLA claims that some of the followers of Theodotus have "simply rejected the Law and Prophets"[30] and Epiphanius claims they "also fabricate spurious books for their own deception."[31] From the proof-texts dossier preserved by Epiphanius it seems likely that Theodotus accepted Deuteronomy, Isaiah, Jeremiah, Matthew, Luke, John,[32] Acts, and 1 Timothy. The "new doctrine" of Theodotus the Banker regarding Melchizedek seems based upon Hebrews,[33] which presumably was also

---

[29] Eusebius, *Ecclesiastical History*, 198 (5.23).

[30] Eusebius, *Ecclesiastical History*, 202 (5.28).

[31] Epiphanius, *Medicine Chest*, 2:79 (55.1.5).

[32] Epiphanius claims that the Theodotians arose as an offshoot of a previous sect that denied the Gospel of John. He equates the denial of the Gospel of John with denial of "the divine Word who it <declares> was 'in the beginning' " (*Medicine Chest*, 2:73 [54.1.1]). Epiphanius takes the prologue of the Gospel to be a proof-text for the divinity of Christ and so equates the denial of the divinity of Christ with the denial of the Gospel. This need not imply that the Gospel was rejected by the followers of Theodotus, who, no doubt, reconciled the prologue with their own understanding of Jesus.

[33] Cf. *Against All Heresies*, 654 (8).

accepted. This sampling from Old Testament and New Testament is almost certainly not exhaustive, and we may assume he accepts other books generally received by the wider church at this time. This stands at odds with claims of LLA and Epiphanius.

The former claim (that of LLA) may be correct as it is only applied to some followers rather than Theodotus himself; perhaps some of his followers did reject the Old Testament. However, it seems more likely that this claim is merely LLA's characterization of the Theodotians, equating their doctrines with a rejection of the scriptures (that is, a rejection of the doctrine he believed was contained within those scriptures). The latter claim (that of Epiphanius) is unsubstantiated by reference to any titles of these purported works. Epiphanius is unsure whether the "Theodotians" still exist, so it is evident he has no firsthand acquaintance on which to base his claims. Given the repeated associations with the Ebionites, Cerinthus, and the Gnostics, it is possible that Epiphanius simply assumes that the "Theodotians" also created rival scriptures like these other heretics had done. The fact is that there are no known pseudepigrapha ascribed to Theodotus or his followers. Neither claim is repeated by Hippolytus, which makes both unlikely.

ARTS OF UNBELIEVERS

LLA accuses the followers of Theodotus of "abandoning the whole Scripture of God" in favor of Euclidean geometry, Aristotle (384–22 BCE) and Theophrastus (c. 371–287 BCE). Further, "some virtually worship Galen."[34] Galen (129–c. 200), who wrote on philosophy and medicine, was a court physician to Roman emperors, and consequently lived in Rome from the reign of Marcus Aurelius till his own death. He knew about Christians and compared their self-control and contempt for death with that of philosophers.[35] It is likely that he was acquainted with Christians[36] and it is possible that there was some contact between Galen

[34] Eusebius, *Ecclesiastical History*, 202 (5.28).
[35] Arabic fragments cited Walzer, *Galen*, 15.
[36] Grant, *Heresy and Criticism*, 60.

and the followers of Theodotus.[37] Galen set store by the propositional geometry of Euclid (fl. c. 300 BCE), and praised the works on logic by Aristotle and Theophrastus.[38] Galen is also known for his use of textual criticism on the Hippocratic writings,[39] perhaps something the followers of Theodotus were attempting to emulate.

LLA writes that, "In using the arts of unbelievers for their heresy, they corrupt the simple faith of the Scriptures and claim to have corrected them."[40] This would indicate that what LLA is complaining about is the use of geometry, logic, and perhaps also the citation of pagan sources in the writings of the followers of Theodotus. Reading beyond the rhetoric, the claim is simply that the followers of Theodotus made reference to pagan writers in their works. When he says, mockingly, that Galen was "almost an object of worship," he presumably means that they cite him often. Such dependence on Galen, perhaps even contact between Galen and the followers of Theodotus, would also explain their use of Euclid, Aristotle, and Theophrastus. Lampe speculates, "when the Theodotians set out to explain the Christian faith in the terminology of post-Aristotelian Hellenistic logic . . . they are attempting to apply precisely Galen's program of logic to their theology."[41] Without seeing their texts; however, we cannot know to what purpose the followers of Theodotus put these pagan sources. The selection of pagan authorities makes it probable that it was syllogistic logic that was being utilized, rather than citing texts on metaphysics to support their theology. This would contrast with the use of pagan sources made by apologists like Justin and Theophilus of Antioch, who appeal to synergies between Christian and pagan views as part of their apologetic for Christianity. It is telling that LLA regards Justin as orthodox. Was Justin "corrupting the simple faith"

---

[37] Lampe, *Christians at Rome,* 347; cf. Löhr, "Theodotus der Lederarbeiter," 103, note 6.

[38] Grant, *Heresy and Criticism,* 67.

[39] These are ancient medical writings traditionally attributed to the physician Hippocrates (c. 460–375 BCE).

[40] Eusebius, *Ecclesiastical History,* 202 (5.28).

[41] Lampe, *Christians at Rome,* 347–48.

when he cited pagan sources, or had not LLA read Justin's apologetic books?

SYLLOGISTIC LOGIC

LLA writes, "if anyone challenges them with a text from divine scripture, they examine it to see whether it can be turned into a conjunctive or disjunctive syllogistic figure."[42] Attempts have been made to read the fragments of Theodotus as syllogisms, though none are presented in that form. For example, 'The apostles said, "a male approved among you by signs and wonders," and did not say, "a God approved"'[43] is not a syllogism but presents a simple challenge: why do the scriptures refer to Christ as a man in passages where one might expect reference to him as a god?

Fragment 3 is sometimes presented as an example of Theodotus's use of syllogisms:[44]

1. 'The Law also said of him, "The Lord will raise up to you a prophet of your brothers who is like me; listen to him." But Moses was a man.
2. Therefore, the Christ whom God raised up was also a man, for he was descended from them.'

However, this is not as it stands a valid form. To be a valid syllogism, it would need to be something like:

1. Christ was to be the same kind of being as Moses.
2. Moses was a man.
3. Therefore, Christ was a man.

---

[42] Eusebius, *Ecclesiastical History*, 177 (5.28).

[43] Fragment 7; cf. Acts 2:22.

[44] Cf. Bertrand, "L'argumentation," 157–158; Grant, *Heresy and Criticism*, 71.

A second fragment which has been taken to imply a syllogism is Fragment 2,[45] though as written it is clearly not in a valid form. Attempting to conform these fragments to formal syllogisms may be too crude an approach. Löhr suggests that the "school" of Theodotus may have used logic as a preliminary exercise before exegetical study, in a similar way to the philosophical schools of the second century.[46]

Whatever the case with these fragments, LLA implies that syllogistic logic was being used to interpret passages that implied Jesus was a god, not the passages that state Jesus was a man as are the extant fragments. We can only speculate about how these syllogisms went. Perhaps they sought to demonstrate some contradiction between divine and human nature, for example:

1. God cannot be tempted.[47]

2. Jesus was tempted.[48]

3. Therefore, Jesus is not God.

Or perhaps they pulled apart proof-texts for Christ's divinity, for example:

1. "He is the image of the invisible God."[49]
2. An image is different from the thing it represents
3. Therefore, Jesus is not God.

---

[45] Cf. Bertrand, "L'argumentation," 156. Fragment 2 (preserved in Epiphanius, *Medicine Chest*, 54.2.3) is: "He asserted Christ himself said, 'All blasphemies shall be forgiven men,' and 'Whoever speaks a word against the Son of Man, it shall be forgiven him, but he who blasphemes the Holy Spirit, it shall not be forgiven' " (author's translation). Cf. Matt. 12:31.

[46] Löhr, "Theodotus der Lederarbeiter," 103, note 6.

[47] "No one, when tempted, should say, "I am being tempted by God"; for God cannot be tempted by evil and he himself tempts no one" (James 1:13, NRSV).

[48] "Then Jesus was led up by the Spirit into the wilderness to be tempted by the devil" (Matt. 4:1, NRSV).

[49] Col. 1:15.

In the absence of the relevant parts of the works of Theodotus or his followers, we cannot know how syllogistic logic was employed. LLA seems to think this use of logic to be inappropriate for a Christian, believing that "simple faith" in Jesus as a god is the clear teaching of Scripture (without any need for logic); I doubt many modern commentators would consider the use of logic, in and of itself, to be heretical.

TEXTUAL CRITICISM

LLA also writes that the followers of Theodotus claim to have corrected the scriptures, making emendations to the text. He says that they have produced numerous copies but that these texts do not agree with one another. He equates this process with the falsification of the text. LLA does not give us any examples of these emendations or of the inconsistencies between their various versions, so we are unable to judge the degree of these changes.

In a series of commentaries on the works ascribed to Hippocrates Galen manifests his critical method for discerning the genuine works of Hippocrates from the large collection of materials ascribed to him. This method not only involved deciding which books were authentic and which were spurious, but also diagnosing interpolations in authentic books. The general procedure seems to have been to identify an authentic core of Hippocratic doctrine and judge other passages against that core. While Galen does deal with a few textual issues, his approach is largely literary critical.[50]

It is possible that Theodotus and/or his followers adopted their critical method from Galen. If this is the case then it might imply that they did not restrict themselves to trying to correct faulty passages but sought to identify spurious books and interpolations.[51] While presented as offensive by LLA, such enquiries are pursued by modern scholars and are the basis of the Greek critical text underlying all modern translations of

[50] Grant, *Heresy and Criticism,* 61–67, 69.
[51] Löhr, "Theodotus der Lederarbeiter," 104, note 8.

the Bible. From what we can deduce from the "canon" of the Theodotians (see above), it seems they accepted a good number of New Testament books as authentic. This is in contrast to Marcion who rejected a large number of New Testament books based upon his view of what the authentic doctrine was. It is also worth noting that according to LLA, the followers of Theodotus attempted to re-interpret proof-texts for the divinity of Christ, which implies that they did not simply dismiss texts that they found problematic as spurious.

Comparison of the fragments from Theodotus with a modern critical New Testament text does not reveal a large number of changes. Bertrand identifies only one intentional change in fragment 4, where "Holy Spirit" has been changed to "Spirit of the Lord." The motivation, according to Bertrand, was to guard against a trinitarian reading by emphasizing that the Spirit is a power of God rather than a discrete person.[52] However, "Holy Spirit" and "Spirit of the Lord" were effectively synonyms in Christian usage (cf. Luke 4:18) so this may only reflect a paraphrase rather than an emendation. A second variant is the change from angel (*angelos*) to gospel (*euangelion*), but this may be due to copyist error; there certainly seems no plausible motivation for this change. Grant asserts that Theodotus also omitted the "therefore" from Luke 1:35, separating the overshadowing of the Spirit from a prediction of being called the Son of God.[53] This seems to be a misreading of Epiphanius's report, who seems to be setting up straw men to knock down. In this fragment Theodotus is actually defending the received reading (*epeleusetai epi se*) against a potential variant (*genesetai en soi*). But we have no evidence of a manuscript containing such a variant, and it seems more likely that Theodotus is rejecting a certain Christology. Nevertheless, it testifies to his interest in establishing the correct text.

LLA claims that he has seen the copies made by the followers of Theodotus and compared them. Further he asserts that he has compared earlier copies with later ones, and this demonstrates that they have undergone further manipulation. Grant proposes that this represents a

---

[52] Bertrand, "L'argumentation," 158.
[53] Grant, *Heresy and Criticism*, 72.

genuine attempt by the followers of Theodotus to address the issue of textual variants amongst extant manuscripts.[54] Without being able to compare the copies for ourselves it is impossible to assess whether their methodology was sound and their conclusions valid.

Whatever the merits of their critical approach to this or that passage, Theodotus and his followers, in contrast to other heretics, seem concerned to establish the authentic texts rather than rejecting or replacing them. Unlike the Ebionites they did not create their own gospel; unlike Marcion they did not choose their own canon; presumably one of the things their critics found so frustrating was that they shared the same scriptural basis but had reached a different conclusion.

GENERAL THEOLOGY

Hippolytus credits Theodotus with partly keeping to the doctrine of the "true church" because he acknowledges God as creator, unlike the Gnostics.[55] From the testimony of Hippolytus we may also deduce that Theodotus accepts the virgin birth of Jesus, his baptism, his miracles, and his resurrection from the dead. The suggestion that some of the followers of Theodotus might have thought that Jesus was "made a god" after the resurrection is perhaps best understood as a reference to the ascension and exaltation of Jesus to the right hand of God, which presupposes they also accepted this doctrine. The author of *Against All Heresies*, describing the "new doctrine" of Theodotus the Banker, implies that they regarded Christ as advocate of human beings,[56] which would also seem to imply the ascension of Jesus and his continued existence as advocate before the throne of God.

LLA might be taken to imply that Theodotus rejected the association of Jesus with the Logos (cf. John 1:1–4), when he attempts to rebut him by citing hymns to Christ as the Logos.[57] However, since Theodotus accepts

---

[54] Grant, *Heresy and Criticism*, 69.

[55] *Refutation of All Heresies*, 571 (7.35.1).

[56] *Against All Heresies*, 654 (8).

[57] Eusebius, *Ecclesiastical History*, 201 (5.28); cf. Epiphanius, *Medicine Chest*, 2:73 (54.1); cf. Löhr, "Theodotus der Lederarbeiter," 105.

the Gospel of John, it seems unlikely that he rejected the opening chapter. More likely is that LLA, like others of his day, viewed the Logos as a personal pre-existent being, a second god. Theodotus may have rejected this view, perhaps seeing the Logos as an impersonal power. After all, it is possible to read John 1:1–13 without concluding that the Logos was a personal being prior to becoming flesh in v.14 (see Chapter Thirteen). Indeed, the use of the neuter pronoun in v.5 might recommend an impersonal reading. But in the final analysis, there is insufficient data available to reconstruct Theodotus's views regarding the Logos.

Hippolytus claims Theodotus appropriated his views from the Gnostics, Cerinthus, and the Ebionites.[58] This is not a claim repeated by the author of *Against All Heresies* or LLA. Like Irenaeus before him, Hippolytus is attempting to interconnect the various heresies and, noting the similarities in Christology, attempts to connect Theodotus with these other "heretics." It is important to be aware of this fact when evaluating the testimony of Hippolytus, as he may well be manipulating the views of Theodotus to make them appear closer to Cerinthus.[59] What Hippolytus records is that Theodotus held that Jesus was a man born of a virgin by the will of God. This coheres with his use of Luke 1:35 in fragment 4. This immediately differentiates Theodotus from Cerinthus, who denied the virgin birth.[60]

Hippolytus describes the rest of Theodotus's Christology as follows:

> He lived a life common to all people yet became the most pious. Later, at his baptism in the Jordan, he received the Christ, who descended from above in the form of a dove. Thus before the Spirit (which he calls "Christ") descended and was shown to be in Jesus, "the miracles were not activated in him." But they do not want him to have become a god when the Spirit descended. Others say that he became a god after he rose from the dead.[61]

---

[58] *Refutation of All Heresies*, 571 (7.35).
[59] Löhr, "Theodotus der Lederarbeiter," 107.
[60] Löhr, "Theodotus der Lederarbeiter," 106.
[61] *Refutation of All Heresies*, 571 (7.35).

Hippolytus seems perturbed by the idea that the followers of Theodotus denied that Jesus had "become a god" when the Spirit descended, and that only after this he began to perform miracles. For modern readers, the possibility of becoming a god will seem like a contradiction as "God" refers to the being who is eternal and uncreated. The New Testament writers almost completely use god-language in this way. However, Hippolytus and others of this period used god-terms more flexibly. Being "a god" meant displaying the characteristics of a god, such as performing miracles or being seated in heaven. It would have seemed natural to Hippolytus that if Jesus gained miraculous powers at his baptism then he "became a god" at that time. Or, by virtue of the same line of thought, when Jesus ascended into heaven, he must have been made a god. Hippolytus does not equate being a god with being an uncreated and eternal being.

The fact that Theodotus and his followers rejected the idea that Jesus "became a god," though perplexing to Hippolytus, suggests that they may have demarcated the term "god" differently (i.e. only the Father should be called that).

In fragment 4, Theodotus states of Luke 1:35, "it did not say, 'The Spirit of the Lord shall come to be in you.' " This seems to be an explicit rejection of a type of incarnation. Though the modern doctrine of incarnation has the Son, not the Spirit, incarnated in Mary's womb, in the second century many Christians conflated God's Logos and his Spirit. Although Theodotus affirms the virgin birth, he rejects the idea that it is an incarnation of a pre-existent person. Presumably, then, Theodotus viewed Jesus as Son of God by virtue of his birth and therefore he cannot correctly be categorized as an Adoptionist.

SPIRIT-MAN CHRISTOLOGY

Hippolytus ascribes to Theodotus the view that "Christ" was a spirit (or just possibly, the Spirit) which descended on the man Jesus at his baptism. A number of "heretics" held a form of Spirit-Man Christology, whereby Jesus was indwelt by a spirit (or the Spirit) descending from heaven (or the spiritual realm). Such "heretics" include Cerinthus[62] and the Ebionites (at least, according to Goulder).[63] This Spirit-Man Christology is also found in the *Epistle of Barnabas* and *The Shepherd of Hermas*. (I explore this Christology in greater depth in Chapter Nine.) Given Hippolytus's aim to link "heretics" together (and ultimately, link them all back to pagan sources), there is a possibility that he has made assumptions about Theodotians based upon their supposed dependence on Cerinthus.

The claim that Theodotus identified "Christ" as a spirit-being separate from Jesus seems inconsistent with his own extant statements. In fragment 1, he states "You see that Christ is a man", and again, in fragment 3, he writes "Christ whom God raised up was also a man." He seems to identify Christ as the Son of Man[64] and the coming prophet[65]; in none of the extant fragments does he imply that Jesus is someone distinct from "Christ." Also, the statements of Theodotus entail that the Spirit is something separate from Christ, for instance when he contrasts Son of Man and Spirit in fragment 2. There is nothing in these fragments covering the baptism of Jesus; if Theodotus had adapted the gospel of accounts to say that "Christ" rather than the Holy Spirit descended on Jesus, then Epiphanius would have called out such an obvious corruption of the text.

Hippolytus may be correct in one regard; Theodotus may have believed that Jesus was unable to perform miracles before his baptism. Old Testament characters, like Samson, were only able to do miraculous feats when God's spirit came upon them; the apostles only started speaking in tongues when the spirit descended on them at Pentecost. Since no miracles are recorded of Jesus before his baptism, it would be a reasonable conjecture for someone to make.

Theodotus seems to explicitly reject at least one form of Spirit-Christology when he writes of Luke 1:35 "it did not say, 'the Spirit of the

---

[62] Cf. Irenaeus, *Against the Heresies (Book 1)*, 90 (1.26.1).

[63] Michael Goulder terms this form of Christology "Possessionism," but this term is misleading, as it might imply that Jesus was overcome by a controlling spirit. Instead I will use the term "Spirit-Man Christology."

[64] Fragment 2.

[65] Fragment 3; cf. Deut. 18:15.

Lord shall enter into you.' "[66] Here Theodotus is rejecting the view that the Spirit was incarnated in Mary. Epiphanius accuses Theodotus of stupidity since the orthodox view, of his own day (i.e. fourth century) is that it was the Son, not the Spirit, who was incarnated in Mary's womb.[67] However, Justin seems to hold the very view that Theodotus is rejecting because he identifies the spirit in Luke 1:35 with the Logos.[68] It is possible that Justin understood Luke 1:35 as speaking of *a* holy spirit rather than identifying the Logos with *the* holy spirit (that of God himself); neither Justin nor Luke uses the definite article.[69] For Justin the Logos both causes the incarnation and is himself incarnated. Theodotus seems to object to this, saying that were this the case, the gospel should speak of the Spirit entering into Mary. Here then, we see a direct dispute between Theodotus and his contemporaries in Rome, who would have been successors to Justin's Logos Christology.

Grant proposes that the implication of fragment 4 is that the Spirit did not enter into Mary but did enter into Jesus at his baptism (cf. Mark 1:10).[70] In this Grant is influenced by the assumption that Theodotus was an Adoptionist as defined by Harnack, which included the descent of the Spirit into Jesus at his baptism. However, we have no knowledge of how Theodotus understood Mark 1:10, or even whether he considered this a text in need of emendation based on comparison with the other synoptic gospels. Here Grant seems in danger of falling into the same folly as the heresiologists, believing that all "heretics" must have sprung from the same root. The fact is, we have no reason to suppose Theodotus was in any way connected with the Ebionites.

MELCHIZEDEK

According to Hippolytus, the followers of Theodotus of Byzantium, specifically Theodotus the Banker, added a new doctrine to the teaching

---

[66] Fragment 4.

[67] Epiphanius, *Medicine Chest*, 2:75 (54.3.9).

[68] Justin, *First Apology*, 46 (33.6).

[69] Minns and Parvis, *Justin*, 173, note 6.

[70] Grant, *Heresy and Criticism,* 72.

of the former Theodotus. This new doctrine was that the greatest power is Melchizedek, that this power was greater than Christ, and that Christ is in the likeness of this power.[71] The author of *Against All Heresies* adds that Melchizedek was seen as an advocate and intercessor for angels; a role Christ emulates for men, quoting Ps. 109:4. He also quotes Heb. 7:3 regarding Melchizedek having no father or mother.[72] Epiphanius seems to expand these reports into an account of a new sect, whom he dubs the Melchizedekians. He says that the Melchizedekians took Ps. 109:4 to imply that Christ was younger than Melchizedek and "second in line."[73] They took literally the claim that Melchizedek was "without father, without mother, without lineage" (Heb 7:3),[74] and saw Melchizedek as a heavenly being descended on the earth.[75] He also claims that they "fabricate spurious books for their own deception."[76] A little later Epiphanius states that the Melchizedekians make offerings in the name of Melchizedek as a heavenly high priest.[77]

Despite the ardor of these heresiologists, it seems likely that the issue over Melchizedek has been completely overblown. It is unlikely that there ever was a separate sect named the Melchizedekians; this seems to be Epiphanius's invention, extrapolating from the reports of Hippolytus and of *Against All Heresies*.[78] LLA says nothing about this new doctrine, even though he does mention Theodotus the Banker. Neither does he give any indication of a split between the followers of Theodotus over this issue. As Fred Horton queries, "we may legitimately question whether this doctrine was in any way fundamental to the sect, or the belief was made more of by those who wrote in opposition to the sect."[79] All the

---

[71] *Refutation of All Heresies*, 573 (36.1).

[72] *Against All Heresies*, 654 (8).

[73] Epiphanius, *Medicine Chest*, 2:78 (35.1.3).

[74] Epiphanius, *Medicine Chest*, 2:78–79 (35.1.4).

[75] Epiphanius, *Medicine Chest*, 2:81 (35.4.1).

[76] Epiphanius, *Medicine Chest*, 2: 79 (35.1.5).

[77] Epiphanius, *Medicine Chest*, 2:84 (35.8.1).

[78] Pearson, "Melchizedek," 189.

[79] Horton, *Melchizedek Tradition*, 97. Later Horton engages in speculation about a division within the Theodotians over the question of Melchizedek and suggests that the view that Melchizedek was a heavenly being arose to "kick" the issue "upstairs" (100).

information reported by Epiphanius seems based upon early reports. "Even the detail about the sect's offerings in Melchizedek's name . . . can be construed as a misunderstanding of what is said in [*Against All Heresies*] about the intercessory role of Melchizedek."[80] The fact that we have no other evidence of the followers of Theodotus engaging in this kind of cultic activity also indicates that this is a misunderstanding on Epiphanius's part.[81] It is not clear whether the author of *Against All Heresies* is reporting the views of the followers of Theodotus, or conjecturing based upon Ps. 109:4 and Heb. 7:3, which he quotes. Nor is it obvious that Hippolytus is reliably reporting their views, rather than embellishing them to fit his presupposition that the Theodotians were Gnostic in origin. Above, I questioned Hippolytus's assertion that Theodotus regarded Christ as a power that descended upon Jesus. The same error may be active in his assertion that the followers of Theodotus regarded Melchizedek as a greater power.

There would be nothing particularly shocking about the proposal that Melchizedek was a heavenly being. Origen, among others, believed Melchizedek to be an angel;[82] one reading of Heb. 7:3 gives license for such a view. The idea that Christ was in the likeness of Melchizedek is taken straight out of Heb. 7:15 but need not imply that Christ was also a heavenly being (assuming that Melchizedek was seen as a heavenly being), as likeness in Heb. 7:15 seems to refer to likeness of priesthood rather than likeness of nature. The idea that Melchizedek intercedes on behalf of angels may be a deduction from the premises that Melchizedek is (a) a priest and (b) in heaven (and perhaps (c) an angel); however, this deduction may be that of the author of *Against All Heresies*, rather than the followers of Theodotus. If the comparison is with intercession made by Christ on behalf of other human beings, then this would be a further indication that Christ was not viewed as a heavenly being, in the same sense as Melchizedek (i.e. an angel). The claim that Melchizedek is greater than Christ is likely derived from the idea that if someone was "after the order of" someone else, then the latter was secondary to the former. It may

---

80 Pearson, "Melchizedek," 190.
81 Horton, *Melchizedek Tradition,* 95.
82 Jerome, *Letter 73,* 2.

also be derived from the idea that Melchizedek was without parents, but Jesus was born. While any suggestion that Melchizedek (or anyone else for that matter) was greater than Christ would have been offensive to those like Hippolytus, we can well imagine such a proposal resonating with the Theodotian view that Christ was a man. Indeed, it seems plausible, probable even, that the original intent was to provide another proof of the humanity of Christ, and that the heresiologists, like Hippolytus, extrapolated some heinous heresy from this proposal. After all, on the face of it, Melchizedek was a human being (Gen. 14:17–18).

In summary, it is possible that Theodotus and his followers believed Melchizedek was an angel, and possible that they believed he interceded on behalf of angels. These views may be unusual but are not outside the bounds of mainstream Christianity, and are unrelated to Gnosticism.[83] In any case, their views about Melchizedek are unlikely to have been a fundamental doctrine of their movement, rather than a proof text for their Dynamic Monarchian views.

ORIGINS

There are a number of views suggested by the heresiologists, as well as by modern scholars, for the origins of Theodotus's beliefs. From the preceding analysis we can see that all but one of these explanations (a, b, and c) are unlikely, being motivated by polemical concerns.

(A) ANCIENT VIEWS

The author of *Refutation of All Heresies* claims that Theodotus appropriated his views from other heretics, such as the Gnostics,[84] but to the contrary, Theodotus seems not to have been a Gnostic, but was rather close to the "orthodoxy" of his time. His views on creation, the virgin birth, the resurrection, and the ascension of Jesus, and also his canon, seem to have been consistent with those of the Roman Church (and with later

---

[83] Pearson, "Melchizedek," 190.
[84] *Refutation of All Heresies*, 571 (7.35).

orthodoxy). His Christology, though sometimes miscategorized as "Adoptionist," differed from Cerinthus in several important respects, and does not clearly show any significant influence from Gnostic sources.

Epiphanius claims that Theodotus invented his views as an excuse for denying Christ during persecution.[85] Although we cannot rule out the possibility that Theodotus apostatized at one point, the story of his creating a Christology to legitimize his apostasy is most likely an invention of Epiphanius.

LLA claims Theodotus was the first to declare that Christ was merely human, which is demonstrably not the case and indicates a blinkered view of Christian history. The Ebionites and Cerinthus also denied the deity of Jesus, though they approach the question from different positions. Throughout the succeeding chapters, I will build the case that Theodotus is by no means the first to deny the pre-existence of Jesus but rather that this view long predates him.

(B) APOLOGETIC DEVELOPMENT

A number of scholars have attempted to explain Theodotus as a development away from orthodoxy in response to a certain theological milieu. For example, Carrington writes

> it was a serious attempt to form a Christian theology out of traditional materials, preserving the monarchian idea of the indivisibility of God, and dispensing with the idea of the incarnate deity.[86]

Similarly, Peppard argues that the pagan milieu recommended this christological development, and

> we can say that the adoptive imagery of the Theodotians would have been especially resonant in urban areas of the second-century Roman Empire because of the established adoptive imperial ideology.[87]

---

[85] Epiphanius, *Medicine Chest*, 73 (54.1.3–7).
[86] Carrington, *Early Christian Church*, 2:416.
[87] Peppard, *Son of God*, 147.

Walzer suggests that Theodotian Christology was an attempt to restate Christian doctrine in a way that might appeal to the pagans like Galen.[88] Justin acknowledged that giving "second place after the unchangeable and eternal God" to "a crucified man" was a stumbling block for pagans.[89] Similarly many of the second century apologists are coy regarding the man Jesus; Theophilus of Antioch does not even mention Christ in his surviving apologetic book.[90] Therefore, one might argue that the Theodotians' denial of the deity of Christ was an apologetic strategy to make Christianity more acceptable to a pagan audience.

I have questioned to what extent Theodotus and his followers made use of pagan sources. It is entirely plausible that Theodotus and/or his followers had a special interest in the works of Galen and even were personally acquainted with him. Nevertheless, it appears that their interest was primarily in logic and textual criticism, neither of which necessarily imply heresy. Any use of pagan sources would need to be compared with that by "orthodox" writers like Justin. Yet it is not clear whether affirming that Christ as a "mere" man would be a sufficient concession, even for a sympathetic pagan like Galen. Galen's criticisms of Christianity were that they relied on faith rather than demonstration, and that they believed God could create out of nothing.[91] Affirming Christ as a "mere" man does not address either of these concerns. Nor does Theodotus seem to have been influenced by them; as far Hippolytus is concerned Theodotus's account of creation was orthodox. Galen, while accepting a designing providence, was unwilling to make specific claims about whether that providence was a god; in one place he identifies providence with Nature.[92] Theodotus seems to have made no attempt to accommodate such agnosticism within his theology. Justin is aware that the virgin birth is also a potential

---

[88] Walzer, *Galen*, 75–86.

[89] Justin, *First Apology*, 31 (13).

[90] Theophilus, *To Autolycus*.

[91] Galen's comments on Christians are made in works no longer extant, but a few portions are preserved in quotations by a later Arabic writer. For English translation of these fragments see Walzer, *Galen*, 10–16.

[92] Galen, *Doctrines*, 9.9.2; 9.8.27.

embarrassment in the eyes of pagans,[93] but Theodotus affirms it. Theodotus believed in the ascension of Jesus and some of his followers equated this with the (in some sense) divinization of Jesus; it is not clear that this would be any more acceptable to a pagan audience than the deity of Christ.

(c) PRE-EXISTING TRADITION

Theodotus was originally a member of the Roman church and his views differed from what would become orthodoxy only significantly with regards to his Christology. One might suppose that his views were a development away from a pre-existing orthodoxy. However, such a view implies that the Roman church of this period was uniform in its Christology. This is unlikely to have been the case. Justin refers to some Christians (probably Jewish Christians) who affirmed Christ as a "mere" man.[94] Although he states that he does not agree with them, the fact that Justin describes them as being Christians, rather than in the unfriendly terms he uses against Marcion (for example), implies that he did not regard them as heretics. It is probable that the Christian community in Rome included such views as were held by Theodotus.[95] We do not know whether Theodotus came to his views while in Rome or whether there were those with similar views in Byzantium, but in either case there is little justification for regarding Theodotus as the "father" of this Christology. According to LLA, the followers of Artemon claimed that "the apostles themselves taught what they do and that the true teaching was preserved until the time of Victor."[96] We do not know on what basis they made this claim. It is possible that they regarded the apostles (as represented by the New Testament) as teaching the same as Theodotus and simply assumed

[93] Justin, *First Apology*, 37–38 (21).

[94] Justin, *Dialogue with Trypho*, trans. Halton, 73–79 (48.3). There is textual variant for this passage, between "our race," that is Christians, and "your race," that is Jews. The scholarly consensus favors the latter.

[95] Carrington also cites Hermas as a precursor to Theodotus. However, as detailed below, I think Hermas holds a Spirit-Man Christology that Theodotus would have rejected (Carrington, *Early Christian Church,* 2:416).

[96] Eusebius, *Ecclesiastical History*, 201 (5.28).

there was a continuous tradition in the intervening period. After all, neither the synoptic gospels nor the book Acts seem to teach either the literal pre-existence or the deity of Christ. However, it is possible that the followers of Artemon had access to sources no longer extant which would broaden our knowledge of Christology in the second century. We have already noted three geographically disparate figures (Paul of Samosata, Artemon, and Beryllus) who all denied the pre-existence of Jesus. To this picture we may now also add Theodotus. Whether he came to his Christology in Byzantium or in Rome, he is an independent representative of Dynamic Monarchian belief. Although we cannot rule out that he came to his views through his own contemplation of the scriptures, the emerging pattern is highly suggestive of a widespread Dynamic Monarchian tradition.

CHAPTER 6

The Other Ebionites

T
HE EBIONITES WERE A GROUP of Jewish Christians who were considered heretical by the writers who mention them. Our earliest reference to the Ebionites is found in Irenaeus's *Against Heresies,* where he states that "in regard to the Lord they hold the same opinion as Cerinthus and Carpocrates."[1] This is usually taken to mean a denial of the pre-existence of Jesus and of the virgin birth. Hippolytus records something similar, perhaps having no source other than Irenaeus.[2] These Ebionites fall outside the purview of this book, as they deny the virgin birth and are better regarded as Adoptionists, (or perhaps, affirming a Spirit-Man Christology—see Chapter Eight). However, there is some evidence of a second group of Ebionites who did not deny the virgin birth, and who therefore would qualify as Dynamic Monarchians. They are the subject of this chapter.

Origen mentions the Ebionites on several occasions. He does not regurgitate what Irenaeus wrote and seems to have independent information. He introduces the Ebionites as those who accept Jesus but live according to the Law.[3] Although he may have all Jewish Christians in view, in this section he seems to be discussing groups that he considers to be outside the Church. Significantly, he says the Ebionites are a "twofold

---

[1] Irenaeus, *Against the Heresies (Book 1),* 90 (1.36.2).
[2] *Refutation of All Heresies,* 569–71 (7.34).
[3] Origen, *Against Celsus,* 311–12 (5.61).

sect," the distinction being that some affirm the miraculous conception of Jesus but others deny it.

Elsewhere he writes of the Ebionites as "those Jews who believe in Jesus" and repeats the distinction: "who sometimes think him to be of Mary and Joseph, and sometimes of Mary alone and the divine Spirit, but not at all holding the teaching about his divinity."[4] The caveat in the second clause ("but not at all holding the teaching about his divinity") implies that these Jewish Christians, despite believing in the virgin birth, held opinions regarding Jesus that Origen considered to be unorthodox. Specifically, he says they reject teaching about the divinity of Christ. While he does not say more, it is likely this meant that they, like all Ebionites, denied the pre-existence of Jesus.

Eusebius also distinguishes two groups called "Ebionites."[5] The first group is characterized as denying the virgin birth and observing the Mosaic Law. The second group is also characterized by their observance of the Law but, he states, they deny the pre-existence of Jesus and they accept the virgin birth. Eusebius does have some additional remarks about the Ebionites, but it is unclear whether these apply to only one of the groups or to both. He says that they reject all the epistles of Paul and accept only the Gospel according to the Hebrews (more on this below). They observe both the Sabbath and the Sunday Eucharist.

But are the testimonies of Origen and Eusebius reliable? And who are these "other" Ebionites?

THE NAZARENES

It is generally held that the church fathers from the third century onwards used the term "Ebionite" to refer to anything Jewish-Christian.[6] So, it is argued, the second group of Ebionites described by Origen and Eusebius were not part of the Ebionite sect but were other Jewish Christians conflated with the Ebionites by these writers. Some scholars have

---

[4] Origen, *Commentary on Matthew*, 249 (16.12)

[5] Eusebius, *Ecclesiastical History*, 116–17 (3.27).

[6] Häkkinen, "Ebionites," 266; Lichtenberger, "Syncretistic Features," 91; Luomanen, *Recovering*, 25.

identified the second "Ebionite" group of Origen and/or Eusebius with another set of Jewish Christians known as the Nazarenes.[7]

Epiphanius describes the Nazarenes as a Jewish-Christian sect.[8] Epiphanius seems unsure of much about the Nazarenes, such as the date and circumstance of their origins; he notes that "at that time all Christians alike were called Nazarenes."[9] He does not know what they believed about the birth of Jesus. It is certainly questionable whether Epiphanius has had any contact with a distinct group named "Nazarene"; it seems more likely that Epiphanius is constructing this "heresy" from earlier sources. Luomanen writes "it is doubtful in my opinion if the kind of separate group of the Nazarenes that Epiphanius describes in *Panarion [Medicine Chest]* 29 ever existed."[10]

"Nazarene" was a name applied to the early Christians (Acts 24:5). It was used by Jews to describe the Christians.[11] Jerome uses "Nazarene" to describe Jewish Christians.[12] It is possible, then, that the Nazarenes were not a separate group, as Epiphanius supposes, but rather "Nazarene" was the name applied to Jewish Christians (and/or Syriac-speaking Christians).[13] The use of the name "Nazarene" from the first century to the fourth century may indicate that the Nazarenes were a continuation of primitive Palestinian Christianity, persisting with the observance of the Law or some other "Jewish" practices.

The most distinctive feature recorded about the Nazarenes by Jerome is that they used a Hebrew gospel,[14] which he calls the "Gospel of the

---

7 Bauckham, "Origin," 163. Also see Paget, *Jews, Christians,* 353 for references.

8 Epiphanius, *Medicine Chest,* 1:123–30 (29).

9 Epiphanius, *Medicine Chest,* 1: 123 (29.1.3).

10 Luomanen, *Recovering,* 26.

11 Tertullian, *Against Marcion,* 354 (4.8).

12 Jerome, *Commentary on Isaiah,* 5.18–19.

13 Luomanen, *Recovering,* 26.

14 Jerome, *On Illustrious Men,* 10 (3.2); Jerome, *Commentary on Matthew,* 88 (6.11), 141–42 (12.13), 267 (23.35).

Hebrews"[15] and ascribes to Matthew.[16] In one place Jerome states that this gospel is used by both the Nazarenes and the Ebionites,[17] though given that this assignment to the Ebionites is uncharacteristic for Jerome, it is possible that this is based solely on Eusebius's testimony,[18] rather than direct information. Scholars usually distinguish the *Gospel of the Hebrews* from the *Gospel of the Ebionites* known through citations by Epiphanius. Given that Jerome quotes the *Gospel of the Hebrews* for variants of the *Gospel of Matthew,* and given many marginal notes in manuscript copies of *Matthew* referring to variants in the "Jewish copy,"[19] it seems plausible that the *Gospel of the Hebrews* was a Hebrew or Aramaic version of the *Gospel of Matthew.* It is entirely plausible that the *Gospel of the Hebrews,* unlike the *Gospel of the Ebionites,* included the virgin birth narrative.

It is worth noting the alternative theory proposed by James R. Edwards that the Hebrew gospel known to Jerome as the "Gospel of the Hebrews" and the "Gospel of the Nazarenes" is the earliest gospel and is the source for (what textual scholars have dubbed) "Special Luke" (i.e. that material unique to Luke's gospel). He argues that the terms "Gospel of the Ebionites" and "Gospel of the Nazarenes" are neologisms of modern scholars; Epiphanius speaks only of "the Hebrew Gospel used by the Ebionites"; Jerome speaks of the "Hebrew Gospel used by the Nazarenes."[20] Instead he argues for a single unified tradition of a *Hebrew Gospel,* near-universally ascribed to Matthew. (Edwards also argues that, although the *Hebrew Gospel* may have been authored by the apostle Matthew, the first gospel in the canon is misattributed).[21] Edwards argues, against the usual consensus, that the gospel used by the Ebionites was not dependent on the synoptics, but rather its similarity with the synoptic

---

[15] *Commentary on Matthew,* 88 (6.11); *Commentary on Isaiah,* Preface to book 18; Jerome, *Dialogue Against the Pelagians,* 249 (3.2).

[16] Jerome, *Tractate on the Psalms,* 262 (on Ps. 135). Jerome even states about this Hebrew gospel that "many call [it] the authentic Gospel of Matthew" (*Commentary on Matthew,* 141 [12.13]).

[17] Jerome, *Commentary on Matthew,* 141–42 (12.13).

[18] Eusebius, *Ecclesiastical History,* 116–17 (3.27).

[19] Elliott, *Apocryphal New Testament,* 13–14.

[20] Edwards, *Hebrew Gospel,* 121–22

[21] Edwards, *Hebrew Gospel,* 252–58.

tradition is because of the dependence of Luke upon the *Hebrew Gospel*.[22] He does not, however, dispute that the gospel used by the Ebionites had been altered by them from the *Hebrew Gospel*.[23] Edwards does not attempt to reconstruct the contents of the *Hebrew Gospel* from extant sources. If we accept his proposal that Special Luke, and specifically those portions rich in Semitisms,[24] is dependent on the *Hebrew Gospel*, then it probably contained a virgin birth narrative.[25] This may be confirmed if we understand Epiphanius to be comparing the gospel used by the Ebionites with the *Hebrew Gospel*, which he knows from the Nazarenes[26] when he says that the Ebionites had falsified the gospel to change its beginning.[27]

It might be that the two groups of Jewish Christians that Origen and Eusebius have in mind are the Ebionites and the Nazarenes. When Eusebius writes that they "thought that the letters of the apostle [Paul] ought to be rejected totally, calling him an apostate from the Law. They used only the so-called *Gospel of the Hebrews* and accorded the others little respect,"[28] he is quoting Irenaeus's report except that he substitutes *Gospel of the Hebrews* for *Gospel of Matthew*.[29] Luomanen suggests that Eusebius could have read how the *Gospel of the Hebrews* refers to the Holy Spirit as "mother" and drawn the conclusion that those Ebionites who accepted the virgin birth must have used the "Gospel of the Hebrews."[30] Alternatively, Eusebius may have simply assumed that when Irenaeus

[22] Edwards, *Hebrew Gospel*, 107–12.

[23] Edwards, *Hebrew Gospel*, 27, 123.

[24] A Semitism is a grammatical or syntactical behavior in a language which reveals that the influence of a Semitic language.

[25] See Edwards, *Hebrew Gospel*, 294–99 for a chart of the Semitisms in this portion of Luke's gospel.

[26] Epiphanius, *Medicine Chest*, 130 (29.9.4).

[27] Epiphanius, *Medicine Chest*, 1:141–42 (30.13.2–3; 30.14.3).

[28] Eusebius, *Ecclesiastical History*, 116–17 (3.27). All that has survived of this gospel is a few patristic quotations; these are collected in Elliott, *Apocryphal New Testament*, 9–10. One of these is in Origen, *Commentary on John*, 116 (2.87).

[29] Irenaeus, *Against the Heresies (Book 1)*, 90 (1.26).

[30] Luomanen, "On the Fringes," 269. He adds "it would have been embarrassing had a heretical group based its teaching on the Gospel of Matthew. After all, in Eusebius's view, heretics tended to use gospels of their own" (270).

refers to Jewish Christians using the *Gospel of Matthew,* he must mean the Hebrew gospel often attributed to Matthew (i.e. *Gospel of the Hebrews*). If Edwards's theory is correct, then when Irenaeus says the Ebionites use only "the Gospel according to Matthew"[31] he may be referring to the *Hebrew Gospel*; when Eusebius amends Irenaeus's report to "the Gospel called according to the Hebrews" he is merely trying to distinguish the *Hebrew Gospel* from the canonical Matthew. A third possibility is that Eusebius was aware, either directly or through earlier reports, of a group of Jewish Christians who accepted the virgin birth and used the *Gospel of the Hebrews;* he (incorrectly) attributes Irenaeus's comments about the Ebionites to this second group, updating his comment about their gospel. As Jewish Christians who use the *Gospel of the Hebrews,* the Nazarenes referred to by Jerome would fit Eusebius's description of this second group.

However, Jerome does not state that the Nazarenes denied the pre-existence of Jesus. The known fragments of the *Gospel of the Hebrews* shed little light on any distinctive Christology. (Of course, a gospel closely akin to the synoptic tradition would not reflect a belief in the pre-existence of Jesus). Origen and Jerome refer to a passage in the *Gospel of the Hebrews* where Jesus describes the Holy Spirit as "my mother."[32] It is not obvious whether this should be taken as a statement of Jesus' origins and, if so, whether it is consistent with the virgin birth. Jerome preserves a fragment from the baptismal narrative where the Holy Spirit descends on Jesus and says to him "my son, in all the prophets I expected that you might come and that I might rest upon you. You are my rest, you are my firstborn Son, who reigns in eternity."[33] The depiction of the Spirit as both a mother and as a descending heavenly being has resonances with Gnosticism. However, the personification of the Spirit as a woman is not unique to Gnosticism. In the *Odes of Solomon* the Spirit is described as a woman who took the milk of the Father (!) and deposited it within the virgin's womb.[34] Jerome suggests the maternity of the Spirit is based on the Hebrew word

---

[31] Irenaeus, *Against the Heresies (Book 1),* 90 (1.26).

[32] Origen, *Commentary on John,* 116 (2.87); Jerome, *Commentary on Isaiah,* 11.9.

[33] Jerome, *Commentary on Isaiah,* 11.2.

[34] *Odes of Solomon,* 752 (19:2), 6. Also see Klijn, *Jewish-Christian,* 54–55.

for spirit, presumably because "spirit" is feminine in Hebrew (it is neuter in Greek). This description of two female figures (Mary and the Spirit) being instrumental in the conception of Jesus might lay behind the description of the Spirit as a mother in the *Gospel of the Hebrews*. It is likely that the *Odes* are of Jewish-Christian provenance. The words of the Spirit might be read as implying that Jesus did not pre-exist but was merely expected by the prophets; however, the latter statement ("who reigns in eternity") might be taken to imply eternal existence, or might be a statement about the future.

Assuming that the *Gospel of the Hebrews* was approximately the same as the *Gospel of Matthew* and that this was the only gospel they used, it would not be improbable that the Nazarenes accepted the virgin birth but denied the pre-existence of Jesus, since the former is explicit in the *Gospel of Matthew* but the latter is not.[35] If the same *Gospel of the Hebrews* was used by the Ebionites, as well as the Nazarenes, as stated by Jerome,[36] then it probably did not record the virgin birth at all. If, following Edwards, the *Hebrew Gospel* is the basis of *Special Luke*, then it is likely to have contained a virgin birth narrative. This gospel was used by the Nazarenes (who therefore probably accepted the virgin birth) and used in an altered form by the Ebionites (who reportedly rejected the virgin birth).

Having said all of this, there are significant problems with identifying the second Ebionites of Eusebius with the Nazarenes of Jerome. Eusebius states that the Ebionites rejected Paul's epistles, but Jerome states that the Nazarenes accepted them.[37] Also Origen, though stating that he has made a thorough examination of sects, does not mention a group called the "Nazarenes."[38] In any case, the possibility that the other Ebionites could be Nazarenes rests on the assumption that Origen conflated all Jewish Christians under the name "Ebionite" but, in fact, he doesn't.[39]

---

[35] Cf. Paget, *Jews, Christians,* 353.

[36] Jerome, *Commentary on Matthew,* 140 (12.13).

[37] Luomanen, *Recovering,* 27.

[38] Finley, "Ebionites," 155.

[39] Finley, "Ebionites," 187.

EVALUATING THE SOURCES

Neither Irenaeus nor Hippolytus[40] display any knowledge of the Ebionites being a two-fold sect;[41] neither list the Nazarenes in their catalogues of heresies; neither mention a Jewish-Christian group that accepts the virgin birth but denies the pre-existence of Jesus. While Irenaeus does not include any Dynamic Monarchians in his *Against the Heresies,* Hippolytus includes Theodotus in his *Refutation,* indicating that he would have included other Dynamic Monarchian groups had he known about them. This being said, it is doubtful how significant this absence of evidence is. Finley judges that "from what Irenaeus wrote and what he omitted from his writing, it seems relatively plain that he did not have abundant personal experience with the Ebionites."[42] Hippolytus closely follows Irenaeus's account of the Ebionites, which makes it unlikely that he had independent acquaintance with the group. In addition, J. Gresham Machen writes, "Irenaeus and Hippolytus, since they lived in the West, can hardly be expected to give minute information about a Jewish Christianity that existed wholly or chiefly in the East."[43] Our two sources for a second group of Ebionites are Origen, who describes the Ebionites as a "two-fold sect,"[44] and Eusebius, who describes "others ... [who] had the same name."[45]

Eusebius does not claim any direct contact with the Ebionites. He places his discussion of the Ebionites in the reign of Trajan and largely speaks of them in the past tense. Some of his descriptions are copied from early sources, such as Irenaeus. This raises the possibility that the second group described by Eusebius is based on confusion. There is a known variant of Irenaeus's description of the Ebionites that negates the statement that they held the same beliefs as Cerinthus. Klijn and Reinink propose that Eusebius read this variant text and concluded that Irenaeus

---

[40] That is, either the historical Hippolytus or the author of *Refutation of all Heresies.*
[41] Finley, "Ebionites," 86.
[42] Finley, "Ebionites," 106.
[43] Machen, *Virgin Birth,* 22–23.
[44] Origen, *Against Celsus,* 311–12 (5.61).
[45] Eusebius, *Ecclesiastical History,* 116 (3.27).

knew of a group of Ebionites who did not deny the virgin birth. His description of the first group would be based on another source, such as Hippolytus.[46] But such a confusion seems unlikely for two reasons. Firstly, Hippolytus's description of the Ebionites is largely the same as Irenaeus's, so it seems unlikely that anyone would read these two sources as describing separate groups. Secondly, Irenaeus's account says nothing of "their refusal to acknowledge his pre-existence as God the Word and Wisdom"[47] (as Eusebius records) which makes it unlikely he is the source of the second group.

Pritz suggests that Eusebius follows Origen in positing two groups of Ebionites.[48] This seems more plausible, since otherwise we would have an unexplained coincidence between two reports. However, as already observed, Origen does not explicitly ascribe the rejection of the pre-existence of Jesus to either Ebionite group (though it is not unlikely they rejected this belief). Pritz proposes two possible sources for this element: Justin's *Dialogue with Trypho* 48.2 or Origen's *Commentary on Titus*.[49] Neither passage explicitly identifies those whose views are under discussion. Many scholars have supposed Justin is referring to the Ebionites, especially those scholars who read "of *your* race [i.e. Jews], who admit that he is Christ," as opposed to "of our race," amending the text of the *Dialogue*. Yet even if Eusebius read this passage as referring to the Ebionites, it is by no means obvious that he would conclude that they accepted the virgin birth but denied the pre-existence of Jesus. Justin introduces those "of our" or "your" race as an example to justify his claim that "the fact that this man is the Christ of God is not to be denied, even if I were unable to prove that he, being God, pre-existed as the Son of the Creator of the universe and became man through a virgin."[50] So, it seems

---

[46] Klijn and Reinink, *Patristic Evidence,* 26.

[47] Eusebius, *Ecclesiastical History* 91 (3.27); contrast with Irenaeus, *Against the Heresies (Book 1),* 90 (1.36.2).

[48] Pritz, *Nazarene Jewish Christianity,* 26.

[49] This commentary is known through surviving fragments; the relevant one here is found in Pamphilus, *Apology for Origen,* 57–58 (33).

[50] Justin, *Dialogue with Trypo,* 73 (48.2).

unlikely that Eusebius should have read this passage as referring to a second group.

The passage from Origen's *Commentary On Titus* does mention Word and Wisdom, but these concepts are frequently cited in the discussions of the pre-existence of Jesus, so he may be responding to any group. In fact, Origen explicitly distinguishes "the Ebionites and Valentinians" from this other group who deny the pre-existence of Jesus. I have proposed that this passage most likely refers to Artemon and his followers (see above Chapter Three). In any case, since Eusebius was aware of both Theodotus and Artemon, he had no reason to assume that this passage refers to the Ebionites.

Pritz does not argue for the accuracy of either of these passages. He writes, "the important point is that he has mixed together more than one source, and perhaps even several sources from several authors. The result is confused and confusing."[51] Perhaps so. Eusebius may be drawing from some other source no longer extant for his second group.[52] Yet why assume that because Eusebius is drawing on several sources that he is doing so ineptly? And why assume that his source for the second group of Ebionites is in error? If Origen is the most likely source for the concept of two groups of Ebionites then perhaps he is also Eusebius's source for the beliefs and practices of the second group.[53]

It seems entirely plausible that Eusebius's report of two groups of Ebionites is based on the testimony of Origen (supplemented, haphazardly, with other sources). Could Origen be the source for the claim that there was a group who accepted the virgin birth but denied the pre-existence of Jesus? In one place Origen mentions "Jews who believe in Jesus, who sometimes think him to be of Mary and Joseph, and sometimes of Mary alone and the divine Spirit, but not at all holding the teaching about his divinity."[54] It is possible that Eusebius would have understood this second group mentioned as holding to some kind of unorthodox Christology and that he assumed that Origen had denial of the pre-

51 Pritz, *Nazarene Jewish Christianity*, 27.
52 Eusebius, *Ecclesiastical History*, 116–17 (3.27).
53 This is suggested by Broadhead, *Jewish Ways*, 196.
54 Origen, *Commentary on Matthew*, 249 (16:12).

existence of Jesus in mind. After all, the Ebionites did deny the pre-existence of Jesus; it is no stretch to conclude that this is what Origen is implying, and such a summation on Eusebius's part would likely be correct. It is also possible that Eusebius is quoting directly[55] from some text of Origen's that is no longer extant, since we know Eusebius had access to works of Origen that have not been preserved.

Origen seems to have direct acquaintance with Jewish Christians. He knows of those who "appear to have taken up the name of Christ" and practice circumcision.[56] He knows of Christians who keep Yom Kippur.[57] He is aware that the Ebionites follow Jewish dietary laws.[58] He thinks others will be acquainted with Jewish Christians, both those who deny the virgin birth and those who accept it.[59] His descriptions do not appear to be based on earlier reports, but suggest direct knowledge.[60] Only in *Against Celsus* does he state that the Ebionites are a twofold sect, with one part accepting the virgin birth.[61] Origen is here responding to accusations made by Celsus, who says that some Christians believe their God is the same as that of the Jews and others do not. Origen's approach is to distinguish those who "belong to the Church" from heretics, and to argue that it is wrongheaded for Celsus to ascribe the views of heretics to those who belong to the Church. In such a context, it is understandable that Origen would seek to group together and label as heretical all Jewish Christians that he disagreed with. This may be disingenuous of Origen, since he seems to imply that there were Jewish Christians within the Church.[62] Nevertheless, there seems no reason to doubt the key claim that he was aware of Jewish Christians who accepted the virgin birth.

[55] Eusebius, *Ecclesiastical History*, 116–17 (3.27).

[56] Origen, *Genesis Homily III*, 95 (5).

[57] Origen, *Homily 10*, 204 (2). See Stökl Ben Ezra, " 'Christians' Observing," 69.

[58] Origen, *Commentary on Matthew*, 75 (11.12)

[59] Origen, *Commentary on Matthew*, 249 (16.12).

[60] Broadhead, *Jewish Ways,* 195. Luomanen's suggestion that Origen's report of two groups of Ebionites was based upon two different versions of Irenaeus's report seems most unlikely (Luomanen, *Recovering*, 28).

[61] Origen, *Against Celsus*, 311–12 (5.61).

[62] Origen, *Homily 10*.

Given that Origen's knowledge of Jewish Christians seems based on direct acquaintance, there seems no reason to doubt his report of a second Ebionite group who accepted the virgin birth. Finley writes that "the fact that some Ebionites held an orthodox view of the virgin birth goes against Origen's assertion that they, as a wider group, did not properly interpret Scripture," so the fact that he ascribes to them this orthodox belief "supports the view that Origen was historically accurate on this point."[63] It seems reasonable then to accept Origen's testimony that there were Ebionites who accepted the virgin birth. These other Ebionites were Dynamic Monarchian in their Christology but differed in other respects from other Dynamic Monarchians we have considered, as they kept the Law and rejected the writings of Paul.

ORIGINS

We have one clue to explain the two groups of Ebionites and that is the gospels they use. Irenaeus records that the Ebionites use the Gospel of Matthew, which explicitly mentions the virgin birth.[64] Eusebius says the Ebionites (or perhaps just the "other" Ebionites) use the *Gospel of the Hebrews*, which is often presented as a Hebrew (or Aramaic) version of Matthew.[65] Epiphanius states that the Ebionites used a version of Matthew's gospel, which is "corrupt and mutilated."[66] Scholars have sometimes separated Epiphanius's quotations from other reports of a Hebrew gospel as though they came from a *Gospel of the Ebionites;* Epiphanius does not use this term.[67] Epiphanius implies that this gospel did not include an infancy narrative, but began with the baptism of John.[68] Generally, the gospel quoted by Epiphanius is judged to be dependent on three canonical synoptics. This gives the impression that the

---

[63] Finley, "Ebionites," 188.
[64] Irenaeus, *Against the Heresies (Book 1)*, 90 (1.26.2).
[65] Eusebius, *Ecclesiastical History*, 117 (3.27).
[66] Epiphanius, *Medicine Chest,* 1:141 (30.13.2).
[67] Elliot, *Apocryphal New Testament*, 14–16.
[68] Epiphanius, *Medicine Chest,* 1:141 (30.14.4).

Ebionites originally used the *Gospel of Matthew* (or an edited version of it) and later devised their own gospel to suit their Christology. [69]

Alternatively, if we accepted Edwards's proposal about the *Hebrew Gospel*, then Jewish Christians (both Nazarenes and Ebionites) used the *Hebrew Gospel*, which was the earliest of the gospels and written by the apostle Matthew. This gospel is not related to the canonical Matthew but is the source of *Special Luke*, which makes it likely that it contained a virgin birth narrative. The Ebionites, however, used an altered form of this gospel, having changed the beginning. This proposal does not significantly change the conclusion. It would imply that Jewish Christians originally used a gospel that taught the virgin birth and that the Ebionites altered this gospel to suit their Christology. On either theory, the implication is that the Ebionites originated from a group that accepted the virgin birth and later deviated from that doctrine.

This would indicate that the "other" Ebionites were actually chronologically prior to those more commonly known as "the Ebionites." Though we may not be able to identify these other Ebionites as Nazarenes, the existence of those known to Jerome as "Nazarene" may also be indicative that the majority of Jewish Christians accepted the virgin birth and that only one part, those commonly known as Ebionites, demurred from this position. It may be that when Origen refers to the "other" Ebionites he is referring to this (non-Ebionite) Jewish-Christian majority. This might be taken as suggestive that the first century Christianity community in Palestine was Dynamic Monarchian in Christology, though on this point we would be reaching beyond what this meager evidence alone will bear.

The relevance of these "other" Ebionites for the argument that I am presenting is that they are representative of another patch of Dynamic Monarchian belief that cannot be plausibly connected to Theodotus, or any other of the Dynamic Monarchians considered so far. Given that our testimony about these "other" Ebionites comes from Origen, presumably

---

[69] The gospel used by this group survives only in the quotes and descriptions given by Epiphanius (*Medicine Chest*, 1:131–65 [30]). For the relevant quotations collected and presented as "The Gospel of the Ebionites," see Elliot, *Apocryphal New Testament* 14–16.

they were active in the third century and somewhere in the East; we cannot be more specific. Yet if, as I have suggested, these "other" Ebionites were prior to those more commonly known as "the Ebionites" then they may be examples not only of Dynamic Monarchian belief in the third century, but in the second and first centuries too.

CHAPTER 7

Other Indicators

I N FOUR CHAPTERS I have examined four figures commonly cited as representatives of Dynamic Monarchianism. In Chapter Six I added the evidence of the "other" Ebionites. In the final chapter in this section, I will examine some other possible indicators of Dynamic Monarchianism in the third and late second centuries, namely, the bishop Heraclides, the Alogi, and anti-monarchian textual emendations.

HERACLIDES

The *Dialogue with Heraclides* is a stenographic report of a synod held because of the bishop Heraclides. This text was only rediscovered in the modern age, in 1951, at Tura in Egypt. From the text it seems evident that Origen took the lead at the synod, adopting a didactic role, both in the brief dialogue and in subsequent responses to questions from the bishops. Indeed, from the text it would seem that the *Dialogue* was only a small part of the synod. Like the synods already discussed in this book, over Paul of Samosata and Beryllus of Bostra, this type of synod was intended to be a dialogue which would convince the subject to change his views.

The text begins "When the bishops in attendance had expressed their worries about the faith of the bishop, Heraclides,"[1] indicating that the synod began with some opening statements from the bishops that had

---

[1] Origen, *Dialogue*, 57 (1.5–6).

gathered to the synod. These comments are not recorded, so we are not told explicitly what Heraclides was accused of. We may attempt to diagnose what the accusations were from what is recorded.

Origen refers to two current opinions. The first, of those who have been "cut off from the Church," is that of unicity (Greek: *monarchias*), which denies that the Son is distinct from the Father.[2] That is to say, they take the view that Father and Son are numerically the same. The second "impious doctrine" is that which "denies the divinity of Christ."[3] The theme of Origen's questioning seems to be to establish that Jesus is both distinct from the Father and is also divine. Origen formulates his questioning as follows, "we do not hesitate to speak in one sense of two Gods, and in another sense of one God,"[4] and Heraclides affirms that Christians profess two gods who are one in power.[5] After this Origen remarks "since our brothers are shocked at the statement that there are two Gods,"[6] which might indicate that there was significant disquiet among the bishops on hearing Origen's line of questioning. Origen proceeds to explain what he means.

Thus far we might assume the accusation against Heraclides was that he denied that the Son was distinct from the Father, that is, the first heresy described by Origen—what we now call Modalistic Monarchianism. However, there are indications that it was the second heresy that was at issue—what we now call Dynamic Monarchianism.

Origen twice asks Heraclides if Jesus was "God" (or "a god") before he came into the body,[7] perhaps indicating that there was some doubt about

[2] *Dialogue*, 60 (4.6–9).
[3] *Dialogue*, 60 (4.10–11).
[4] *Dialogue*, 58 (2.6–8).
[5] *Dialogue*, 59 (2.26–27).
[6] Origen goes on to explain how sometimes things which are two can be spoken of as *if* they were one, e.g. Adam and Eve become "one flesh" (though each has their own flesh) and a Christian is "one spirit" with Christ (though in fact they are not the same spirit, but rather two spirits). His point is that though the Father and the Son are in fact two gods, they can be spoken of as "one god." (Origen, *Dialogue*, 59–60 [2.29–4.19]). Although they misfit later orthodoxy, these views cohere with what Origen expresses elsewhere, e.g. his *Commentary on John*, 98–101 (2.12–27) and his *Against Celsus*, 377 (6.61).
[7] Origen, *Dialogue*, 58 (1.35–36, 38–39).

this. Heraclides begins his first statement by quoting John 1:1–3, a common proof text for the pre-existence of Jesus. Heraclides quotes this text saying, "Thus we share the same faith."[8] This suggests that Christ's literal pre-existence was the point of contention. The two proof texts Origen alludes to, Phil. 2:6[9] and Col. 1:15,[10] would also suggest it was the issue of Christ's alleged pre-existence that was under dispute.

In his most extended answer Heraclides agrees that Jesus "is God" (or "a god") but qualifies this statement saying that God is the Almighty and the Son of God is the Logos; he describes Jesus as being "God [or, a god] according to the Spirit, and man from being born of Mary."[11] This feels like Heraclides is reserving a special status for the Father, while only agreeing that Jesus is "a god" inasmuch as he was born of the Spirit. (He may have had a what-is-born-of-God-is-god style of argument in mind.) This would explain why Origen emphasizes the question of whether Jesus was a god before he came into the body, in an attempt to distinguish the idea that Jesus was a god from birth from the idea that Jesus was a god before his birth. It is possible that Heraclides could agree that Jesus "was a god" before he came into the body in the sense that the Word "was God," hence his quotation from John 1:1–3—though there are many senses in which one could say the Logos "was a god."

An alternative is that Heraclides is under pressure and knows what he is expected to say. Regardless of what he personally believed, he knows that Origen is expecting him to affirm two gods. So Heraclides can concede that the Logos is another god[12] and that God created through this second god.[13] Origen suspects Heraclides of something and pushes him to be sure of his responses. Heraclides concedes enough to satisfy Origen, but his reticence may make us doubt how committed he is to those statements.

---

[8] *Dialogue*, 57 (1.15–16).

[9] *Dialogue*, 58 (1.34).

[10] *Dialogue*, 58 (2.6).

[11] *Dialogue*, 58 (2.13–14).

[12] *Dialogue*, 58 (1.40–2.3).

[13] *Dialogue*, 58 (2.13).

The dialogue proceeds with Origen addressing other issues; Heraclides is not mentioned again, and it is not clear whether any of Origen's teaching in the rest of the dialogue is intended to speak to the concerns about Heraclides. Justifying his statement that there are two gods, Origen feels the need to respond to Is. 43:10[14] and Deut. 32:39.[15] He rejects the idea that these refer to God "in his purity . . . apart from Christ";[16] he claims this is what "the heretics would say." This claim is not directed against Heraclides himself, so it is probable that he had others in mind. Reading between the lines, we might be seeing examples of how Dynamic Monarchians were responding to Origen's Christology. Biblical affirmations of the unity of God would be ready ammunition against Origen's two-god theories.

Origen then addresses two attendant issues, which may have been motivating factors for the present synod. First is the question of prayer; Origen teaches that prayer is made to God (the Father) through Jesus rather than twice, once to each.[17] Second is the question of how Christ can be a god and yet become a corpse.[18] The fact that Maximus[19] raises a subsequent question about how the corpse of Jesus rose if his spirit had separated from it (cf. Luke 23:46) demonstrates that this was a live debate.[20]

The teaching about prayer clearly presupposes some problem connected with the divinity of Christ.[21] The issue of whether to pray to Jesus is here linked to whether he is a god. Perhaps Heraclides queried why Jesus was not addressed in prayer equally with the Father, thus arguing for subordination from the conventions of Christian prayer. More probably, Heraclides came under suspicion because of the way he prayed, perhaps for failing to "maintain the duality" of gods in prayer that Origen alludes

---

[14] "Before me no god was formed, nor will there be one after me." (NIV)

[15] "There is no god besides me." (NIV)

[16] Origen, *Dialogue*, 60 (4.12–17).

[17] *Dialogue*, 60–61 (4.31–34). This fits with his *On Prayer*, 269–71 (15.1–16.1).

[18] *Dialogue*, 61 (5.13–16).

[19] Probably Maximus of Bostra (fl. mid-3rd c.) (*Dialogue* [trans. Chadwick], 432).

[20] *Dialogue*, 62 (6.15–22).

[21] *Dialogue*, 60 (4.4–5).

to.[22] Ultimately, Origen judges that the conventions of praying to the Father through Jesus should be kept, but he argues for this from ecclesiastical order, not from the nature of Christ.[23]

The teaching about the resurrection is less clearly linked to the divinity of Christ, though Origen attests that he has been criticized for affirming the resurrection of a dead body while affirming the divinity of Christ.[24] He reasons that a spiritual body cannot become a corpse, else resurrected believers might rightly fear some future death.[25] He also objects that the salvation of the human body for believers would be impossible if the pre-resurrection Christ had had a spiritual body.[26] Therefore it seems that some connected the divinity of Christ to him possessing a spiritual (and not a physical) body.[27] Perhaps some found it easier to conceive of the resurrection of a spiritual body; perhaps some assumed that Origen must have ascribed a spiritual body to Jesus on the grounds that a truly mortal, physical, body could not be reconciled with Jesus' purported divinity.

Origen attests that another issue was current at this place and "in the surrounding regions," those who deny the immortality of the soul.[28] The question of Dionysius, "is the soul blood?"[29] is essentially a question about one proof text for the mortality of the soul.[30] Those defending the mortality of the soul, according to Origen, believe that "the soul lies in the tomb with the body,"[31] whereas Origen would claim that the soul goes to be with Christ. This, presumably, has relevance for the divinity of Jesus

[22] *Dialogue*, 60 (4.4–5).

[23] *Dialogue*, 61 (4.34–5.11).

[24] *Dialogue*, 61 (5.13–16).

[25] *Dialogue*, 61–62 (5.28–6.7).

[26] *Dialogue*, 63 (7.8–9).

[27] Second and third century Christians speculated in various ways about Jesus not having the sort of physical or fleshly body that other humans now have. See Ashwin-Siejkowski, *Clement*, 95–111.

[28] Origen, *Dialogue*, 65 (10.23–11.3).

[29] *Dialogue*, 65 (10.20).

[30] "For the life of a creature is in the blood, and I have given it to you to make atonement for yourselves on the altar; it is the blood that makes atonement for one's life" (Leviticus 17:11, NIV).

[31] Origen, *Dialogue*, 75 (23.11–12).

because if the soul of Jesus was unconscious in the tomb with his body for three days, then this would be inconsistent with the innate immortality implied by his divinity. Origen believes that the soul of Jesus was immortal and did not remain with the corpse of Jesus; his soul descended into Hades[32] and his spirit was given in deposit to the Father.[33] This assumes a tripartite division of a human being body, soul, and spirit,[34] as was held by other Christians in this period. Origen's response to Maximus's question is, essentially, that while the soul of Christ returned to his body to wait to be resurrected, his spirit remained in heaven until the ascension.[35]

Once again, we see the issue of the immortality of the soul raised in the context of questions about the divinity of Jesus. Eusebius equates the view that Jesus was a "mere man" with the view that Jesus had a human soul (Eusebius himself believed the Logos took the place of the soul in Jesus).[36] The question of whether Jesus was endowed with a human soul also seems to have been an issue at the synod for Beryllus.[37] In Origen's *Dialogue* the question of the soul of Jesus seems related to reconciling his purported divinity with the reality of his resurrection. For Origen, the problem is overcome, in part, by his belief in the universal immortality of the soul; for Jesus to have a human soul does not entail that his soul be mortal.

It is difficult to establish from the extant record what Heraclides's views about Christ were. It is possible that his views were orthodox (by Origen's standards); there is certainly no mention of Heraclides being excommunicated. However, the fact that Heraclides is asked to account for his beliefs before a gathering of clergy is indicative of the doctrinal milieu. Origen describes two Monarchian heresies and is concerned that Heraclides may be guilty of one or other of them, that is either denying

---

[32] *Dialogue*, 63 (7.23–24).

[33] *Dialogue*, 63 (7.24–29). That is, the man Jesus' human spirit—something which was mysteriously united with the divine Logos before the Incarnation as a reward, according to Origen's unique speculations. (See Martens, "Origen's Christology.")

[34] *Dialogue*, 62–63 (6.23–7.7).

[35] *Dialogue*, 63–64 (8.4–21).

[36] Eusebius, *Ecclesiastical Theology*, 203 (1.20).

[37] Socrates, *Ecclesiastical History*, 81 (3.7).

that the Son is distinct from the Father or denying the divinity of Christ.[38] I have proposed that a possible reconstruction of Heraclides's views is that he denied the personal pre-existence of Jesus. He does not say this explicitly, but if he had he may have faced excommunication or other sanction. Regardless, this raises a number of issues associated with the divinity of Christ that were clearly yet to be resolved. Perhaps neither Heraclides nor any of the others in attendance were Dynamic Monarchian *per se*, yet in the recorded dialogue and the issues that they raise we see that questions around the divinity of Christ and his personal pre-existence were still live and controversial.

Perhaps such issues had arisen fresh in this area, but the alternative explanation that recommends itself is that these issues had yet to be addressed as the emerging theology of Origen had yet to take root.

THE "ALOGI"

One group sometimes included amongst Dynamic Monarchians are the so-called "Alogi," a group mentioned by Epiphanius. Epiphanius says that this group rejected the Gospel of John, ascribing it to the heretic Cerinthus. He calls them "Alogi" because they reject the Logos and he considers them dumb (*alogoi*, i.e. without reason).[39] He does not discuss their view of Christ in detail but does associate the Alogi with Theodotus, whom he describes as an "offshoot" of the Alogi.[40] Neander writes, "the Alogi were induced by their aversion to the mystical element in Christianity, and the doctrine of the divinity of Christ, to declare themselves against the Gospel of John."[41]

However, there are strong reasons for doubting that the Alogi ever existed. After careful examination of the evidence, Scott Manor concluded that "the heresy known as the *Alogi* is actually an amalgamation of various testimonies that Epiphanius conflates under a single rubric."[42]

---

[38] Origen, *Dialogue*, 60 (4.5–11).

[39] Epiphanius, *Medicine Chest*, 2:28–29 (51.2.3–3.1), 2:60 (51.28.4).

[40] Epiphanius, *Medicine Chest*, 2:73 (54.1.1).

[41] Neander, *History of Christian Dogmas*, 1:161.

[42] Manor, "Epiphanius' Alogi," 16.

The earliest reference we have to Christians rejecting John's gospel is from Irenaeus.[43] As Fisher writes,

> it is plain from what Irenaeus says, that they were a set of persons whom a reaction against the enthusiastic ideas of Montanism, especially its doctrine of ecstatic prophecy, moved to discard John's Gospel.[44]

Neander had argued that it is "improbable that they would reject John's Gospel merely because the Montanists appealed to it, since they would in other ways be easily refuted."[45] Nonetheless, Irenaeus does not mention any other motive.

Fragmentary testimony remains of one individual who rejected John's gospel, a man named Gaius.[46] Dionysius Bar Salibi (d. 1171) records that "Hippolytus of Rome said, 'There was a man named Gaius who claimed that neither the Gospel nor the Apocalypse was John's but belonged to the heretic Cerinthus.'"[47] Consistent with this report is the fact that one of the lost works of Hippolytus is reported to be his defense of John's gospel and the Apocalypse.[48] The objections of Gaius, as recorded by Dionysius, are all based upon apparent inconsistencies either between John and the other evangelists[49] or between the Apocalypse and other eschatological statements in the New Testament.[50] This is consistent with Epiphanius's quotations from the "Alogi," which also seem to be largely concerned with such inconsistencies.[51] There is no indication in any extant

---

[43] Irenaeus, *Against the Heresies (Book 3)*, 55, (3.11.7), 57–58 (3.11.9).

[44] Fisher, "Alogi," 2.

[45] Neander, *History of Christian Dogmas,* 1:161.

[46] The fragments for Gaius are collected together in Grant, *Second Century Christianity*, 83–86. I follow his numbering in these references. Fragments 14–17 are quoted from a twelfth century commentary by Dionysius Bar Salibi.

[47] Grant, *Second Century Christianity,* 86 (fr. 14). Also cited in Stevenson, *New Eusebius,* 153. Also see Gaius's *Dialogue with Proclus,* quoted in Eusebius, *Ecclesiastical History,* 117 (3.28).

[48] Fisher, "Alogi," 5.

[49] Grant, *Second Century Christianity,* 86 (fr. 15).

[50] Grant, *Second Century Christianity,* 86 (frs. 16–17).

[51] Epiphanius, *Medicine Chest,* 2:29–62 (51.4.5–51.35.4).

testimony of Gaius that he rejected the pre-existence of Jesus or was motivated by such views to reject these writings.

One clue to Gaius's motives for rejecting John's writings, aside from any claimed inconsistencies, comes from his *Dialogue with Proclus,* preserved in four quotations by Eusebius. Gaius complains that the Apocalypse says that Christ's Kingdom will be on the earth and implies that in the Kingdom the saved will be serving fleshly pleasures again.[52] Clearly Gaius held that such pleasures were sinful and did not consider them appropriate for the Kingdom. We can also assume that another motivation was his rejection of Montanism, since Proclus was a Montanist.

It is generally considered likely that Epiphanius drew his information for the Alogi from Hippolytus's refutation of Gaius. [53] In the process of elaboration, Epiphanius dropped the name Gaius and employed the derogatory term "Alogi." Manor rejects the idea that Epiphanius's report was based upon testimonies about Gaius and proposes that Epiphanius derives his information from Irenaeus, confusing the word "others" (Greek: *alli*) for Alogi.[54] Yet whatever the case, little credence can be given to the idea that there was a sect named the "Alogi." Of those, like Gaius, who rejected John's gospel, there is no indication that they rejected the pre-existence of Jesus. As we have seen, many of the Dynamic Monarchians accepted the Gospel of John. Although heresiologists like Epiphanius may have considered the Gospel of John to contain unequivocal statements of Jesus' pre-existence and divinity (as modern apologists are often wont to declare), the Dynamic Monarchians saw no contradiction between their views and the Gospel of John.

ANTI-ADOPTIONIST TEXTUAL EMENDATIONS

Another indication of the significance of those who denied the pre-existence of Jesus in the second and third centuries is the textual

[52] Eusebius, *Ecclesiastical History,* 117 (3.28).

[53] Fisher, "Alogi," 3.

[54] Manor, "Epiphanius' Alogi," 96.

emendations that were made to New Testament texts during this period. As Bart Ehrman discusses in *The Orthodox Corruption of Scripture*, these are variants found in one or more manuscripts that seem to be deliberate changes to the New Testament text to help refute or guard against ideas that scribes thought were heretical.

The wealth of manuscript witness to the New Testament texts has allowed textual scholars to categorize manuscripts into textual groups, and so to propose when and where an emendation is likely to have been first made. I have selected a handful of examples which are likely to have originated from the second or third century and may represent attempts of scribes to guard against Dynamic Monarchianism.

Where the earliest and best manuscripts for Matthew 1:18a ("now the birth of Jesus Christ took place in this way") have *genesis*, other manuscripts have *gennesis*. Ehrman observes,

> the orthographic and phonetic similarity between the two words in question could certainly have led to some confusion. It seems unlikely, however, that a simple slipup would have occurred, one way or the other; both variants appear in wide stretches of the textual tradition, a fact difficult to explain as simple coincidence.[55]

Both words can be used for birth, so the change does not dramatically alter Matthew's birth narrative, but the change does affect the significance of the story because, while *gennesis* is more commonly used of birth, *genesis* refers to a beginning in time. For those adamant that Jesus pre-existed, the original text of Matt. 1:18a was uncomfortably close to an explicit contradiction of that claim.

Later in Matthew Jesus explicitly places a limit on his own knowledge by stating that neither the angels nor the Son know the day or the hour of the coming of the Son of Man (Matt. 24:36). Though omitted by some manuscripts, the words "nor the Son" are well attested, and are almost certainly original. The omission of words in some witnesses is unlikely to be coincidence. Ehrman writes:

[55] Ehrman, *Orthodox Corruption,* 89.

it is lacking in the *Diatesseron*[56] and Origen, and in a range of versional witnesses whose convergence is inexplicable apart from the existence of their common text at least as early as the late second century.[57]

It seems that this emendation sought to remove the implication that Christ was limited in knowledge.

Looking at the variants for John 1:18, at first glance the witnesses seem evenly divided between *monogenes huios* ("only Son" or "only-begotten Son") and *monogenes theos* ("only god" or "only-begotten god") for the one who reveals the Father. The former would be consistent with John's usage elsewhere,[58] but the latter is often preferred by textual critics, because it is the more "difficult" reading. However, as Ehrman points out, *monogenes theos* is not widely attested outside the Alexandrian tradition.[59] This variant is found in manuscripts dating back to the third century, and is attested by writers from the late second century. As well as being witnessed in the Alexandrian text-group of manuscripts, this variant is attested amongst both orthodox Christians (e.g. Clement of Alexandria [c. 150–215], Origen) and Gnostics (e.g. Ptolemy, Heracleon [fl. 145–80]) from Alexandria. This data gives a strong indication of the origin of this variant: "the variant was created to support a high [i.e. divine] Christology in the face of widespread claims, found among adoptionists recognized and opposed in Alexandria."[60] Later in John's gospel Pilate says of Jesus "Behold the man" (John 19:5). It is possible that this suggestion of Jesus' humanity (and mortality) was troubling to some who held a divine Christology because one manuscript (P66) omits this phrase.[61] This manuscript was discovered in Egypt, dates from around 200 CE, and is of the Alexandrian text-type.

[56] The *Diatesseron* was a harmonization of the four New Testament gospels composed by the second-century Syrian apologist Tatian. For a translation of a Arabic translation of this see Tatian, *Diatesseron*.

[57] Ehrman, *Orthodox Corruption*, 108.

[58] See for example John 3:16, 18 and 1 John 3:1–2.

[59] Ehrman, *Orthodox Corruption*, 93.

[60] *Orthodox Corruption*, 96. Note that Ehrman uses the term "Adoptionist" here to refer to those who are probably better referred to as "Dynamic Monarchian" (see Introduction.)

[61] Ehrman, *Orthodox Corruption*, 111.

One other type of variant worth noting is where scribes have changed the text to designate Jesus as "god" or "God." For example, in four uncial manuscripts of 1 Tim. 3:16 *hos* ("who") has been later corrected to read *theos* ("god"), so as to describe Jesus as "god manifested in flesh" rather than "who was manifested in flesh." The fact that manuscripts have been deliberately corrected indicates that the change was not accidental. Ehrman writes, "the change must have been made fairly early, at least during the third century, given its widespread attestation from the fourth century on."[62] A second example is found in a third century papyrus (P72) which changes 1 Pet. 5:1 from "sufferings of Christ" to "sufferings of god."[63] This variant is not widely attested and is almost certainly not original. It is also difficult to explain simply as a copyist error as the words "Christ" and "god" are not similar in Greek. This Alexandrian-type manuscript reflects a theological shift as Jesus came to be regarded as a "god."

The pattern revealed by these and other examples is that scribes who were copying out the New Testament texts were, sometimes, making changes to the text. We should not exaggerate the extent of these changes. These copyists were not rewriting large portions of text. Nor has the presence of these variants made the original text irrecoverable. Instead we find changes here and there as scribes found the presence of some words, or the absence of others, challenging. Extrapolating from the presence of variants to the intentions of the copyists who made them is, of course, risky. It is possible that these copyists, fully convinced of their own Christology, were only seeking to correct the text to reflect what they presumed must have been the original meaning. However, as Ehrman suggests, the presence of these variants is highly suggestive that orthodox scribes were reacting to the perceived problem of those who denied the pre-existence of Jesus and that, in turn, suggests that those who held this position were not limited to a handful of "heretics." The fact that a number of these variants come from Alexandrian-type manuscripts (though not exclusively so) suggests that in Alexandria, or thereabouts, the

---

[62] *Orthodox Corruption*, 92.
[63] *Orthodox Corruption*, 104.

challenge of Dynamic Monarchianism was felt keenly. This should not be surprising given the activity of Origen against Beryllus and Heraclides, and the presence of Origenists at the deposition of Paul of Samosata. It indicates that Dynamic Monarchianism in the East was more widespread than just these few individuals.

It would be interesting to know to what extent those who *denied* the pre-existence of Jesus were also making changes to the text to reflect their position. We know that the followers of Theodotus were accused of emending manuscripts to suit their own ends (see Chapter Five above). Unfortunately, we have no means to judge the extent of this practice, as no manuscripts produced by Dynamic Monarchians have survived. Ehrman explains,

> because it was the victorious part of later centuries that by and large produced the manuscripts that have survived antiquity, we should not expect to find in them a large number of textual modifications that support an adoptionistic Christology.[64]

---

[64] Ehrman, *Orthodox Corruption*, 114.

Part One Summary

IN THIS FIRST PART I have examined the evidence for Dynamic Monarchians in the third and late second centuries. This examination has covered some usually included under that heading (Paul of Samosata, Artemon, Theodotus) and some who are not (Heraclides, the "other" Ebionites). Viewed from one perspective, it may seem a rather meager sampling: a handful of individuals, whose works (if they wrote any) are not extant and who are known largely, if not completely, from the comments of their critics. Yet viewed from another perspective, the evidence is highly suggestive of a much broader phenomenon.

Consider the geographical distribution: Theodotus in Rome, Artemon somewhere in the western portion of the Roman Empire (probably not Rome), Paul at Antioch in Syria, Beryllus at Bostra in Arabia, Heraclides in Arabia, the "other" Ebionites somewhere in the eastern portion of the Roman Empire, and others causing serious concerns to the Alexandrian scribes in Egypt. What makes this distribution all the more significant is that there seems to be no connection between these disparate representatives of Dynamic Monarchianism. Paul of Samosata did not learn his views from Artemon or the Ebionites; Beryllus did not come to his ideas from Heraclides or Theodotus. In the absence of evidence, we cannot rule out the possibility that these individuals arrived at their ideas independently, but the distribution suggests a more plausible alternative: that Dynamic Monarchianism was widespread throughout the Christian world in the late second and third centuries. These representatives are known to us only because they attracted sufficient attention to earn them criticism from those who represented an opposing Christology.

One of the recurring themes in what we have examined thus far is the claim that Dynamic Monarchianism has a long pedigree and that the opposing view is more recent. For example, Theodoret records of Artemon that "he claimed that the apostles also proclaimed these things" (i.e. his views about Jesus).[1] Similarly *The Little Labyrinth* repeats the claim of the followers of Artemon that

> all their predecessors and the apostles themselves taught what they do and that the true teaching was preserved until the time of Victor [r. 189–99], the thirteenth bishop of Rome after Peter, but that the truth had been perverted from the time of his successor, Zephyrinus [r. 199–217].[2]

In the synodal letter Paul of Samosata is accused of banning all hymns to Jesus as "recent compositions,"[3] indicating that he thought that Christian tradition up to that point had not treated Jesus as a god, or even as God himself. And Origen seems to talk on a similar theme when he says in the *Dialogue* that prayer should be offered to God *through* Jesus, not *to* Jesus, following the conventions, suggesting that this was an issue at the time of that dialogue, and that Christian tradition up to that point had indeed not prayed to Jesus in this same way.

This repeated theme provokes a question. Of course, it was common apologetic strategy for Christians of whatever stripe to appeal to apostolic authority to justify their doctrinal positions. Yet the comments considered seem indicative of something more. Not only did the Dynamic Monarchians defend their views from the New Testament books ascribed to the apostles, but they also perceived that something was changing in their own day, that there was a doctrinal shift underway that was not consistent with the Christian tradition as they saw it.

The remaining two parts of this book are about exploring that possibility, that Dynamic Monarchianism was not a new phenomenon, but part of the existing Christian tradition, that in the second and third centuries something happened that shifted Christian orthodoxy away

---

[1] Theodoret, *Compendium*, 208 (2.4)
[2] Quoted in Eusebius, *Ecclesiastical History*, 201 (5.28).
[3] Quoted in Eusebius, *Ecclesiastical History*, 277 (7.30).

from this Dynamic Monarchian position such that it came to be viewed as heretical, and that the views of the Dynamic Monarchians were shared by earlier generations even as far back as the earliest Christians.

PART TWO
Projecting Backwards

Part Two Introduction

IN HIS SEMINAL WORK *Orthodoxy and Heresy in Earliest Christianity (Rechtgläubigkeit und Ketzerei im ältesten Christentum)* Walter Bauer opened a powerful new paradigm for understanding early Christianity. He argued that orthodox Christianity was not an enduring monolith from which heretics had deviated but rather that what eventually became orthodox Christianity was just one of a number of versions of Christianity competing for adherents. Attempting to reconstruct the history of early Christianity in different locations, Bauer argued that in some places what was later considered heresy was the first form of Christianity at that location. These forms of Christianity, including Gnosticism, were often very different from what became orthodox Christianity.

Bauer's thesis has more recently been influential in forming a new paradigm in the understanding of early Christian history, particularly on scholars like Helmut Koester, Elaine Pagels, and Bart Ehrman, but has also had traction outside the academy. It has been argued by some that the diversity of early Christianity tells against the claims of mainstream Christianity and/or that given the diversity in the early church the modern church should be more tolerant of difference. I think this line of reasoning is misguided for at least two reasons. Firstly, it would be incorrect to read the early centuries of Christianity as a more tolerant age, as though Gnosticism and other forms of Christianity happily coexisted. The earliest records we have about Gnostics portray them as being opposed by other Christians. The fact that diverse forms of Christianity existed and flourished is not evidence that these were tolerated, but only that the early Christians had neither the evangelistic success nor the temporal power to eliminate Gnostic or other "heretical" ideas. Secondly, the fact that diverse forms of Christianity existed is not a reliable indicator of whether those forms of Christianity are true. (Perhaps some postmodern people do not concern themselves with the truth of religious beliefs, but I think most people have a preference for avoiding false beliefs where possible). When, for example, modern scholars attempt to reconstruct the life and teaching of Jesus, while they might question the conclusions of orthodox Christianity, I know of no sensible historian who would turn to the works of the Gnostics as source material.[1]

Subsequent work has undone a lot of Bauer's thesis. Research on the locations covered by Bauer, including Asia Minor[2] and Alexandria,[3] have revealed that, contrary Bauer's thesis, Gnosticism and other "heretical" forms of Christianity were not prevalent prior to orthodoxy. Another staple objection against Bauer's original thesis is that so much of it depended on an argument from silence, to the degree that one critic described the results as the *konstruktive Phantasie des Verfassers* ("constructive fantasy of the author").[4] Nevertheless, despite the criticisms of many of the details of Bauer's thesis, his paradigm-shifting proposal that alternative forms of Christianity co-existed during the early period continues to be influential and has formed the basis of much modern scholarship into early Christianity.

In this book I have been seeking to identify early Christians who shared Dynamic Monarchian beliefs. My interest in these Dynamic Monarchians is largely doctrinal and I have made no attempt to engage in sociological analysis, except insofar as this enlightens something about the origins or nature of their doctrine. In attempting to explain the existence of these Dynamic Monarchian Christians in the second and third century I find it implausible that they all developed their views independently and with no prior tradition. As we've seen, several of them claim that their doctrines are more primitive than the non-Monarchian views of their

---

[1] The one exception is the *Gospel of Thomas*, which is sometimes considered in historical studies of Jesus and which is sometimes considered Gnostic (though it is not the Gnostic parts of *Thomas* that are considered historical). For the remnants of this see Elliot, *Apocryphal New Testament*, 123–47.

[2] Robinson, *Bauer Thesis Examined*; Hultgren, *Rise of Normative Christianity*.

[3] Pearson, *Gnosticism and Christianity*; Roberts, *Early Christian Egypt*.

[4] Altendorf, "Zum Stichwort."

critics. In Part Two of this book, I shall explore the proposal that Dynamic Monarchian views existed within second century Christianity alongside the emerging Logos Christology. This might be read as a version of Bauer's thesis, and there are some similarities, however there are several important differences. Firstly, I am not claiming that there were several versions of Christianity, each with an equal claim to be primitive. I presuppose that there was a single primitive Christianity (that of Jesus and his immediate followers), and will argue that various forms of Christianity can be traced from that primitive form. Secondly, I am not claiming that the Dynamic Monarchians existed alongside other Christians as a separate church. We see no evidence of this until Theodotus is excommunicated from the church in Rome (c. 190). My thesis is that the Dynamic Monarchian views existed within Christian communities, though not formally identified as "other" until another form of Christology had gained dominance. Thirdly, my only interest in Gnostic Christianity is as evidence of the sort of Christology that preceded it.

This project faces a number of methodological problems. The Dynamic Monarchians considered in Part One were all defined as heretical by their critics and so were easily distinguishable. In contrast, if and when the Dynamic Monarchian position was not considered heretical, then it would be less easy to distinguish those holding that view from other Christians. Most of what we know about divergent doctrinal views in the early Christianity comes from the reports of those who define those views as heretical. Further, a good deal of what we know about the views of the church fathers themselves comes from their attempts to define orthodoxy against something they consider heretical. If divergence of opinion is only articulated when it is already considered heretical, then there will be little evidence of "acceptable" (non-heretical) divergence. We are faced with a significant methodological problem: without the ancient writers themselves identifying divergence for us, how can we detect it?

There is a related problem in the silence of sources on a particular topic. Imagine an early Christian text, say an uplifting homily or a letter dealing with a number of pastoral issues. Imagine that this text never directly addresses the issue of Christology. And imagine that viewed through the lens of post-Nicene Christianity it has every appearance of orthodoxy; it cites only canonical sources, it recommends chaste and temperate conduct, it shows appropriate reverence of God, Jesus, and the apostles. How would such a work be treated by post-Nicene Christians? It would probably be lauded for its orthodoxy, preserved for future generations for their edification, and perhaps even regarded as canonical (if it was traditionally purported to be apostolic). And yet this presents us with a methodological problem, because the text I have described would appear the same whether written by a Dynamic Monarchian or by an "orthodox" Christian. And this is not a hypothetical problem, because most Christian texts prior to the mid-second century were practical and/or exhortational in nature; there were no systematic treatises on Christology. The Dynamic Monarchians examined in Part One were all broadly orthodox on most matters, except Christology, and so any text that is silent on Christology will appear consistent with later orthodoxy even if it is Dynamic Monarchian in provenance. The problem is compounded by the fact that Dynamic Monarchians, as observed in Part One, could call Jesus "Lord" and even "a god" (in some sense), despite denying his pre-existence. In most regards a Dynamic Monarchian can sound as orthodox as any other Christian.

This leaves us with a dangerous silence. Dangerous because, in the absence of evidence, we might conclude that there were no Dynamic Monarchians or that there were many, depending on which way our inclination bends. This would not be a sound way to conduct historical investigation.

In Part Two, I will attempt to present what evidence there can be, despite this silence. On the one hand I will demonstrate that Dynamic Monarchianism would not have been regarded as heretical prior to the mid to late second century and thus there *could* have been Dynamic Monarchians in the early second century who have gone unreported. On the other hand, I will present what positive evidence is available for the existence of Dynamic Monarchianism in the first and early second centuries. The former question will be considered in Chapter Eight, in which I will consider the attitudes of Justin and Irenaeus, two early heresiologists, towards those who denied the pre-existence of Jesus. Furthermore, I will consider the ecclesiastical situation within second century Christianity, focusing on Rome, since here the most evidence is available. I argue that, in part, it was a changing ecclesiastical situation in Rome that led to the excommunication of Theodotus; the implication is that prior to this change, Dynamic Monarchian views could have co-existed with other Christologies. The emergence and success of Justin's Logos Christology had a significant impact on what was regarded as heretical.

In Chapter Nine I explore some of those earlier texts that affirm the pre-existence of Jesus and consider their motivations for doing so. This analysis reveals that although earlier Christians did affirm the pre-existence of Jesus, they did not have consistent reasons for doing so. Indeed, some of these reasons would have been rejected by both the earliest Christians and by later orthodoxy. This is representative of the fact that ideas about the pre-existence of Jesus were still emerging throughout the second century and were far from settled.

The positive evidence for Dynamic Monarchianism in the late first and early second centuries is, admittedly, tentative and suggestive, rather than conclusive. This should not be surprising, and it is consistent with the methodological problems sketched above. It is also helpful to remember that I am not attempting to evidence a separate Dynamic Monarchian church or movement; there were no ancient Christians who called themselves "Dynamic Monarchians." Indeed, that label was coined by nineteenth century scholars, not ancient Christians. I am only seeking to evidence the presence of Dynamic Monarchian views.

Chapter Ten explores a proof-text dossier whose existence can be hypothesized from the shared arguments of Theodotus and Tertullian. I argue that the existence of such a document may be indicative of the Dynamic Monarchian tendency of its author(s).

Chapter Eleven attempts to reconstruct early Christian Christologies by "projecting backwards" from Gnostic (and other "heretical") Christologies to the non-Gnostic Christology from which they deviated. Such a procedure is inevitably speculative, but not to the point of being purely imaginative. The core assumption is that one can identify a key element of the Gnostic (or other "heretical") Christology and determine what that Christology would have looked like were that key element removed (that is, what it would have looked like prior to that key element being introduced). It is possible that such an assumption is unwarranted, but the results are at least interesting and highly suggestive.

Chapters Twelve and Thirteen examine two Christian writers usually claimed for orthodoxy. Re-examination of their writings calls into question this orthodox label. Both cases are significant given the prominence these writers are given in histories of Christian dogma. If either Ignatius of Antioch or John the evangelist were Dynamic Monarchians, or had significant leanings in that direction, then this has significant implications for how the history of dogma in this period should be written.

Perhaps the most we can say with confidence is that there was room for Dynamic Monarchians in this period, and some indications that they existed. Yet this may be all that we need to establish. If there was a significant Dynamic Monarchian tradition in the late second and third centuries, and if the views of the earliest Christians were Dynamic Monarchian, then the tentative dotted line across the intervening period is probably sufficient to connect the two phenomena into a single doctrinal tradition.

CHAPTER 8

When Was Dynamic Monarchianism Considered Heretical?

T HE EARLIEST INDIVDIUAL modern historians describe as a Dynamic Monarchian is Theodotus of Byzantium. He was excommunicated by the church in Rome around 190 and subsequently considered heretical by several writers, including Hippolytus and the author of *The Little Labyrinth.* This provides us with a date marker; we can say that by this time at least some Christian churches considered Dynamic Monarchians to be heretical. But what was the situation before this? Would Dynamic Monarchianism always have been condemned as heresy whenever it was proposed? Or were such views accepted alongside others? In this chapter I will explore the possibility that Dynamic Monarchians would not have been condemned until the late second century. I will begin by looking at two figures, later considered to be orthodox, who, although explicitly affirming the pre-existence of Jesus, may not have condemned those who did not. I will then proceed to explore the ecclesiastical situation in the second century, focusing on the situation in Rome, and argue that there were not yet the institutional systems in place to maintain orthodoxy by exclusion. I will explore the possibility that the changing ecclesiastical situation gave rise to the circumstances under which Theodotus could be excommunicated.

IRENAEUS OF LYONS

Around 180 Irenaeus of Lyons wrote his *Against the Heresies* (a.k.a. *Against Heresies*). Writing a decade or more before Theodotus of Byzantium was active in Rome, there is no reason to suppose Irenaeus would have been familiar with his views. Though Irenaeus is attempting to reply to all heresies,[1] he does not list (and thereby condemn) anyone for holding views akin to those of Theodotus. The closest comparator to these would be the Ebionites,[2] though as we shall see, his condemnation of the Ebionites does not focus on the issues for which Theodotus was excommunicated, namely denying the pre-existence of Jesus.

There are, broadly speaking, two reasons why Irenaeus might have omitted any reference to Dynamic Monarchian type Christians in his list of heresies. Either it is because he was not aware of any (perhaps because there were none) or because he did not consider them to be heretical. It is not a matter of dispute that Irenaeus believed in the pre-existence of Jesus. He says that it was the Logos that walked in Eden with man, who spoke with Abraham, who wrestled with Jacob, who spoke with Moses and appeared to Balaam. He writes that "it is not the Father of all, who is not seen by the world . . . [it is not] this One who, standing in a very small space, talked with Abraham, but the Word of God."[3] Irenaeus believed that the Logos was the "Maker of all things" and the "Creator of the world."[4] However, how might Irenaeus have considered those who denied the pre-existence of Jesus?

The Ebionites are often grouped together with Theodotus and others as denying the pre-existence of Jesus. They are usually considered under the category "Adoptionists," supposing that they share the belief that Jesus was born a normal human being, but was at some point in his life adopted by God to be his Son. Yet this category is misleading, because it

[1] Irenaeus, *Against the Heresies (Book 1)*, 81 (1.22.2).

[2] *Against the Heresies (Book 1)*, 90 (1.26.2).

[3] Irenaeus, *Demonstration*, 70 (45). See also 47 (12), 69 (44), 66 (40); 70 (46), and Irenaeus, *Fragments*, 577 (fr. 53 and fr. 54), 572 (fr. 23).

[4] Irenaeus, *Against Heresies*, 539 (5.12.6), 546 (5.18.3).

overlooks the important distinction that the Ebionites rejected the virgin birth as well.

Irenaeus has a number of complaints against the Ebionites: that they accept only Matthew's gospel, that they reject the writings of Paul, that they interpret the prophets "in a rather curious manner," and that they practice circumcision and keep the Law of Moses. But first and foremost, Irenaeus condemns the Ebionites because "in regard to the Lord they hold the same opinion as Cerinthus and Carpocrates."[5] In none of his complaints does Irenaeus mention denial of the pre-existence of Jesus. According to Irenaeus, both Cerinthus and Carpocrates believed that something of Jesus Christ pre-existed his birth,[6] so were Irenaeus concerned about this question he is unlikely to have classed the Ebionites as similar to these others. Rather the point on which they are similar is their shared rejection of the virgin birth.

In several passages in *Against the Heresies* Irenaeus refers to those who assert Jesus was a "mere man." These are the earliest known occurrences of this term in such a context. This is the charge later levelled against Dynamic Monarchians like Theodotus, Artemon, and Paul of Samosata. However, it is clear from Irenaeus's usage that he is concerned about those who deny the virgin birth. Irenaeus writes of those "who bluntly assert that He is a mere man, begotten of Joseph."[7] The target is clearly those who deny the virgin birth. His objection is that those who deny the virgin birth "defraud humankind of its ascent to God," because, he writes,

> how could we be united with imperishability and immortality unless imperishability and immortality had first become what we are, in order that the perishable might be swallowed up by imperishability, and the mortal by immortality.[8]

He thus speculates that somehow it is the union of immortality with mortality through the virgin birth that results in eternal life. (Modern

---

[5] Irenaeus, *Against the Heresies (Book 1)*, 90 (1.26.2).

[6] *Against the Heresies (Book 1)*, 90 (1.26.1), 87–90 (1.25)

[7] *Against the Heresies (Book 3)*, 92 (3.19.1).

[8] *Against the Heresies (Book 3)*, 93 (3.19.1)

readers are unlikely to be impressed by this argument, not least because it implies that God is incapable of conveying immortality through his power alone.) Later in the same chapter he reinforces the pre-eminence of Jesus' birth, quoting John 1:13 ("who was born not of the will of flesh nor the will of man").[9] Irenaeus states that Jesus would not have been called "God" or "Lord" if he had been a mere man, but only if he had a pre-eminent birth from both the Father and from the virgin.[10] A few chapters later Irenaeus cites Isaiah 7:14 ("Behold, the Virgin shall be with child and bear a Son") as proof that "the Holy Spirit carefully pointed out His birth from the Virgin." Irenaeus equates this proof of the virgin birth with a denial that Jesus is "a mere man."[11]

Although Irenaeus himself firmly believed in the pre-existence of the Logos as a personal being who communed with the patriarchs, at no point does he condemn anyone for denying the pre-existence of Jesus. For Irenaeus it is the virgin birth, not pre-existence, that differentiates Jesus as being more than a mere man, which is why he considered denial of the virgin birth to be heretical. If he was aware of any Dynamic Monarchians, he would not have considered that they held Jesus to be a "mere man" because they affirmed the virgin birth.

JUSTIN MARTYR

Writing in his *Dialogue with Trypho* a few decades earlier than Irenaeus, Justin also refers to those who deny the virgin birth. Unlike Irenaeus, he does not use the phrase "mere man"; this phrase may have been Irenaeus's

---

[9] This reading of John 1:13 is based on a textual variant which makes this phrase a reference to the birth of Jesus, rather than to the rebirth of believers. This textual variant has been rejected by modern textual critics; see Ridderbos, *Gospel of John*, 46–48.

[10] Irenaeus, *Against the Heresies (Book 3)*, 93 (3.19.2).

[11] *Against the Heresies (Book 3)*, 100 (3.21.4).

invention. Instead, Justin uses the phrase "man from men."[12] However, it seems that he, like Irenaeus, is describing the Ebionites, though he does not name them.

Like Irenaeus, Justin's major objection to the Ebionites is their denial of the virgin birth. In chapter 54 of the *Dialogue,* Justin quotes a prophecy of Jacob about the blood of the grape (Gen. 49:11) to demonstrate that Jesus was born of God. He equates the blood of the grape to the Holy Spirit and so argues that Christ received his blood from the power of God, rather than man. This, he argues, "shows that Christ is not a man of mere human origin" [more literally: "not a man of men"].[13] Further in chapter 76, Justin takes Daniel's vision of one "as a Son of Man" (Dan. 7:13) and Isaiah's prophecy "Who shall declare his generation?" (Is. 53:8) as proofs that he was a man but not "a man of men."[14] For Justin, that Jesus was "a man of men" was the understanding of those who denied the virgin birth, not of those who denied the pre-existence of Jesus.

In chapter 48 of the *Dialogue,* Justin is debating with Trypho about whether Jesus is the Christ and Trypho is objecting to Justin's claim that Jesus pre-existed as a god and submitted to be born as a man. Justin responds that even if he is unable to prove to Trypho that Jesus pre-existed, he would still succeed in his proof that Jesus is the Christ. Justin asserts that there are some "of your race"[15] who acknowledge Jesus as the Christ but hold that he is "a man of men." Just prior to this line he introduces the concept of Jesus becoming Christ "by the Father's choice," which indicates that the people he has in mind are Adoptionists.[16] This conclusion is supported by the fact that elsewhere he uses the expression

[12] Justin, *Dialogue,* 118 (76.2); unfortunately, this recent translator too freely renders the Greek for "a man from men" as "mere man." Elsewhere he renders similar phrases more accurately as "of human origin" (73–74 [48.3–4], 74 [49.1]) or "a man of mere human origin" (81 [54.2], 103 [67.2]). In one place Justin spells out the idea more fully, that Jesus was "born as a result of human intercourse like any other first-born son" (130 [84.1]).

[13] *Dialogue,* 81 (54.2).

[14] *Dialogue,* 118 (76.2), translation modified—see note 12 above.

[15] Or "of our race;" scholars differ on the correct reading of the Greek text here. See the translator's comment at Justin, *Dialogue,* 73–74, note 3.

[16] Justin, *Dialogue,* 73 (48.3).

"man from men" with reference to those who deny the virgin birth. These seem likely to be the Ebionites.

However, Justin's description of the Ebionites seems far more sympathetic than Irenaeus's, and certainly far more charitable than his own condemnation of the followers of Marcion and Valentinus (c. 100–c. 160).[17] He describes the Ebionites either as being "of our race" (i.e. Christians) or as being "of your race" (i.e. Jewish Christians),[18] which implies that Justin regarded them as fellow Christians and gives no indication that he thought they should be excommunicated. If this was his attitude towards the Ebionites, then it seems improbable he would have regarded Dynamic Monarchians as heretics.

ECCLESIASTICAL SITUATION

It seems that neither Justin nor Irenaeus regarded (or would have regarded) Dynamic Monarchians as heretical. These writers were influential, both in their own day and, through their writings, on subsequent generations. However, while a writer might have the power to persuade, the power to excommunicate rested with the clergy, or at least by the end of the second century it did, when Theodotus was excommunicated by Victor. How then would the Dynamic Monarchians have fared in earlier generations?

We do not have much evidence for the ecclesiastical situation in the early and mid-second century. Perhaps the most evidenced and most discussed is the ecclesiastical situation at Rome, which I will take as a test case. Of course, it would be inappropriate to assume that the situation at Rome was necessarily the same as in Christian communities elsewhere; indeed, there are indications that the ecclesiastical arrangements differed in important ways in other locations. However, Rome is significant both because of its later prominence and because the earliest known excommunication of a Dynamic Monarchian occurred at Rome.

---

[17] *Dialogue*, 55 (35.5–8).
[18] See note 15 above.

One oft-discussed question is whether there was a monarchical episcopacy at Rome prior to the second half of the second century. Tradition has it that Rome had a succession of bishops dating back to the apostle Peter. Modern scholars have often argued that monarchical bishops were a later development; and, specifically, Rome had no such role until the second half of the second century. For example, Peter Lampe argues that "before the second half of the second century there was in Rome no monarchial episcopacy for the circles mutually bound in fellowship."[19] All who attempt to address this question would be wise to heed Bernard Green's warning: "the early evidence is so imprecise and fragmentary that readers can impose upon it whatever they expect to find."[20] With this warning in mind, I will briefly summarize the evidence. There are two episcopal succession lists dating from the second century. Hegesippus (c. 110–80) writes, "After arriving in Rome I compiled the succession down to Anicetus . . . Anicetus was succeeded by Soter and he by Eleutherus."[21] He implies, though does not name, a succession of bishops prior to Anicetus (r. 155–66). He states that he had to piece together this list, indicating that it was not well-established or well-known. Irenaeus does present a full list from bishop Linus, implicitly numbered as the first bishop, through to Eleutherus (d. 189), who is explicitly numbered as the twelfth.[22] Lampe argues that the emphasis on the number twelve, underscored by the fact that the only other bishop numbered is the sixth, shows that the list was written according to this overriding structure, and therefore dates from the time of Eleutherus.[23] Yet, though the composition of Irenaeus's form of the list may have been recent, this does not of itself undermine the historicity of the succession presented. Both Hegesippus and Irenaeus present these lists in the context of denouncing heresy; the succession links the present orthodoxy, as represented by the bishop, with the apostles. Green argues that

---

[19] Lampe, *Paul to Valentinus,* 397.

[20] Green, *Christianity in Ancient Rome,* 92.

[21] Quoted in Eusebius, *Ecclesiastical History,* 157 (4.22).

[22] Irenaeus, *Against the Heresies (Book 3),* 32–33 (3.3.3).

[23] Lampe, *Paul to Valentinus,* 405.

these anti-gnostic arguments would have been exploded embarrassingly easily had they not been based on a common opinion that there was a recognised tradition of leadership going back a long way behind Anicetus.[24]

However, Hegesippus says that he himself pieced together the succession list, so it is not clear how much weight Green's argument holds.

Lampe argues that Ignatius, in his letter to the Roman Christians, does not mention a monarchical bishop, even though this was his ecclesiastical experience in the East. Further he argues that Marcion, prior to his separation, defended his position to a synod of presbyters, not to a single bishop.[25] In contrast, Green argues that Ignatius did not refer to presbyters either in his letter to Rome, but does claim elsewhere that no group without a bishop could be called a church.[26] He also cites the example of Noetus (fl. 230), who was judged before a synod of presbyters even though Smyrna had a bishop.[27] However, Lampe and Green seem to essentially agree that Rome was led by a team of presbyters with a single spokesman, as indicated both in Clement's (fl. late 1st c.) letter[28] and by Hermas (fl. early to mid-2nd c.),[29] and that this senior presbyter was recognized as a bishop by analogy to the practice in Asia Minor and later accepted as such in Rome.[30] The succession lists, therefore, may record the names of real individuals, but their role may have been misinterpreted, with the later concept of bishop being projected back onto them.

A related question regards the diversity and multiplicity of the congregations at Rome. Lampe puts forward the proposal that Rome was not a single church but rather a number of house-churches, each operating independently while recognizing themselves as part of a larger fellowship. He derives his evidence from two main sources. Firstly, he refers to Paul's letter to the Romans, where Paul seems to refer to five or more separate

---

[24] Green, *Christianity in Ancient Rome,* 95.

[25] Lampe, *Paul to Valentinus,* 399.

[26] Ignatius, *To the Trallians,* 259 (3); Green, *Christianity in Ancient Rome,* 93–94.

[27] Green, *Christianity in Ancient Rome,* 94.

[28] Clement, *First Letter,* 113–15 (44.1–6).

[29] Hermas, *Shepherd,* 191–93 (*Visions* 2.4 or 8).

[30] Lampe, *Paul to Valentinus,* 398; Green, *Christianity in Ancient Rome,* 93.

groups within the city (Rom. 16:5, 10, 11, 14, 15).[31] Secondly, he refers to the *tituli* (i.e. private buildings used as churches throughout Rome) from post-Constantinian synod lists as indicative of the plurality of pre-Constantinian churches within Rome. [32] Regarding this first argument, Green objects that,

> even if several house churches could be detected in the list of names Paul supplies at the end of the letter, there would still be no reason to think that those churches survived Nero's persecution of 64.[33]

Regarding the second argument, we should be cautious of attempting to extrapolate backwards from these synod lists to the existence of churches in the second century. Nevertheless, there is nothing implausible about the proposition that there was more than one meeting place for Christians in Rome, though, as even Lampe acknowledges, the Christians in Rome were treated as unity by those outside (e.g. Paul, Dionysius of Corinth (fl. c. 171), Ignatius).[34]

Perhaps more problematic is the implication Lampe draws from the multiplicity of congregations at Rome that this arrangement both accommodated and nurtured theological pluralism.[35] In the absence of a monarchical episcopacy, and of a centralized and unified congregation, diverse opinions could co-exist within the city without challenging the mutual recognition of other groups as Christian. Lampe argues that

> before the end of the second century, specifically before the episcopacy of Victor (c. 189–99 CE), hardly any Roman Christian group excluded another group in the city from the communion of the faithful—apart from a few significant exceptions.[36]

---

[31] Lampe, *Paul to Valentinus*, 359.

[32] *Paul to Valentinus*, 360–5.

[33] Green, *Christianity in Ancient Rome*, 92.

[34] Lampe, *Paul to Valentinus*, 398.

[35] *Paul to Valentinus*, 381–84.

[36] *Paul to Valentinus*, 385.

Lampe's most significant example is that of the Valentinians, who seem to have existed within the Christian community at Rome. Lampe refers to the Valentinian Florinus (fl. late 2nd c.), who was a presbyter, apparently without objection, and was free to circulate his writings. It is Irenaeus, not Victor, who first attempts to expose and rebut the teaching of Florinus.[37]

Similarly, Valentinus seems to have gone unchallenged in Rome for a long period.[38] Lampe notes that Justin has an apparent change of attitude towards Valentinus, who is not mentioned in Justin's *Apologies* but whose teaching is explicitly condemned a decade later in the *Dialogue with Trypho*.[39] Yet it is not obvious that the evidence can only be interpreted in terms of toleration of the Valentinians. As Lampe acknowledges, the Valentinians themselves were happy to continue meeting with what they called "psychic" (or merely "soulish") Christians, that is, non-Valentinian Christians.[40] (The Valentinians considered themselves to be "pneumatic" or "spiritual" Christians.) They were also happy to withhold their full beliefs when conversing with these "psychic" Christians; Ptolemy's *Letter to Flora* is an example of this coyness.[41] Irenaeus suggests that previous anti-Valentinian writers were unsuccessful because of their lack of familiarity with Valentinian teaching,[42] indicating both that Valentinians were condemned by others prior to Irenaeus and that there was general ignorance among Christians about the full teaching of Valentinus. This being the case, it is not clear that Valentinus or Valentinians were tolerated rather than just being assumed to be orthodox. The Valentinians were not tolerated by Justin, Irenaeus, or Hegesippus, all of whom condemned Valentinianism as heresy. (The fact that Justin does not explicitly condemn Valentinianism in his apologies is not strong evidence of an earlier more tolerant attitude towards these views).

---

[37] Lampe, *Paul to Valentinus*, 389; Eusebius, *Ecclesiastical History*, 195 (5.20).

[38] Irenaeus, *Against the Heresies (Book 3)*, 35–36 (3.4.3); cf. Epiphanius, *Medicine Chest*, 1:165–208 (31).

[39] Lampe, *Paul to Valentinus*, 390.

[40] Irenaeus, *Against the Heresies (Book 3)*, 76–77 (3.15.2).

[41] Quoted in Epiphanius, *Medicine Chest*, 1:216–21 (33.3.1–7.10).

[42] Irenaeus, *Against Heresies*, 462 (Book 4, Preface, 2).

Lampe presents the Marcionites as a contrasting, and perhaps exceptional, example of a group that was not tolerated. [43] Marcion was originally in fellowship with other Christians at Rome, but disturbed other believers with his views and was expelled.

At Marcion's own initiative he met with a synod of the Roman presbyters to discuss his views, and this led to his break with the church.[44] Lampe argues that Marcion caused separation by trying to reform other Roman congregations,[45] the implication being that Marcion's views could be tolerated by other Christians at Rome, but not the attempt to change to received doctrine of the majority. However, like the Valentinians, the Marcionites were not tolerated by the second century heresiologists, like Justin, Irenaeus, and Hegesippus.

Yet the fact that neither the views of Marcion nor Valentinus were acceptable within the Christian community at Rome should not be surprising. Marcion taught that there were two gods, and that the god of the Old Testament was different from the god of the New Testament. In no stretch of the imagination was this part of the teaching of the earliest Christians; this is an innovation of the early second century. Valentinus taught that the material world is evil and was created by a "demiurge" (a divine craftsman), not God. Again, this was not part of the teaching of the earliest Christians, but is an innovation of Valentinus, influenced by other gnostic teachers. The teachings of Marcion and Valentinus are so radically different from the teachings of traditional Christians that it would be genuinely surprising if such views were accepted and tolerated by them. Regardless of whether Rome had a monarchical episcopacy or was a single church, the views of Marcion and Valentinus would not have been tolerated within the Christian community at Rome, and if it took many years before these thinkers and their followers were excommunicated this is more easily explained by the practicalities of the situation, not a supposed more tolerant attitude.

If the views of Marcion and Valentinus would not have been tolerated by the Christian community at Rome, what about the views of Dynamic

[43] Lampe, *Paul to Valentinus*, 394.
[44] Epiphanius, *Medicine Chest*, 1:295 (42.1.7).
[45] Lampe, *Paul to Valentinus*, 394.

Monarchians? We know that Victor excommunicated Theodotus around 190, but what about the earlier ecclesiastical situation? Neither Justin, nor Irenaeus, nor Hegesippus condemn any Dynamic Monarchian group, and while this might be because they did not know any, we found nothing in the writings of Justin or Irenaeus that would lead us to expect that such views would be condemned (though they obviously differed from their own).

I will argue that Dynamic Monarchianism preceded the views of Christology affirmed by Justin, Irenaeus, and others (that Christ preexisted), and if this is the case, then Dynamic Monarchianism is different from Marcionism and Valentinianism. No credible historian, however unorthodox, believes that either the views of Marcion or Valentinus cohered with the teaching of the earliest Christians; it is unsurprising that those in the tradition of the earliest Christians viewed Marcion and Valentinus as, at best, mistaken and, at worst, heretics. But the situation is different with the Dynamic Monarchians. It is arguable, and I will be arguing, that Dynamic Monarchianism stood very much within the tradition of the earliest Christians, because it was the Christology of the earliest Christians or else a reasonable inference from it. We should not expect Dynamic Monarchianism to be condemned as heretical until such time as a new Christology became dominant. This new Christology was the Logos Christology of Justin, which was influential both on Irenaeus and on Hippolytus, the latter of which is the earliest known writer to condemn a Dynamic Monarchian of heresy.

If the emergence and success of Justin's Logos Christology explains how Dynamic Monarchian views fell into disfavor, we have still not explained why Victor excommunicated Theodotus. Why did these views not continue to be tolerated at Rome? Part of the reason, it seems, must lie with the promptings Victor received from others. For example, Eusebius records that Irenaeus, despite being based in Lyons, wrote various letters to those in Rome whom he considered heretical, including Blastus (fl. late 2nd c.) and Florinus.[46] The implication of Irenaeus's sending such letters is that the ecclesiastical authorities at Rome had not

---

[46] Eusebius, *Ecclesiastical History*, 195 (5.20).

yet acted to excommunicate these persons. Florinus, it seems from Irenaeus's letter, was a presbyter and therefore under the oversight of the bishop of Rome. Yet it seems that Irenaeus felt compelled, despite the distance, to write directly to Florinus to condemn him. Now we may allow that the circumstances were more complicated than our extant sources describe, and that Irenaeus's interjection into the situation was preemptive, presumptive, and/or misjudged.

We find the opposite situation in Victor's action over the celebration of Easter. Victor sought to excommunicate all the Asian dioceses after they had written to him to express their intention to celebrate Easter according to the tradition they had received. These "Quartodecimans" celebrated Easter on 14th day of Nisan; other Christians did not. In this case Irenaeus writes to Victor to admonish him for his actions.[47]

The difference between the two situations does not seem caused by apostolic tradition. Were that the key factor then Florinus would have been quickly rebuked, or excommunicated, for his Valentinian views whereas the Quartodecimans would not have been castigated, given they could claim, on the testimony of Polycarp, that their practice was apostolic.[48] Rather, the significant difference between the two situations is that in the latter case Victor is prompted into action by the letter from the Asian dioceses. The excommunication of the Asian dioceses is reactive. Victor does not seem to be proactively weeding out heretics, like Florinus, but reacting to situations as they arise. Perhaps Victor perceived the Quartodecimans as defiant or rebellious, or perhaps Victor saw them as threatening the unity of the Church.

The Little Labyrinth implies that Theodotus was the first to claim that Jesus was a "merely human."[49] This is plainly false because, as we have seen, Irenaeus ascribes this view of the Ebionites. Justin accepted the Ebionites as Christians, even while rejecting their views. Therefore, the apparent sequence of events presented by *The Little Labyrinth,* as though Theodotus was the first to proclaim such views and was quickly excommunicated doesn't ring true. More likely, something prompted

---

[47] Eusebius, *Ecclesiastical History*, 197–200 (5.23–24).
[48] *Ecclesiastical History*, 198 (5.24).
[49] Quoted in Eusebius, *Ecclesiastical History*, 201 (5.28).

Victor into action. This might have been Theodotus himself, if Victor perceived him as causing disruption, or this may have been external prompting, as with Irenaeus's letters about others. There is no denying that the theological context was changing; Justin's views about the Logos was gaining dominance in some quarters. But Justin himself had tolerated the views of the Ebionites and would have, presumably, tolerated any Dynamic Monarchians. Alongside the theological changes, there were also ecclesiastical changes and differences that at one time coexisted were now being hounded out as heresy.

CONCLUSION

Theodotus of Byzantium is the earliest example extant of someone who was excommunicated for Dynamic Monarchian beliefs. Prior to this we have no evidence that Dynamic Monarchianism would have been considered heretical. Indeed, the evidence from Justin and Irenaeus gives us no reason to think they would have condemned Dynamic Monarchians (though there is no definitive evidence that they knew any). The ecclesiastical situation in Rome prior to the episcopacy of Victor does not indicate a highly centralized hierarchy. This does not that mean no one was cast out of the church on doctrinal grounds; Marcion and Valentinus were, but these were extreme cases. The evidence of Victor's behavior is suggestive that the excommunication of Theodotus was reactive, and the same outcome may not have resulted in different circumstances. Yet after Theodotus had been excommunicated, he was listed by his critics amongst the heretics, and thus began the process of defining orthodoxy against that other.

The excommunication of Theodotus not only represents a change in the ecclesiastical situation, but also is symptomatic of a theological shift that was taking place in this period. As we shall explore in the next chapter, the concept of the pre-existence of Jesus was taking root within the Christian community and being endorsed by some of its prominent thinkers. The Logos theology of Justin gained traction in the Roman community; this theology was adopted by Hippolytus, who condemns Theodotus as a heretic. The irony is that already by the end of second century, the doctrinal pendulum had swung on further with the emergence of Modalistic Monarchianism, endorsed by Victor's successor. As Carrington writes,

> at the end of the episcopate of Victor, therefore, the theology of incarnation had won a resounding victory over the theology of adoption; and when Zephyrinus succeeded him, a 'Monarchian' theology of this type became the official theology of the Roman church.[50]

[50] Carrington, *Early Christian Church,* 2:416–17. On the Modalistic Monarchianism of bishop Zephyrinus see Vinzent, "Zephrinus to Damasus," 274–76, 286.

CHAPTER 9

The Emergence of Ideas about Pre-Existence

IT WOULD BE SIMPLE AND CONVENIENT for my thesis if the emergence of ideas about the pre-existence of Jesus could be tied to Justin's Logos Christology or, even better, to the Platonic ideas that influenced much of Justin's thought, but the evidence does not bear out this facile proposal. Undoubtedly Justin and his Logos Christology were very influential on the development of Christian views about the nature of Jesus and his relationship to Father and Spirit, and undoubtedly Platonic concepts and language framed much of Justin's thought about God, about the Logos and much else besides,[1] but when it comes to the pre-existence of Jesus it is evident that others held these views before Justin. Though I will argue that the Dynamic Monarchian tradition originated with the earliest Christians and continued in the second and third centuries, it would be too crude to suppose that this was the only Christology until the mid-second century, as though Justin, Victor and whoever else could impose something completely new and different upon the whole Christian community. Leaving aside the New Testament, which I will consider later in the book, there are examples of Christian texts from the late first and early second centuries which are indicative of early ideas about the pre-

---

[1] Gaston, "Why Three?"

existence of Jesus within the Christian tradition. However, in these examples we will also see a mix of different views about Christ's pre-existence, rather than a monolithic doctrinal unity centered around a trinitarian Christology. As we shall see, although some Christian thinkers in this period (late first and early second centuries) did believe Jesus pre-existed, it was not because they believed Jesus was God or that he was as divine as the Father.

Before proceeding we should note some methodological problems with sources from this period. The selection of texts and fragments extant from the late first and early second century is patchy and cannot be taken as representative of the full spectrum of Christian thought. Often the texts survived because they were nearly included in the canon, and so were reasonably well known. Whatever else might have been written in this period is lost to us. Even though these texts are not uniformly orthodox (by later standards), they were clearly orthodox enough for some copies to have survived. We should hardly expect explicitly Dynamic Monarchian texts from this period, if there were such, to have survived.

Moreover, with those texts that have survived it is usually difficult to determine the date and location of the composition with any degree of certainty. In part this is because these texts are often misattributed, yet even if a text is correctly attributed, this provides limited assistance if there is not biographical information available about the author. The sources that I will consider in this chapter are conventionally dated to the late first or early second century. Those dates seem plausible enough to me and I do not, for my purposes, require anything more specific. Nevertheless, given that such texts are often dated by the feel of their doctrine and practice, there is always a danger of circularity when using these texts to illustrate a sequence of doctrinal development. The best we can do is to note the problem and proceed with the caveat in mind.

EPISTLE OF BARNABAS

The first example is a text misattributed to a companion of Paul. The epistle may be dated with reasonable confidence to the period 70–135. It refers to the ruins of the Temple in Jerusalem[2] so must post-date its destruction but probably predates the erection of a Roman temple upon that site in reign of Hadrian (76–138; r. 117–38).[3] J. A. T. Robinson dates it to around 75,[4] however its developed Christology may indicate a later date (c. 125). Its composition is sometimes placed in Alexandria, Egypt, although this is only an educated guess. This pseudonymous epistle seems likely to be a product of a Jewish-Christian tradition. It is akin to the *Didache*, sharing the Two Paths material and a preference for the Gospel of Matthew.[5] It omits any reference to the Pauline corpus and makes no effort mimic his style, as Polycarp and Ignatius do; this epistle comes from a different tradition. The epistle itself is very critical of Jewish practices, but this reactionary attitude from the author may well indicate that he came from a Jewish-Christian background himself.

Despite having no apparent affinity with Pauline or Johannine Christianity and their purported high Christologies, the Epistle of Barnabas does contain explicit reference to the pre-existence of Jesus. For example, the author describes Jesus as having been "the Lord of the entire world, the one to whom God said at the foundation of the world, 'Let us make a human according to our image and likeness.' "[6] He also explains that the Son of God had to come in flesh, otherwise humans could not have looked at him and survived, "For they cannot even look intently at the sun, gazing directly into its rays, even though it is the work of his hands."[7] These passages have the implication that the Son was with God at creation and was the creator (or, perhaps, co-creator, or the one through whom God created). One might be tempted to read the Epistle of Barnabas as affirming a form of incarnation Christology, with the pre-existent Son taking on flesh or a "human nature" to save mankind.

---

[2] *Epistle of Barnabas*, 71 (16:3–4).

[3] Ehrman, *Apostolic Fathers*, 2:6–7.

[4] Robinson, *Redating*, 353.

[5] *Epistle of Barnabas*, 75–81 (19–20), 25 (4:14).

[6] *Epistle of Barnabas*, 27 (5:5); Gen. 1:26.

[7] *Epistle of Barnabas*, 29 (5:10).

However, closer examination reveals that the author presupposed a different Christology, what we might term a Spirit-Man Christology.[8] Concerning the law on fasting, the author writes, "For the Lord gave the written commandment that 'Whoever does not keep the fast must surely die,' because he himself was about to offer the vessel of the Spirit as a sacrifice for our own sins."[9] The "Lord" in this verse is, presumably, the Father but the "sacrifice" is obviously a reference to Jesus. The translation "the Spirit" is preferable to "his spirit"[10] given the absence of *autou* ("of him"), and this reinforces the point that it is the Holy Spirit, and not the spirit of Jesus, that is being referred to. As God is offering "the vessel of the Spirit" as the sacrifice, then Jesus must be identified as that "vessel."[11] To describe Jesus as "the vessel of the Spirit" implies this Spirit acts through the man Jesus This suggests that the author did not regard Jesus as divine in himself, but rather as a human vessel for the Holy Spirit.

Given a Christology that identifies the divine person dwelling within Jesus as the Holy Spirit, it is natural that the author should believe that this person existed with God at creation and was the creator because neither point would have been controversial for Christians. Genesis is explicit that the Holy Spirit was present at creation (Gen. 1:2) and elsewhere in the Old Testament the creative activity of the Spirit is affirmed (cf. Ps. 104:30). The proposal that God was speaking to the Holy

---

[8] The term "Possessionist" is one coined by Michael Goulder to describe the view that Jesus was a mortal man who was possessed by the Holy Spirit, usually at his baptism. Goulder ascribes this Christology to the Ebionites, to Petrine (i.e. Jewish) Christians (who are responsible for the books of Matthew, James and some "strands" of Revelation) and to the opponents of Ignatius (usually identified as Docetists). For myself, I am not persuaded that Possessionism is the correct understanding of the Ebionite Christology, nor do I believe there is compelling evidence to warrant projecting Ebionite views onto early Jewish Christians more generally, nor do I believe that there is evidence of this same Christology in the opponents of Ignatius. Nevertheless, I can see the applicability of this concept for the Christology expressed in the *Epistle of Barnabas* and the *Shepherd of Hermas*. I am using the term "Spirit-Man Christology" for this view. On these ideas see Goulder, *Tale of Two Missions*, 107–34; Goulder, "Pre-Marcan Gospel," 456–57; Goulder, "Poor Man's Christology"; Goulder, "Ignatius' 'Docetists'," 16–30.

[9] *Epistle of Barnabas*, 37 (7:3).

[10] Contrary to one translator of this letter (*Epistle of Barnabas* [trans. Kleist], 47).

[11] *Epistle of Barnabas*, 55 (11:9).

Spirit when he said "Let us make" (Gen 1:26) is not stated in the Genesis text, but is a natural corollary of ascribing that creative role to the Spirit. The only aspect that might require explanation is the personhood of the Spirit, as for Jews and the early Christians, the Spirit was not understood as a separate person in addition to God himself. However, once one had taken the step to understand Jesus as a man possessed by the Holy Spirit then adding personhood to the understanding of the Spirit may have seemed a natural implication.

THE SHEPHERD OF HERMAS

A second text that seems to stand in the same tradition as the *Epistle of Barnabas* is the *Shepherd of Hermas*. Like the *Didache* and the *Epistle of Barnabas*, the *Shepherd* makes use of the Two Paths material[12] and seems to be a product of the Jewish-Christian tradition.[13] The text may be tentatively dated to c. 110–40.

It is surprising how little attention Hermas gives to the life of Jesus, in contrast to contemporary writers like Ignatius. The name "Jesus" is never mentioned. The title "Christ" is used three times in doubtful manuscript variants.[14] Osiek explains these omissions as "reverential avoidance,"[15] but actually there seems no reference to the historical Jesus at all.[16] This would seem to indicate that for the author, the man Jesus was of little significance. Yet, like the Epistle of Barnabas, Hermas explicitly affirms the pre-existence of the Son, saying "the Son of God is older than all his creation, and so he became the Father's counsellor for his creation."[17]

---

[12] Ehrman, *Apostolic Fathers,* 2:164; Osiek notes one possible allusion to the *Didache* in Hermas (Osiek, *Shepherd of Hermas,* 27).

[13] Hermas, *Shepherd,* trans. Snyder, 16.

[14] Hermas, *Shepherd,* 189 (*Visions* 2.2.8 or 6.8), 209 (*Visions* 3.6.6 or 14.6), 435 (*Parables* 9.18.1 or 95.1). The structure of this book is idiosyncratic, and scholars have used two ways of marking its sections, so both locations will be given for each reference to this book. On its organization see Ehrman, *Apostolic Fathers,* 2:163–65, 171–72. In the Ehrman-translated volumes cited here what older editions call "Similitudes" are called "Parables."

[15] Osiek, *Hermas,* 34.

[16] Hermas, *Shepherd,* trans. Snyder, 107.

[17] Hermas, *Shepherd,* 419 (*Parables* 9.12.2 or 89.2)

Though Hermas does not quote Gen. 1:26, this conversation would be the obvious source for the idea that the Son was the Father's "counsellor" in creation. But even though Hermas affirms the pre-existence of the Son, it seems that he meant something different by this than later trinitarians would mean.

The Christological material in Hermas is largely confined to Similitudes/Parables 5. In this section the angel tells Hermas a parable about a field. The owner of the field plants a vineyard and then chooses a slave to build a fence around the vineyard while he is on a journey. The slave does more than his master requires, also weeding the vineyard. When the master returns, he is pleased and calls his "beloved son," and other advisors, and they congratulate the slave. So, the owner makes the slave fellow heir with his son, and his son approves.[18]

Now this parable has many familiar elements from the synoptic parables (e.g. Matt. 21:33–45). This comparison would lead us to expect that the owner would represent God, the son would represent Jesus, and the slave would represent God's servants. However when the parable is explained to Hermas he is told "the son is the Holy Spirit and the slave is the Son of God."[19] Now while the phrase "the son is the Holy Spirit" is only included in the Vulgate,[20] there is every reason to suppose it was in the original. No alternative identity for the son is given in the other variants, and all the witnesses identify the slave as "the Son of God." Snyder reasons that it was the presence of two sons in the passage that led later copyists to omit the phrase in an attempt to avoid confusion.[21] In any case, it is clear from the angel's explanation that the Holy Spirit is the son of the parable:

God made the Holy Spirit dwell in flesh that he desired, even though it preexisted and created all things. This flesh, then, in which the Holy Spirit

[18] *Shepherd*, 321–25 (*Parables* 5.2.1–11 or 55.1–11.)

[19] Hermas, *Shepherd*, 333 (*Parables* 5.5.2 or 58.2).

[20] That is, from manuscripts of an early Latin translation of the *Shepherd*. The phrase is omitted from the Codex Athous (15th century), the two Palatine manuscripts (15th century), and the Ethiopic version (6th century).

[21] Hermas, *Shepherd*, trans. Snyder, 106.

dwelled, served well as the Spirit's slave, for it conducted itself in reverence and purity, not defiling the Spirit at all. Since it lived in a good and pure way, cooperating with the Spirit and working with it in everything it did, behaving in a strong and manly way, God chose it to be a partner with the Holy Spirit. For the conduct of this flesh was pleasing, because it was not defiled on earth while bearing the Holy Spirit. Thus he took his Son and the glorious angels as counselors, so that this flesh, which served blamelessly as the Spirit's slave, might have a place of residence and not appear to have lost the reward for serving as a slave.[22]

In this passage Jesus is described rather impersonally as "this flesh." *Sarx* (flesh) is a feminine word in Greek and the pronouns in the passage are also feminine, though translated as neuter above. The slave in the parable is given masculine pronouns. His possession by the Holy Spirit is explicitly described. The intriguing conclusion of the parable describes how "this flesh" (i.e. Jesus) was rewarded for his conduct bearing the Spirit with him to "a place of residence," perhaps referring to the ascension of Jesus. It seems evident, then, that when Hermas says "the Son of God is older than all his creation" he is not referring to Jesus but rather to the Holy Spirit that "pre-existed and created all things."[23] In contrast, Hermas did not regard Jesus as the Son from birth (or from eternity) but that this status was bestowed on Jesus because of his conduct.[24]

Both Hermas and the author of the Epistle of Barnabas seem to affirm the view that the Holy Spirit is the pre-existent Son, and that Jesus was an ordinary man who was indwelt by the Holy Spirit. Hermas, if not the *Epistle of Barnabas*, implies that the Holy Spirit was also a person. There are parallels with the Christology of Cerinthus, though these authors do not see the need to speculate about existence of otherwise unknown spirit beings (like Cerinthus's Christ). One might speculate that the views of Cerinthus were a development upon something like the views endorsed by these authors. It is also not difficult to conceive of how this Spirit-Man Christology arose. The early Christians affirmed that Jesus could perform

---

[22] Hermas, *Shepherd*, 335–37 (*Parables* 5.6.5–7 or 59.5–7).

[23] *Shepherd*, 419 (*Parables* 9.12.2 or 89.2), 335 (*Parables* 5.6.5 or 59.5).

[24] *Shepherd*, 323 (*Parables* 5.2.5–6 or 55.5–6.)

miracles by the Spirit, that the Spirit had descended on Jesus at baptism; it is an understandable, if crude, interpretation to suppose that Jesus not only used the power of the Holy Spirit but that he was possessed by it. Yet since the Holy Spirit did not originate with Jesus, but was known to be present at creation, then to say that Jesus was possessed by the Spirit was to say that something in him had pre-existed.

SECOND CLEMENT

What is commonly known as *Second Clement* is almost certainly misattributed and is also misidentified as an epistle. It is best described as "an early Christian homily."[25] There are various speculations as to the location of composition, including Rome, Corinth, Syria and Egypt,[26] and various theories as to the identity of the author, including Clement (Harnack),[27] Soter (Hilgenfeld), Julius Cassianus (fl. c. 170) (Harris) and the elders at Corinth (Donfried).[28] As to date, Tuckett judges that "a date some time around the middle of the second century seems to create the least number of problems,"[29] given the possible allusions of Origen and Irenaeus on the one hand and the lack of quotations of Paul and John on the other. This date also seems appropriate in terms of theology (unnuanced) and ecclesiology (presbyters but no single bishop).[30]

Though the main concern of this homily is not Christology, the author clearly presupposes that Christ pre-exists in some sense:

the Bible and the apostles indicate that the church has not come into being just now, but has existed from the beginning. For it existed spiritually, as did

[25] Ehrman, *Apostolic Fathers,* 1:154.

[26] Tuckett, *2 Clement,* 58–62; Ehrman, *Apostolic Fathers,* 1:158; cf. Donfried, "Theology of Second Clement," 499; Lightfoot, *Apostolic Fathers,* Part 1, 2:197.

[27] See Hermas, *Shepherd,* 143 (*Visions* 2.4.3 or 8.3).

[28] Tuckett, *2 Clement,* 15–16.

[29] Tuckett, *2 Clement,* 64.

[30] Ehrman, *Apostolic Fathers,* 1:159–60. Donfried connects the *Second Letter of Clement* with *First Letter of Clement* and so dates the composition the second shortly after the reception of the first in Corinth (c.98–100); see Donfried, "Second Clement," 499.

our Jesus; but he [or it] became manifest here in the final days so that he [or it] might save us.[31]

The author believes that Jesus existed from the beginning, that he was sent by the Father,[32] and that he underwent some change of nature ("first a spirit and then became flesh").[33] However, he does not explicitly describe Jesus as "a god." The homily does begin "we must think about Jesus Christ as we think about God,"[34] but this is explicitly in relation to the judgment being entrusted to Jesus (cf. Acts 10:42; 1 Pet. 4:5), rather than being a statement about Jesus' nature.[35] When the author says Jesus pre-existed, this is not because he believes that Jesus is God or a divine person. In the quotation above[36] he compares the pre-existence of Jesus with the pre-existence of the Church. It is conceivable that by "spiritually" he means something like "figuratively" (cf. Rev. 11:8) but given what he says elsewhere it seems evident that "spiritually" means as a spirit-being. For example, Jesus is said to have been "first a spirit" and then flesh.[37] (The implication of this might be that Jesus stopped being a spirit when he became flesh, though there is a danger of reading too much into this one line). While it might seem odd that the author should hold that the Church pre-existed as a spirit being, he seems clear that this was the case. He writes, "we will belong to the first church, the spiritual church, the church that was created before the sun and moon,"[38] and again, "the church was spiritual, it became manifest in Christ's flesh."[39] Now we might be tempted to ease the peculiarity by proposing that he is being figurative, that the church pre-existed as an idea in the foreknowledge of God, except that he says that Jesus pre-existed in the same way. So, our

---

[31] *Second Letter of Clement*, 187 (14.2).

[32] *Second Letter of Clement*, 199 (20.5).

[33] *Second Letter of Clement*, 179 (9.5); Tuckett, *2 Clement,* 69.

[34] *Second Letter of Clement*, 165 (1.1).

[35] Ehrman, *Apostolic Fathers,* 1:155.

[36] *Second Letter of Clement*, 187 (14.2).

[37] *Second Letter of Clement*, 179 (9.5).

[38] *Second Letter of Clement*, 187 (14.1).

[39] *Second Letter of Clement*, 187 (14.3).

choice of readings is either that Jesus only pre-existed in a figurative sense (and not literally) or that the Church pre-existed as a spirit-being.

Talk of "spirit beings" might make one suspect that *Second Clement* is influenced by Gnosticism. Indeed, scholars have frequently argued for allusions to Gnosticism (or more specifically, Valentinianism[40]), either as something the author promotes or rejects.[41] Affinities with Valentinianism might explain the concept of the Church pre-existing as a spirit-being. According to Irenaeus, in the mythology proclaimed by Valentinus, one of the aeons of the primal ogdoad was named "Ecclesia" (Church). This aeon was the consort to Anthropos (Man), and from this consort pair emerged twelve powers.[42] In a later Valentinian text, *The Tripartite Tractate* (3rd century), Church is the third member of the primal triad that "exists from the beginning."[43] In this text Church is a composite entity "of many people, which preexists the eternities."[44] In this sense, Church is not a single aeon but rather a composite of individual aeons.

Although there are some reasons for suspecting some kind of interaction with Gnosticism, such as the emphasis on Jesus' flesh and on ethical behavior,[45] it is difficult to read *Second Clement* as a polemic against Gnosticism. The author never directly addresses or criticizes false teachers, and he never implies that the role of God as creator is in doubt or that his opponents regarded the material world as evil.[46] Even when the author uses a saying which is similar to one used in *Gospel of the Egyptians* and *Gospel of Thomas*[47] he neither gives a Gnostic interpretation nor does he use the quotation to directly combat Gnosticism.[48] Tuckett concludes,

---

[40] Warns, "Untersuchungen zum," 76–90.

[41] Donfried, "Second Clement," 490.

[42] Irenaeus, *Against the Heresies (Book 1)*, 51 (1.11).

[43] *Tripartite Tractate*, 173 (57.34–35).

[44] *Tripartite Tractate*, 173 (58.30–31).

[45] See Pratscher, *Der zweite Clemensbrief*.

[46] *Second Letter of Clement*, 189–91 (15.1–5); Tuckett, *2 Clement*, 50–53.

[47] *Second Letter of Clement*, 183 (12.2).

[48] Tuckett, *2 Clement*, 54.

If one is permitted to "mirror read" what is said here (at least in general terms) and postulate "libertine" tendencies in the community, it does not clearly point to a Gnostic background: not all Gnostics were necessarily libertines, and not all libertines were necessarily Gnostic . . . given what is said, as well as what is not said and what seems to be accepted by all sides in the discussion, it is hard to see the "opponents" here as Gnostics.[49]

Focusing specifically on the question of the Church as a spirit being, "the author here gives no hint that he disapproves in any way of the sentiments or claims being made about the church."[50] This makes it unlikely that the author is seeking to correct "a gnostic misunderstanding of the church," as Donfried proposes. [51] On this view the author is combatting those who hold that they already belong to the spiritual church because they had already been saved. [52] Yet this still leaves the author affirming that the Church is a spirit being (or collection of spirit-beings), something he might be more coy about were he combatting Gnosticism.

Though Tuckett has reservations about concluding that the author is combatting Gnosticism, he nonetheless seems persuaded that the author is operating "in the context of some kind of (Valentinian?) Gnostic milieu."[53] Donfried also posits that *Second Clement* is on a "Gnosticizing trajectory" leading to Valentinian Gnosticism. [54] We may speculate (and it can only be speculation) that *Second Clement* is a sort of missing link between Pauline Christianity (say) and Valentinianism. The author does not reject the material world, nor does he posit a malignant creator, but perhaps his ideas about spirit beings provide a basis for Valentinian aeons. Of course this analysis is too crude. Valentinianism developed in a wider Gnostic context, with its own aeonology, but perhaps some precedent in the milieu represented by *Second Clement* explains the designation of one of the Valentinian aeons as "Church." Whatever the case, the possibility that the ideas expressed in *Second Clement* were part of a conceptual

---

[49] Tuckett, *2 Clement*, 55, 56.

[50] Tuckett, *2 Clement*, 249.

[51] Donfried, "Second Clement," 493.

[52] Donfried, "Second Clement," 495.

[53] Tuckett, *2 Clement*, 252.

[54] Donfried, *Setting of Second Clement*, 1, 164; cf. Danielou, *Jewish Christianity*, 302.

trajectory towards Valentinianism does not explain those ideas, and specifically does not explain why the author believes the Church (and Jesus) to have been pre-existent.

Both Tuckett and Donfried trace the origins of the pre-existent spiritual Church to Ephesians 1:4,[55] where Paul speaks about believers having been chosen in Christ before the foundation of the world. This speaks somewhat to the idea of pre-existence, but only in the sense of the foreknowledge of God, and that was not unique to Paul's letter to the Ephesians. Nor is Paul talking about the pre-existence of the Church, but only the pre-selection of believers. This doesn't get us very far along the road to explaining the idea of the Church as a pre-existent spirit or collection of spirit-beings.

Donfried provides an additional explanation from Galatians 4:26 and Paul's reference to the "Jerusalem above," which Donfried argues finds precedent elsewhere.[56] There is a connection here between Paul's quotation of Is. 54:1 with reference to the Jerusalem above (Gal. 4:27) and the use of that same quotation in *Second Clement* with reference to the Church.[57] Donfried proposes that Paul is engaged in aeon speculation, yet neither Galatians, nor the comparison texts, talk about Jerusalem as a spirit-being. In *The Fourth Book of Ezra* and Revelation, the heavenly Jerusalem is the promise of an eschatological renewal, of spiritual Israel revealed, not a pre-existent spirit-being. In *2 Baruch*, the heavenly Jerusalem is the heavenly pattern or ideal, of which the temporal Jerusalem is a shadow (cf. Heb. 8:5). Of these, it seems more likely that Paul is speaking of Jerusalem in the latter mode, as the ideal of what Jerusalem should be, instead of what it has become while shackled by the Law. Given the shared allusion to Is. 54:1 and given that the shift from Jerusalem to the Church is natural (cf. Rev. 21:2), then it is likely that *Second Clement* does derive its ideal of the spiritual Church from Galatians. It is just possible that what the author means by the spiritual Church is something like Paul's idea of the heavenly ideal, the church as it should be. But given the

---

[55] Tuckett, *2 Clement*, 248; Donfried, *Setting of Second Clement*, 164.

[56] Donfried (*Setting of Clement*, 192) cites as precedents: *Fourth Book of Ezra*, 537 (7:26); *1 Enoch*, 71 (90:28–29); *Book of Elijah*, 38–39; *2 Baruch*, 622 (4:2–7). Cf. Rev. 21:2.

[57] *Second Letter of Clement*, 167 (2.1); Donfried, *Setting of Second Clement*, 198.

comparison between the pre-existence of the Church and the pre-existence of Jesus, it seems more probable that the author has moved beyond Paul, substantiating or reifying talk of God's ideals into discrete spiritual entities. In such a mindset, anything that was previously said to pre-exist in the foreknowledge of God might be given existence as a spirit-being, and Jesus is the most obvious candidate for this treatment.

Once again in *Second Clement* we have an early Christian text, which while appearing to agree with later orthodoxy about the pre-existence of Jesus, in fact has very different reasons for positing this conclusion. The author thought in terms of spirit beings, a mode of thinking that may have fed into Gnostic speculation, and in that mode of thinking the pre-existence of Jesus as a spirit being is a natural corollary.

DIALOGUE OF JASON AND PAPISCUS

The *Dialogue of Jason and Papiscus* (hereafter *JP*) is the earliest known example of a genre of Christian texts in which a Christian and a Jew debate Christianity. *JP* is known only from quotations in later sources, the largest of which was only recently discovered.[58] Based upon the testimony of John of Scythopolis (early 6th c.),[59] *JP* has usually been attributed to Aristo of Pella (fl. c. 135–78). John claims that his source for this information is Clement of Alexandria, though noting that Clement says the author was Luke.[60] This latter claim is also repeated by Sophronius (c. 560–638)[61] but has always seemed doubtful. The discovery of the new fragment has allowed textual comparison with the gospel, on the basis of which Lukan authorship can be ruled out.[62] The text is usually dated on two grounds. Firstly, it must date before Celsus's anti-Christian polemic *True Account* (c. 177–80) which cites it. Secondly, since Aristo was alive during the reign of the emperor Hadrian (r. 117–38),[63] it was likely

---

[58] Bovon and Duffy, "New Greek Fragment," 457–65.

[59] Migne, *Patrologia Graeca*, 4:421c; previously attributed to Maximus the Confessor.

[60] Varner, "Trail of Trypho," 555.

[61] Bovan and Duffy, "New Greek Fragment," 462.

[62] "New Greek Fragment," 463.

[63] Eusebius, *Ecclesiastical History*, 138 (4.6).

composed around this time. Varner dates *JP* to 135–65.[64] This date means that this dialogue is contemporaneous with or earlier than Justin's *Dialogue with Trypho*.

Celsus Africanus (late 3rd c.) gives a brief outline of *JP*, saying that Jason is a Hebrew Christian and Papiscus is an Alexandrian Jew who at the end of the dialogue is converted and receives baptism.[65] In terms of the actual contents of the dialogue, we have only a few testimonies. John of Scythopolis records that the dialogue includes mention of the seven heavens.[66] Origen states that the dialogue "shows that the prophecies concerning the Messiah apply to Jesus."[67] Jerome gives two apparent quotes: "in the Son God made the heavens and the earth," an apparent textual variation on Gen. 1:1,[68] and "The one who is hanged is a curse in the eyes of God" or "Because God was hanged in a disgraceful manner."[69] Lastly we have the fragment in the works of Sophronius which concerns the question of why Christians celebrate Sunday as opposed to the Sabbath.

It is worth also considering the relationship between *JP* and later texts of this genre. Lahey has proposes remnants of *JP* can be found in the triple tradition shared by *Athaneaeus and Zacchaeus* (late 4th c.), *Timothy and Aquila* (5th c.) and *Simon and Theophilus* (5th c.), and that is not dependent on either Tertullian's *Against the Jews* or Cyprian's *Testimony*.[70] If true, this would imply that the contents of *JP* could be partially sketched by reference to this triple tradition. Skarsaune has proposed *JP* as a source for Justin's *Dialogue with Trypho*.[71] Rutherford

---

[64] Varner, "Trail of Trypho," 557.

[65] Varner, "Trail of Trypho," 556.

[66] Migne, *Patrologia Graeca*, 4:421c.

[67] Origen, *Against Celsus*, 227 (4:52).

[68] Jerome, *Hebrews Questions on Genesis*, 30 (1.1).

[69] Jerome mentions those two renderings of the same Greek sentence (Jerome, *Commentary on Galatians*, 141 [2.3.13b–14]).

[70] Rutherford, "*Altercatio Jasonis*," 141. Varner also notes echoes of *JP* in later dialogue texts ("Trail of Trypho," 558).

[71] Skarsaune, *Proof from Prophecy*, 234. He further speculates that Marcion made critical comments about *JP* in his *Antitheses,* which would explain some of the

explores this proposal with reference to Justin's "second god" argument, attempting to find parallels between the triple tradition identified by Lahey and Justin's *Dialogue*.[72] Though Justin does make use of some of the same proof-texts, given the difference in order and usage, Rutherford concludes that Justin is not dependent on *JP* for these arguments. Instead he suggests that *JP* and the *Dialogue with Trypho* have parallels due to broader tradition which Justin expands creatively.[73] Varner is also unconvinced of any dependence by Justin on *JP*, arguing that the two texts are "in the same conceptual trajectory" and that any parallels are due to having the same subject matter and format.[74] None of the other dialogues in the genre show literal dependency on the recently discovered fragment; Bovon and Duffy say that the closest comparator is Justin's *Dialogue with Trypho,* which expresses similar concerns.[75]

These analyses suggest two things. Firstly, while we may not be able to use later texts to determine the precise contents of *JP*, it is likely that *JP* contained arguments and proof texts used by them. Secondly, *JP* is unlikely to have originated these arguments, though it may have been the first text to incorporate them. Rather *JP* is representative of the Christian side of Jewish-Christian discourse from the early second century.

For our purposes the pertinent questions are whether *JP* affirmed the pre-existence of Jesus and, if so, what was the background of this affirmation. The former question may be answered in the affirmative on two scores. Firstly, the fragments of *JP* suggest a commitment to the pre-existence of Jesus. Jerome's quotation of the variant of Gen 1:1 "in the Son God made the heavens and the earth" entails that Jesus, or else a divine being later united to Jesus, was present at creation. Similarly, the fragment preserved by Sophronius states that the creative word which proceeds from God "was Christ, the son of God through whom all the other things as well came to be." It is just possible that in this second case Jesus is

apparently anti-Marcionite tendencies of Justin's *Dialogue with Trypho* (*Proof from Prophecy*, 242).

[72] Rutherford, "*Altercatio Jasonis,*" 137.
[73] "*Altercatio Jasonis,*" 144.
[74] Varner, "Trail of Trypho," 558.
[75] Bovan and Duffy, "New Greek Fragment," 460.

identified as the Word in the same sense John does, as an impersonal abstraction that was embodied in Jesus (see Chapter Thirteen), but given the quotation from Jerome this seems unlikely.

Secondly, there is the triple tradition identified by Lahey. A key part of this core is back-and-forth between the Christian and the Jew over specific proof texts. "Beginning" in Gen. 1:1 is identified with the Son; "let us make" in Gen. 1:26 is taken to refer to God speaking to the Son; Prov. 8 is taken show that the Son was with the Father at creation.[76] Although we cannot be certain that *JP* included this sequence, it is at least significant that *JP* attests the same understanding of Gen. 1:1. This interpretation also recurs in *Discussion of Zacchaeus and Apollonius*.[77] It is attested by Irenaeus and likely by Justin too when he identifies Wisdom as a Beginning.[78] Furthermore Rutherford argues that *JP* may have included the "second god" proof text Gen. 19:24,[79] and perhaps also Ps. 109:1 and Ps. 44:7–8.[80]

Given these proof-texts, the explanation of *JP*'s affirmation of the pre-existence of Jesus is likely the utilization of rabbinic interpretations by Aristo (or by those Christians engaged in discourse that gave rise to this use of the proof-texts that JP represents). The identification of "beginning" with the Son may seem odd to modern readers but, according to Williams, is in accordance with Rabbinic methods (citing Rashi).[81] Moreover, Skarsaune writes that the "combination of Prov 8:22 and Gen 1:1 is commonplace in rabbinic literature."[82] If Wisdom was being

---

[76] Rutherford, "*Altercatio Jasonis*," 142.

[77] Williams, *Adversus Judaeos*, 297, 308.

[78] Irenaeus, *Demonstration*, 68 (43); Rutherford, "*Altercatio Jasonis*," 140.

[79] "Then the LORD rained down burning sulphur on Sodom and Gomorrah—from the LORD out of the heavens." While the original does not imply two LORDS, a misguided reading of the text distinguishes the first LORD from the LORD-in-the-heavens. For this text as an example of widespread Old Testament "illeism" see Malone, "God the Illeist."

[80] Rutherford, "*Altercatio Jasonis*," 137.

[81] Williams, *Adversus Judaeos*, 33. The first word of Genesis *bereishit* ("in the beginning") was treated as two words, *bar* and *reishit*, by Rashi (11th century rabbnic scholar). *Bar* means "son," though rabbinic scholars took this to refer to Israel.

[82] Skarsaune, *Proof from Prophecy*, 388.

identified as the beginning within rabbinic Judaism, then it was a small step from Christian interpreters to identify the Son as the beginning, given that Jesus was already associated with Wisdom in the first century. Similarly the question of the plurality of "Lords" within Gen. 19:24 is known to have been a matter of dispute amongst the rabbis c. 150.[83] Skarsaune also demonstrates the rabbinic background for Justin's arguments for the pre-existence of Jesus in the *Dialogue with Trypho.*[84] It is worth emphasizing the conclusion that the use of these proof-texts is not dependent on Philo.[85] Rather it is rabbinic ideas of the late first and early second century that seem to be the source for these arguments. Not that the Rabbis affirmed the pre-existence of Jesus, but they did believe in the pre-existence of "the name of the Messiah" (and, possibly, in the pre-existence of the Messiah), and in the role of Wisdom in creation, and in other elements that could be taken over and applied to Christ. Taking up these arguments, Christians were able to argue for the presence of Christ in the Old Testament, and thus in favor of Christianity in general. It would, of course, be too crude to suggest that certain Christians adopted the pre-existence of Jesus for narrow evangelistic purposes. But Christians did hold the Old Testament to be authoritative and were predisposed to find Christ in the Old Testament. The influence of Rabbinic Judaism on certain Christians seems likely to have shaped how they interpreted the Old Testament.

JUSTIN AND LOGOS CHRISTOLOGY

In the earlier parts of this chapter I outlined several early occurrences of the pre-existence of Jesus in Christian texts and explored the likely background for these ideas. In retrospect we can see that although these ideas were on the trajectory towards later orthodoxy, by themselves they would not have been influential in fixing Christian views about the pre-existence (or otherwise) of Jesus. The pre-existence of Jesus achieved its central position within Christianity in no small part due to the work of

[83] Skarsaune, *Proof from Prophecy,* 412.
[84] E.g. Skarsaune, *Proof from Prophecy,* 381.
[85] Skarsaune, *Proof from Prophecy,* 410, 413; Rutherford, "*Altercatio Jasonis,*" 137.

Justin and the adoption of his views within Western Christendom. Part of Justin's argument for the pre-existence of Jesus comes from Old Testament theophanies. He was convinced that it was impossible that the unbegotten God could have come down to a specific place on earth and conversed with men;[86] these Old Testament theophanies must be ascribed to someone else, and for Justin that someone was the Logos. Though it is possible that this argument from theophanies was an original contribution by Justin (perhaps directed against Marcion),[87] it was simply an extension of Jewish and Christian thought about intermediaries acting on God's behalf.[88] Justin's Jewish dialogue partner Trypho proposes the role of the Angel of the Lord in such theophanies.[89] In this sense Justin exhibits the same tendency as *JP* of reading Christ into the Old Testament. However, there is another motivation for Justin's affirmation of the pre-existence of Jesus and that is his identification of Jesus as the Logos.

As we saw in an earlier chapter, Justin draws a sharp distinction between the unbegotten God and his begotten creation. This leads to a problem familiar from contemporary Platonic philosophy (and Justin was a Platonist before he became a Christian) of how to reconcile the essential transcendence of God with the immanence of God in his activity.[90] Justin claims that God does not change, is unbegotten, and only interacts indirectly with the world.[91] Justin describes his own conversion as coming to realize that he could not hope to "gaze upon God" through the pursuit of philosophy because the begotten human soul has no natural affinity with unbegotten God.[92] For Justin the Logos resolves the problem of how the human soul can come to knowledge of God if it has no innate

---

[86] Justin, *Dialogue*, 191–92 (127), 83–88 (56); 92–93 (60); Justin, *First Apology*, 68–69 (63).

[87] Skarsaune, *Proof from Prophecy*, 422.

[88] For example, Hos. 12:4 asserts that Jacob wrestled with an angel (cf. Gen. 32:22–32) and Heb. 13:2 implies that it was angels that spoke to Abraham (cf. Gen. 18).

[89] Justin, *Dialogue*, 92 (60.1).

[90] Goodenough, *Theology of Justin*, 139.

[91] Justin, *Dialogue*, 8 (3.5), 13 (5.6), 191–92 (127).

[92] *Dialogue*, 6 (2.6), 9–11 (4), 11–13 (5).

affinity with God. The seed of the Logos (*spermatikos logos*[93]) is implanted in the whole human race,[94] and through this seed each person is able to see "what is connatural [*suggenes*] to it" (i.e. Christ) and through the seed Christ is in everything.[95] This seed is human reason, the imitation of divine reason, through which the philosophers before Christ achieved knowledge of God.[96] For Justin, the Logos is not just God's mind or reason (an impersonal faculty or activity); the Logos is a person and one-and-the-same person as Christ.

It would be too simplistic to say that Justin remained a Platonist after his conversion or adopted stock Platonic concepts and dropped them unchanged into Christianity. Justin has a rich variety of sources and traditions behind his views and a good deal of originality to his thought. However, Justin represents a shift in Christian thought whereby the Johannine Logos has morphed from a divine abstract embodied in Jesus into a knowing and creating being in addition to God. The conceptual framework for this change, if not the concepts themselves, is Platonic. Although Justin shares with later orthodoxy the affirmation of the pre-existence of Jesus, he does so for different reasons. For Justin, Jesus is not God. Jesus is the Logos, the rational power of God and the intermediary for God in the world; he necessarily is not God, but is a separate and lesser being. Since the Logos is necessary for this mediating function between God and the world, then he must have existed prior to creation, and so if Jesus is the Logos (and Justin has resources in the Johannine tradition for affirming this) then Jesus must have pre-existed.

[93] The term *logos spermatikos* was used in Stoicism with reference to the supposed gaseous element in sexual reproduction, and by extension to God as the active element in matter (Goodenough, *Theology of Justin*, 161), however it seems unlikely that Justin took the term directly from the Stoics (Edwards, "Justin's Logos," 277).

[94] Justin, *First Apology*, 44–46 (32); Justin, *Second Apology*, 79 (8).

[95] *Second Apology*, 83 (13); 81 (10).

[96] *Second Apology*, 80–81 (10), 77 (6), 79 (8), 83–84 (13); Minns and Parvis, *Justin*, 65–66.

CONCLUSION

In this chapter we have examined a selection of early Christian texts and discovered that while they affirm the pre-existence of Jesus, their reasons for doing so are not those of later orthodoxy. The *Epistle of Barnabas* and the *Shepherd of Hermas* represent a Spirit-Man (sometimes called "Possessionist") Christology which was presumably endorsed by others in this period; they affirm that Jesus was a man possessed by the Holy Spirit. These Christians affirm the pre-existence of Jesus in the sense that the Holy Spirit (i.e. the divine element in Jesus) pre-existed and was active in creation. *Second Clement* represents a different form of Christianity which might be regarded as somewhere on the trajectory towards Gnosticism, teaching that there were spirit beings that included Jesus and the Church. These Christians affirm the pre-existence of Jesus in the sense that he was one of many pre-existing spirit beings. The *Dialogue of Jason and Papiscus* represents an ongoing discourse of parts of Christianity with Rabbinic Judaism, engaging with and being influenced by those interpretations of the Old Testament as they sought to understand the role of Jesus prior to his birth. These Christians affirm the pre-existence of Jesus in the sense that he was ascribed the role of the Messiah, of the Angel of the Lord, and of Wisdom. Finally, Justin marks the beginnings (though perhaps not the very beginnings[97]) of Christian engagement with Platonism and the contextualization of Christian ideas in a Platonic conceptual framework. Justin affirms the pre-existence of Jesus in the sense that he was a second and lesser god (=the Logos), performing a mediating function between God and the world both in creation and in our coming to knowledge of God.

These findings are significant for a number of reasons. Firstly, though these texts anticipate later orthodoxy by affirming the pre-existence of Jesus, the reasons for these affirmations are not those of later orthodoxy and are certainly not trinitarian (i.e. tripersonal-God affirming). The Spirit-Man Christology of *Barnabas* and *Shepherd* did not identify Jesus as God or as one Person of a triune Godhead. Those holding a Spirit-Man Christology may have affirmed the personhood of the Spirit centuries before this was established in the creeds, but the Spirit was not a co-equal

---

[97] See Gaston, "Influence of Platonism," 573–80.

and co-eternal Person in addition to the Father. Furthermore, Spirit-Man Christology would seem to entail that Jesus, far from being an eternal divine Person, was a mortal man who was indwelt by the Spirit. The ideas assumed by *Second Clement* about spirit beings would seem to entail that Jesus was not God, but was rather a spirit-being, presumably of a lower order (though the text gives little by way of theology or Christology). Justin is adamant that God and Jesus must be separate because it is impossible for the transcendent God to appear on earth; the Logos is an intermediary for God and therefore something separate. Justin did not affirm the pre-existence of Jesus because he believed that Jesus was God, but rather because he believed that (in some sense) God's eternal rationality was externalized and became another divine being just prior to creation. It may be that these thinkers, especially Justin, were influential (indeed instrumental) in the development of what became orthodox doctrine, but they were not trinitarians in the post-Nicene sense of the term.

Secondly, the motivations for affirming the pre-existence of Jesus presupposed by these texts are also different from those of the earliest Christians. The earliest Christians did not identify the Spirit as the Son of God, nor did they ascribe personhood to the Spirit, nor did they view the relationship between Jesus and the Spirit as a divine person possessing (or: indwelling, or cooperating together with) a human person. The earliest Christians did not consider the Church to be a spirit-being, nor did they consider Jesus to be a spirit-being, although they acknowledged the existence of angels and perhaps other spirit-beings. It is debatable to what extent the earliest Christians identified Jesus with Wisdom, or with the Angel of the Lord, or with other "second god" Old Testament passages. It seems likely that much of the Rabbinic interpretation that the author of *Dialogue of Jason and Papiscus* depended on did not exist at the time of Jesus and his immediate followers. The earliest Christians had little if any acquaintance with Platonism, and did not understand God or Jesus (or anything else) in that conceptual framework. While Jesus was seen as an intermediary in terms of the Atonement and being God's prophet and Messiah, the earliest Christians had no problem with the idea of God being known directly or creating directly; there was no conceptual space for a Platonic intermediary. The emergence of these affirmations of the pre-existence of Jesus arose as Christianity (or certain parts of it) was developing away from its earliest roots.

Thirdly, it is possible that these various Christological strands actually provide evidence for the presence of Dynamic Monarchianism in early Christianity. If those holding a Spirit-Man Christology believed that the Holy Spirit was the pre-existent Son who indwelt Jesus, then it follows that they believed that Jesus, prior to his indwelling, was an ordinary man and not a pre-existent person. If we accept that the Spirit-Man proposition (that the Spirit was the pre-existent Son) was a later accretion, then we may speculate about what sort of Christology preceded it. This depends upon when Jesus was supposed to have been indwelt by the Spirit. The moment of Jesus' possession by the Spirit is not stated in *Barnabas* or in the *Shepherd of Hermas.* The corrective statement of Theodotus[98] that the Spirit came "upon" Mary, not into Mary, suggests the existence of those who believed that the Spirit entered Jesus at his conception. Such a view is sometimes ascribed to the Valentinians. The other plausible opportunity afforded by the gospel narratives is Jesus' baptism, when the Spirit descended on Jesus. The former alternative would suggest that Spirit-Man Christology was a development on a Christology that affirmed the virgin birth while not yet affirming the pre-existence of Jesus. The latter alternative would suggest that Spirit-Man Christology was a development on an Adoptionism-type Christology. Given that the *Epistle of Barnabas,* at least, shows a preference for the Gospel of Matthew, there may be some reason to prefer the former alternative.

Second Clement says nothing about the birth of Jesus, except the cryptic phrase "Jesus Christ . . . was first a spirit and then became flesh."[99] However, given the dependence on the canonical gospels, it is not unlikely that the author presupposed the virgin birth. Presumably, a special birth is entailed in a spirit-becoming-flesh. The author places significance on Jesus being flesh ("so also we will receive the reward in this flesh") so presumably had something like incarnation (or, at least, transformation), rather than Docetism, in mind. If we accept that the schema of spirit-

[98] Fragment 4 (= Epiphanius, *Medicine Chest*, 2:75 [54.3.5]).
[99] *Second Letter of Clement*, 179 (9.5).

beings presupposed by the author is a later accretion, then we can speculate about the sort of Christology that preceded it. This would be a Christology that did not view Jesus as a spirit-being and thus would be a Christology that affirmed the virgin birth without affirming the pre-existence of Jesus.

Little has survived of the *Dialogue of Jason and Papiscus*. The fragment from Sophronius states that "on this day [i.e. Sunday] Christ was manifested on earth."[100] It is not clear that this means that Jesus was born on a Sunday, though this seems likely. As stated above, it would be too crude to suggest that the simple addition of Rabbinic interpretations converted certain Christians from something like Dynamic Monarchianism to a Christology that affirmed the pre-existence of Jesus. Similarly, it would be too crude to suppose that Justin only affirmed the pre-existence of Jesus because of the influence of Platonism. He had several and varied reasons for this affirmation, and it was almost certainly part of the Christian tradition that he learnt. However, we can see how this affirmation became more central and more entrenched within Christian thought due to engagement both with Rabbinic Judaism and with Platonism. Christology was changing on a trajectory towards later orthodoxy, and the pre-existence of Jesus had become a central plank of that Christology.

[100] Bovon and Duff, "New Greek Fragment," 462.

CHAPTER 10

Proof-Text Dossier

T HE THIRD CENTURY APOLOGIST TERTULLIAN wrote a treatise *On the Flesh of Christ* in which he sought to repudiate those who deny the resurrection. His rationale for focusing on the flesh of Christ is that if Christ's flesh was genuine then his resurrection must have been genuine. (By "flesh" Tertullian is referring a complete human person; he is affirming that Jesus was truly human.) In chapter 2 his target is Marcion, who denied the flesh and nativity of Christ. In chapter 15 his target is Valentinus, though Tertullian believes his remarks are applicable to all heretics. The key for Tertullian was to prove that the flesh of Jesus was human, not some other kind of substance, for one "who has refused to believe it [i.e. Christ's flesh] human can fashion it into anything he likes," such as Valentinus, who supposed Christ's flesh to be a "spiritual flesh."[1] In chapter 15 Tertullian cites a series of seven biblical texts to demonstrate that Jesus was truly human. Of course Tertullian is not seeking to deny the pre-existence of Jesus; however, it is notable that the seven texts he cites parallel in part the eight proof-texts used by Theodotus, as cited by Epiphanius (see Table 1 below).[2] Having cited the seven texts, he writes that these "texts by themselves ought to have been sufficient . . . evidence of his flesh being human and derived from man,"[3] though he does

[1] Tertullian, *Flesh of Christ*, 53 (15).
[2] Bertrand, "L'argumentation," 161–63; cf. Löhr, "Theodotus der Lederarbeiter," 110.
[3] Tertullian, *Flesh of Christ*, 53 (15).

continue to provide further arguments. The coincidence with the proof-texts cited by Theodotus, suggests that Tertullian was working from a pre-existing dossier of scriptural texts. The question for this chapter is whether Tertullian was referring to the work of Theodotus, or whether they were both citing from a third source. If a third source, then what did it contain, and is it an indicator of Dynamic Monarchian belief?

Table 1: Comparing the proof-texts for Tertullian and Theodotus

Tertullian, *On the Flesh of Christ*, 53 (15):	Theodotus, cited in Epiphanius, *Medicine Chest*, 2:73–78 (54.1–6):
1) John 8:40 2) Matt. 12:8 3) Is. 53:3 [LXX][4] 4) Jer. 17:9 [LXX] 5) Dan. 7:13 6) 1 Tim. 2:5 7) Acts 2:22	1) John 8:40 2) Matt. 12:31 3) Deut. 18:15 [LXX] 4) Luke 1:35 5) Jer. 17:9 [LXX] 6) Is. 53:3 [LXX] 7) Acts 2:22 8) 1 Tim. 2:5

COMPARISON

The texts of Tertullian and Theodotus offer little by way of comparison. Tertullian's summary is little more than a series of quotations introduced by who said them. Epiphanius does record some of the surrounding context when he preserves the quotations used by Theodotus, but little distinctive phraseology. Despite this small sample, we can be clear that Tertullian does not quote the words of Theodotus.

[4] "LXX" signifies a quotation from the Septuagint, an ancient Greek translation of the Hebrew Old Testament; sometimes this text and its chapter and verse numberings differ from modern translations, which are based primarily on a critical Hebrew text.

There are also variations between the quotations. In particular, Theodotus offers a longer quotation from Isaiah and the two quotations from Acts differ in the words included. Were Tertullian dependent on Theodotus for his quotations, then the shortening of the Isaiah quote might be explicable, but the change in the Acts quotation would not.

Finally, Tertullian includes two quotations not used by Theodotus (at least, not in the selection given by Epiphanius). Assuming that he did not get these quotations from a section of Theodotus's text unknown to us, then it seems unlikely that he is depending on Theodotus at all.

Table 2: Textual Comparison of Tertullian and Theodotus

Tertullian, *On the Flesh of Christ*, 53 (15). (re-ordered)	Theodotus, quoted in Epiphanius, *Medicine Chest*, 2:73–78 (54.1–6).
(A) if it was not human and not derived from man, I cannot see what substance Christ himself was referring to when he declared himself both man and the Son of Man: *Now therefore ye seek to kill a man who hath spoken to you the truth*, and, *The Son of Man is lord of the Sabbath*.	[Theodotus] said, [for example], "Christ said, 'But now ye seek to kill me, a *man* that hath told you the truth.' "You see," he said, "that Christ is man."[5]
	"For," says [Theodotus], "Christ himself has said, 'All manner of blasphemy shall be forgiven men,' and 'Whoever speaketh a word against the Son of Man, it shall be forgiven him; but he that blasphemeth the Holy Ghost, it

[5] Quoted in Epiphanius, *Medicine Chest*, 2:73–74 (54.1.9).

	shall not be forgiven him here or in the world to come.' "[6]
	And this same Theodotus says, "The Law too said of him, '<u>The Lord will raise up unto you a prophet of your brethren, like unto me; hearken to him</u>.' But Moses was a man. Therefore the Christ whom God raised up was this person but, since he was one of them, was a man just as Moses was a man."[7]
	Next Theodotus says, "And the Gospel itself said to Mary, '<u>The Spirit of the Lord shall come upon thee</u>'; it did not say, 'The Spirit of the Lord shall enter into thee.' "[8]
(C) and Jeremiah, *And <u>he is a man, and who hath known him</u>?*	The wretched Theodotus . . . says by way of allegation, "Jeremiah too said of him, '<u>He is a *man* and who will know him?</u>' "[9]
(B) Moreover it is of him that Isaiah says, *A man under chastisement, and knowing how to bear weakness*	Then Theodotus says in turn, "Isaiah too called him a man, for he said, '<u>A *man* acquainted with the bearing of infirmity; and we knew him afflicted with blows and abuse, and he was despised and not esteemed</u>.' "[10]

[6] *Medicine Chest*, 2:74 (54.2.3).

[7] *Medicine Chest*, 2:74–75 (54.3.1).

[8] *Medicine Chest*, 2:75 (54.3.5).

[9] *Medicine Chest*, 2:76 (54.4.1).

[10] *Medicine Chest*, 2:76 (54.5.1).

(F) again Peter in the Acts of the Apostles, *Jesus of Nazareth, a man appointed by God for you*	Theodotus . . . says, "The holy apostles called him 'a <u>*man* approved among you by signs and wonders</u>;' and they did not say, 'God approved.' "[11]
(E) also Paul the apostle, <u>*A mediator of God and men, the man Christ Jesus*</u>	[Theodotus's] next allegation is that "The apostle called him <u>the mediator between God and man, the *man* Christ Jesus</u>."[12]
(D) and Daniel, <u>*And behold, above the clouds as it were a son of man*</u>	

There are two plausible explanations for the coincidence of these proof-text summaries. One alternative is that these texts are truly independent and the work of two men well-versed in their scriptures. After all, a modern biblical unitarian would probably reach for some of these texts were he seeking to demonstrate the humanity of Jesus.[13] Tertullian is seeking to provide quotations that couple Jesus with "man" (or "son of man"); any scholar armed with a concordance or a Bible computer program would reach similar results.

However, there are some odd things about Tertullian's selection. Firstly, although he uses several scriptural texts that connect "Jesus" and "man," his list is by no means exhaustive (e.g. Matt. 9:8, Luke 4:4, John

[11] *Medicine Chest*, 2:77 (54.5.9).
[12] *Medicine Chest*, 2:77 (54.6.1).
[13] For example see Buzzard and Hunting, *Doctrine of the Trinity*: Dan. 7:13 (206–8), 1 Tim. 2:5 (79, 81, 97, 99, 102, etc.) and Acts 2:22 (51, 69, 81).

19:5). A text like Romans 5:12–17[14] would have been a substantial aid to his case, but he doesn't cite it. Given the wider pool of possible proof-texts, the coincidence between Tertullian and Theodotus's proof-texts is more significant.

Secondly, there is the fact that both Tertullian and Theodotus cited Jer. 17:9. Both cite the ancient Greek Septuagint translation; our Hebrew Masoretic text does not mention "a man." Yet even the Greek text does not have obvious Christological significance. Whereas one might immediately call Is. 53:3 to mind when thinking about the humanity of Christ, I'm not sure one would naturally associate Jer. 17:9 with Jesus. It is, nevertheless, a useful proof text when taken out of context, because it contains the statement "he is a man." That both Tertullian and Theodotus should strike upon this unusual proof text independently seems most unlikely. This lends credence to the idea that both writers had a shared source.

The selection of texts used by Tertullian and Theodotus do differ, but that difference is not beyond explanation. The first difference is Tertullian's use of Matthew 12:8 as opposed to verse 31, which Theodotus uses. Yet this change is explicable when one considers Tertullian's purpose, which is to provide texts where Jesus is referred to as a "man" or "son of man." Matthew 12: 31–32, which designates Jesus as "Son of Man," also includes the implication that Jesus has a lower status than the Holy Spirit. Such an implication is in line with Dynamic Monarchianism but muddies the waters somewhat for Tertullian's purposes. There seems no particular reason for Tertullian to use Matthew 12:8, as opposed to any other of the Son of Man texts, and one cannot rule out the possibility that he simply shifted from verse 31 to the next available Son of Man verse.

[14] "Therefore, just as sin came into the world through one man, and death came through sin, and so death spread to all because all have sinned . . . But the free gift is not like the trespass. For if the many died through the one man's trespass, much more surely have the grace of God and the free gift in the grace of the one man, Jesus Christ, abounded for the many . . . If, because of the one man's trespass, death exercised dominion through that one, much more surely will those who receive the abundance of grace and the free gift of righteousness exercise dominion in life through the one man, Jesus Christ" (NRSV).

Tertullian's desire to include texts referring to Jesus as "son of man" would also explain the addition of Daniel 7:13, which adds little to the argument.

The omission of Deuteronomy 18:15 may also be explained on this basis that, while it might imply that the Christ would be a man (as Theodotus argues), it does not contain any explicit mention of "man" or "son of man." The final omission, Luke 1:35, is the most obvious change for Tertullian to make because it has no direct relevance to the question of Jesus' humanity but only to his pre-existence. Theodotus uses the passage to argue against the idea that a pre-existent person entered Mary's womb and was incarnated. He notes, quite rightly, that there is no suggestion in Luke 1:35 of anyone descending from heaven into Mary. Tertullian, however, is not interested in this point, and in any case would have disagreed with Theodotus on this matter.

THE HYPOTHESIZED SOURCE

It seems plausible then that Tertullian and Theodotus shared a source. What can we say about this source?

- Since it is used by Theodotus c. 190, then it must have been composed earlier than this—let's say mid-second century or earlier.
- Since it is used by both Theodotus and Tertullian, then it is more likely a document of Western Christianity, perhaps even Roman Christianity, though we should be cautious of imposing artificial geographical constraints on the dissemination of texts.
- It must, at very least, have contained the five passages the two writers have in common (John 8:40, Is. 53:3 [LXX], Jer. 17:9 [LXX], 1 Tim. 2:5, and Acts 2:22). I am inclined to think it likely that this text also contained Matt. 12:31, Deut. 18:15 [LXX], and perhaps even Luke 1:35, though this is less easy to determine with confidence.
- Given the absence of textual parallels outside the passages cited, it seems unlikely that this dossier included a large amount of

commentary on the passages cited. Its form may have been more notes than treatise.

Finally, what, if anything, would the existence of such a proof text dossier imply for Dynamic Monarchianism in the second century? Above I argued against Tertullian's dependence on Theodotus on textual grounds, but there is also an *a priori* expectation that Tertullian would not be dependent on Theodotus, who by Tertullian's time was widely regarded as a heretic. By the same measure, it would seem unlikely that Tertullian would make use of any source that was associated with what he believed to be heresy. This indicates that the proof text dossier was a work of "orthodox" Christianity or came from a time when Dynamic Monarchianism was not outside the Christian mainstream. I have argued above that in the mid-second century Dynamic Monarchianism was not yet distinguished as a heresy. In this sense it would not be implausible for Tertullian to use a text that had been written by someone with Dynamic Monarchian views.

What, then, was the original purpose of this proof text dossier? Tertullian uses it in his rebuttal of Valentinianism, and the teachings of Valentinus may have been the prompt for its original compilation. The argument Theodotus utilizes from Luke 1:35 would have been just as pertinent for Valentinus's view that Jesus descended into Mary as for the emerging "orthodox" views of incarnation. However, Valentinus was not the only one proposing that Jesus was not truly human, and some other teacher may have been the original target. The only text used by Theodotus that would not fit this purpose would be Matthew 12:31, which seems most naturally applied as an argument for the subordination of Jesus to God. Given it is not possible to determine whether the hypothesized dossier included Matthew 12:31 or not, it may not be possible to determine with confidence the original purpose and scope of the proof text dossier. Nevertheless, the best explanation would seem to be that the proof text dossier was intended to prove the humanity of Jesus against those who questioned it, whether Valentinians or others.

CHAPTER 11

Precursors to Gnosticism and Other "Heresies"

O
UR SOURCES FOR SECOND CENTURY CHRISTOLOGY are meager, and those sources that have been preserved were usually those consonant with later orthodoxy. Trying to achieve a balanced view of the doctrinal landscape in second century Christianity is virtually impossible, given that so many of the pieces are missing. However, our efforts are not entirely hamstrung. In addition to the second century "fathers" such as Justin and Irenaeus, we also have reports about those whom later orthodoxy came to consider as "heresiarchs." These thinkers are important indications of the complex religious milieu in which early Christianity developed, and the wide range of ideas, theologies, and mythologies that existed in this period which had some kind of connection to Christianity. But they are also important as witnesses to the Christian milieu that gave rise to their ideas. For my purposes I am interested in the Christology of these "heresiarchs" not so much because of their own views (they are not Dynamic Monarchian) but because of what their views imply about the Christianity that produced them.

It will be useful to say something here about methodology. For example, the majority view among recent historians seems to be that Sethian Gnosticism had its origins in Judaism and was only later Christianized. (A few scholars, like Simone Petrement and Alastair Logan, demur from this position.) Yet whether Sethian Gnosticism had its origins in Judaism or in Christianity, at some point it took on Christological elements, and so regardless of its origins, it is appropriate to ask what sort of Christianity gave rise to this sort of Gnostic Christology.

There are some caveats to be noted. Firstly, this approach assumes that these heresies are divergences from some more primitive form of Christianity and are not the primal form of Christianity. In most cases this will not be controversial, and I hope in later chapters to give some idea about what I consider to be the primitive forms of Christianity. Secondly, this approach is necessarily speculative; we are trying to extrapolate from existing evidence to areas where evidence is lacking. I hope, however, that this approach will, at least, not be considered wildly speculative, and that the consistency of the results will in some measure speak to their accuracy. Thirdly, our sources for the heresiarchs are in large part not primary sources but rather the reports from their adversaries.

DOCETISM

Around the end of the second century the bishop of Antioch Serapion (fl. late 2nd–early 3rd centuries) wrote a pamphlet entitled *The So-Called Gospel of Peter*, a refutation of some of the claims made within that gospel. In his pamphlet Serapion refers to those from whom the *Gospel of Peter* originated, whom he calls "docetists" (from *dokein* "to appear").[1] The fragment of the *Gospel of Peter* found at Akhmim seems to imply that Jesus did not truly suffer on the cross.[2]

Petrement distinguishes four types of Docetism: (1) that Jesus' sufferings were only apparent, (2) that Jesus' human form was only apparent, (3) that Jesus and Christ were separate beings, and (4) that Christ was too special to be contaminated by matter.[3] In this section I am

---

[1] Serapion, quoted in Eusebius, *Ecclesiastical History*, 216 (6.12).

[2] "But he held his peace as (if) he felt no pain." (*Gospel of Peter*, 155 [4 or 10]). (This work has been divided into sections by modern scholars in two different ways.) Despite Serapion's report some modern scholars are not willing to ascribe any sort of Docetism to the *Gospel of Peter* given how little of it is extant. (e.g. Schneemelcher, *New Testament Apocrypha*, 1:220).

[3] Petrement, *Separate God*, 145–51.

concerned with the second view, that Jesus was not human but some other thing.

Perhaps the earliest form of Docetism is to be located in the unnamed "false prophets" (1 John 4:1) and "antichrists" (1 John 2:18, 2:22, 4:3; 2 John 1:7) condemned by John in his letters. He says that "every spirit that confesses Jesus Christ has come in the flesh is from God" and that the contrary view is the "spirit of the antichrist" (1 John 4:2–3). In these verses John contrasts confessing that "Jesus Christ has come in the flesh" with not confessing Jesus and so it has been suggested that the operative issue is confessing Jesus, not whether he was in the flesh or not. It seems to me that this view is mistaken for two reasons. Firstly, John elsewhere talks about "those who do not confess that Jesus Christ has come in the flesh" (2 John 1:7). Secondly, it is not unexpected that John should consider Docetism fundamentally the same as denying Jesus; he explicitly says that they are "antichrist."

It is also possible that John had docetists in view when composing his gospel, stating explicitly that "the Word became flesh" (i.e. became a man; John 1:14) as well as recording that Jesus became tired (John 4:6–7), wept (John 11:35), died (John 19:30), and his resurrected body still carried the scars of his execution (John 20:24–29). Nevertheless, John tells us little about these docetists, except that they did not confess that Jesus came in the flesh and that this, for him, was beyond the pale. Plausibly, the opponents of John may have held that Christ was a separate being from the man Jesus, and a number of modern scholars associate the opponents of John with the views of Cerinthus (on which see below).[4] However, Cerinthus did not question the reality of Jesus' flesh; if John is stressing the reality of Jesus' flesh against his opponents then he would seem to have a different heresy in view.

Ignatius also writes against Docetism. He instructs the church at Tralles to guard themselves against this heresy:

> And so, be deaf when someone speaks to you apart from Jesus Christ, who was from the race of David and from Mary, who was truly born, both ate

---

[4] For references see Brown, *Epistles of John,* 65. Also see Irenaeus, *Against the Heresies (Book 3),* 52 (3.11.1), 81 (3.16.5); cf. 34 (3.3.4).

and drank, was truly crucified and died, while those in heaven and on earth and under the early looked on. He was also truly raised from the dead, his Father having raised him.[5]

He writes similar warnings to the church at Smyrna against "unbelievers" who say "that he suffered only in appearance."[6] For Ignatius, the resurrection of Jesus is an integral guarantee of the promised resurrection of believers.[7] More importantly the suffering of Jesus had to be genuine as he suffered "on behalf of our sins."[8] As Robert Grant observes, "If Christ did not really suffer, men could receive no real benefits from his passion. This is why Ignatius is militantly opposed to Docetism."[9]

Given that Ignatius was bishop of Antioch, it would be unsurprising if he had in mind the views like those of Saturninus of Antioch (fl. early 2nd c.). According to Irenaeus, Saturninus claimed that Jesus was "unbegotten [i.e. not born of a woman], incorporeal, and formless; still he was believed to have appeared as man."[10] Similar statements are given in the book sometimes attributed to Hippolytus called *Refutation of All Heresies* ("manifested in human appearance")[11] and in a work falsely attributed to Tertullian called *Against All Heresies* ("had not existed in a bodily substance, and had endured a *quasi*-passion in a phantasmal shape merely")[12], though these authors may not know more than they read in Irenaeus's *Against the Heresies*.

A similar view is ascribed to Cerdo (fl. c. 136–40) in *Against All Heresies*, namely that Jesus was not born, did not suffer, and had only a "phantasmal shape" and not "the substance of flesh."[13] Similarly, according to *Refutation of All Heresies* Marcion rejected the birth of Jesus,

---

[5] Ignatius, *Trallians*, 265 (9:1–2).

[6] Ignatius, *Smyrneans*, 297 (2:1); cf. *Trallians*, 265 (10:1).

[7] *Smyrneans*, 299 (3:2, 4:2), 301 (5:3); *Trallians*, 265 (9:2, 10:1), 267 (11:2).

[8] *Smyrneans*, 303 (7:1); *Trallians*, 267 (11:2).

[9] Grant, *Early Christian Doctrine*, 11.

[10] Irenaeus, *Against the Heresies (Book 1)*, 84–85 (1.24.2). On the meaning of "unbegotten" here see the translator's note (231 note 4).

[11] *Refutation of All Heresies*, 539 (7.28.4).

[12] *Against All Heresies*, 649 (1).

[13] *Against All Heresies*, 653 (6).

as it would imply that he was a creature of the evil creator of this cosmos. For Marcion, Jesus, also called "Logos," descended during the reign of Tiberius. This Jesus was an intermediate between the good god and the bad god, liberated from both their natures.[14] Irenaeus, however, says that Marcion held that Jesus was derived from the Father (i.e. the good god).[15] According to *Against All Heresies*, Apelles (fl. mid-2nd c.) a follower of Marcion, held that Jesus was a spiritual being, who borrowed elements during his descent that he wove together into a starry and airy body.[16]

We have two differing accounts of Basilides (fl. mid-2nd c.), one from Irenaeus and one from the *Refutation of All Heresies*.[17] It is not clear whether they represent two different stages of his thought (or of his followers' thought) or whether one of our sources has misidentified Basilides. In Irenaeus's account, Christ was the "Nous" (i.e. "mind") of an unnamable father. He descends and appears "as a man." He avoids crucifixion by switching places with Simon of Cyrene, transfiguring his appearance to look like Simon. "For, since his was an incorporeal Power and the ingenerate Father's Mind, he was transformed as he willed." Then he ascended.[18] This account implies that Christ had no physical substance and was only man in appearance, and this is how the author of *Against All Heresies* evidently interprets Irenaeus's report.[19]

Theories about the origins of docetic belief vary. For instance, Werner asserts that Docetism appeared early, before the infancy narratives (which, he thinks, were written in response to docetic beliefs), and that it was derived from the belief that Jesus was an angel.[20] Several writers suggest

---

[14] *Refutation of All Heresies*, 561 (7.31.5).

[15] Irenaeus, *Against the Heresies (Book 1)*, 91 (1.27.2).

[16] *Against All Heresies*, 653 (6). According to this report Apelles also taught that when Jesus ascended to heaven after his resurrection he restored these elements to their places so that "He reinstated in heaven His spirit only" (653 [6]).

[17] *Refutation of All Heresies*, 493–537 (7.14.1–7.27.13), esp. 529–31 (7.26.8) and 535 (7.27.8).

[18] Irenaeus, *Against the Heresies (Book 1)*, 86 (1.24.4).

[19] *Against All Heresies*, 650 (1).

[20] Werner, *Formation*, 128–29; also see H. F. Wickings, "Nativity Stories," 457–60.

that Docetism was a natural consequence of a Spirit-man Christology.[21] Others have associated Docetism with Jewish Christianity.[22]

Gedaliahu Stroumsa, noting the common theme amongst Gnostic texts (e.g. Basilides) of Jesus switching forms before the crucifixion and laughing, argues that Docetism originated from the early association between Jesus and Isaac, who also escaped death by substitution and whose name means "he will laugh."[23] Robert Grant finds another possible precedent for the laughing motif in Ps. 2:4.[24] While this background may explain the laughing motif, it does not account for the impulse to deny that Jesus was crucified. Given the significance of the cross for early Christians, it hardly seems likely that some would adopt Docetism only to conform Jesus to an Isaac typology.

Petrement comments that "the desire to accentuate Jesus Christ's divinity as much as possible is the root of Docetism."[25] Goldstein and Stroumsa describe how Greek revisionists used the technical literary device of the *eidōlon* (phantom or ethereal double) to solve theological problems. For example, the Greek poet Stesichorus (c. 632–c. 553 BCE) has Helen's *eidōlon* go to Troy with Paris because her behavior would be unfit for a goddess. They argue that this device provided a ready solution for those who thought the crucifixion to be unworthy of a deity.[26] Yet this would presuppose the beliefs that Jesus was divine and that crucifixion is unworthy of the divine. The latter could derive from Greek philosophers, such as Xenophanes[27] or Plato;[28] the former is an inference some make on the basis of Pauline and/or Johannine texts.

Yet the named docetists we have considered—Saturninus, Marcion, and Basilides—have something else in common, and that is a belief that humanity is tainted. Saturninus believed that humanity was a creation of mere angels, as did Basilides; Marcion held that creation was the product

---

[21] Rudolph, *Gnosis*, 159; Knox, *Humanity and Divinity*, 16.

[22] Goulder, *Tale of Two Missions*, 116–19; Rudolph, *Gnosis*, 307.

[23] Stroumsa, "Christ's Laughter," 275–88.

[24] Grant, "Gnostic Origins," 121–25.

[25] Petrement, *Separate God*, 144.

[26] Goldstein and Stroumsa, "Origins of Docetism," 428–33.

[27] Xenophanes, *Fragments*, 95 (fragments B11, B12, B14, B15).

[28] Plato, *Republic*, 1016–29 (2.377b–391e).

of the evil god. It is not simply that they considered the crucifixion to be unseemly, but rather that human nature itself was unworthy of Jesus.

If we remove this anti-cosmic rationale, then we may get a glimpse of the Christology which preceded these heresies. For Marcion, Jesus is the Son of God. He recognized only his redacted form of Luke's gospel, stripped of the virgin birth narrative. Given the dateline Marcion gives for the descent of Jesus,[29] it is likely his gospel began at Luke 3:1. It is probable that Marcion came to his views in a milieu that accepted the virgin birth and it was his view of human nature that led him to reject it. Since for Marcion, the material world (including human bodies) was a creation of the evil god, he would not want to ascribe a real human body to Jesus. It is not clear whether Marcion held that Jesus was created by the Father only briefly before his appearance in Judea or that Jesus was much older.

Our sources about Saturninus don't inform us about when he dated the emanation of Jesus. We know that Basilides regarded Jesus as the first emanation from God, *Nous* (Mind), and presumably Basilides presupposes some of form of Gnostic aeonology (i.e. a hierarchical scheme of numerous spirit-beings). We can assume that the Christology from which they deviated considered Jesus to be special enough for him to be identified as an aeon once the Gnostic aeonology was accepted. However, that is not particularly informative. Gnostics named aeons after a range of nouns (e.g. Church, Life, Word, Mind, Man) and there does not seem any determining factor as to which noun (or pronoun) the Gnostics chose to elevate into aeons. Jesus (or Christ) wouldn't have had to be that special for Gnostics to make him into an aeon.

DESCENDING SPIRIT

Another category of heretical Christology is those who acknowledge that Jesus was genuinely human but attribute his divinity (or specialness) to a descending power or spirit.

---

[29] Irenaeus, *Against the Heresies (Book 1)*, 91 (1.27.2); *Refutation of All Heresies*, 561 (7.29.5); Tertullian, *Against Marcion*, 351 (4.6).

Carpocrates believed that Jesus was the son of Joseph, and so not virgin-born. According to *Against All Heresies*, Carpocrates held that Jesus was only superior "in the practice of righteousness and in integrity of life";[30] Irenaeus and the *Refutation of All Heresies* add that for Carpocrates, the soul of Jesus remembered what it had seen in the sphere of the unbegotten God.[31] It is not obvious whether Carpocrates meant that only the soul of Jesus pre-existed, or that all souls pre-exist but only a pure soul would remember pre-existing. The latter would be explicable as an adoption of common Hellenist doctrine of the transmigration of the soul (reincarnation).[32] Further, Carpocrates claimed that a power descended upon Jesus from the Father so that his soul might escape from the creators of the world. It is not recorded what sort of power this was or when it descended.

Cerinthus believes that Jesus was the son of Joseph but was more righteous than other men. Christ, however, was a separate power that descended upon Jesus at his baptism from the unknown Father. Christ was impassible, and so did not suffer with Jesus, but rather departed from him.[33]

According to the *Refutation of All Heresies*, the Italian school of the Valentinians, including Heracleon and Ptolemy, maintain that Jesus had an animal body, and that at his baptism Logos descended on him from Sophia. It was this Logos that gave Jesus voice and raised him from the dead.[34]

According to Irenaeus, some of the Gnostics believed that Jesus was born of a virgin and was thus more righteous than other men. A spirit-being, Christ, used John the Baptist and his baptism of repentance to ensure that Jesus was a pure vessel. Then Christ, united with *Sophia* (Wisdom), descended into Jesus. Though the disciples were unaware of

---

[30] *Against All Heresies*, 651 (3).

[31] Irenaeus, *Against the Heresies (Book 1)*, 87 (1.25.1); *Refutation of All Heresies*, 563 (7.32.1).

[32] The classic source for this is Plato's dialogue *Meno*, 879–86 (80C–86B).

[33] Irenaeus, *Against the Heresies (Book 1)*, 90 (1.26.1); *Refutation of All Heresies*, 569 (7.33.2).

[34] *Refutation of All Heresies*, 433 (6.35.5–6).

Christ's descent, from that time Jesus began to work miracles and reveal the Father. Christ left Jesus before his death.[35] Though Irenaeus does not explicitly link Christ's descent with Jesus' baptism, this would make most sense of the idea that it was from that time that Jesus began his ministry. According to the *Refutation of All Heresies*, the Gnostics called the Naassenes believe in three qualities—intellectual, animate, and earthly— that make up Geryon, the originating principle of the capacity for knowledge of God. These three qualities descended simultaneously into Jesus, who was born of Mary, and spoke through him.[36]

Leaving aside Carpocrates's doctrine of the transmigration of the soul (reincarnation), both he and Cerinthus have a shared core of views. They both maintain that the world was not created by the true God, that Jesus was born of Mary and Joseph, and that a power descended on Jesus. For Cerinthus this power is a spirit being called "Christ"; our information about Carpocrates is ambiguous as to whether this power was a personal being. These two heretics seem less motivated by their anti-cosmic tendencies than the docetists considered above, as they are willing to acknowledge that a human Jesus could have been righteous (despite being human). Since they seem content with the idea that the power could descend into a human Jesus, it is not obvious that their anti-cosmic tendencies would prompt them to reject the virgin birth. As we know of others who denied the virgin birth (e.g. the Ebionites), this may have been part of the Christology that preceded their views.

It seems likely that Cerinthus's idea of a personal power named "Christ" who descended into Jesus is connected with the Gnostic position of the aeon "Christ" descending into Jesus. This same idea presumably motivated the Christology of the Italian Valentinians. The common thread between these Christologies is a heavenly power descending into Jesus at his baptism, which is no doubt based upon the gospel narratives of the descent of the Spirit at Jesus' baptism—in Mark 1:10 the Spirit descends *eis* (into or upon) Jesus—perhaps via a non-canonical version.[37]

---

[35] Irenaeus, *Against the Heresies (Book 1)*, 100–1 (1.30.12–13).

[36] *Refutation of All Heresies*, 197–99 (5.6.6–7).

[37] E.g. the beginning of the *Gospel of the Ebionites* (Epiphanius, *Medicine Chest*, 1:142 [30.13.6]).

In the biblical narratives the Holy Spirit is almost certainly an impersonal power, as it was first century Judaism. The impersonal nature of the descending power is, perhaps, still seen in the doctrine of Carpocrates and of the Naassenes. For the Gnostics and those influenced by them the transition from impersonal power to personal aeon was natural and unproblematic.

If the transformation of the descending power into a descending spirit-being is a later addition to the narrative, then the preceding Christology was without any of sense of pre-existent Jesus (or Christ). Cerinthus and Carpocrates on the one hand and the Gnostics on the other, differ as to whether Jesus had a human father, but all these Christologies are predicated on the temporal beginning of Jesus and on his humanity, which presumably reflects the Christology they were in the process of diverging from.

However, there must have been another aspect of the Christology that preceded these "descending Spirit" Christologies because each of them is motivated to find some explanation for the specialness of Jesus. Whether through an impersonal power or a personal aeon, there is a clear recognition that something about Jesus needed explaining—there was something spiritual/heavenly/divine about this man. For some reason, the early Christian Christology seemed insufficient to these "heretics."

SPECIAL BIRTH

As noted above, some of those with "descending Spirit" Christologies also accepted the virgin birth but believed that it was at Jesus' baptism that a spirit or power descended into Jesus. For another set of heretics, it was the virgin birth that made Jesus special.

Basilides (as reported in the *Refutation of All Heresies*) describes Jesus as "the son of Mary" who was "illuminated" by the light that descended upon him from the Ogdoad (a group of eight aeons). Although Jesus' miraculous conception is not explicitly mentioned, the descending light is linked to the message of Gabriel to Mary (Luke 1:26-38).[38] While the terms

[38] *Refutation of All Heresies*, 529 (7.26.8).

"Holy Spirit" and "power of the Highest" are interpreted as two powers descending, the core narrative is something divine descending into the womb of Mary, thus making Jesus special.

The Valentinians seem to have had changing views about the origins of Jesus. According to Irenaeus, Valentinus at various times ascribed the production of Jesus to different aeons: Desired, Christ, and "Man and Church."[39] Ptolemy held that the whole pleroma of aeons brought contributions that were united together to form Jesus.[40]

Against All Heresies says that according to Valentinus Jesus descended with a spiritual body and "passed through the virgin Mary as water through a pipe, neither receiving nor borrowing aught hence."[41] The point is that although Jesus was born of a virgin, he did not receive anything of Mary's nature. The *Refutation of All Heresies* ascribes a different view to the Valentinians, that Jesus was born of a virgin but was generated by the Artificer (i.e. the Creator), who supplied his body, and Sophia, who supplied his essence. This scheme is read into Luke 1:35, the "Holy Spirit" being Wisdom (*Sophia*) and the "Most High" being the Artificer. The purpose of this birth was so that there "arose a heavenly Word from the Ogdoad, born through Mary."[42] The author adds that the Eastern school of the Valentinians, including Axionicus (fl. late 2nd c.– early 3rd c.) and Bardesianes (154–222) held that Jesus had a spiritual body and for this reason the Holy Spirit (= Wisdom, *Sophia*) descended on Mary.[43]

Marcus (fl. mid-2nd c.), a Valentinian from Lyons, held that Jesus was generated of a virgin by special dispensation after the likeness of the heavenly *Anthropos* (Man or Human). Marcus correlates the heavenly tetrad—*Anthropos*, *Ecclesia* (Church), *Logos* (Word), and *Zoe* (Life) — that produced the aeons with the four characters in the birth narrative (Gabriel, Holy Spirit, Power of the Highest, and Mary). Later, at the baptism of Jesus, *Anthropos* descended upon Jesus and was made one with

---

[39] Irenaeus, *Against the Heresies (Book 1)*, 52 (1.11.1).

[40] Irenaeus, *Against the Heresies (Book 1)*, 27 (1.2.6).

[41] *Against All Heresies*, 652 (4).

[42] *Refutation of All Heresies*, 431 (6.35.4).

[43] *Refutation of All Heresies*, 433 (6.35.7).

him. It was *Anthropos* who spoke through Jesus and revealed the Father. Marcus seems to distinguish the Savior, whom he identifies as Jesus, from Christ, whom he identifies as *Anthropos*.[44] The author of *Against All Heresies* seems mostly interested in Marcus's use of Greek alphabet to justify his views, but does mention that Christ descended as a dove on Jesus, and that this Christ did not have a physical body.[45]

Gnostic ideas about Jesus seem to have changed over time. Writing in the second century, Irenaeus reports that the Gnostics believed Jesus was born of a virgin through the agency of God, and it was for this reason that he could be wiser, purer and more righteous than other men.[46] Writing in the fourth century, Epiphanius reports that the Gnostics believed that Jesus "is not 'born of Mary' but 'revealed through Mary.' And he has not taken flesh but is only appearance."[47] This later view is similar to the view ascribed to Valentinus in *Against All Heresies*, that Jesus was a spiritual being who merely passed through Mary rather than taking his substance from her.[48]

In general, Gnostics texts, such as those discovered at Nag Hammadi, do not mention the birth of Jesus, who is regarded as a third manifestation of Seth, whom they regard as a spirit-being. *The Holy Book of the Great Invisible Spirit* describes the great Seth mystically preparing Jesus (a "reason-born being" or "a body begotten by the word") through "the virgin."[49] Later Seth was "clothed" with Jesus.[50] This sounds similar to Irenaeus's account of the Gnostics. The *Revelation of Adam* seems to reject the idea of the virgin birth.[51] Instead it says of the great illuminator (= Seth) that "God chose him from all the eternal realms . . . The [great]

---

[44] Irenaeus, *Against the Heresies (Book 1)*, 66 (1.15.3); *Refutation of All Heresies*, 477 (6.51.1–4).

[45] *Against All Heresies*, 653 (5).

[46] Irenaeus, *Against the Heresies (Book 1)*, 101 (1.30.12).

[47] Epiphanius, *Medicine Chest*, 1:99 (26.10.4–5).

[48] *Against All Heresies*, 652 (4).

[49] *Holy Book*, 265 (63).

[50] *Holy Book*, 265 (64).

[51] *Revelation of Adam*, 352 (78). (On the interpretation of this passage about fourteen "kingdoms" see 344).

illuminator has come [from] foreign air, [from a] great eternal realm,"[52] which, whatever else it might mean, does not mean virgin birth. Epiphanius reports that the Sethians said this about Jesus (who is for them the third Seth): "from Seth by descent and lineage came Christ, Jesus himself, not by generation but by appearing miraculously in the world. He is Seth himself, who visited men then and now because he was sent from above by the Mother."[53]

Each of these "special birth" Christologies seems to adapt the pre-existing idea of the virgin birth for one of three reasons. Firstly, there are those like Basilides for whom the virgin birth was the opportunity for some power to descend into Jesus. For Basilides neither Jesus nor the light that illuminated him in the womb pre-existed. The virgin birth is not an instance of incarnation; rather, the virgin birth makes Jesus special and able to lead souls, benefited by the third sonship, into the celestial realm.

Secondly, there are those like the Eastern Valentinians, Marcus and some Gnostics, for whom the virgin birth was the means by which a special body could be created or prepared. For the Eastern Valentinians, the virgin birth of Jesus was a way of ascribing to Jesus a spiritual body rather than an animal body. For the Gnostics, according to Irenaeus, the virgin birth made Jesus more righteous; this was part of his preparation for receiving the Christ-aeon. This same basic narrative recurs in *The Holy Book of the Great Invisible Spirit,* where the virgin birth prepares Jesus for the descent of Seth. The Valentinians also thought that a spirit descended on the virgin-born Jesus, either *Logos* or *Anthropos* (Marcus). For these heretics, the virgin birth is also not an incarnation but rather a preparation for the later descent of a spirit being, usually at Jesus' baptism.

Thirdly, there are those for whom the virgin birth is an opportunity for a spirit being to descend into the world, rather than an act of creation. This view is ascribed to Valentinus in *Against All Heresies* and seems to be behind Epiphanius's report about the Gnostics. It may also be that Epiphanius's report about the Sethians is explained by Jesus being apparently born by Mary but really being the descended Seth. In these cases, we have a pre-existent Jesus (or Seth), but no incarnation, because

---

[52] *Revelation of Adam,* 354–55 (82).
[53] Epiphanius, *Medicine Chest,* 1:278 (39.3.5).

he does not take on flesh, that is, become a real human being. This may have been motivated by anti-cosmic sentiments. It also seems explicable as a simplification of the second view described above. Rather than create a spiritual body into which a spirit later descends, we have a spirit descending and taking non-physical form all at once.

Of these three types of special-birth Christology, the first and second both have as a core narrative a virgin birth by some sort of divine intervention for the creation of Jesus. The description of the divine intervention varies according to the system in question—light for Basilides, varying aeons for the Gnostics and Valentinians—but each of these can be understood as rooted either directly or indirectly in the biblical narrative. The second type has an additional narrative point when a pre-existent spirit or power descends into Jesus, as with the descending-spirit Christologies considered above. As above, we can see the descending-spirit narrative as being rooted in the biblical baptismal narratives. Therefore, the virgin birth narrative in these Christologies has no pre-existent being or spirit who is the same person as the man Jesus. In other words, Jesus does not pre-exist, nor is he incarnated in these accounts—the virgin birth is an act of creation.[54]

The third type of special-birth Christology does contain a pre-existent being, a pre-human Jesus instead of the created man Jesus. The urge to preserve the virgin birth story while rejecting its implication of Jesus' creation suggests a syncretic or apologetic tendency, an attempt to reconcile a spiritual Jesus/Seth with the tradition of the virgin birth. I have proposed above that this is a later adaption of the second type. Alternatively, it might be an adaptation of Docetism, conforming it to Christian tradition. Given the evidence, it seems most plausible that the third type is later than the second.

If this analysis is correct, then these special-birth Christologies seem to be based, directly or indirectly, on a shared virgin birth narrative in which Jesus is created in the womb of the virgin Mary by the intervention of God's spirit. It seems unlikely that this narrative depicted Jesus as a pre-existent being, because this is an element that we would have expected

---

[54] Brown, *Birth of the Messiah*, 140–41, 314, 432.

these heretics to preserve had they known it. It does seem likely that this narrative contained the concept of Jesus being in some way special by virtue of his miraculous conception.

SUMMARY

We have examined a number of heretical Christologies from around the second century and found a number of indications of what sort of Christology these heretics deviated from. The descending spirit Christologies presuppose a strong emphasis on the Christological significance of Jesus' baptism. For several heresies, the baptism of Jesus was the moment when a spirit-being descended into Jesus. The presentation of his baptism in the New Testament gospels might provide sufficient precedent for these ideas (once combined with a belief in aeons or other spirit-beings), but emphasis on the status-changing, perhaps adoptive, nature of the event would have given added impetus to the descending spirit Christologies. Some of these Christologies rejected the virgin birth, while others accepted it.

Those heretical Christologies that accept the virgin birth do not seem to employ any concept of incarnation (i.e. a spirit coming to be human or to in some sense gain a human nature). For example, in the earlier forms of Gnostic Christology, the virgin birth is part of the preparation for Jesus, but does not involve a pre-existent being descending into the womb. In latter forms a pre-existent being does descend into Mary, but does not take on flesh; rather, that being proceeds to cooperate with the man he has entered. These special birth Christologies would seem to indicate the existence of a virgin birth Christology, but they do not witness to the motifs of incarnation or of a pre-existent Jesus. Although it is possible that the concept of the incarnation existed but was rejected by these heretics, one would expect them to readily accept the idea of a pre-existent being descending into the womb of Mary.

The docetic Christologies are the most difficult to draw significant conclusions from since by rejecting the reality of Jesus' body they reject all but a semblance of the biblical Jesus. Marcion presumably knew but rejected a virgin birth Christology. It also seems plausible that Marcion did not believe in the pre-existence of Jesus, but rather that Jesus, though not material, was a creation in time. With other docetists, we have insufficient data to judge, but we should not assume that by eschewing Jesus' body and birth these docetists necessarily held that Jesus existed for a significant amount of time prior to his manifestation. However, if some docetists believed in the pre-existence of Jesus, it is plausible that this is something they introduced themselves. If Jesus did not have a human birth, then there would be no reason for him not to exist for an unspecified amount of time prior to his manifestation. Therefore, although it is plausible that Marcion deviated from a form of Christianity that did not affirm the pre-existence of Jesus, it is impossible to tell whether other docetists deviated from a form of Christianity that did affirm the pre-existence of Jesus.

Docetism seems predicated on the elevated status of Jesus, and so presumably the Christology from which docetists deviated had an elevated view of Jesus. What is not clear is *how* special Jesus would have to be for someone to feel compelled to reject his crucifixion (and birth) and consider Jesus to be a spirit being rather than a man. The key issue is about Jesus' status, and particularly his righteousness, rather than his longevity. If one believed that Jesus was quintessentially pure and that the material world was evil, then denying the material body of Jesus seems an appealing conjecture. The theology of Paul and/or John might seem a starting point for such conjectures,[55] but the issue of whether or not Jesus pre-existed seems to have little relevance for the origins of Docetism.

In summary, I have shown that a number of the early Christian heresies presuppose a Dynamic Monarchian Christology, that is, a Christology which affirms the virgin birth but not the pre-existence of Jesus. From those heresies considered, there is no unequivocal evidence of a Christology that *did* affirm the pre-existence of Jesus, though such Christologies might have formed the basis of some of the heresies considered. What is evident from this chapter is that Dynamic Monarchianism did not emerge fresh in the late second century with Theodotus, but that this type of Christology preceded many of the early

---

[55] Petrement, *A Separate God,* 144.

Christian heresies, and so was widespread in the early second and late first century.

CHAPTER 12

Ignatius of Antioch: Proto-Orthodox or Monarchian?

GNATIUS WAS A BISHOP of Antioch in Syria,[1] where he was arrested and sent over land to Rome to face death in the teeth of the beasts of the arena. During his journey through Asia Minor he stayed briefly in Smyrna and became acquainted with its bishop Polycarp. From there he wrote three letters to churches that had made contact with him (*Ephesians, Magnesians, Trallians*) and wrote a further letter to Rome, asking them not to interfere with his martyrdom. He had further stop-offs in Troas, where he wrote three letters (*Philadelphians, Smyrneans and Polycarp*), and in Phillipi. The church at Phillipi requested the Ignatian letters from Polycarp, which he sent with his own covering letter; "it may well be that our present collection of all seven letters derives from this collection made by Polycarp himself."[2]

The textual history of the Ignatian letters is complicated and fraught with difficulty. Three versions of the Ignatian letters are extant, known as "long" (including six other letters), "short" (extant in Syrian only), and "middle"; recent scholarly consensus accepts the latter as authentic. [3] In addition to the Greek manuscripts, there are also translations extant in Latin, Armenian, Syriac, Coptic, and Arabic. It is possible that one or

[1] Ignatius, *Romans*, 273 (2:2).
[2] Ehrman, *Apostolic Fathers,* 1:205.
[3] Ehrman, *Apostolic Fathers,* 1:210.

197

more of these translations reflects an earlier version of the Greek text which is no longer extant.[4] While modern scholars favor the middle version, it is generally recognized that this version also includes alterations dating from the fourth century.[5] Conversely, while the long version is viewed as inauthentic, some of its textual variants have sometimes been judged closer to the original than the middle version.[6] Gilliam's extensive study of the Ignatian letters in relation to the fourth century Arian controversy concludes that variants in the middle version are by a pro-Nicene editor. The longer version was composed around 350 by a non-Nicene writer in response to perceived changes to the text, first attempting a recover the original text, as the writer saw it, and then expanding upon it.[7] The upshot of these textual issues is that we must have a healthy skepticism about passages that seem to reflect a later Nicene orthodoxy, especially where there are known variants in other manuscripts.

The martyrdom of Ignatius is conventionally dated, on the testimony of Eusebius, to the mid-reign of Trajan (c. 110–117 CE), making Ignatius contemporary with the letters of Pliny (61–c. 113) to Trajan.[8] Those opposing this date (and the authenticity of the letters) have generally done so because of certain theological innovations, like monarchical episcopacy, which appear too developed for letters coming hard on the heels of some New Testament texts. Others, such as Lechner, have pointed to parallels with Valentinian mythology to argue for a date of 165–75.[9] More recently scholars have questioned the reliability of Eusebius's testimony.[10] If we accept the conventional date for the letters of Ignatius then these works

---

[4] Gilliam, *Ignatius,* 21–22.

[5] Gilliam, *Ignatius,* 9; see 11–12 for list of significant variants.

[6] Gilliam, *Ignatius,* 18.

[7] Gilliam, *Ignatius,* 225.

[8] Ehrman, *Apostolic Fathers,* 1:203–5.

[9] Cf. Foster, "Epistles of Ignatius (Part 1)," 490–91.

[10] Eusebius does not mention a date for Ignatius's martyrdom, and his reason for placing it in the reign of Trajan may well be derived from Origen's testimony that Ignatius was the second bishop of Antioch (Origen, *Homily 6,* 24 (4); see Eusebius, *Ecclesiastical History,* 110 (3.22) and the assumption of a continuous succession from Peter (*Ecclesiastical History,* 123 [3.36]); Foster, "Epistles of Ignatius (Part 1)," 490; Barnes, "Date of Ignatius," 126.

are the most substantial body of literature from a Christian author dating from the first half of the first century. Though it cannot, of course, be assumed that Ignatius is representative of all Christians in this period (or even most of them), his position as bishop of Antioch means that he represented that church and the reception of his letters probably indicates that his views were not widely divergent from many of those to whom he wrote.

As many scholars have noted, the circumstances of writing mean that we should not expect carefully developed theological treatises from Ignatius, but rather the bald and unadorned Christianity of second century Antioch.[11] For this reason, we should be cautious about viewing Ignatius as a sort of theological transitional species between the New Testament and the early Christian "fathers" (that is, prominent Christian thinkers of the period from the mid-second century to the Council of Nicaea).[12] On the other hand, this sample of bald and unadorned Christianity is unlikely to be coy or guarded, as an apologetic work or a treatise written in the midst of controversy might be.

The preservation of Ignatius's letters indicates that these letters were considered orthodox by later Christians, or at least their language did not offend later orthodox sensibilities. Therefore, he might be assumed to represent a proto-orthodox form of Christianity. However, scholars have noted that Ignatius's theology tends towards (modal) Monarchianism.[13] We should ask whether or not Ignatius's Christology is essentially consistent with later orthodoxy. In this chapter I will argue that Ignatius's theology has only a superficial resemblance to later orthodoxy, and that instead his views are entirely consistent with Dynamic Monarchianism.

---

[11] As Corwin observes, "the theology of St Ignatius of Antioch was wrought in struggle, not in the study" (Corwin, *St Ignatius,* vii). And Barnard warns us that "Ignatius was not writing in the leisurely manner of the academic scholar" (Barnard, "Background," 193).

[12] Barnard, "Background," 195.

[13] Schoedel, *Ignatius,* 20. This was noticed in antiquity too. Gilliam argues that the creator of the long version started with the middle version and then "where the figures of Father and Son were merged together close enough to cause discomfort . . . introduced Christological demarcation into his version of the Ignatian letters" (Gilliam, *Ignatius,* 96).

USE OF NEW TESTAMENT

Before proceeding it will be useful to say something about Ignatius's use of the New Testament. It is generally accepted that he knew Matthew's gospel, or at least oral traditions preceding it, and Paul's first letter to the Corinthians.[14] Beyond that, opinions diverge. Schoedel is inclined to ascribe many apparent allusions to the use of "traditional materials," rather than the New Testament texts themselves.[15]

By his own admission Ignatius knew several letters of Paul;[16] his statement that Paul mentions the Ephesians in every epistle, often considered hyperbole, is taken by Foster to indicate Ignatius knew only 1 Corinthians, Ephesians, 1 Timothy and 2 Timothy.[17] Ehrman, however, notes possible allusions to Romans, Galatians, Philippians, Colossians and 2 Thessalonians (see Table 1). The question of allusions to other gospels also provokes diverging views. Ehrman, like others, notes possible allusions to Luke and John, as well as Matthew (see Table 2). Richardson reaches no final judgment regarding allusions to John, noting that much of the apparently Johannine teaching could be derived from Paul.[18] Barnard suggests that Johannine teaching was used in the church at Antioch but the gospel wasn't yet known (else why not quote it directly).[19]

Table 1: Ignatius's allusions to the Pauline Epistles

PAULINE EPISTLES	IGNATIAN EPISTLES
Rom. 8:5, 8	*Ephesians*, 227 (8:2)
1 Cor. 1:20, 23	*Ephesians*, 237 (18:1)

[14] Schoedel, *Ignatius,* 9; Barnard, "Background," 203–5.
[15] Schoedel, *Ignatius,* 10.
[16] Ignatius, *Ephesians*, 233 (12:2).
[17] "An examination of the text of the seven letters appears to support the hypothesis that Ignatius knew the very four Pauline letters which explicitly make mention of the Ephesians" (Foster, "Epistles of Ignatius (Part 2)," 9–10).
[18] Richardson, *Christianity of Ignatius,* 68–75.
[19] Barnard, "Background of Ignatius," 203–5.

1 Cor. 2:10	*Philadelphians*, 289 (7:1)
1 Cor. 3:1–2	*Trallians*, 261 (5:1)
1 Cor. 3:16	*Ephesians*, 235 (15:3)
1 Cor. 4:4	*Romans*, 275–77 (5:1)
1 Cor. 6:9	*Ephesians*, 235 (16:1)
1 Cor. 6:9–10	*Philadelphians*, 287 (3:3)
1 Cor. 9:27	*Trallians*, 267 (12:3)
1 Cor. 15:8–9	*Romans*, 281 (9:2)
Gal. 6:14	*Romans*, 279 (7:2)
Eph. 4:2	*Polycarp*, 311 (1:2)
Eph. 5:25, 29	*Polycarp*, 315 (5:1)
Eph. 6:11–17	*Polycarp*, 317 (6:2)
Phil. 3:15	*Smyrneans*, 307 (11:3)
Col. 1:16	*Trallians*, 261 (5:2)
2 Thes. 2:4	*Romans*, 271 (2:1)
2 Tim. 2:4	*Polycarp*, 317 (6:2)

Table 2: Ignatius's allusions to the Gospels

GOSPELS	IGNATIAN EPISTLES
Matt. 3:15	*Smyrneans*, 297 (1:1)
Matt. 10:16	*Polycarp*, 313 (2:2)
Matt. 12: 33	*Ephesians*, 233–35 (14.2)
Matt. 19:12	*Smyrneans*, 301 (6:1)
Matt. 26:7	*Ephesians*, 237 (17:1)
Luke 24:39	*Smyrneans*, 299 (3:2)
John 3:8	*Philadelphians*, 289 (7:1)
John 4:10, 14	*Romans*, 279 (7:2)
John 10:7,9	*Philadelphians*, 293 (9:1)
John 16:28	*Magnesians*, 249 (7:2).

The danger with these considerations is concluding too much from too little. There are only two direct quotations in the Ignatian letters that are prefaced as such and both are from Proverbs.[20] The probable reason for this is that Ignatius did not have any biblical text in front of him while he wrote; Proverbs, at least, is composed of many pithy statements that could be easily recalled. That Ignatius misquotes Luke's gospel (24:39), writing "I am not a bodiless daimon,"[21] is not surprising, and does not necessarily indicate familiarity with non-canonical gospels. Though he does not quote John's gospel, his allusions make it likely that he was aware of it. He calls Jesus the Word (*logos*) of God,[22] presumably based on John 1, but shows no evidence of the concept of the Logos developed later by Justin and his followers. The most likely explanation is that one from Antioch travelling through Asia Minor was familiar with the writings of both Paul and John.

MONOTHEISM

Ignatius affirmed Jewish monotheism. He writes that the Jewish prophets "lived according to Jesus Christ," that is, lived as Christians before Christ, and convinced the "disobedient" that "there is one God."[23] Thus, Ignatius subsumes Jewish monotheism into Christianity, while rejecting the idea of living according to Judaism. The added significance of this passage is the way Jesus relates to the one God: "one God, who manifested himself through Jesus Christ his Son." The very sentence structure implies the one God is someone different from Jesus.[24] This concept of manifestation is also expressed where he writes that "God became manifest in a human way."[25]

---

[20] Proverbs 3:34 in *Ephesians*, 225 (5:3); Proverbs 18:17 in *Magnesians*, 253 (12).

[21] Ignatius, *Smyrneans*, 290 (3:2).

[22] Ignatius, Magnesians, 249 (8:2).

[23] *Magnesians*, 249 (8:2).

[24] Schoedel (*Ignatius*, 120) worries that this passage is "close to modalism," supposing that the "gracious gift" that inspired the prophets was from Jesus; in fact, the preceding verse makes it clear that it is "God's gracious gift" (*Magnesians*, 249 [8:1]).

[25] Ignatius, *Ephesians*, 239 (19:3).

It is possible that Ignatius's monotheism is one of the motivating concerns in his apparent monoepiscopacy.[26] He describes God as "bishop of all."[27] Yet if such a hierarchy is envisaged then it is significant that Jesus is, in the analogy, a servant of the bishop. Believers should not act "apart from the bishop," "just as the Lord did nothing apart from the Father,"[28] and they must "be submissive to the bishop . . . as Jesus Christ was to the Father."[29]

The analogy is not consistently used; elsewhere Jesus "alone will oversee [*episkopaesei*]" the church at Antioch and God is to "shepherd,"[30] and the letter Polycarp has both God and Jesus as Ignatius's bishop.[31] Nevertheless, there is the impression in the Ignatian letters as a whole that God tops both the ecclesiastical and the divine hierarchies.

JESUS AS "GOD"

One thing that distinguishes Ignatius from those who preceded him, is his boldness in calling Jesus "a god" (*theos*), which he does on several occasions.[32] Barnard asserts that his "manner assumes that this is a natural and uncontested designation, at least among the recipients of his letters,"[33] though the fact Polycarp does not use this designation in his "covering letter" should give pause to his assertion. Gilliam observes that of the fourteen instances in the middle version of the Ignatian letters where Jesus

---

[26] "the model that Ignatius deems as normative is leadership in the form of a single *episkopos* (overseer, bishop) supported by a presbytery (eldership) along with those filling the role deacon" (Foster, "Epistles of Ignatius (Part 2)," 2).

[27] *Magnesians*, 245 (3:1).

[28] *Magnesians*, 247 (7:1); cf. *Philadelphians*, 291 (7:2); *Smyrneans*, 303 (8:1).

[29] *Magnesians*, 253–55 (13:2).

[30] *Romans*, 281 (9:1).

[31] Ignatius, *Polycarp*, 311 (salutation).

[32] "our God" (*Ephesians*, 235 [15:3], 237 [18:2]; *Romans*, 269 [Introduction]; *Romans*, 273 [3:3]; *Polycarp*, 321 [8:3]); "my God" (*Romans*, 279 [6:3]); "Jesus Christ, the God who made you so wise" (*Smyrneans*, 297 [1:1]). The double genitive in *Smyrneans*, 305 (10:1) allows two renderings, as in Ehrman: "Christ of God [or Christ, who is God]."

[33] Foster, "Epistles of Ignatius 2," 5–6.

is referred to as "a god," eleven have significant textual variants.[34] Nevertheless, it is clear that Ignatius was comfortable with using *theos* to refer to Jesus.

For some, this is taken as evidence of Ignatius's consistency with later orthodoxy. Jefford writes that Ignatius "speaks of Jesus Christ as divine, distinctly identifying the Messiah with God in a sense that far exceeds the monotheistic confession of Judaism."[35] Similarly, Steenborg concludes that "such passages, along with a host of others, demonstrate Ignatius's firm conviction that the Father and the Son abide in an eternal unity."[36] We should be cautious of over-interpreting the use of such a designation. The occasions where the designation is used do *not* allow us to assume that "under all conditions he thought of Christ as God" or that "θεός [*theos*] stands for God the Father and Jesus Christ together."[37] In fact, Ignatius does not designate Jesus as "God" in an unqualified way; usually he is "our god," which implies "a function distinct from God simply as God."[38] When he uses *theos* without qualification, he is referencing God alone, as is indicated in the passages that speak of both Father and Son.

Richardson explains this qualified use of *theos* for Jesus as a natural development for Gentile Christians, given the wide semantic field of the word *theos* in Greek. "Once Christ was called 'Lord' . . . to the Gentile Christians there would be little difficulty in predicating him with 'God.'"[39] In the Gentile thought world the word *theos* did not refer exclusively to Yahweh, as in Judaism, but to a wide range of superhuman beings and it is probably in this sense that Ignatius uses the term.[40] Similarly, Ignatius does not speak of Father and Son being the same God

---

[34] Gilliam, *Ignatius,* 224.

[35] Jefford, "Ignatius," 115, citing Ignatius, *Ephesians,* 227 (7:2) and Ignatius, *Romans,* 279 (6:3).

[36] Steenborg, "God," 243, citing Ignatius, *Magnesians,* 249 (7:2) and Ignatius, *Ephesians,* 225 (5).

[37] Contrary to Richardson, *Christianity of Ignatius,* 40.

[38] Schoedel, *Ignatius,* 22.

[39] Richardson, *Christianity of Ignatius,* 43.

[40] *Christianity of Ignatius,* 45.

(or as the same substance). [41] But he does write of Jesus being "spiritually united" with the Father after his resurrection. [42]

TRINITARIAN?

It is generally recognized that there are three apparent "trinitarian" (or triadic) formulas in the Ignatian letters, though their significance is debated.

In one passage Ignatius uses a metaphor of temple construction.

> You are stones of the Father's temple, prepared for the building of God the Father. For you are being carried up to the heights by the crane of Jesus Christ, which is the cross, using as a cable the Holy Spirit; and your faith is your hoist, and love is the path that carries you up to God. And so you are all traveling companions bearing God, bearing the temple, bearing Christ, and bearing the holy things, adorned in every way with the commandments of Jesus Christ. [43]

Here the temple stands for the church as a whole. The other metaphors are just as obvious: stones = believers, crane = cross, cable = Spirit, hoist = faith, and path = love. This passage is "trinitarian" only in the sense that the Father, Jesus, and God's spirit are mentioned together, but the passage is not strictly speaking triadic (more than three things are mentioned) nor does it imply a tripersonal God. The passage is of soteriological, not ontological, significance; it "adds nothing to our understanding of his views of distinct functions within the godhead."[44] The metaphor illustrates how through faith and love believers come near to God, but it is through the action of God's spirit, and especially the cross of Christ that believers are elevated to a position within the temple of God. Were we to insist on an ontological interpretation, we would necessarily assume that

---

[41] *Christianity of Ignatius,* 40.

[42] Ignatius, *Smyrneans,* 299 (3:3).

[43] Ignatius, *Ephesians,* 229 (9:1).

[44] Corwin, *St Ignatius,* 142, contrary to the anachronistic statement of Schoedel, *Ignatius,* 66 note 6: "the passage shows how firmly trinitarian language was rooted in the Christianity known to Ignatius."

the Father alone is God (the object of the temple), while both Jesus and the spirit (or Spirit) function are intermediaries.

The two other so-called "trinitarian" formulas both occur in *Magnesians* 13. The first is a series of couplets: ". . . that you may prosper in everything you do in flesh and spirit, in faith and love, in the Son and the Father, and in the Spirit, in the beginning and end."[45] The Spirit (or spirit) stands alone in the passage, separated from the previous couplet by "in" (*en*). The inclusion of the Spirit disrupts the rhythm of the text, leading to the suspicion that it is not original.[46] If the words are authentic, then two opposing conclusions are possible. Either the triadic formula was so significant to Ignatius that he included it "even when by doing so the rhythm was destroyed,"[47] or since his rhetorical purposes took precedence, the triad was "of secondary importance to him."[48] Perhaps a better conclusion is that this passage doesn't witness to an established trinitarian formula, but does witness to conviction that the Spirit is of sufficient significance for it to be listed and listed alongside Father and Son.

Later in the passage, Ignatius writes about submission to bishops, citing the examples of Jesus' submission to the Father, and of the apostles "to Christ and to the Father [and to the Spirit]".[49] This text is textually difficult; the words "and to the Spirit" are omitted in the Armenian and Arabic.[50] The passage appears to present a hierarchy of Father-Christ-apostles which is disturbed by the addition of the Spirit. The suspicion must be that this was "an addition made in the interest of trinitarianism."[51]

It is important also to notice what Ignatius does not write; he does not include triadic formulas in passages where they might be expected.[52] For example, Ignatius parallels the three church offices—deacon, bishop,

---

[45] *Magnesians*, 253 (13:1).

[46] Schoedel, *Ignatius*, 130. The words "and in the Spirit" are omitted in the Arabic version.

[47] Corwin, *St Ignatius*, 143.

[48] Schoedel, *Ignatius*, 130.

[49] *Magnesians*, 253–55 (13:2).

[50] Gilliam, *Ignatius*, 45. Ehrman unaccountably omits the words from his Greek text but includes them in his English translation (Ehrman, *Apostolic Fathers*, 1:254–55).

[51] Schoedel, *Ignatius* ,131.

[52] Cf. Corwin, *St Ignatius*, 142.

presbyter—with Jesus, the Father, and the apostles respectively.[53] Elsewhere we find a triad of church-Jesus-Father in "symphonic union."[54] On the other hand, passages about unity do not appeal to the unity of three divine persons where later writers might have done so.[55] In conclusion, we do not see this sort of consistent triadic language that we would expect to see from someone who believed in a tripersonal God.[56]

SUBORDINATION

Schoedel writes "there are a number of passages that have a 'subordinationist' ring, but appearances are probably deceiving in this regard,"[57] but it is not clear what reason we have to suspect Ignatius of being misleading. He exhorts the Philadelphians to be "imitators of Jesus Christ as he is of his Father,"[58] the Smyrneans to follow the bishop "as Jesus Christ follows the Father",[59] the Magnesians to do nothing apart from the bishop "as the Lord did nothing apart from the Father,"[60] and to be submissive to the bishop "as Jesus was to the Father according to the flesh."[61] This last phrase needs some comment as the phrase "according to the flesh" might imply that Jesus was only subordinate during his time on earth, an idea contradicted by the two former citations which both have the present tense. Schoedel thinks that this phrase "looks suspiciously like an addition made by an interpolator bent on eliminating any suggestion of subordinationism in the text."[62]

[53] Ignatius, *Trallians*, 259 (3:1).
[54] Ignatius, *Ephesians*, 225 (5:1).
[55] Ignatius, *Philadelphians*, 287 (4:1); Ignatius, *Magnesians*, 249 (8:2).
[56] "none of these passages adds anything to an understanding of what the Trinity meant to Ignatius, and we are forced to conclude that it was a very undefined belief indeed" (Corwin, *St Ignatius,* 143). "Ignatius occasionally uses Trinitarian formula, but he makes little of them theologically" (Schoedel, *Ignatius,* 20).
[57] Schoedel, *Ignatius,* 20
[58] Ignatius, *Philadelphians*, 291 (7:2).
[59] Ignatius, *Smyrneans*, 303 (8:1).
[60] Ignatius, *Magnesians*, 247(7:1).
[61] *Magnesians*, 255 (13:2).
[62] Schoedel, *Ignatius,* 131; also see Gilliam, *Ignatius,* 40–45.

This subordinationism—an assumption that Jesus is less divine and/or less great than the Father—also seems apparent in the metaphors used to describe Christ's relationship to God. Christ is the door, altar, mouth, word, and will of God. [63] Jesus Christ is the means by which believers gain access to God; he is, in this sense, an intermediary. In Ignatius's letters Jesus "always stands in a place secondary and inferior" to God.[64] This is not how you would expect someone who believed in the full deity of Christ to write.

GOD-MANIFEST

In these letters we frequently encounter the concept of manifestation. He writes of Jesus being "manifest [*ephane*] at the end."[65] But he also writes of God being manifest through Jesus. He writes about "one God, who manifested [*phanerosas*] himself through Jesus Christ his Son."[66] This manifestation was, in part, through the actions of Jesus, "who was pleasing in every way to the one who sent him." But for Ignatius, this process is much more intimate, such that he can talk of the time "when God became manifest [*phaneroumenou*] in a human way."[67]

In *Ephesians* 7:2 Ignatius describes Jesus as "God come in flesh" (as per Greek and Latin MS). There is significant variant in the Syriac and patristic quotations: "in man, God". (The Armenian has "God and Son of Man".[68]) Of these two main options, both are problematic and later textual alteration has been proposed for both. [69] Either one, taken out of

---

[63] Richardson, *Christianity of Ignatius,* 42.

[64] Richardson, *Christianity of Ignatius,* 44.

[65] Ignatius, *Magnesians,* 247 (6:1).

[66] *Magnesians,* 249 (8:2).

[67] Ignatius, *Ephesians,* 239 (19:3).

[68] Gilliam, *Ignatius,* 36.

[69] The phrase "God come in the flesh," or 'God become incarnate', is the reading in Greek and Latin MS, but the patristic quotations read "in man, God." Grant argues that the latter is the original as it is more coherent with Ignatius's style, while the former shows signs of later Christology (Grant, *Early Christian Doctrine,* 39). Schoedel disagrees, suspecting that the patristic reading was a later change made "to avoid any suggestion of

context, might be taken to imply incarnation. However, given Ignatius's repeated statements about manifestation, it is simpler to conclude that this is his sense here.

Schoedel explains the rationale of Ignatius's talk of manifestation by arguing that the transcendence of God in Ignatius implied a need for intermediaries, as others will conclude in the second century. Jesus is "the atemporal and invisible God manifesting himself in space and time."[70] This is probably true, though perhaps misleading, as it implies that for Ignatius the problem was how a transcendent God could interact with the world. He gives no sense of that. Rather for Ignatius the "problem" is how Jesus can meet two different functional requirements. Jesus had to be passible so that he could suffer for believers, but Jesus also had to reveal God to men. For Ignatius, Jesus is not God-incarnate but rather God-manifest, that is, a human manifestation of God.

CONCEPTION

Given Ignatius's aim to repudiate docetic Christology, it is not surprising that he gives so much space to describing the conception of Jesus, which for Ignatius underscores the humanity of Jesus. He was born a man that he might suffer.[71]

Corwin writes "he has in mind the union of the divine and human in the God-man and thus anticipates the classical two-nature christology." Further, Corwin argues, this marks a development upon New Testament Christology, with an added emphasis on the transcendence of God. Further,

> The development evidently presupposes a description of divine transcendence in metaphysical terms . . . for such a description opens up a

an Arian or Apollinarian Christology which denied a human soul to Christ" (Schoedel, *Ignatius,* 61).

[70] Schoedel, *Ignatius,* 20.

[71] Ignatius, *Ephesians,* 237 (18:2).

gulf between God and humanity that requires something as paradoxical as the incarnation for God and humanity to meet.[72]

However, as noted above, Ignatius does not seem to give any indication of being aware that the transcendence of God might pose a problem for his interaction with the world. The problem Ignatius identifies is not a metaphysical one but an epistemological one: how can God be known by humans? The solution is that Jesus reveals God, he in that sense "is" the knowledge of God.[73]

For Ignatius this solution requires the virgin birth. Jesus was the product of two kinds: "from the family of David according to the flesh, Son of God according to the will and power of God."[74] The expression "according to the flesh" might be taken to imply Adoptionism,[75] were Ignatius not explicit elsewhere about Jesus being "from both Mary and God,"[76] "from the seed of David, but also from the Holy Spirit."[77] Ignatius, then, is more explicit even than the New Testament infancy narratives that Jesus was "conceived" [ekuophorethe] of Mary and by the Holy Spirit[78] The meeting of humanity and divinity in Jesus is important for Ignatius, but he says nothing of incarnation. It is in the special conception of Jesus that this union takes place.

Did Ignatius understand Jesus as coming into being at the moment of his conception? He is not clear on this point. He does refer to "the divine plan that leads to the *new* person Jesus Christ,"[79] though this may just be allusion to Paul's Adam Christology (also see Eph. 2:15) and may not entail a temporal beginning for Jesus. *Ephesians* 7:2 describes Jesus as both "born and unborn," which might be taken to pre-empt post-Nicene ideas of Jesus as "born, but not begotten." However, the reference here is more likely to his dual origins, "from both Mary and God." The next lines read,

---

[72] Schoedel, *Ignatius,* 20.

[73] Ignatius, *Ephesians,* 237 (17:2).

[74] Ignatius, *Smyrneans,* 297 (1:1).

[75] Schoedel, *Ignatius,* 20.

[76] Ignatius, *Ephesians, 227 (7:2)*; also see *Ephesians,* 241 (20:2).

[77] *Ephesians,* 237 (18:2).

[78] *Ephesians,* 237 (18:2).

[79] Ignatius, *Ephesians,* 239 (20:1), emphasis added.

"first subject to suffering and then beyond suffering," which would imply that Jesus only became impassible (and thus divine) *after* his resurrection. Corwin counters that in *Polycarp* 3:2 impassible is noted first,[80] but this passage refers to Christ post-ascension and so does not decide the question.

PRE-EXISTENCE

There are a handful passages that may indicate that Ignatius believed in the pre-existence of Christ, either before his birth or before creation. It is, at very least, significant that "nothing is said of his agency in creation."[81] Schoedel points to *Magnesians* 6:1;[82] Richardson adds *Polycarp* 3:2 and *Ephesians* 7:2.[83] Let's look at these in reverse order.

In Ephesians Ignatius writes, "For there is one physician, both fleshly and spiritual, born and unborn, God come in the flesh, true life in death, from both Mary and God, first subject to suffering and then beyond suffering."[84] This passage says nothing explicitly about pre-existence. It is possible that "born and unborn" might be taken to mean that Jesus had a pre-incarnate existence. However, given the contrast Ignatius is developing is between the fleshly and the spiritual, between the human (from Mary) and the divine (from God), it seems more likely that "born and unborn" is reference to his special birth. Since Ignatius states that Jesus was passible before he became impassible, this would seem to rule out pre-existence.

In his letter to Polycarp Ignatius tells him to

Await the one who is beyond the season, the one who is timeless, the one who is invisible, who became visible for us, the one who cannot be handled,

---

[80] Corwin, *St Ignatius,* 93.

[81] Richardson, *Christianity of Ignatius,* 41.

[82] Schoedel, *Ignatius,* 20.

[83] Richardson, *Christianity of Ignatius,* 41.

[84] Ignatius, *Ephesians,* 227 (7:2).

the one who is beyond suffering, who suffered for us, enduring in every way on our account. [85]

This text lists a number of attributes now possessed by the exalted Jesus in heaven: "beyond the season," "timeless," "invisible," "untouchable," "impassible." Ignatius intersperses these attributes with two others, each referring to the period before the resurrection: "visible for us" and "passible for us." Since it has "invisible" before "visible," and "impassible" before "passible," the passage might be taken to imply pre-existence, i.e. that Jesus was first invisible and then became visible. Ehrman renders this phrase "the one who is invisible, who became visible for us." By adding "became", he strengthens the impression that a change of state occurred, from invisible to visible. The Greek simply says *ton di hemas horaton*[86] There is no temporal marker in this passage to imply that one state preceded the other. In contrast *Ephesians* 7:2 explicitly says "first passible and then impassible."[87]

In *Magnesians* Ignatius refers to Jesus as one "who was with the Father before the ages and has been manifest at the end,"[88] which strongly suggests the personal pre-existence of Jesus before the formation of the world. There is slight possibility that here Ignatius is once again repudiating the Valentinians, asserting the pre-eminence of Christ over the aeons. However, better sense is made by interpreting *pro aionon* (before the aeons or ages) temporally. The New Testament parallel is in 1 Corinthians, a text that Ignatius alludes to frequently, where Paul writes of the wisdom of God decreed "before the ages [*pro aionon*]" (1 Cor. 2:7; cf. 2 Tim. 1:9, Tit. 1:2). Two other parallels, though not verbal allusions, may be adduced. 1 Pet. 1:20 (NKJV) says of Jesus, "He indeed was foreordained before the foundation of the world but was manifest in these last times for you." Given the loose verbal parallel and the frequent

---

[85] Ignatius, *Polycarp*, 315 (3:2).
[86] Hence Schoedel's more literal translation: "for our sakes visible" (*Ignatius*, 266).
[87] Schoedel, *Ignatius*, 59.
[88] Ignatius, *Magnesians*, 247 (6:1).

occurrence of this concept in early Christian writings,[89] we need not suppose that Ignatius was alluding directly to 1 Peter. However, comparison of the two texts is revealing. 1 Peter speaks only of the foreknowledge of God, not the actual pre-existence of Jesus. This presents us with two possible readings of Ignatius. Either by "with the Father before the ages" he means only to refer to Jesus existing in the foreknowledge of God, or, alternatively, this verse may witness to an evolution in Christian thought, interpreting existence in the foreknowledge of God to be existence in substance as well.

It is plausible that Ignatius, in calling Jesus "Word" (*logos*),[90] is referring either directly to John 1:1 or to a cognate Christian tradition. Associating Jesus with the pre-existent Word would justify his language in *Magnesians* 6:1 without implying personal pre-existence since for John the pre-existent Word was not a personal being (on which see Chapter Thirteen).

SUMMARY

Given the paucity of any reference to Jesus' existence as a person prior to his birth, McGuckin suggests that "it is possible that [Ignatius] envisaged the divinity [of Christ], until the time of the incarnation, as 'indistinguishable' " from the Father, so that only at the incarnation was "the 'Sonship' historically manifested."[91]

This would imply Ignatius tends towards Modal Monarchianism. This proposed interpretation ignores a more straightforward solution, the one argued for in this chapter. Since Ignatius does not state that the Son is one substance with the Father, nor that he "is God" or is divine in the sense

---

[89] "The Son of God is older than all his creation . . . he has been revealed in the last days" (Hermas, *Shepherd*, 419 [*Parables* 9.12.2–3 or 89.2–3]). Elsewhere in Hermas the Son of God is identified as the Holy Spirit, while the man Jesus is described as the flesh in which the Spirit dwelt (*Shepherd*, 323–37 [*Parables* 5.6.1–8 or 59.1–8]). This may indicate that the author held a Spirit-Man ("possessionist") Christology in common with the Ebionites (Irenaeus, *Against the Heresies (Book 1)*, 90 [1.26.2]; cf. Epiphanius, *Medicine Chest*, 1:133 [30.3.3]. Also see Irenaeus, *Against the Heresies (Book 1)*, 50 [1.10.3].)

[90] Ignatius, *Magnesians*, 249 [8:2].

[91] McGuckin, "Christ," 261.

that the Father is, but strongly implies that Jesus is subordinate to and separate from the Father, then it may be that for Ignatius Jesus had no pre-existence, except his pre-existence in the foreknowledge of God. Ignatius strongly emphasizes the meeting of humanity and divinity in the miraculous conception of Jesus. Jesus derives attributes from Mary and from the Spirit. If I read Ignatius correctly, he does not mean that Jesus is fully human and fully God, in a Chalcedonian sense, but rather the product of a human and of God, by his Spirit. If this is the case then Ignatius, while saying enough "orthodox" things to be received by later Christians, would be better classified as a Dynamic Monarchian.

CHAPTER 13

Gospel of John:
The Fly in the Ointment?[1]

I HAVE HITHERTO BEEN ARGUING that the Christology of the Dynamic Monarchians of the second and third centuries was not a late deviation from an established orthodoxy but has legitimate claim to be a primitive Christian tradition. However, there would seem to be a fly in the ointment in the shape of the Gospel of John. This gospel is commonly known for its "high" Christology (or more specifically, "divine Christology"[2]), for its purported radical claims that Jesus is equal with God, bears the divine name ("I AM") and is, in fact, God. Surely, it might be argued, the Gospel of John is clear evidence that by the end of the first century both the pre-existence and the divinity of Jesus were safely in the doctrinal bag. Those who accepted the Gospel of John as canonical (and this includes the followers of Theodotus) must also have either accepted the divine Christology of this gospel or else strained every sophistic muscle to overturn its (apparently) plain meaning. Does the Gospel of John sink the thesis I am proposing?

---

[1] The material in this chapter has been adapted from Gaston, "Does the Gospel."

[2] The term "high Christology" encompasses of wide variety of perspectives, from the idea that Jesus was worshipped to the idea that Jesus was fully divine in a post-Nicene sense. To avoid ambiguity, I will use the term "divine Christology," that is, the view that Jesus was divine in same sense that the Father is divine.

In this chapter I will present a rather radical departure from the common approaches to the Gospel of John. I will argue that many of the features the gospel commonly read as presupposing or advocating a divine Christology are actually entirely consistent with a low(er) Christology. Specifically, I am concerned with the claims that according to this gospel, Jesus is divine in the sense that the Father is divine, and more broadly that it ascribes literal pre-existence to Jesus. I will conclude that some passages that are often considered to be proof texts for pre-existence are not as compelling as sometimes thought. Though it is not possible in a single chapter to give the full consideration that could be devoted to this topic, this chapter will be sufficient to show that another reading of the Gospel of John is possible and arguably more plausible than conventional readings.

THE WORD

John opens his gospel (1:1) with a prologue regarding "the Word" (*ho logos*). Given the apparent discontinuity caused by the mentions of John the Baptist (1:6–8, 15), many scholars have concluded that the prologue was originally an independent hymn. The possibility that the prologue might not originate with the evangelist but with a later redactor might seem favorable to the case I am presenting, since often the prologue is the primary proof text cited for John's divine Christology. However, as Hengel reminds us, it is possible that John was author of the prologue, and it was most likely he who chose this beginning for his gospel.[3] Barnabas Lindars proposed that the evangelist added the prologue to the "second edition" of his gospel.[4] This being plausible, any reading of John's gospel needs to account for the prologue and why John (or his redactor) feels the prologue is important context for his message. Presumably, John (or his redactor) believe that the prologue presents information necessary to understand some or all of the rest of the gospel, particularly with regard to Christology. On the other hand, the notable absence of the Logos in the

[3] Hengel, "Prologue," 268.
[4] Lindars, *Gospel of John*, 76–77

remainder of the gospel underscores the fact that a fundamental change of state has occurred in verse 14, "the Word became flesh." The popular reading of "Word" as the proper noun for a person who "was with God" and "was God" is rightly ignored by scholars.

It was previously common for scholars to identify John's Logos as an allusion to the Stoic or Platonic Logos, an attempt by John to engage with a Hellenistic audience. More recently, scholars have become convinced of the Semitic character of the gospel. John's gospel is fundamentally Semitic in character and shows intimate knowledge of Jewish customs and Judean geography. Whereas Mark includes explanatory notes about certain Jewish practices for his Gentile audience (e.g. Mark 7:11), John makes no effort to do so, using imagery such as the sacrificial Lamb without as much as a footnote (John 1:29, 1:36). He also quotes readily from the Old Testament, though admittedly less frequently than the synoptic writers. Burney argues that John's gospel was originally written in Aramaic and is a product of Aramaic thought.[5] Some scholars, like Buchanan, go further and pinpoint the Samaritans as the specific group for which John is writing,[6] based upon such evidence as the favorable inclusions in the narrative of incidents in Samaria and the unfriendly presentation of those John calls "the Jews," but Cullmann urges caution, seeing the Samaritan question as only one factor in the origins of John's gospel.[7] Whatever the precise circumstances of the authorship of the gospel, there are more than sufficient precedents for John's Logos within Jewish writings.

There is an obvious allusion to Gen. 1:1 ("In the beginning") and the creative word of God that brought forth light out of darkness (cf. Gen. 1:1–5). In this account of creation, all things were made through the word of God, and without it nothing was made (cf. John 1:3). Evidently, the creative word is not a person, but is rather an activity of God. However, John wants to do something more than just recounting the creative commands of God. The Logos is a source of life and light in John 1:5 and

---

[5] "The author's language is cast throughout in the Aramaic mould. He is thoroughly familiar with Rabbinic speculation. He knows his Old Testament, not through the medium of the LXX, but in the original language" (Burney, *Aramaic Origin*, 127).

[6] Cullmann, *Johannine Circle*, 51.

[7] *Johannine Circle*, 52.

is described in anthropomorphic terms in John 1:10–13, and arguably in John 1:1b too.

The Johannine Logos also has precedent in Jewish Wisdom literature, which should not be surprising given the Christological allusions to Wisdom in the writings of Paul. Thus, the prologue alludes to a second creation narrative, in which Wisdom (personified as a woman, Prov. 7:4) was with God at creation and all things were created through her (Prov. 8:22–31). Though personified, Wisdom is not understood to be a literal person (Prov. 3:19–20; 9:10–11). In the *Wisdom of Sirach*[8] we see part of the transition from Wisdom to Logos, where Wisdom says, "I am the word [*logos*], which was spoken by the Most High" (*Sirach* 24:3). Here Wisdom is also identified with the Law and is described as dwelling in the Tabernacle (*Sirach* 24:23; 24:10–11). Similarly, in *Wisdom of Solomon*[9] we find that Wisdom, though still personified as a woman (*Wisdom* 6:12–21), is called *logos* (*Wisdom* 9:1–2). Wisdom remains the agent of creation (*Wisdom* 9:1–2, 9) but does not constitute a second divine person; "for 'thy Almighty Word' one can substitute 'God' without altering the meaning of the verse."[10]

John's prologue can be plausibly regarded as a piece of Wisdom literature, ascribing the same functions of creation and spiritual enlightenment to an anthropomorphized divine "Word" (i.e. Wisdom). The preference for *logos* (word) over *sophia* (wisdom) is probably explained as being more harmonious with both the allusion to Genesis and with the transition from Word to Word-made-flesh. John's description of the Word as the agent or catalyst of creation (1:2–3), as coming to men and being received by them (1:10–13), and "was God" (1:1), are not revolutionary or scandalous in the context of Second Temple

---

[8] This piece of Hebrew wisdom literature (also called *Ecclesiasticus*, or *The Wisdom of Jesus Son of Sirach, The Book of Ben Sira*) from around 200–180 BCE is included in Eastern Orthodox Bibles and in Catholic Bibles as a "Deuterocanonical" book, but is not in Protestant Bibles.

[9] The *Wisdom of Solomon* was written in Greek c. 250–150 BCE and is included in Orthodox and Catholic but not in Protestant Bibles.

[10] Clarke, *Wisdom of Solomon,* 121. For further texts and arguments see Tuggy, "What John 1 Meant."

Judaism (especially when compared with Philo). Before verse 14, John has not said anything that a first century Jew would not say "amen" to.[11]

As such, John's prologue is not a strong proof-text for the pre-existence of Jesus—quite the reverse in fact. The allusions noted by scholars both to Genesis and to the Wisdom literature argue against the idea that the Word is a pre-existent person. As Thompson writes, "Wisdom is not an 'agent' of God in the same way that prophet or angels are," nor "a separate being and entity that must be 'related' to God but is in fact the expression of God's mind, will or ways." From this it follows that "to speak of Jesus as God's Wisdom incarnate is to say that he is God's self-expression."[12] Though Hengel argues that the prologue "transcends all the parallels behind it" because the Word has "an inalienable personality,"[13] it is not obvious that the personal language used in regards to the Word in John 1:1–13 is more significant than that in *Proverbs*, *Sirach*, or *Wisdom*. When Jesus self-identifies as "the light of the world" (8:12),[14] he retains a masculine pronoun; in contrast, when John identifies the Word as "the light of men" (1:5) he uses the neuter pronoun (which is equivalent to our using the impersonal pronoun "it"). This seems a strong indicator of impersonality of the Word. Read in the light of Jewish precedents, "the Word became flesh" is a reference to the creation of a new person, one who embodies the expression of God's will, a declaration of God (cf. 1:18), not the incarnation of a pre-existent person.

GOD

It is often claimed that John identifies Jesus as God; if true, this would indicate an early divine Christology and be fatal to my argument. However, the situation is not so clear cut as often presented. Of the three occasions in the gospel when, it is claimed, Jesus is called "God," one is a

---

[11] Dunn makes the same point when he says "prior to v.14 nothing has been said which would be strange to a Hellenistic Jew familiar with the Wisdom tradition" (*Christology in the Making*, 241). See also Boyarin, "Logos," 691.

[12] Thompson, *God of the Gospel*, 134–35.

[13] Hengel, "Prologue," 272.

[14] Unless otherwise stated, all quotations from the Gospel of John are from the ESV.

reference to the pre-incarnate Word (1:1; see above), another is textually difficult (1:18),[15] and in the remaining passage it is far from clear what Thomas means by his exclamation "my Lord and my God" (20:28). Throughout the gospel Jesus prefers the self-designation "Son of Man" (e.g. 1:51; 3:13; 9:35) but never "God." Other characters in the narrative understand Jesus as "Son of God" (e.g. 1:34; 1:49; 11:4; 11:27; 19:7) but never "God" (except possibly 20:28). The evangelist stipulates his purpose for writing as "that you may believe that Jesus is the Christ, the Son of God" (John 20:31). The frequency and usage of these designations in John's gospel is not too far removed from that of the synoptics, and certainly not a strong indicator of a radically different Christology.

In contrast, there are passages that explicitly distinguish Jesus from God, such as John 17:3. Barrett notes that

> those notable Johannine passages that seem at first sight to proclaim most unambiguously the unity and equality of the Son with the Father are often set in contexts which if they do not deny at least qualify this theme.[16]

In John 1 God is unknowable, but Jesus is the revelation of God (1:18); in John 5 Jesus is obedient to his Father's will (5:19); in John 10 unity with God accommodates a real distinction.[17] The Gospel of John contains some of the most explicit subordinationist statements in the whole New Testament (e.g. "the Father is greater than I," 14:28; cf. 5:19, 8:28, 8:50). Subordinationism does not simply occur as a sort of qualification on claims that Jesus is divine but is a consistent theme throughout the gospel. God is the sender; Jesus is the sent (3:34; 4:34; 5:23–24, 30, 36; 6:29, 38, 57;

---

[15] The textual witnesses seem reasonably evenly split between *huios* (son) and *theos* (God or god). Following a central principle in the field of textual criticism, some scholars prefer *theos* as the more difficult reading; others prefer *huios* as it conforms to John's usage elsewhere (John 1:14; 3:16, 18; 1 John 4:9). For arguments that the reading *huios* is more likely correct see Ridderbos, *Gospel of John*, 59; Ehrman, *Orthodox Corruption*, 92–96; and Perry, "John 1:18.

[16] Barrett, *Essays on John*, 23.

[17] *Essays on John*, 23–25.

7:16; 8:18, 42; 9:4; 11:42, etc.).[18] Jesus recognizes that everything comes from God, his Father (17:7), including his mission (5:36, 17:4, 18:11), his words (7:16, 17:8), his disciples (6:39, 10:29, 17:9), his power and authority (5:26–27, 10:18, 17:2) and his glory (17:22–24). This recognition of Jesus' dependence upon God is explicitly stated by Jesus throughout his mission: "the Son can do nothing of his own accord" (5:19; cf. 5:30, 8:28). He repeatedly declares that the Father is greater than the Son (10:29, 14:28), recognizing that the one who is sent is not greater than the one who sent him (13:16). Although many read these subordinationist statements as a consequence of the humanity of Jesus alongside his divinity,[19] the more obvious alternative is that John intends to make a significant distinction between Jesus and God in his gospel.

More potentially significant are those passages where Jesus is purportedly identified with God. John 5:17–18 is often cited, in which the Jews seek to kill Jesus for "making himself equal with God." It is important to note however that Jesus does *not* claim this. The claim that the Jews react so violently against is that "God was his Father" because *they thought* this meant that Jesus was claiming to be God (or a god). Though Jesus does not respond by directly refuting the idea that he is a god, his response underlines John's belief in the Son's subordination; "the Son can do nothing of his own accord, but only what he sees the Father doing" (5:19). Similarly, in John 10:30–33 Jesus says, "I and the Father are one" and it is his adversaries that (mis)understand him to be making himself God. Jesus' response is particularly significant. Using Psalm 82:6, Jesus cites scriptural precedent for mortals being called "gods." Then, having shown from Scripture that even if he was just a holy man he could legitimately be called "god," Jesus proceeds to restate his own claim: "I am *the Son of* God." Then he concludes by explaining how he is one with the Father: "though you do not believe me, believe the works, that you may know and

---

[18] van der Watt, *Johannine Gospel*, 36.

[19] Barrett, *Essays on John*, 26–27; Hengel, "Prologue," 269; van der Watt, *Johannine Gospel*, 48. Barrett's own solution to the "problem" of subordinationism is by way of analogy to the "messianic secret" in Mark: just as it was expedient for Jesus to conceal his messiahship, so it is expedient for Jesus to downplay his deity "majesty veiled in humility" (Barrett, *Essays on John*, 30–32).

understand that the Father is in me and I am in the Father" (10:37–38). By only claiming the title "Son of God," when he could legitimately be called "god," Jesus emphasizes that he is subordinate to the Father, and thus John tacitly denies the deity of Christ.

The absence of any explicit statements regarding the deity of Christ seems inconsistent with the purported divine Christology, as do those statements distinguishing Jesus from God. The tacit rejection of the deity of Christ, alongside the claim that even mortals can be called "gods," seems indicative of a "low" (i.e. human and not divine) Christology (perhaps adopted against the contrary accusations of Christianity's opponents).

"I AM" SAYINGS

It is often argued that the "I am" sayings in John's gospel, in particular John 8:57–58, ascribe deity to Christ. Some scholars argue that in John 8 Jesus ascribes to himself the name of God: "I am who I am" (Ex. 3:14). Brown asserts, "no clearer implication of divinity is found in the Gospel tradition."[20] Similarly Ball writes, "surely it is this ἐγὼ εἰμί [*ego eimi*, I am] more than any other which forces the reader to see Jesus' words as a claim to divinity."[21] Some translations capitalize "I AM" to emphasize the point.

However, it is improbable that *ego eimi* here functions as name. Bultmann writes "It would mean that *ego* would have to be both subject and predicate!"[22] While it is possible that *ego eimi* is an allusion to Ex. 3:14, the Septuagint, Philo and Josephus all render the divine name as *ho on* ("he who is," or "the being").[23] The meaning of *ego eimi* when used without a predicate is determined by the context (i.e. "I am the person you are

---

[20] Brown, *Gospel According to John*, 367. Yet another commentator writes that "it is not necessary to suppose that they saw in 'I am' the Divine Name, though no doubt the evangelist would have his readers note the allusion" (Sanders, *Commentary*, 236n).

[21] Ball, *'I am'*, 197.

[22] Bultmann, *Gospel of John*, 327n; cf. Thompson, *God of John*, 92.

[23] Balz and Schneider, *Exegetical Dictionary*, 393; Bauckham, *Beloved Disciple*, 246; Thompson, *God of John*, 89.

talking about").[24] Therefore the use of *ego eimi* in 8:58 should be read in the context of the rest of passage. That Jesus' reference is already unclear in 8:24 is indicated by the response of the Jews, "who are you?" (8:25). In 8:28 Jesus says, "when you lift up the Son of Man, then you will know that I am he [*ego eimi*]." Bauckham rejects the idea *ego eimi* here could mean "I am the Son of Man" declaring such a meaning "too enigmatic,"[25] though it must be stressed that there is no other available predicate for *ego eimi* in the passage and, as noted above, "Son of Man" is Jesus' preferred self-designation throughout the gospel. The rules of grammar seem to require us to read Son of Man as the predicate for *ego eimi*, thus ruling out an allusion to Ex. 3:14.

However, other possible allusions have been proposed. A number of scholars have seen parallels to the "I am" sayings in Deut. 32:39 and Is. 41:4, 43:10, and 46:4.[26] These parallels are particularly strong with *The Isaiah Targum*, which talks of God declaring the future to Abraham.[27] A further intertextual link with the 2nd c. BCE book *Jubilees* has been noted by Mary Coloe,[28] in which Abraham celebrated the Feast of Tabernacles[29] and "knew and perceived that from him there would be a righteous planting for eternal generations and a holy seed from him so that he might be like the one who made everything. And he blessed and rejoiced."[30] In *Jubilees*, Abraham saw the coming of "a holy seed"; in John Jesus claims that what Abraham saw was him. *The Isaiah Targum* speaks of the Messiah in whom God delights; Jesus speaks of himself as pleasing God.[31] If these

---

[24] Williams, "Self-Declaratory Pronouncements," 344, citing 2 Sam. 2:20 (LXX), Mark 14:42, John 9:9, and the *Testament of Job*, 853 (29:4, 31:6); cf. b. Ketibbot 63a (Aramaic).

[25] Bauckham, *Beloved Disciple*, 245.

[26] Bauckham, *Beloved Disciple*, 246.

[27] Ball, '*I am*', 196, citing *The Isaiah Targum*, 84–85 (43:10–12); cf. John 8:56–58. *The Isaiah Targum* is an Aramaic expansive translation and commentary on the Hebrew book of Isaiah written over a course of centuries starting some time in the first century BCE.

[28] Coloe, "Role of Abraham," 1–11. *Jubilees*, written in Hebrew in the 2nd c. BCE, is supposed to contain God's revelation to Moses described in Exodus 24:18.

[29] *Jubilees*, 89 (16:21); cf. John 7:2.

[30] *Jubilees* 89 (16:26–27); cf. John 8:58.

[31] *The Isaiah Targum*, 84 (43:10), John 8:29.

passages are a background to John 8, then they support the interpretation that the figure Jesus is identifying himself with is the Messiah (rather than God). It is commonly suggested that Jesus identified himself as both Messiah and God, but this is not what Jesus says. He says "[I] speak just as the Father taught me" (8:28), "he who sent me is with me" (8:29), "I speak of what I have seen with my Father" (8:38) and "I do not seek my own glory" (8:50). In the absence of an explicit claim to be God (which, we have noted, is something John tacitly rejects), the claim to be Messiah would naturally be read as a claim to be someone other than God.

It is true that Deut. 32:39 and Is. 41:4, 43:10, and 46:4 put the words *ego eimi* in the mouth of God, but this phrase simply means "I am he" and so carries no theological weight of itself. How else would a Greek speaker say "I am he"? For all the bold claims of some modern commentators, John's meaning is plain: Jesus is claiming to be the Son of Man.

It is sometimes claimed that the exchange between Jesus and the Jews in John 8:56–58 points to the pre-existence of Jesus. Jesus' statement "before Abraham was, I am" is interpreted as indicating that he was temporally prior to Abraham. Bultmann comments that "one might expect" *emen* (I was) rather than *eimi* (I am),[32] and the existence of one textual variant to that effect demonstrates that some in the early church also thought that this would be more natural.[33] A number of scholars argue that the present tense strengthens Jesus' claim from pre-existence to timeless (or eternal) existence.[34] Yet such a reading ignores the allusions to *The Isaiah Targum* and *Jubilees* noted above and ignores the grammatical need to find a predicate for *ego eimi* (I am). When proper attention is given to both these factors, John 8:56–58 is read as an unequivocal statement by Jesus to be the prophesied Messiah, not just foretold to Abraham but foreknown from creation. It is interesting to note that, again, it is Jesus' adversaries who leap to the conclusion that Jesus is claiming to have existed at the time of Abraham; Jesus does not claim this.

[32] Bultmann, *John,* 327 n. 4.

[33] *prin Abraam genesthai, ego emen* ("before Abraham came to be, I was") [miniscule 157, Rome 7th c.] (Swanson, *Greek Manuscripts: John,* 124).

[34] Westcott, *Gospel,* 2:28; Sanders, *John,* 236; Ball, *'I am',* 195; Thompson, *God of John,* 92.

One final "I am" saying should be noted. In John 18:6 we find Jesus saying *ego eimi* (usually rendered "I am he"), which causes the arresting soldiers to draw back and fall to the ground. The claim is that the reaction of the soldiers be read as a recognition that Jesus was using a divine self-designation. Yet this reading seems odd. Jesus says "I am he" to identify himself *as Jesus of Nazareth* (18:5, 7–8). It stretches credulity to believe that "I am Jesus of Nazareth" should be taken as divine self-designation. Whatever the narrative purpose of the falling back of the soldiers, it does not seem intended to indicate a divine Christology.

FROM HEAVEN

Throughout John's gospel, Jesus consistently presents himself in terms that at first glance seem to indicate descent from heaven following some pre-existent state. Some of these statements are stronger than others. For example, the frequent descriptor of Jesus as having been "sent" by God[35] are often no stronger than the statement that John the Baptist was "sent from God" (1:6). Surely, John the Baptist was not previously in heaven.

Somewhat stronger are those passages which describe Jesus as "from above" (3:31, 8:23), "from heaven" (6:32–33, 38), and "from God" (6:46, 8:42, 13:3; cf. 7:39, 16:28). However, none of these phrases necessitate movement from one location (i.e. heaven) to another (i.e. earth.) James writes about gifts and wisdom "from above" (James 1:17, 3:13–15); the phrase denotes the source, not the initial location (cf. John 19:11). The fact that Jesus describes his adversaries as being "from below" while he is "from above" illustrates that these phrases are not used spatially but morally/spiritually. This same contrast occurs in John 3:31–32.

[35] John 3:34; 4:34; 5:23–24, 30, 36; 6:29, 38, 57; 7:16; 8:18, 42; 9:4; 11:42, etc.

Strongest of all are those passages where Jesus parallels his post-resurrection ascension with his previous descent (6:62; cf. 3:13)[36] and that might be taken to imply some kind of conscious experience in his pre-existent state. These sayings connect a statement of Jesus' origins with some activity. For example, "He who comes from heaven is above all. He bears witness to what he has seen and heard" (3:31–32) and "not that anyone has seen the Father except he who is from God; he has seen the Father" (6:46). In other passages, Jesus speaks of having been "taught" by the Father (8:28; cf. 12:50); he says, "I speak of what I have seen with my Father" (8:38).

It is interesting to note that scholars have not been unanimous in interpreting John 6:62 ("what if you were to see the Son of Man ascending to where he was before?") as a reference to a pre-incarnate state. For example, Robinson proposes that John envisions Jesus ascending into heaven at the beginning of his ministry to receive his commission.[37] This might make sense of the pre-resurrection Jesus speaking of having "ascended" (past tense) into heaven (3:13), though such an ascent is otherwise unattested in the gospel or in any known material John might have presupposed as context. Other suggestions are that 6:62 refers to Jesus' ascension of the mountain where he fed the 5000[38] or to Jesus' ascension to Jerusalem.[39] It is also possible that Jesus does not refer to ascension, but to a coming up out of the ground, that is, his resurrection.[40]

Furthermore, the presupposition that when Jesus speaks of being taught by the Father he is referring to a pre-incarnate tutorial goes beyond

---

[36] John 3:13 ("no one has ascended into heaven, except the one who descended from heaven") may be a polemic against Jewish apocalyptic speculations, which proposed that Enoch (amongst others) had ascended into heaven. See Charlesworth, "Enoch Tradition," 223.

[37] Robinson, *Priority of John*, 371. This proposal ("the pre-ascension ascension") was an interpretation put forward by Socinus (1539–1604) and was common amongst the Polish Brethren.

[38] Perry, *Before He Was Born*, 238–39.

[39] Mackay, *John's Relationship with Mark,* 264; Dodd, *Interpretation*, 385 note 1; Brodie, *Gospel According to John*, 52.

[40] "John 6:62 Commentary."

what is explicitly stated in John's gospel.[41] Other sayings in John's gospel portray Jesus as describing his teacher-learner relationship with his Father as a present reality. For example, "the Son can do nothing of his own accord, but only what he sees the Father doing . . . the Father loves the Son and shows him all that he himself is doing" (5:19–20). Similarly, "he who sent me is with me. He has not left me alone, for I always do the things that are pleasing to him" (8:29). These passages speak of an intimate relationship between the Father and Jesus during his ministry; Jesus, while on the earth, sees the actions of the Father and mimics them. Given the clear presentation in the gospel that Jesus has learnt from the Father while on the earth, it would seem presumptive to assume that there must also have a been heavenly learning experience in a pre-existent state.

In John 3 there is a possible play on words. The word *anothen* can be translated both "from above" and "again." When Jesus tells Nicodemus, he must be "born *anothen*", he may mean "born again" or "born from above." When the gospel writer refers to Jesus as being "from above" in verse 31, he uses the same word. The comparison of Jesus with baptized believers as both being "from above" tells against any suggestion of pre-existence.

In John 6 Jesus is speaking about himself as the bread from heaven (6:58) in contrast to the manna the Israelites received in the wilderness. The manna is described as bread "from heaven" (John 6:31), meaning, of course, that was a gift from God, not that it had previously existed in heaven. Once again, his adversaries mistake his meaning; they take him to mean he didn't have a real birth and family (John 6:41–42). Jesus tacitly rejects that meaning when he explains that he is speaking of himself as the manifestation of the Father (John 6:44–46).

There is one further passage worthy of note. Jesus prays, "Father, glorify me in your own presence with the glory that I had with you before the world existed" (17:5; cf. 17:24). This can be easily read as implying personal pre-existence: Jesus was with God in glory before the world

---

[41] In some manuscripts "is above all" is missing from the end of verse 31, and so would read "He who comes from heaven bears witness to what he has seen and heard." This might imply pre-existence. This variant is not accepted by most textual critics.

began. However, we can point to several other examples from the New Testament which describe events before the world. Paul writes that believers were chosen by God as "before the foundation of the world" (Eph. 1:4). Revelation declares that the names of the saved were written in the book of life "before the foundation of the world" (Rev. 13:8; cf. 17:8). First Peter makes explicit the concept at work in these passages: "he was foreknown before the foundation of the world but was made manifest in the last times for the sake of you" (1 Pet. 1:20). Scholars have noted that in pre-Christian Jewish thought the future was seen as already present in the foreknowledge of God.[42] This concept seems to have been adopted by the New Testament writers, often signaled by this expression "before [the foundation of] the world." The prayer of Jesus in John 17 seems to follow the same logic. Jesus asks to be glorified with the glory he had with God before the world (17:5). Later he says he *is* glorified in his followers (17:10) and, further down, that he *has given* his followers the glory with which his Father glorified him (17:22). In each case, he speaks prophetically, as it were moving back future events to the present or the past. Although Jesus speaks of having glory "before the world," this glory is actualized through accomplishing God's work in the lives of his followers. Jesus explains his future glorification as a consequence of having been loved by God "before the foundation of the world" (17:24). God foreknew Jesus and fore-loved him, and thus Jesus was glorified before the world in the foreknowledge of God. This mode of speaking about the future as a present or even a past reality emphasizes the unchangeableness of it.

MISUNDERSTANDING MOTIF

It has been frequently observed by scholars that there is a "misunderstanding motif" throughout the narrative of John's gospel.[43] Repeatedly characters that encounter Jesus misunderstand his statements, often taking an overly literal interpretation instead of the intended meaning. They are then corrected by Jesus (or sometimes, by the narrator).

---

[42] Hamerton-Kelly, *Pre-Existence*; T. Givens, *Souls*.
[43] Thatcher, "Anatomies"; Skinner, "Misunderstanding."

When Jesus tells Nicodemus that one must be "born again," Nicodemus is perplexed by impossibility of a literal rebirthing (John 3:3–4). When Jesus declares himself to be "the living bread," his opponents quarrel over the implied cannibalism (John 6:51–52). And so on. These repeated misunderstandings highlight the importance of giving attention to Jesus' self-revelation.

It is, then, significant that those statements of "high Christology" in John's gospel follow this pattern of the misunderstanding motif and are placed on the lips of Jesus' opponents in the gospel, "the Jews." When Jesus says that both he and his Father have been "working," "the Jews" interpret him to mean that he is equal with God. Jesus corrects their misunderstanding, stating that the Son can "do nothing of himself" (John 5:17–19). When Jesus says "I and my Father are one," "the Jews" take it as a claim that he is God. Jesus corrects their misunderstanding, claiming instead to be the Son of God (John 10:30–36). When Jesus says that Abraham saw his day, "the Jews" assume he must mean super longevity (or pre-existence). Jesus corrects this misunderstanding, restating his claim to be the Son of Man (John 8:56–58).

Far from being proof-texts for the deity of Christ, these claims are presented by John as misunderstandings, as false interpretations that Jesus has to correct. Through use of the misunderstanding motif, and placing these statements in the mouths of Jesus' opponents, John is actually denying the claims being made. John denies that Jesus is equal with God; John denies that Jesus is God; John denies that Jesus pre-existed. And since John denies these claims, he is (by implication) affirming the alternatives.

CONCLUSION

John's gospel does not teach a divine Christology if it does not teach that Jesus existed before his human career. It must be acknowledged that to the modern English reader, many passages in John's gospel read naturally as entailing the personal pre-existence of Jesus. However, a number of considerations nuance these appearances and make an alternative reading more credible.

Reading John's prologue in the context of Jewish Wisdom literature, it seems unlikely that the Logos is supposed to be a pre-existent person. Since John chose this prologue to introduce his gospel, and since he describes Jesus as the Word-made-flesh, much of the pre-existence language of John's gospel seems open to an interpretation that does not entail Jesus' personal pre-existence.

Common proof-texts for the deity of Christ, such as the confrontations with the Jews in chapters 5 and 10 or the "I am" sayings in chapter 8, do not, upon examination, provide solid proof for the divinity, and thus for the pre-existence, of Jesus. Ironically, statements apparently endorsing a divine Christology are placed in the mouths of Jesus' opponents ("the Jews") and presented as misunderstandings. It is "the Jews" who think Jesus makes himself equal with God (5:18); it is "the Jews" who think Jesus is claiming to be God (10:33); it is "the Jews" who think Jesus is claiming to have seen Abraham (8:57). Given that in each case Jesus does not affirm their assertions but rather seems to demur (cf. 5:19–23; 10:34–36; 8:54–56), these make very precarious proof-texts. By presenting them as misunderstandings, John implicitly affirms the contrary.

Of all the passages considered, those that have the strongest appearance of affirming the pre-existence of Jesus are those that speak of descent from heaven, but even these seems to yield to more satisfying explanations. In sum, the evidence of divine Christology within the Gospel of John is minimal, at best, if not entirely non-existent.

The implications of this finding are significant, as it suggests the Gospel of John may be closer in Christology (and perhaps in date[44]) to the synoptics than is commonly recognized. For our purposes, the key implication is that the Gospel of John is not a pillar of (proto-)orthodoxy, nor is it indicative that something like orthodox Christology was current by the end of the first century. The fact that later Christians would use the Gospel of John to defend the pre-existence and the divinity of Christ neither implies that the evangelist did so nor that his earliest readers did so. On the contrary if, as I have argued, the Gospel of John does not advocate the personal pre-existence of Jesus, then we should not expect its

---

[44] Robinson dates the Gospel of John to 40–65 (*Redating*, 352).

earliest readers to do so, and we should not be surprised to find those who accepted the canonicity of the Gospel of John while denying the pre-existence of Jesus (as is the case with the followers of Theodotus). Rather than sinking the thesis I am proposing, the Gospel of John is consistent with it.

Primitive Christology

Part Three Introduction

IN THE FIRST PART OF THIS BOOK I described those usually identified as "Dynamic Monarchians" and put forward the proposal that their distribution makes it unlikely that they arrived at their views independently. Yet their lack of apparent connection indicates that the origin of their views was not dependence on each other, but rather a shared tradition. In the second part I sought to project backwards from this evidence for Dynamic Monarchianism in the third and late second centuries, arguing that there are reasons for thinking that Dynamic Monarchian views were part of mainstream Christian tradition in the second and late first centuries. In this third and final part, I intend to push back one stage further into the first century to explore whether Dynamic Monarchianism can be traced back to the earliest Christians.

In this part I will be focusing on Christianity from around 70 CE back till the earliest Christians (including Jesus himself). Almost all of the evidence for Christianity in this period comes from the New Testament, either because the texts were written in this period or because they contain evidence that witnesses to those in this period (or both). There are also some non-canonical Christian texts that may possibly date from this period, most notably the *Didache*.[1] However, since the *Didache* contains little by way of Christology, it will not be relevant for the issue at hand.

I have presented Dynamic Monarchianism as the Christology that affirms the virgin birth while denying the pre-existence of Jesus. This differs, on the one hand, from those who affirm the pre-existence of Jesus, such as proponents of Logos Christology (and, later, trinitarians), and, on

---

[1] For Greek text and translation see Ehrman, *Apostolic Fathers*, 405–43. Ehrman dates the *Didache* to c. 100, though dates as early as c. 40 have been proposed.

the other hand, from those who deny the virgin birth, which would include the idea that Jesus became the Son by adoption ("Adoptionist") or through possession by the Holy Spirit ("Possessionist"). In dealing with the earliest Christians, I will be seeking to demonstrate that they did not affirm the pre-existence of Jesus but did affirm the virgin birth.

This is not, to my knowledge, a position often pursued by scholars. Broadly, historians of early Christianity and New Testament scholars seem divided into two "schools": the "Early High Christology Club" (as represented by scholars such as Larry Hurtado, Richard Bauckham, Martin Hengel and others) and those scholars who think divine Christology developed later. Yet this debate is about whether Jesus was worshipped as God or as a god early or later, and only secondarily about whether Jesus pre-existed. Those who argue that the early Christians believed in the pre-existence of Jesus are usually more amenable to the idea that the early Christians believed in the virgin birth; in contrast those scholars who argue against the one usually argue against the other too. The idea that the earliest Christians may have been Dynamic Monarchian, affirming the virgin birth yet denying the pre-existence of Jesus, is rarely pursued.

I will explore this question across three successive chapters. Firstly, I will address the question of whether the earliest Christians believed in the pre-existence of Jesus (Chapter Fourteen). It is broadly accepted that much of the New Testament, especially the synoptic gospels (Matthew, Mark, and Luke), does not explicitly affirm the pre-existence of Jesus. There have been efforts to find language there that indicates an assumption of pre-existence, and I will briefly address those passages which are often cited as proof-texts for early high Christology. Then I will discuss some isolated passages in the writings of Paul. I will argue that, rightly understood, they do *not* provide evidence for early high Christology.

Having addressed the question of Jesus' pre-existence in earliest Christianity, I will then turn to the opposing view that the earliest Christology was Adoptionist (Chapter Fifteen). The proposed evidence for this early Adoptionism comes from two fronts: projecting backwards from reports about the Ebionites and identifying "Adoptionist" pre-literary texts within the New Testament. I will push back against both fronts. The Ebionites are more likely a later phenomenon and are unlikely to be representative of Jewish Christians in the early to mid-first century. The evidence from pre-literary texts does not support the view that Jesus was the Son of God by adoption; often, some other status is in view. Having dismantled the case for early Adoptionism, there is very little to recommend it, if a more plausible proposal can be established.

The final chapter of the book attempts to date belief in the virgin birth. One may think that the belief dates to its occurrences in the Gospel of Matthew and the Gospel of Luke, which are conventionally dated to around 80 CE. However, upon investigation this cannot be the case. Firstly, these gospels may well date earlier, but secondly and more importantly, the shared tradition requires that the belief be dated earlier than its appearance in these gospels. Following this line of reasoning, I argue that the absence of a virgin birth narrative from Mark's gospel does not entail that belief in the virgin birth must post-date the composition of that gospel, or of Paul's letters for that matter. Indeed, there may be indications that the virgin birth was assumed by both Mark and Paul. Lastly, Jesus' own filial consciousness may be indicative that the virgin birth was part of Jesus' own self-understanding. This completes the historical arc of the book, having traced Dynamic Monarchian belief from the "heretics" of the third century all the way back to Jesus himself.

CHAPTER 14

Did the Earliest Christians Believe in the Pre-Existence of Jesus?

THE BROAD SCHOLARLY CONSENSUS is that the notion of the pre-existence of Jesus is not to be found in the synoptic gospels (Matthew, Mark, and Luke). Certainly, these gospels do not include any narrative of events that occur before Jesus's birth, nor any saying of Jesus indicating his memories of such a time, nor any explicit statement equivalent to the claim that Jesus existed before his human career. This same scholarly consensus would find pre-existence in the Pauline epistles (usually dated prior to the synoptics) and in the Gospel of John (usually dated later than the synoptics).[1] There is an interesting incongruity in the chronology of this evidence, which would seem to disrupt simplistic ideas about Christological development.[2] Such incongruity might be resolved if one allows that Paul did not, in fact, hold

---

[1] Gathercole summarizes this consensus as follows, "a preexistent Messiah is a feature of early Jewish texts such as *1 Enoch* and *4 Ezra* and of some early Christian writers like Paul and John, but is certainly not an idea held by the Synoptic Evangelists" (Gathercole, *Pre-existent Son,* 2).

[2] Ehrman writes, "How could Paul embrace 'higher' views of Christ than those found in later writings such as Matthew, Mark and Luke? Didn't Christology develop from 'low' Christology to a 'high' Christology over time? . . . And I simply did not get it, for the longest time" (Ehrman, *How Jesus Became God,* 251–52). He concludes that Paul and the authors of the synoptics held different Christologies, even though they were contemporaries.

that Jesus pre-existed. More on this below. An alternative is that the synoptics *do* presuppose the pre-existence of Jesus. Though this view is not wildly held among scholars, it is worth exploring before moving to the more controversial question of pre-existence in the writings of Paul.

I will focus in this section on the proposals of Simon Gathercole, who has given the best developed defense of the claim that the synoptics presuppose the pre-existence of Jesus. His thesis centers on the claim that the "I have come" sayings of Jesus give the "clearest indications" of pre-existence within the synoptics, though he does consider some other indicators.[1] He rejects attempts to find Wisdom Christology within the synoptics as a "blind alley."[2]

Gathercole identifies ten "I have come" sayings within the synoptics: Mark 1:24 (parallel: Luke 4:34), Matt. 8:29, Mark 1:38 (cf. Luke 4.43), Mark 2:17 (parallels: Matt. 9:13, Luke 5:32), Matt. 5:17, Luke 12:49, Matt. 10:34 (parallel: Luke 12:51), Matt. 10:35, Mark 10:45 (parallel: Matt. 20:28), and Luke 19:10.[3] He argues that this formula ("I have come" + purpose) implies a deliberate act of coming to our realm from somewhere else in order to do something.[4] He draws parallels with the "I have come" sayings used by angels to announce their purpose of visit,[5] where the implication is that the angel was previously in heaven and was sent to earth for a specific purpose. Gathercole argues that when Jesus uses the "I have come" formula he is announcing the purpose of his life's work and indicating that he has come from somewhere else.[6] He concludes that

---

[1] Gathercole, *Pre-existent Son,* 18.

[2] Gathercole, *Pre-existent Son,* 19.

[3] Gathercole, *Pre-existent Son,* 84. He dismisses as irrelevant Matt. 11:19a (parallel: Luke 7:34), Luke 9:55, and Mark 1:45 (Gathercole, *Pre-existent Son,* 88–91).

[4] Gathercole, *Pre-existent Son,* 87.

[5] His cited parallels include: Dan. 9:22–23; Dan. 10:12, 14, 20, 11:2; *Tobit* 5:5; *Fourth Book of Ezra,* 535 (6:30), 536 (7:2); *2 Baruch,* 130 (71:3) (Gathercole, *Pre-existent Son,* 119–37). Gathercole also explores traditions about the coming of Elijah. "It is noteworthy that here again there is an eschatological ministry that is envisaged as having a cosmic scope, which, again, is difficult to imagine outside of a coming from heaven" (Gathercole, *Pre-existent Son,* 138).

[6] Gathercole, *Pre-existent Son,* 117.

> there is a consistent use of the 'I have come' + purpose formula *which is not conventionally used in early Judaism by human figures to describe the totality of their life's work.* Instead, the formula refers *to the totality of the heavenly figure's earthly visit, and to the purpose of that visit.*[7]

Although the meanings of the "I have come" sayings are not directly about pre-existence, in the case of Jesus coming from heaven they would imply his pre-existence. Gathercole also argues that "I have been sent" sayings probably imply the same thing, though these could also be statements about a prophet's commission.

Gathercole dismisses several alternative explanations for the "I have come" sayings. For example, the proposal that "I have come" is a declaration of a prophetic advent is dismissed given the lack of examples of the formula being used in this way. 1 Samuel 16:2, 5 is rejected as not referring to the prophet's advent; *Pesikta Rabbati* 20, from a collection of midrashim from the 9th century CE, is rejected as not being explicitly about prophets.[8] Similarly Gathercole rejects the proposal that the "I have come" sayings have messianic connotations ("the coming one"), arguing that the emphasis of the "I have come" sayings is on the purpose, not on the coming. He summarizes,

> the messianic interpretation falls foul of the same problem as both of the prophetic interpretations: they rely heavily on 'coming' being a technical or semi-technical term as opposed to referring to a coming from 'a' to 'b.'[9]

This thesis rests on two claims. Firstly, it must be true that "I have come" + purpose had become idiomatic by the time of the composition of synoptics. Secondly, the "I have come" sayings of Jesus must be more naturally understood as involving literally coming from a location, rather than in any other sense. The first of these claims is plausible enough, though "I have come" sayings are not reserved for heavenly beings (e.g. Luke 13:7). Yet the second claim founders on the fact that the concept of

---

[7] Gathercole, *Pre-existent Son,* 145–46.

[8] Gathercole, *Pre-existent Son,* 102–6.

[9] Gathercole, *Pre-existent Son,* 108.

coming is used in other senses with reference to Jesus. Mark's gospel begins with John the Baptist proclaiming "after me comes he who is mightier than I" (Mark 1:7; cf. Matt 3:11, Luke 3:16). Presumably John does not mean literal travel from one place to another, because John himself did not come from Nazareth (cf. Mark 1:9) and, though Jesus does come to the Jordan, he only remains there temporarily (cf. Mark 1:12). So, in what sense did Jesus "come"? The "after" implies that John (or Mark) is thinking temporally rather than geographically. It also implies that John considers himself to have come at a certain time, but Mark does not present John as having pre-existed. Elsewhere in the synoptic tradition John the Baptist asks Jesus if he is "the one who is to come" (Matt 11:3/Luke 7:19) and, though Gathercole dismisses this example, presumably it is rooted in this same tradition of John speaking about one who was to come after. So in these sayings of John we have a clear example of "coming" used in the sense of a temporal advent of a significant figure. More than that, by introducing his gospel with John predicting the advent of the one who was to come, Mark contextualizes Jesus' "I have come" sayings with a clear temporal marker; Jesus was the one to come *after* John.

There is a possible response to this: John the Baptist is identified as the Elijah who was to come (Matt 11:14, 17:10–12; Mark 9:11–13), and given the common belief that Elijah was in heaven and would come at some significant moment, then John's talk of Jesus coming after would be consistent with the idea that Jesus had literally come down from heaven. However, this response rests on the assumption that John and/or the synoptic evangelists regarded John the Baptist as the same person as Elijah, having descended from heaven. But it is evident that Luke did not. Luke describes the circumstances of John's conception without any whiff of reincarnation or pre-existence. He omits the saying of Jesus that John was the Elijah to come, instead including the prediction that John would go before Jesus "in the spirit and power of Elijah" (Luke 1:17). The other two synoptic evangelists are more coy about John's origins, though again there is no indication that they consider him to be Elijah himself. (Since Jews generally did not believe in reincarnation, it would be surprising if John was believed to be Elijah.) Rather, the impression is given through the events of the transfiguration that Elijah is someone other than John. When

Jesus speaks of the "Elijah who is to come" that very qualification indicates that he is not talking about Elijah himself but rather the role of Elijah in prophetic expectation. So, the coming of John, even in the context of his being "Elijah," does not imply a coming from heaven, but rather an arrival on the world stage at a specific moment in time.

So even though Gathercole is correct that there does not seem to be strong precedent for the use of "I have come" in the context of prophetic or messianic advent, I think there are strong reasons for thinking this is the way this formulae is used in the synoptics. Consequently, I do not think there are any compelling reasons to think the synoptic evangelists presupposed the pre-existence of Jesus. They do not say that Jesus existed before he was a human, and we can reasonably expect that they would have said that had they believed it.

PRE-EXISTENCE IN PAUL

The synoptic gospels are conventionally dated to 70–80, though I think there are compelling reasons for dating them earlier (see Chapter Sixteen). The authentic writings of Paul are dated to the 50s and 60s. Were we looking for a sequence of doctrinal development between these texts, we might be surprised to find that the synoptic gospels do not presuppose the pre-existence of Jesus and the writings of Paul do. Yet this is what we find, at least according to the general consensus of biblical scholars. If this is the case, then the concept of the pre-existence of Jesus emerged early (within two decades of the crucifixion) and was present in the texts that became foundational for many subsequent Christians. If Paul does presuppose the pre-existence of Jesus, then it would be difficult, though not impossible, to argue that the Dynamic Monarchian tradition dates back to the apostolic era. If, on the other hand, Paul does not presuppose the pre-existence of Jesus then the most important plank in the case for "Early High Christology" is removed.

Before proceeding, it is important to note a major methodological issue in Pauline studies. Of the thirteen New Testament letters ascribed to Paul, only five are (near) universally held to be authentic: Romans, 1 Corinthians, 2 Corinthians, Galatians, and Philippians. For a further five letters the authenticity is disputed: Ephesians, Colossians, 1 Thessalonians, 2 Thessalonians, and Philemon. For the remaining three, the "pastoral letters" 1 Timothy, 2 Timothy, and Titus, the consensus is against their authenticity (though there are a number of scholars who do defend their authenticity).[10]

The questions over the authenticity of some of Paul's letters raise methodological issues about how to treat the Pauline corpus when trying to position chronologically the theology expressed within these letters. Any authentic letters will date from within Paul's lifetime (i.e. before c. 66 CE), whereas when certain letters are considered inauthentic, they are sometimes dated as late as early to mid-second century. So for each particular letter the question arises: does this reflect the Christology of Paul (and his milieu) or that of second century Christians? As we have seen, by the second century there were plenty of Christians who believed in the pre-existence of Jesus; if Colossians, say, is dated to the second century then it would be unsurprising if it affirmed the pre-existence of Jesus. In this sense it might be convenient to my argument if those letters with the appearance of high Christology were also those judged inauthentic and dated to the second century. However, I am not convinced by the arguments against the authenticity of any of the Pauline letters; even in the case of the pastoral letters I am at least sympathetic to some of questions raised about the current consensus. In general, I am skeptical about the tendency to date canonical texts to the second century; one suspects that often those proposing such dates are unfamiliar with the literature of this period.

In considering the question of whether Paul believed in the pre-existence of Jesus, I will start with the undisputed letters of Paul and then move on to consider what the disputed letters of Paul might add to the question if they're included in the Pauline corpus. This procedure allows all readers to follow the argument about Jesus' pre-existence whether or not they agree on the authenticity of all of the New Testament letters attributed to Paul.

---

[10] For a defense of their authenticity see Schnabel, "Paul, Timothy, and Titus." For the more skeptical majority view see Ehrman, *Forged*, chapter 3.

PAUL'S UNDISPUTED LETTERS

Before discussing the usual texts cited as evidence for the pre-existence of Jesus in the Pauline letters, it is worth considering the indications that Paul did not presuppose the pre-existence of Jesus. First and foremost, it is worth noting that nowhere does Paul give any description of the (purported) incarnation (i.e. an eternal divine person entering into a hypostatic union with a complete human nature). This is important, because Paul clearly believed that Jesus was born as a man, that he had human ancestors and at least one human parent (Rom. 1:3; Gal. 4:4). Paul presupposes a moment when the earthly life of Jesus began. If, therefore, he believed that Jesus had previously had a heavenly life then some kind of incarnation is necessary to explain the transition from one state to the other. Yet, with the exception of Philippians 2 (which I will discuss below), I don't think there is any passage which could be read as a description of incarnation. A birth without an incarnation reveals Paul's assumption that Jesus came into existence at his conception, and thus tells against pre-existence.

A second, related, indication is Paul's use of cognates of the root word *ginomai* ("to become") in relation to the birth of Jesus (Rom. 1:3; Gal. 4:4). This word can be used of human birth, but it is not the usual word, which is *gennao* and its cognates (Gal. 4:23). Now *ginomai* can have a range of meanings, not just of a temporal beginning, but also of a change of state, so it would be too much to argue that Paul uses this word to signal that Jesus was created at a moment in time, but it is an interesting word choice, and one that would seem unlikely if Paul was sensitive to possibility that he might be denying the pre-existence of Jesus by using a word than can refer to temporal beginnings. If Paul believed in the pre-existence of Jesus one might expect him to be more careful in his use of words so that he would not be misunderstood.

The third indication is Paul's presentation of Jesus as "the last Adam" (1 Cor. 15:45). Just as death entered the world through Adam, so life came through Jesus Christ (Rom. 5:12ff; 1 Cor. 15:22, 45). As we shall see, Phil. 2:5–11 may also contrast Jesus with Adam: one made in the image of God, tempted with equality with God but (unlike Adam) choosing obedience instead. J. D. G. Dunn in particular has strongly emphasized the role of Adam in Paul's Christology, [11] though others feel that this theme has been overemphasized or has "proved a red herring" (i.e. a distraction).[12] Yet regardless of what emphasis we place upon it, it does seem evident that Paul understood Adam to be, in some sense, a type of Jesus. For this typology to have purchase there has to be a real parallel between Adam and Jesus. These parallels would be somewhat muted (to say the least) if Jesus had pre-existed in heaven, but these parallels are that much stronger if Paul regards Jesus as a creation. Just as Luke describes Adam as the "son of God" (Luke 3:38) to highlight the comparison between Adam and Jesus, so the Christological significance Paul gives to Adam is more explicable if Paul (like Luke) believed Jesus was conceived through a miraculous act of God.

We should not take from these points that Paul believed that Jesus was just a good man, an eschatological prophet, or a wise teacher. Paul makes very bold claims for Jesus, that he is the Son of God, that he has been exalted into heaven, and that he has astounding power and authority now.[13] But Paul emphasizes that Jesus' exaltation came after, and as a consequence of, his earthly life, his obedience to God even through a terrible death, and his resurrection.

For those who argue that Paul presupposed the pre-existence of Jesus there are some common proof-texts in Paul's undisputed letters. The two most significant passages are Phil. 2:6–11 and 1 Cor. 8:6. Larry Hurtado also identifies 1 Cor. 15:47 ("is from heaven"), 2 Cor. 8:9 ("became poor"), Gal. 4:4 ("sent"), Rom. 8:3 ("sending") and 1 Cor. 10:4 ("the rock was Christ"; cf. Exod. 17).[14] These passages need not detain us much as none is particularly strong, nor are these the mainstay of the case of those arguing for Early High Christology. While "sending" (Rom. 8:3, Gal. 4:4) might refer to a directive given by God to a pre-existent Jesus, it can also

[11] Dunn, *Christology in the Making*; Dunn, *Theology of Paul*, 283–86; cf. Ziesler, *Pauline Christianity*, 45.

[12] Bauckham, *Jesus and the God*, 41; cf. Hurtado, *Lord Jesus Christ*, 121 note 98.

[13] For a perceptive discussion of the exalted Jesus' current power and knowledge see Emyln, *An Humble Inquiry*, 69–89.

[14] Hurtado, *Lord Jesus Christ*, 119.

refer to the sending of a human prophet to a community, and so it need not imply pre-existence. While becoming poor (2 Cor. 8:9) might refer to Jesus laying aside some sort of pre-existent glory, it may also refer to laying aside the honor rightfully due to the Son of God to live in poverty and humility. 1 Cor. 15:45–48 is contrasting Adam (made out of dust) with Jesus (not made out of dust); "from heaven" could refer as much to Jesus' cause or his moral qualities as to his location (cf. Mark 11:30). Finally, although it is just possible, I suppose, that Paul thought that the pre-existent Jesus descended to the Earth to inhabit a rock, as many commenters have observed, it seems more likely that Paul is talking allegorically (or typologically) rather than literally in 1 Cor. 10.[15]

PHILIPPIANS 2:6–11

The Christ-hymn in Philippians 2 is a key passage of contention in the question of "Early High Christology." A common way of reading this passage is that Jesus was God (i.e. was fully divine) but did not attempt to hold on to his status of equality with God, instead humbling himself, taking on human nature and submitting to death on the cross. This reading presupposes that Jesus both pre-existed and is, in some sense, God.

In response to this common reading a number of possibilities have been suggested. Ziesler suggests three possible sources for the ideas in this "Christ-Hymn," of which he favors the latter: "a Gnostic Redeemer Myth," the "Wisdom story" and "a contrast between Christ and Adam."[16] Dunn has been a leading proponent of the view that this passage should be interpreted in light of Paul's Adam Christology. Since *morphe* (here translated "form") and *eikon* (usually translated "image") were "used as near synonyms" in Greek,[17] Paul may be making the comparison between the first Adam, made in the "image of God" (Gen. 1:26–27),

---

[15] E.g. Norris, *Acts and Epistles*, 349. Craig Keener observes that "In some Jewish traditions the well [in Exodus 17:1–7] followed the Israelites in the wilderness... In Paul's midrashic application, what the rock did for Israel corresponds to what Christ did for the Corinthians" (Keener, *Bible Background Commentary*, 473).

[16] Ziesler, *Pauline Christianity*, 45.

[17] Dunn, *Christology in the Making*, 284; Ziesler, *Pauline Christianity*, 45.

with the last Adam. The first Adam was tempted with being "like God" (Gen. 3:5); in contrast, Jesus did not grasp after equality with God, choosing humility instead. Therefore, in this passage Paul may be presenting Jesus as an antitype of Adam with the reverse outcome; believers are challenged to consider which example to follow. This reading would undermine claims of a high Christology: "Adam was certainly not thought of as pre-existent . . . so no implication that Christ was pre-existent may be intended."[18]

Dunn's proposal has not been universally accepted and has faced significant challenge. For example, Larry Hurtado writes "the question is not whether the general meanings of *morphe* and *eikon* have resemblances, but whether the specific expression *en morphe theou* [in the form of God] is actually used interchangeably with *eikon theou* [image of God] in Greek texts."[19] He points out that *morphe* is not used in the Greek translations of the Old Testament for Gen. 1:26–27, nor is it used in any other Greek text as an allusion to that passage. "The alleged use of *en morphe theou* as an allusion to Adam in Philippians 2:6 would be a singular phenomenon, and a particularly inept one as well."[20] He also argues that there is no other allusion to the Genesis story in Phil. 2:5–11. Further, "equality with God" is not used elsewhere as an allusion to Gen. 3:5, but is rather a description of human hubris (John 5:18; 2 Macc. 9:12).[21] Instead, he argues, the "equality with God" here is intended to be the equivalent of being "in the form of God."[22]

Dunn has responded to these and similar criticisms by saying that such analysis treats the concept of allusion "too woodenly." He argues Paul is using the Genesis as a template to understand one aspect of Jesus. And, "Like other templates . . . the template should not be treated as a rigid

---

[18] Dunn, *Christology in the Making,* 119.

[19] Hurtado, *Lord Jesus Christ,* 122.

[20] Hurtado, *Lord Jesus Christ,* 122.

[21] Also see Philo, *Allegorical Interpretation,* 177 (1.49); Hurtado, *Lord Jesus Christ,* 122.

[22] Hurtado, *Lord Jesus Christ,* 123.

frame that imprisons the meaning of the story . . . but as a suggestive parallel that allows the story to be seen from a different angle."[23]

Although it may be true that *morphe* is not used elsewhere as an allusion to Genesis, this does not answer the question as to why Paul chooses this word. This word does not mean "very nature," as the NIV mistranslates it; it normally refers to external appearance, not to a thing's inner essence or substance. Mark uses this word in a short post-resurrection episode, in which Jesus "appeared in another form [*morphe*]" (Mark 16:12). This does not mean Jesus changed his "very nature"; it means his appearance was different, which is why the two disciples did not recognize him (cf. Luke 24:16). In the first century *morphe* was used to refer to a condition rather than an essence.[24] Paul uses this same word when he says here that Jesus took the "form of a servant"; in this case he cannot mean nature or essence, because the property of being a servant was not understood in ancient philosophy to be a defining essence, but rather as a condition one may gain or lose, something more like appearance or role. (This would seem apt, since Jesus was not actually a bondservant to anyone, though he did serve others). If Paul had meant to say of Jesus "he was God" (NLT; cf. "was truly God" CEV), or even "he was *a* god," then he had straightforward phrases at his disposal to say those things. Presumably Paul chose the word *morphe* because he was intent on saying something else, and one thinks about why Paul might have wanted to describe Jesus as having the appearance or condition of God, then the background of Gen. 1:26 seems inviting. This may, as Hurtado says, be a "singular" choice for alluding to Genesis; still, it has greater explanatory value than its alternatives.

The idea that we should understand "being in the form of God" as the equivalent of "being equal with God" rests on the idea that Paul speaks of equality with God as something that Jesus had but did not seek to retain, rather than to something he lacked and did not seek to attain. The word *harpagmos* (to be grasped) is notoriously difficult to translate because it is used so rarely in Greek literature, and it occurs nowhere else in the New

---

[23]Dunn, *Did the First Christians,* 137n.
[24] Keown, *Philippians,* 387; Hellerman, "*Morphe Theou,*" 784–86.

Testament.[25] Lightfoot, after extensive evaluation of its uses, concluded that the instance of *harpagmos* here implies neither necessarily, either holding on to what one already has or reaching out for it is something one wants to gain.[26] Roy Hoover argues that when the complement to the object of a verb of thought, *harpagmos* is an "idiomatic expression [that] refers to something already present and at one's disposal."[27] Yet in the conclusion of the Christ-hymn Paul says that Jesus exalted by God because of his obedience and received from God "the name that is above every name" (Phil. 2:9), which is difficult to square with the reading that Jesus had (this sort of) equality with God from the start. Indeed, even at the end of this Christ-hymn Jesus does not have equality with God because every knee bows to Jesus "to the glory of God the Father" (Phil. 2:11).

Finally, some recent English translations may lead us to read Phil. 2:5–11 as saying that Jesus in some sense laid aside his divinity, was incarnated, and became obedient to death. This is commonly called "Kenosis Theory," based on the Greek word *kenosis* behind "emptied" in this passage.[28] It refers to the idea that a pre-existent Jesus was able to somehow "empty" himself of divine nature and take on the limitations of human nature. Whether such a procedure is metaphysically possible is an issue for a different book.[29] We can set aside that question since that is not what Paul is saying here.

Yes, he "emptied" himself or made himself of "no effect," but given the outcome was taking the role of a servant, this is more likely to refer to

[25] "where it does appear it denotes 'robbery' " (Fee, *Letter to the Philippians*, 205).

[26] Lightfoot, *Epistle to the Philippians*, 111.

[27] Hoover, "*Harpagmos* Enigma, 95–119.

[28] On the 19th century origins of such interpretations, see Thompson, "Nineteenth Century Kenotic Christology." For some carefully-developed recent variants see Evans, *Exploring Kenotic Christology*, chs. 5–8. For how any Kenosis Theory goes against the mainstream creedal traditions about Christ, see Pawl, *Incarnation*, 43–44.

[29] One analytic theologian observes that some divine attributes seem to be in principle un-give-up-able, which casts doubt on Kenosis Theory as a way to show how a divine being can temporarily have the limitations shared by ordinary humans (Morris, *Logic of God Incarnate*, 61–62, 89). Another problem is that for any two-natures theorist, Christ is still both divine and human, but since his post-resurrection exaltation is no longer "emptied" (Pawl, *Incarnation*, 43–44).

becoming humble than giving up divine nature. While *ginomai* (became) may refer to birth in other contexts, as this is secondary to becoming a servant and as it is in reference to Jesus' likeness, rather than his nature, it is better understood as becoming like others. Similarly, being found in human *schema* is unlikely to refer to taking on human nature, but rather the way his manner of life appeared to others. Therefore, at no point in this hymn does Paul use words or phrases that lead us to conclude that a change of nature has taken place. He does not say that Jesus became a human being, which would lead us to expect that prior to that Jesus had been something else, but says that Jesus changed the appearance and manner of his life, despite his right to have "dominion . . . over every living thing" (Gen. 1:28). Rather, Paul says, Jesus was given lordship, in heaven as well as on earth, as a consequence of his obedience.

Primarily Paul's point is a practical one, an exhortation to believers to be humble and to look to the interests of others (Phil 2:3–4). Therefore, one would expect a meaningful correspondence between the example he is giving and the behavior he expects of believers. Pre-existent glory and incarnation in flesh would be beyond the personal experience of his readers, which lends weight to the idea that instead he is speaking of Jesus in his earthly obedience, culminating in his death on the cross. This example of service and humility would be familiar to Paul and his readers from traditions of Jesus they had received (and known to us through the gospels); there is no independent witness that these traditions contained anything about the supposed pre-existent life of Jesus. The resonance with Gethsemane, where Jesus refuses to call upon the divine legions and rejects his own desires to escape death, may well be the background to Paul's words here. This explanation has the obvious advantage that Gethsemane was part of the Jesus tradition, which cannot be said of the hypothesized "Early High Christology."

1 CORINTHIANS 8:6

The second key passage for Early High Christology is 1 Corinthians 8:6.[30] Richard Bauckham suggests that Paul has deconstructed and reconstituted the Shema (Deut. 6:4), ascribing it jointly to both God and Jesus. He writes "the only possible way to understand Paul as maintaining monotheism is to understand him to be including Jesus in the unique identity of the one God affirmed in the Shema."[31] Yet here Bauckham has overstated his case. Given that Paul uses the phrase "Lord Jesus Christ" on 47 other occasions (e.g. 1 Tim. 6:3, 14), it is unlikely that here "Lord" should be interpreted as *Yahweh*.[32] It would also be decidedly odd if Paul divided *Elohim* and *Yahweh* across two persons, since the point of the Shema is to affirm that *Yahweh* is *Elohim*. By identifying only one person as the "one God," Paul explicitly separates Jesus from "the unique identity of the one God." "Lord" is an important title and elevates Jesus above ordinary men but not to equality with God. Ziesler writes "it could mean divinity in a somewhat reduced sense, and would not necessarily say anything unique or even highly unusual about Jesus."[33] And Dunn observes that "*kyrios* is not so much a way of identifying Jesus with God, but if anything more a way of distinguishing Jesus from God."[34]

Perhaps a more significant consideration is Paul's ascription to Jesus: "through whom are all things." Many take this as implying that Jesus was the agent of creation, which would mean his pre-existence is presupposed.[35] Dunn writes of this passage "Paul's readers could have little doubt that Paul was attributing a role in creation to the 'one Lord Jesus Christ.'"[36] Paul has already stated that all things are "from" (*ek*) God; the word used of Jesus is "through" (*dia*). If referring to creation, this

---

[30] Also see Gaston and Perry, "Christological Monotheism."

[31] Bauckham, *God of Israel*, 38. For a critique of Bauckham's concept of "divine identity" see Tuggy, "On Bauckham's Bargain."

[32] Ziesler, *Pauline Christianity*, 37.

[33] Ziesler, *Pauline Christianity*, 37.

[34] Dunn, *Theology of Paul*, 254.

[35] Hurtado, *Lord Jesus Christ*, 123.

[36] Dunn, *Theology of Paul*, 268.

might indicate that God is the ultimate source and Jesus was the instrument. The word *dia* can also be used causally or even to refer to purpose, so it is possible that Paul is saying that Christ was the predestined purpose of creation, but if Paul had meant "for whom we exist" then he had words by which to say that. So many conclude that Paul is saying Jesus was the instrument of creation.[37]

It is worth emphasizing that this (apparent) declaration from Paul that Jesus participated in creation comes out of the blue. Gordon Fee writes "there is nothing like this to be found in Paul's Jewish heritage as such."[38] There is no indication in Genesis that God had an instrument, personal or otherwise, through which he created. The role of Christ in creation was not a feature of Jesus' own teaching. Paul gives no indication in any of the other undisputed letters that God had or needed an instrument by which to create (e.g. Rom. 1:20). This passage in the letter to Corinthians about meat offered to idols would be a strange place to introduce such a radical new doctrine.

Fee concludes that "the adjustment most likely had its origins for Paul in his own encounter with the risen Christ."[39] However, though Paul's experience was no doubt formative for him and for his theology, it would be an enormous leap to go from "Christ ascended to heaven" to "Christ participated in creation." It is not surprising therefore that scholars have concluded that the background "if anything" is Wisdom literature.[40]

Wisdom (of God) appears in Proverbs, Sirach, and Wisdom personified as a woman. She is identified with the Law (Prov. 7:1–4; Sir. 24:22–23), with the word of God (Sir. 24:3; Wis. 9:1–2) and with God's creative activity (Prov. 8:30; Sir. 42:21; Wis. 9:1–2, 9). Though it has sometimes been argued that Wisdom was worshipped as a goddess by the ancient Israelites, or by the diaspora in preference to local goddesses, the evidence is not forthcoming; Wisdom has neither altars, nor temples, nor images, nor cult, and she is not described as a goddess in the Jewish Bible

[37] Conzelmann, *1 Corinthians*, 144.
[38] Fee, *Pauline Christology*, 92.
[39] Fee, *Pauline Christology*, 92.
[40] Dunn, *Theology of Paul*, 273; also see Ziesler, *Pauline Christianity*, 34, Conzelmann, *1 Corinthians*, 145.

or in extra-biblical literature.[41] In Proverbs the character Wisdom exhorts us to be wise, in contrast to the path of the unrighteous personified in the harlot Folly. The close association between Wisdom and God, as his first creation (cf. Prov. 8:22, 25) and "chief workman" (Prov. 8:30), emphasizes the appeal of wisdom for God's servants. In Sirach and Wisdom, Wisdom takes on as aspect of mediation for God, a mode by which the transcendent God is immanent in the world, but never in any other sense than an extended metaphor.[42]

We have already seen how Wisdom may be background for the Word in John 1. Paul may also be influenced by this same tradition; he writes that for the "called" Jesus is "the power of God, and the wisdom of God" (1 Cor. 1:24,30).[43] The temptation needs to be resisted to describe Wisdom as a hypostasis or emanation from God; as Dunn says, this is "anachronistic and imposes a distinction which, so far as we can tell, never occurred to first century Jews."[44] Paul happily combines the feminine *sophia* with the masculine pronoun (1 Cor. 1:30), indicating that he did not take the personification of Wisdom literally. Paul takes the extended metaphor, presumably known so well to his readers, and sees it embodied in Christ. The Gentiles seek after the wisdom of world, but God has made the wisdom of world foolish by confounding their expectations and sending Christ to be crucified. Christ then appears as foolishness to the Gentiles, but to believers he has become the wisdom of God (1 Cor. 1:20–25, 30–31). The wisdom that is hidden from the world was revealed in Christ (1 Cor. 2:7–8), or though the Spirit of God (1 Cor. 2:10). It is possible, therefore, that when Paul says all things were created "through" Jesus, he means that all things were created through Wisdom, which is now embodied in Jesus. This would mean 1 Cor. 8:6 would not imply personal pre-existence. [45]

---

[41] See Gaston, "Wisdom and the Goddess," 53–57. Contrary to the aspersions of earlier scholarship, the ancients were well able to conceive of personified concepts and distinguish them from their gods and goddesses.

[42] Dunn, *Theology of Paul,* 35, 270.

[43] Dunn, *Theology of Paul,* 274.

[44] Dunn, *Theology of Paul,* 272.

[45] Dunn, *Theology of Paul,* 75.

Hurtado agrees that Wisdom is a possible background for Paul but argues that Paul does not give any indication of speaking about Wisdom in 1 Cor. 8:6.[46] Fee also criticizes this proposal: "there is nothing in this passage or in its surrounding context that would ever remotely suggest that Jewish Wisdom lies behind Paul's formulation."[47] He argues that the context of the passage is knowledge, not wisdom (1 Cor. 8:1–3). He also notes that 1 Cor. 1:18–31 "has nothing to do with personified Wisdom"; the contrast is between the apparent foolishness of the crucifixion and its wisdom in the purpose of God for the called. He suggests that it would be difficult for Paul's original readers to find Wisdom in this passage since Paul is opposed to those who consider themselves wise.[48]

The problem commentators face in trying to say anything about 1 Cor. 8:6 is that Paul says so little. Hurtado writes, "Paul's brief statement of this also seems to presuppose that the idea was already known to his readers, thus requiring no elaboration from him here."[49] Fee argues that this statement about Christ "will work *only* if this is in fact a shared assumption between Paul and the Corinthians."[50] Furthermore it seems unlikely that 1 Cor. 8:6 is "ad hoc"[51]; the poetic balance indicates something that is almost creedal in nature. But if Paul had received a creedal tradition from the apostles that Christ was the instrument of creation, it is without witness anywhere else in the New Testament; certainly not in the preaching recorded in Acts, where we might expect such a radical idea.

So, on the one hand, in his undisputed letters Paul gives little reason to suppose that he was influenced by the Wisdom literature, yet on the other hand, we have no evidence (except the passage itself) that the role of Christ in creation was part of the teaching of Paul or of the other apostles. There is a third possibility: that 1 Cor. 8:6 does not refer to creation at all. It is assumed rather too readily by some scholars that "all things" must be

---

[46] Hurtado, *Lord Jesus Christ*, 126.
[47] Fee, *Pauline Christology*, 93.
[48] Fee, *Pauline Christology*, 600.
[49] Hurtado, *Lord Jesus Christ*, 124.
[50] Fee, *Pauline Christology*, 504.
[51] Fee, *Pauline Christology*, 503.

a reference of the natural creation. In fact, "all things" (*ta panta*) is a broad and flexible term. Paul uses "all things" to refer to the spiritual benefits of discipleship (Rom. 8:28, 32; 1 Cor. 3:21; 2 Cor. 9:8), to the "new creation" (Col. 1:16–17, 20—see below), even to an eschatological reality (1 Cor. 15:27–28; cf. Eph. 1:10–11, 22). There is no verb in 1 Cor. 8:6 that means "to create"; there seems insufficient reason to suppose the context here has anything to do with creation. There is a long list of things that Paul says come to believers "through" Christ, including "redemption" (Rom. 3:24), "peace" (Rom. 5:1), "reconciliation" (Rom. 5:11), "eternal life" (Rom. 5:21), "victory" (1 Cor. 15:57), "comfort" (2 Cor. 1:5), "confidence" (2 Cor. 3:4), "adoption" (Eph. 1:5), "righteousness" (Phil. 1:11), "salvation" (1 Thes. 5:9), and the Holy Spirit (Tit. 3:6). Since Paul believes that such an "abundance of grace" has been given through Jesus Christ (Rom. 5:17), is there actually anything to explain about this statement that "all things" are "through" Christ? Given how inexplicable a creation reading of 1 Cor. 8:6 would be, and given the lack of precedent for such an idea, there can be no justification for forcing this meaning on the text when Paul's own writings suggest a different reading. There is, therefore, no reason to see pre-existence in this text.

PAUL'S DISPUTED LETTERS

Within Paul's disputed letters there is one standout passage that has become a favored proof-text for the pre-existence of Jesus. Aside from John 1, perhaps no other text is as trumpeted as Colossians 1:15–20. Unlike 1 Cor. 8:6, the language of creation is explicit. He is "firstborn over all creation," "by him all things were created," "all things were created through him and for him," he is "the beginning," and in all things he has the "pre-eminence."

It is worth stating that this passage does not identify Jesus as God. Here Jesus is described as the *eikon* ("image") of God (cf. Matt. 22:20) not the substance. This is emphasized by the juxtaposition between God as invisible one and Jesus as image. Jesus represents God, who cannot be directly perceived.

The term "firstborn" (*prototokos*) might be taken to mean that Jesus was the first created thing, making him pre-existent but not eternal. However, many scholars conclude that firstborn is used to refer to Jesus' status, giving him pre-eminence over creation, as the firstborn son was given pre-eminence in the household. This is entirely consistent with the idea that Jesus gained this status only after his resurrection and ascension. If so, then nothing about pre-existence is implied. Similarly, though one might read the phrase "he is before all things" temporally, as *pro* ("before") can be used with reference to time, it seems more likely that here too, Paul (or whoever) is referring to Christ's pre-eminence. After all he says Jesus "is" before all things, rather than "was." Though one might be inclined to suppose that pre-eminence requires temporal priority, we have seen from Philippians 2 that in the Pauline tradition Jesus was given such a status after his death and exaltation.

Nevertheless, the passage certainly would entail the pre-existence of Jesus if it is saying that Jesus is the creator, or agent of creation. All things were created "through" (*dia*) him, but also "in" (*en*) him and "for" (*eis*) him; not "from" (*ek*) him, the role 1 Cor. 8:6 ascribes to God. If the "all things" that are created through Jesus are the elements of the world then this passage presupposes that Jesus was present at that creation. Dunn asserts that " 'all things' (*ta panta*) was a familiar way of speaking about 'everything, the universe, the totality of created entities' "[52] citing 1 Cor. 15:27–28, Eph. 3:9 and John 1:3. However the "all things . . . in heaven and on the earth" that Jesus creates (Col. 1:16) are, presumably, the same "all things . . . whether in heaven or on earth" that Jesus reconciles to God (Col. 1:20). Since it is believers that are reconciled to God, it may be creation referred to here is not the Genesis creation, but the new creation in Christ. [53]

Though it may seem a little strange to the modern reader, it is clear that in both Paul's undisputed and disputed letters, creation language is used to talk about the spiritual re-birth of the believer (2 Cor. 5:17; Gal. 6:15; Eph. 2:10,14–15, 4:24; Col. 3:10). In fact, this passage is more easily

---

[52] Dunn, *Christology in the Making*, 267.

[53] As per Whiteley, *Theology of St Paul*, 110. There are those who still advocate this approach: see Perry, *Before He Was Born* and White, *Doctrine of the Trinity*, 223–26.

understood as referring to the new creation. Gen. 1:1 describes God creating the heavens and the earth; Col. 1:16 refers only to things "in" heaven and "on" earth, not heaven and earth themselves. "Thrones or dominions or principalities or powers" are not the sort of things that Genesis 1 talks about God creating, but these very terms are used in the New Testament to talk about the new creation, that is, the community of believers (cf. Eph. 3:10, 6:12; Col. 2:10). The phrase "all things" (*ta panta*) is also used by Paul in the context of spiritual regeneration (2 Cor. 5:17–18; Eph. 1:22–23; Col. 1:20), as is the phrase "in heaven and on earth" (Eph. 1:7–15; Col. 1:20). Believers are created "in" (*en*) Christ (Eph. 2:10, 15) and created by Christ (Col. 3:10).

This new creation reading is not common among scholars; the more common view of this passage is that it draws on Wisdom literature, as with John 1. For Dunn the source of this language and imagery can be quite confidently asserted as being "drawn from earlier Jewish reflection on divine Wisdom."[54] In pre-Christian Jewish literature, God's agent of creation was Wisdom.[55] In the same way that Paul describes all things being made 'through' Jesus, so Jewish writers describe all things being made 'through' Wisdom (Ps. 104:24; Prov. 3:18; Wis. 9:2).[56] Wisdom is also described as been the firstborn of creation (Prov. 8:22, 25; Sir. 24:9),[57] as being the image of God (Wis. 7:26),[58] as being before all things (Sir. 1:4), and as holding all things together (Wis. 1:6–7; cf. Sir. 43:26).[59] Wisdom, though personified, was never regarded as a person nor as being truly separate from God. It seems unlikely that Paul means that Christ was a pre-existent person or was literally with God at the beginning of creation. One way of seeing Paul's statement is as expressing the fact that Jesus was

---

[54] "indeed, few issues in recent New Testament theology have commanded such unanimity of agreement" (Dunn, *Christology in the Making*, 269).

[55] Clarke, *Wisdom of Solomon*, 46.

[56] See Philo, *That the Worse*, 239 (54).

[57] Philo, *On Drunkenness*, 333–35 (30–31); Philo, *Questions and Answers on Genesis*, 381 (4.97).

[58] Philo, *Allegorical Interpretation*, 175 (1.43).

[59] Dunn, *Theology of Paul*, 269; Clarke, *Wisdom of Solomon*, 55; Schweizer, *Letter to the Colossians*, 64–66.

the purpose of creation, the manifestation of God's power and character. Dunn concludes that Paul writes

> not of Christ as such present with God in the beginning, nor of Christ as identified with a pre-existent hypostasis or divine being beside God, but of Christ as embodying and expressing (and defining) that power of God which is the manifestation of God in and to his creation.[60]

In conclusion, we have two possible readings of this passage: the new creation reading or the Wisdom reading. Which would be the more natural reading for its original readers? Dunn asserts, "it is hard to imagine any first-century reader interpreting the first strophe [i.e. "for by him all things were created, in heaven and on earth"] except as a reference to the 'old' creation."[61] On the other hand, it might seem odd that Paul, who is fond of quoting scriptures, never once quotes from the Wisdom literature. On either reading, Paul doesn't feel the need to explain himself to his audience, so presumably he took it for granted that they would understand his meaning. The concept of Wisdom would have been known to Jews of the Second Temple period so, perhaps, Paul could have taken that background for granted. It is not clear how widespread new creation language would have been at the point this letter was written. If Paul is writing to his own converts, then there may be a lot of information that Paul assumes that he shares with his readers.

This problem is complicated further by the conclusion of many scholars that Colossians 1:15–18 (and Philippians 2:5–11) are pre-literary hymns that Paul has incorporated into his letters.[62] While this does not

---

[60] Dunn, *Christology in the Making*, 194.

[61] Dunn, *Christology in the Making*, 190.

[62] "The passage is widely regarded as a hymn quoted and adapted by the writer" (Dunn, *Christology in the Making*, 268). "It is no longer a matter for dispute that we have in these verses a hymn which has been taken over by the author" (Schweizer, *Colossians*, 55). "Because of its condensed and memorable form, more obvious in Greek than in translation, this is widely believed to be a piece of early liturgical tradition that Paul is quoting" (Ziesler, *Pauline Christianity*, 44). "Since the seminal work of Lohmeyer, the vast majority of interpreters have assumed the present passage to be an early hymn (whether by Paul or otherwise) in honor of Christ" (Fee, *Philippians*, 192).

mean that these hymns were known by Paul's original readers, presumably they were already fairly well diffused among the Christian community. Paul may have been able to assume, therefore, that the ideas he used in these hymns to express were, at least, not controversial to his readers and may have been well known. Indeed, it is possible that the original hymn was written about Wisdom and only later applied to Jesus when Jesus became associated with Wisdom;[63] there would be no way to say definitively either way.

What are the implications then? If we follow the modern scholarly consensus and interpret Colossians 1:15–17 as speaking about Christ as the embodiment of God's Wisdom, then no personal pre-existence is implied. The passage would be about how the Wisdom, with which God created the world, has now become embodied in Jesus Christ. If instead we interpret this chapter through lens of Paul's own new creation language, then also no personal pre-existence is implied. The passage would be about how, following his exaltation, Christ has become preeminent and is the means by which the new creation, that is the Christian community, has come into being. Neither reading can be taken to imply that Jesus was personally present at the creation of the world.

SUMMARY

How, then, should we judge the state of the evidence regarding whether the earliest Christians affirmed the pre-existence of Jesus or not?

The three synoptic gospels, although drawing on the same material, represent three different parts of first century Christianity. Yet the strongest purported evidence for the pre-existence of Jesus in any of these three gospels is the "I have come" sayings of Jesus. By my assessment, those sayings do not entail pre-existence. Aside from these sayings, the evidence is non-existent. None of these writers includes anything about Jesus's (purported) existence prior to his birth, or any sayings indicating his memory of such a period. These writers certainly have nothing to say about Christ existing before creation or having a role in creation. These

[63] Dunn, *Epistles to the Colossians*, 84–86.

gospels, and therefore the earliest records of the sayings of Jesus, are silent as to the purported pre-existence of Jesus. Had the authors believed in such things, surely these would have been worth a mention! Their silence, then, is telling.

When it comes to the letters of Paul, it is noteworthy how scant the purported evidence is. I have examined the three main proof-texts: two from Paul's undisputed letters, and one from his disputed letters. Each of these passages yields to a more satisfying interpretation. Read correctly, Phil. 2:5–11 does not speak about the decision of a pre-incarnate son to empty himself of his divinity and yield to incarnation as a man; this passage is about Jesus's humility in accepting the role of a self-sacrificing servant. 1 Cor. 8:6 actually says nothing about creation, and I see no reason to read creation into this passage. Col. 1:15–18, which primarily concerns Christ in his post-exaltation state, is better read against the background of Pauline new creation language. Even if we were to follow many modern scholars in seeing Wisdom as the background for Col. 1:15–18 and 1 Cor. 8:6, this would not be evidence of the personal pre-existence of Jesus since Wisdom was not considered to be a real person in addition to God.

In conclusion, the total evidence for the claim that the earliest Christians believed in the pre-existence of Jesus is not compelling. The sort of evidence we might expect (e.g. descriptions of what Jesus was doing prior to birth) does not exist. The purported evidence does not withstand examination. Therefore, we must conclude that the earliest Christians did not believe in the pre-existence of Jesus.

CHAPTER 15

Could Adoptionism be the Earliest Christology?

IF THE EARLIEST CHRISTIANS did not believe in the pre-existence of Jesus, then they had something in common with the Dynamic Monarchians of the second and third century. The second key affirmation of Dynamic Monarchians was Jesus' virgin birth. However, the view proposed by Adolf Harnack, and affirmed by many scholars since, is that the earliest Christians understood Jesus' sonship to be adoptive, that Jesus was an ordinary man chosen by God to be called his "son."[1] It was only later that Christians added the idea that Jesus' sonship was not purely adoptive, but was also ontological because of his miraculous birth.

This proposal is appealing to scholars for a number of reasons. Firstly, if you view the historical Jesus as being an ordinary man (say, an apocalyptic prophet) then it is inconvenient to think that Jesus might have actually claimed to be the Son of God (or indeed actually been the Son of God). The claim that early Christians first viewed Jesus' sonship as adoptive and only later as ontological creates a plausible narrative for the transition from this view of the historical Jesus to later Christological

[1] Harnack, *History of Dogma,* 1:190.

developments.[1] Bart Ehrman has popularized this view, theorizing that Jesus claimed to be the Messiah during his lifetime, but that after his death the earliest Christians came to the view that Jesus was adopted to semi-divinity at his resurrection. As time went on, Ehrman argues, this moment of Jesus' divinization was pushed earlier: to his baptism, then to his birth, then to before his birth. [2]

Secondly, an adoptive sonship might seem more consistent with Old Testament precedent. The kings of Israel and Judah were described as "sons" of God (Ps. 2:7; Ps. 89:26; 2 Sam. 7:14), a status, it is argued, that the king acquired at his coronation. Whether this new status is best understood as adoptive is disputed,[3] but clearly these kings were not sons of God in some ontological sense (i.e. each of these kings had a human father). For those who understand Jesus' sonship to be synonymous with (or else originating from) his claim to be the Messiah (i.e. the future king of Israel), it makes sense for his sonship to be analogous to that of the kings of Israel. The idea that Jesus' sonship was a consequence of his miraculous conception would thus be a later embellishment on his claim to be the Messiah.

Thirdly, the existence of groups like the Ebionites in the second century (and perhaps earlier) who denied the virgin birth and who, arguably, viewed Jesus as being adopted at his baptism, has led some to suggest that perhaps these groups preserved something of the earliest Christology. For example, Michael Goulder argued that the Ebionites preserved the "Petrine" Christianity that eventually lost out to the "Pauline" Christianity in the battle to become orthodoxy.[4]

However, the convenience of a theory is not the same as evidence for that theory. The sonship of Jesus was connected with the virgin birth by Matthew and Luke no later than c.80 CE, when those texts were

---

[1] Knox, *Humanity and Divinity*, 8–9.

[2] Ehrman, *How Jesus Became God*.

[3] Collins and Collins, *King and Messiah*, 20–22.

[4] Goulder, *Tale of Two Missions*. It is worth noting that Goulder identifies the Ebionites as "Possessionists," rather than as "Adoptionists," arguing that the Ebionites held that at his baptism the Spirit descended into Jesus and possessed him. In this book, I have used the term "Spirit-man Christology" in preference to "Possessionism."

composed, and since both record it, seemingly independently, then this view clearly did not originate with them. This means that the view that Jesus was only an adopted son of God, if it was the view of the earliest Christians, must have flourished, withered and been supplanted within a single generation. Or if, as seems likely, Paul held that Christ was more than an adoptive son of God, then this must be squeezed into an even tighter timeframe, since Paul's letters date from the 50s and 60s. This requires us to believe that those eyewitnesses to the life and sayings of Jesus did not object to these Christological developments, or else were not consulted, or else were somehow convinced to adjust their memories—all of which seem very unlikely.

When it comes to the evidence for this Adoptionist Christology that, supposedly, predates the New Testament texts, this evidence is not the New Testament texts themselves, but rather what scholars refer to as pre-literary traditions, that is, sayings, creeds or formulae that pre-date the New Testament texts but were incorporated within them. In terms of such pre-literary traditions that are purported to proclaim the adoption of Jesus, there are only a handful. Knox refers only to Acts 2:36.[5] Ehrman, who has no reason for restraint on this issue, cites only four texts that might reflect the idea that Jesus was adopted at his resurrection (Acts 2:36, 5:31, 13:32–33; Rom. 1:3–4). He cites a further two as evidence that Jesus was adopted as his baptism (Mark 1:9–11; textual variants of Luke 3:22).[6] J. C. O'Neill, who carefully considers all possible allusions to Adoptionism, would add only Acts 4:24–27 to this list.[7] In this chapter I will analyze each of these proposed Adoptionist texts and argue that none of these support the view that Adoptionism was the Christology of the earliest Christians.

HOW EARLY WERE THE EBIONITES?

It will be helpful at this point to briefly consider whether the existence of the Ebionites offers any support for the idea that the earliest Christology

---

[5] Knox, *Humanity and Divinity,* 7.
[6] Ehrman, *How Jesus Became God,* 218–41.
[7] O'Neill, *Who Did Jesus Think,* 14.

was Adoptionist. The earliest mention of the Ebionites comes from Irenaeus in the late second century. Broadly, there are two possible theories for understanding the Ebionites. Either they are the remnant of an earliest form of Christianity that had been supplanted by other forms, or they are a deviation from the earlier form(s) of Christianity.

In favor of the former alternative, there have been attempts to link the name "Ebionite" (from the Hebrew for poor) to the early Jerusalem church (cf. Rom. 15:26; Gal. 2:10), to link the asceticism of the Ebionites with that of the earliest Christians (cf. Acts 2),[8] and generally to connect the Jewish-Christian Ebionites with the Jewish-Christian church in Jerusalem. Yet none of these points provides much by way of strong confirmation of the thesis. There were many attempts by the heresiologists, as well as by modern scholars, to explain the origin of the term "Ebionite"; it is more often regarded by modern scholars as linking to a tradition of Jewish piety.[9] In any case, it is only conjecture that the Jerusalem church self-designated as "the poor." The Ebionites were hardly the only group to practice asceticism and the links between this asceticism and the community described in the early part of Acts are largely superficial. While "Ebionite" later became the name for any form of Jewish Christianity,[10] the Ebionites were hardly representative of all Jewish Christians in the second century. We know, at least, of a group called the Nazarenes whose Christology was never condemned by the heresiologists. There are also reports of a second group of Ebionites who *did* affirm the virgin birth (see Chapter Six). So Adoptionism cannot be regarded as characteristic of all early Jewish Christians.

The latter alternative, that Ebionism was a deviation from earlier forms of Christianity, derives significant support from the gospels used by the Ebionites. The gospel known as the *Gospel of the Ebionites* and preserved in quotations by Epiphanius was a Greek gospel that depended on the three canonical synoptics (Matthew, Mark and Luke), though

---

[8] Ehrman, *Lost Christianities*, 100.
[9] Häkkinen, "Ebionites," 247.
[10] Lichtenberger, "Syncretistic Features," 91.

omitting the virgin birth narrative.[11] The textual dependence of the *Gospel of Ebionites* on the synoptics is indicative of doctrinal dependence of the Ebionites upon earlier forms of Christianity. It seems that the Ebionites originated from a form of Christianity that affirmed the virgin birth and deviated from it.[12]

It may be objected that the *Gospel of the Ebionites* was not the earliest gospel used by the Ebionites. Irenaeus records that they used the Gospel of Matthew. However, this does not substantially alter the argument. If the Ebionites did use the Gospel of Matthew, or an edited version of it, then again, their denial of the virgin birth seems secondary to an earlier form of Christianity that affirmed it.

In earlier chapters I referred to the proposal of James Edwards that the gospel, ascribed variously to "the Hebrews," "the Nazarenes" and "the Ebionites," was the earliest gospel and is the source of *Special Luke* (i.e. the content unique to Luke's gospel).[13] On this proposal, the Ebionites used a gospel that was essentially similar to other Jewish Christians except that they had altered it to conform to their own views.[14] Since the *Hebrew Gospel* is likely to have contained a virgin birth narrative (see Chapter Sixteen) then the implications for the origins of the Ebionites are essentially the same. The Ebionites originated from a group who accepted the virgin birth and later deviated from that group altering their gospel to cohere with their views.

If the Ebionites, or at least their Adoptionist Christology, began in the second century, it is natural to suppose that they were reacting against the emergence of various speculations about the pre-existence of Jesus, including the Logos Christology of Justin and others. For these Jewish Christians, any sort of pre-existence may have been viewed as making Jesus in some sense divine and conflicted with monotheism. It is, therefore, conceivable they would have reacted by re-emphasizing that Jesus was "a

---

[11] Ehrman, *Lost Christianities,* 102. For the existing fragments see Elliott, *Apocryphal New Testament,* 14–16.

[12] See particularly Bauckham, "The Origin of the Ebionites," 162–81.

[13] See Edwards, *Hebrew Gospel.*

[14] *Medicine Chest,* 1:141, 143 (30.13.2–3; 30.14.5).

man born of men," as Justin would put it,[15] and concluded that this entailed that Jesus had a biological father.

The evidence we have strongly indicates that Ebionism was not the earliest form of Christianity but was a later deviation.

THE PRE-LITERARY TRADITIONS

Having dismissed the Ebionites, I now return to the purported pre-literary traditions and to whether they provide any evidence for early Adoptionism. Before proceeding, however, it will be useful to note some interpretative issues. When considering the question of adoption, it is important to ask: "Adopted to what?" In this chapter I am considering the view that Jesus' *sonship* was adoptive; that Jesus may have acquired new status at his resurrection, say, is not equivalent. For example, O'Neill argues that "all the terms that have been taken to imply God 'adopted' or 'chose out' Jesus for a new dignity refer without exception to his enthronement as King."[16] He reasons that the words used in these passages do not imply a change in the relationship between Jesus and God, but refer instead to "the public promulgation of his power."[17] He attempts to show that behind all the verses taken as indications of Adoptionism are four Old Testament passages that all have to do with the Israelite king.[18] Interestingly, Adela Collins would agree with O'Neill about the Old Testament precedent while disagreeing with his conclusion. Both O'Neill and Collins connect Jesus' sonship with his kingship, but O'Neill would argue that the earliest Christians had a divine Christology. It is evident that the New Testament writers believed that Jesus did ascend into heaven, and that his status was in this sense changed. Therefore, it is not sufficient to identify texts, pre-literary or not, that state that Jesus acquired new

---

[15] Justin, *Dialogue*, 73 (48.3).

[16] O'Neill, *Who Did Jesus Think*, 14.

[17] O'Neill, *Who Did Jesus Think*, 16.

[18] 2 Sam. 7:14 (Rom. 1:3–4), Ps. 2 (Luke 3:22, Acts 4:25–26, 13:13, Heb. 1:5, 5:5, Rev. 19:14), Ps. 8 (Matt. 21:6, 1 Cor. 15:27, Eph. 1:22, Heb. 2:6–8), Ps. 110 (Matt. 22:44, Mark 12:36, Luke 20:42–43, Acts 2:34–36, 1 Cor. 15:25, Heb. 1:13, 5:6, 7:17–21); O'Neill, *Who Did Jesus Think*, 14.

authority, power or status by his ascension. The issue is the sonship of Jesus and whence that derives.

The other consideration to bear in mind is that one's interpretation will differ depending on whether you believe being the "Son of God" is synonymous with being the "Christ." Given that William Wrede's thesis in his *Messianic Secret* that Jesus did not claim to be the Messiah is now thoroughly discredited and dismissed, if you regard "Christ" and "Son of God" as synonyms then you must regard Jesus as being Son of God prior to his resurrection. If, on the other hand, you think that these titles are not synonyms, then any passage mentioning only messianic status will be irrelevant to the question of sonship.

ACTS 2:36

"Let all the house of Israel therefore know for certain that God has made him both Lord and Christ, this Jesus whom you crucified." (Acts 2:36 ESV)

Luke ascribes these words to Peter on the day of Pentecost (Acts 2:14), but regardless of whether these words can be attributed to Peter, these words are regarded as pre-dating Luke's composition of Acts. These words are taken to affirm that Jesus was made Lord and Christ after his resurrection and ascension (Acts 2:32–33). The aorist tense of "made" is ambiguous and does not require that Jesus was made Christ after his ascension. Nevertheless, the logic of the passage would seem to be that the one murdered by the Jewish authorities has now been elevated to this new status.

Now this verse says nothing of sonship and so would only be evidence of Adoptionism if "Christ" and "Son of God" are synonyms. Yet in either case, this verse would seem to claim too much, since no one wants to say that Jesus did not claim to be Christ during his lifetime. When Peter says Jesus has been made Christ, he cannot mean that he was not Christ before. This verse comes at the end of Peter's speech in which he has argued that Jesus fulfilled the promise to David that one would sit on his throne (Acts 2:30) and that this one would sit at the right hand of God (Acts 2:34–35; cf. Ps 110:1). When Peter says Jesus *has been made* Lord and Christ, the most plausible reading is that Peter means that Jesus has now fulfilled that promise to David, and fulfilled his status as messiah, by now ascending to be enthroned at the right hand of God. Peter does not mean that Jesus was not the messiah before his ascension but that his messiahship was fulfilled by his ascension. Nothing like Adoptionism is implied.

ACTS 5:30–31

The God of our fathers raised Jesus, whom you killed by hanging him on a tree. God exalted him at his right hand as Leader and Savior, to give repentance to Israel and forgiveness of sins. (Acts 5:30–31 ESV)

Again, in the early preaching of Peter we find these words about Jesus being exalted to the right hand of God. Once again, these verses have nothing to do with sonship. Neither do these verses explicitly state that Jesus has *become* Leader and Savior, merely that Jesus *is* Leader and Savior. The emphasis of these words is on Jesus being exalted for the forgiveness of sins; if Peter thinks that Jesus has become a savior by his exaltation, he means that by his exaltation Jesus has saved people from their sins. This has nothing to do with adoption.

ACTS 13:32–33

And we bring you the good news that what God promised to the fathers, this he has fulfilled to us their children by raising Jesus, as also it is written in the second Psalm, "You are my Son, today I have begotten you." (Acts 13:32–33 ESV)

These words ascribed to Paul in Acts 13 are part of a speech where Paul seeks to demonstrate that the resurrection of Jesus fulfilled Scripture. One might therefore think it odd that Paul should use Psalm 2:7, which speaks of birth, as though it spoke of resurrection. This gives grounds for the

Adoptionist reading: Paul is saying that the day of Jesus' resurrection was the "today" on which Jesus was "begotten" as the Son of God.[19]

There is something odd about the proposal that these verses are evidence of Adoptionism. Those who make this proposal know that the author of Acts does not believe that Jesus became the Son of God by adoption. Nor do they think that the "real" Paul (i.e. the Paul of the epistles) believed that Jesus became the Son of God by adoption. The proposal is that Luke (or the anonymous author of Acts, if they prefer) composed the speech that he attributes to Paul, but incorporates within that speech this pre-literary Adoptionist tradition. This is a peculiar suggestion, that either Luke knew that this was an Adoptionist tradition but borrowed it anyway, or he did not know that this was an Adoptionist tradition and failed to spot that when he was copying it. Either case requires us to believe that Luke was very sloppy and did not take time or trouble to compose this speech about a central aspect of the gospel with care. Given the evident implausibility of such a procedure, it would be irresponsible to accept this proposal unless there really was no other explanation forthcoming.

Simon Gathercole argues that the Adoptionist reading is to interpret the words "woodenly" and fails to do justice to the way the New Testament writers cite the Old Testament. He argues that the New Testament writers do not always quote the Old Testament for a literal fulfilment, but sometimes merely for "suggestive similarities." In this case the suggestive similarity would be between the reversal of David's fortunes when he became king and Christ's reversal of fortunes when he was resurrected.[20] Interesting as this analysis is, it doesn't really explain why Paul should choose Ps. 2:7 in addition to his quotations from Is. 55:3 and Ps. 16:10, which speak more explicitly about the parallels with David.

A more satisfying explanation is forthcoming if we see Acts 13:33b–41 as a recapitulation of Acts 13:23–33a. Thus, when Paul introduces his quotation from Ps 2:7, he is not suggesting that this was fulfilled by the resurrection. After all, Paul explicitly introduces his next quotation as referring to the resurrection. Instead, his quotation of Ps 2:7 is a

[19] Ehrman, *How Jesus Became God*, 226.
[20] Gathercole, "What Did the First," 106–9.

counterpart of what Paul says in Acts 13:23, i.e. that God raised up a savior for Israel. Whether Paul here is primarily thinking of Jesus fulfilling Psalm 2 with regard to its ascription of divine sonship or its messianic aspect, there seems no reason for us to understand Paul as endorsing Adoptionism.

ROMANS 1:3–4

concerning his Son, who was descended from David according to the flesh and was declared to be the Son of God in power according to the Spirit of holiness by his resurrection from the dead, Jesus Christ our Lord." (Rom 1:3-4 ESV)

Scholars have long suspected that within these verses is an early Christian creed, given the closely paralleled structure of the six clauses. Ehrman presents these as follows:

A1 *Who was descended*
A2 *from the seed of David*
A3 *according to the flesh,*
B1 *who was appointed*
B2 *Son of God in power*
B3 *according to the Spirit of holiness by his resurrection from the dead* [21]

Other clues that this creed may not have originated with Paul are those elements of discontinuity with the rest of Paul's writings: the phrase "Spirit of holiness," which contrasts with Paul's preferred "Holy Spirit," and, it is argued, the descent of Jesus from David. This latter idea does not seem a particularly strong indication of discontinuity, since Paul undoubtedly understood Jesus to be the Messiah, and thus undoubtedly believed Jesus to be of the line of David (even if he doesn't explicitly mention this elsewhere). Nevertheless, that these clauses may have been a creed that pre-dated Paul's composition of Romans is plausible.

[21] Ehrman, *How Jesus Became God*, 220–21.

This creed would seem to imply Adoptionism. About the word *horisthentos,* Cranfield has pointed out that "no clear example, either earlier than, or contemporary with the NT, of its [the verb: *horizo*] use in the sense 'declare' or 'shown to be' has been adduced." He favors the translations "appoint" or "install."[22]

An early interpretation of this phrase, attested by the textual variant *prohoristhentou*[23] that is Jesus did not become Son of God at his resurrection, but was designated to that role earlier by the Holy Spirit. An alternative is to argue that through the resurrection Jesus achieved the recognition of humanity: that it was humanity (not the Holy Spirit) that designated Jesus Son of God at his resurrection. Neither solution does full justice to these words.

One solution advocated by several commentators focuses on the attribute of the Son: "with power." Jesus was already the Son of God—as implied by the previous clause "concerning his Son"—but after his resurrection he was "appointed the Son of God *with power.*"[24] Peter Stuhlmacher concurs, suggesting that Rom. 1:4 relates to passages (and particularly Ps. 110:1) that talk about Christ's exaltation to the right hand of God. He paraphrases the verse as saying that Jesus "was appointed to that appropriate sovereign rule which appertains to the Son of God."[25] Given that it was a common belief amongst the New Testament writers that Jesus was granted (greater) power from God after his ascension[26] (or after his resurrection),[27] it is not unreasonable to suppose this was Paul's meaning. Adela Collins, who takes both sets of clauses ("seed of David," "Son of God") as referring to Jesus as Messiah, argues that these verses imply that "Jesus was indeed the messiah of Israel during his lifetime, but

---

[22] Quoted Dunn, *Christology in the Making,* 34. Dunn himself takes a middle ground, stating "what is clear, on either alternative, is that the resurrection of Jesus was regarded as of central significance in determining his divine status" (35).

[23] Kittel, *Theological Dictionary,* 5:453.

[24] O'Neill, *Who Did Jesus Think,* 19; Kittel, *Theological Dictionary,* 5:453n.

[25] Stuhlmacher, *Letter to the Romans,* 19.

[26] *dunamis* ("power"): Matt. 24:30, Mark 13:26, Luke 21:27, 2 Thes. 1:7, Rev. 5:12–13; *pneuma* ("spirit"): Acts 2:33; also see Eph. 1:20–22, 1 Pet. 3:22.

[27] *dunamis*: Matt. 28:18.

only a messiah designate."[28] She argues that "Paul considers the epithet 'Son of God' to apply to Jesus in a stronger sense from the moment of his resurrection."[29]

A number of scholars, including Ehrman, have argued that the original creed did not include the words "in power," that these were added by Paul to avoid the Adoptionist implication of the creed. Gathercole rightly describes the argument here as viciously circular: the words "in power" are assumed to be an insertion because they disrupt the Adoptionist reading, the very thing that is in question.[30] It might be argued that the words "in power" lessen the contrast between the clauses A2 and B2, so that the original is less likely to have included them. Yet by the same logic the words "by his resurrection from the dead" should also be seen as a later addition and so we might reconstruct the creed as follows:

> He was descended from the seed of David, according to the flesh
> He was appointed the Son of God, according to the Spirit of holiness
> Jesus Christ our Lord.

This reconstruction seems at least a plausible as any other (and the exercise is a matter of conjecture, however one slices it), but is not Adoptionist, as it does not make the sonship of Jesus contingent on any one event. Therefore, to find a pre-Pauline Adoptionist creed in these verses requires predetermining one's conjecture. Once again, there is something significantly odd about the idea that Paul willfully incorporates an Adoptionist creed into his text after sanitizing it to change its implication. Was Paul really so feeble a rhetorician that he needed to borrow words from traditions he manifestly disagreed with?

The contrast in these verses is between Jesus "according to the flesh" and "according to the Spirit." Elsewhere Paul uses this contrast in two ways. One is about a way of life, either "according to the flesh" (i.e. following the promptings of sinful human nature) or "according to the Spirit" (see Rom. 8:4ff). The other is the contrast between Ishmael, "born

---

[28] Collins & Collins, *King and Messiah*, 117.
[29] Collins & Collins, *King and Messiah*, 117.
[30] Gathercole, "What Did the First," 105.

according to the flesh" (Gal. 4:23) and Isaac "born according the Spirit" (Gal. 4:29), or according to the promise (Gal. 4:23); that is, one was born according to the natural way of things, and the other was born according to the plan and purpose of God. We find a similar contrast elsewhere in Romans where Paul describes Jews as "my kinsman according to the flesh" (Rom. 9:3) and Christ as being descended from the Israelites "according to the flesh" (Rom. 9:5). The implication is that, as well as natural Jews, there are spiritual Jews; those who are Jews, not according to the flesh, but according to the Spirit (that is, by the will of God). The contrast Paul affirms in Rom. 1:3–4 is that Jesus fulfilled the criteria of messiahship by natural descent but, more than that, was Son of God by the will of God. Regardless of whether a pre-Pauline creed is the foundation of Rom. 1:3–4, there is no evidence for Adoptionism here.

MARK 1:9–11

In those days Jesus came from Nazareth of Galilee and was baptized by John in the Jordan. And when he came up out of the water, immediately he saw the heavens being torn open and the Spirit descending on him like a dove. And a voice came from heaven, "You are my beloved Son; with you I am well pleased." (Mark 1:9–11 ESV)

It is sometimes argued that Mark presents Jesus as being adopted as Son of God at his baptism. Some measure of credence might be given to this proposal from the fact that a number of heretical groups from the late first or early second century seem to have identified Jesus' baptism as the moment when an ordinary man became something special, though usually by the descent of a spiritual being into Jesus.

The adoption of Jesus as Son of God at his baptism does not find precedent in the Old Testament usage of the phrase "Son of God," since Jesus' baptism was not his coronation. Adela Collins argues that "you are my beloved Son" is an allusion to Ps. 2:7, and this allusion carries the implication that "God thus appoints Jesus as messiah at the time of his baptism by John."[31] However, given that the baptism was not a coronation, and given that none of the other words in the psalm are used, it is not clear how one can securely identify "you are my . . . son" as an allusion. Which words would God have used if he were *not* alluding to Psalm 2? If Mark was seeking to present an allusion to Psalm 2, he would not have added "beloved."

An allusion to Psalm 2 would have made the baptismal account appear Adoptionist, implying that day was the "today" when God begat Jesus. But the absence of any such allusion, the account is neutral as to Adoptionism. To read God's declaration from heaven as a statement of adoption goes beyond the text. God does not say to Jesus "I am making you my son" or "today you have become my son" but simply "you are my son," says nothing about when Jesus became the Son.

The only redeeming feature of the Adoptionist reading of Mark's baptismal record is that Mark's gospel does not provide any alternative explanation for how or when Jesus became the Son of God. It is simply affirmed that this is the case.

LUKE 3:22 [TEXTUAL VARIANTS]

"and the Holy Spirit descended on him in bodily form, like a dove; and a voice came from heaven, "You are my Son; today I have begotten you.""

This variant is attested by one Greek manuscript (*Bezae Cantabrigiensis* [D]), seven Old Latin manuscripts, and a selection of patristic quotations.[32] The variant is, therefore, not strongly attested, and it is often explained as a unconscious substitution of the original reading with the words of Ps. 2:7. Ehrman makes the case for this variant to have been the original. Firstly, amongst the patristic sources of the second and third centuries this is virtually the only reading found. Secondly, the majority reading can be explained as an attempt to harmonize Luke with the other gospels. Thirdly, Ehrman attempts to argue that the variant

---

[31] Collins & Collins, *King and Messiah*, 127.
[32] Swanson, *Greek Manuscripts: Luke*, 54.

reading is more consistent with Luke's theology, but inconsistent with later orthodox theology.[33]

Yet regardless of whether this variant was original or not, it is manifestly not evidence for Adoptionism. Luke is commonly held to have drawn from Mark's gospel, and Mark's account of Jesus' baptism did not include this quotation of Ps. 2:7. If this variant was original, then Luke has consciously changed the account to make God's declaration a quotation of Ps. 2:7. And if he did that, it was not because he believed Jesus was adopted as the Son of God at his baptism, because Luke believes that Jesus was the Son of God as a consequence of his birth (Luke 1:35). In any case, if this variant was original, then it was original *to Luke's gospel*, and so represents what Luke thought at the point of composition. Because it differs from what Mark said earlier (and from what Matthew records) it clearly does not represent the views of earlier Christians. So, whatever the case with this variant, it provides no evidence for early Christian Adoptionism.

ACTS 4:27

"For truly in this city there were gathered together against your holy servant Jesus, whom you anointed, both Herod and Pontius Pilate, along with the Gentiles and the peoples of Israel" (Acts 4:27 ESV).

One final passage to consider is Acts 4:27, where the apostles say that Jesus was anointed of God. Collins presents this as a reference to Jesus' baptism.[34]

This verse says nothing of sonship or adoption. It says only that Jesus was anointed by God, something that it is unsurprising given that Jesus was called "the Christ," the anointed one. These verses do not allude to Jesus' baptism, nor do they give any chronological marker for his anointing. Even if these verses are referring to Jesus being anointed with

[33] Ehrman, *Orthodox Corruption*, 73–79.
[34] Collins & Collins, *King and Messiah*, 146.

the Holy Spirit at his baptism, there is no support for Adoptionism in that.

CONCLUSION

In this chapter I have reviewed all the purported evidence that is adduced for the claim that the earliest Christians believed Jesus became the Son of God by adoption. None of the proposed evidence stands up to scrutiny. In the absence of any evidence, we have no reason to conclude that the earliest Christians were Adoptionists. If they did not believe that Jesus was the adopted son of God, then they must have understood the sonship of Jesus in some other sense. For many early Christians, Jesus was the Son of God because of his miraculous birth (Luke 1:35; Matt. 2:15). In the next chapter I will explore whether belief in the virgin birth dates back to the earliest Christians.

CHAPTER 16

How Early is Belief in the Virgin Birth?

I T IS A COMMONLY REPEATED CLAIM that belief in the virgin birth was not part of the original Christian preaching and was a later invention. The claim is based upon the idea that the virgin birth is absent from Mark's gospel and the letters of Paul, and is not attested until the gospels of Matthew and Luke. Given that these two gospels are traditionally dated later than Mark's gospel and the letters of Paul, the appearance is given that the virgin birth arrives late on the scene.

This reconstruction parallels another common proposal that the earliest Christologies did not hold Jesus to be the Son of God by birth but only by adoption (or even, didn't regard Jesus as the Son of God at all). It fits this "evolutionary" paradigm to argue that belief in the virgin birth was a later invention. But does this chronology of doctrine have any basis in fact? How early is belief in the virgin birth?

DATING MATTHEW'S GOSPEL

Scholarly convention requires one to nod politely at the consensus that Mark's gospel was written c.70 and the other synoptics c.80 or perhaps a little later. Having paid our dues to convention, we may examine the evidence and comment on the oddity of taking as near axiomatic something that stands on such shaky foundations.

If it is argued that the Olivet Prophecy requires a date of composition after the destruction of Jerusalem, then we are presented with an implied scenario whereby the evangelist, writing, it is supposed, a decade or more after that fateful event, attributed to Jesus the prediction that "*immediately* after the tribulation of those days" the Parousia would occur (Matt. 24:29). So, either the evangelist sees no problem with attributing an obvious falsehood to Jesus, or we should dispense with such absurdity and conclude that the destruction of Jerusalem had not yet occurred. Even if we denied the possibility of predictive prophecy and the authority of Jesus to issue such, it would nevertheless be no great stretch for any Jew in the early first century to observe the political situation and issue the warning about where events were headed (if indeed that is what Jesus was doing).

If it is argued that Matthew's gospel is not cited in other early Christian writings then, first, we must respond that it is,[1] and second, we must ask why would one think it should be. Textual citation presupposes not only a readily available copy to cite from but also knowledge of the same book by the readers of that citation. It is reasonable to suppose that there was a transitional period between the composition of any text and the time when it became useful for textual citations. Yet even if we suppose that no such transitional period was necessary and that the New Testament writers would have taken a freshly penned gospel and cited it immediately, is the absence of citation a reliable indicator that a book was not yet composed?

Take Paul's pastoral letters, which, if authentic, probably date from the early 60s. The UBS 4th edition indexes only two quotations from this corpus (Deut. 25:4 / 1 Tim. 5:18; Num. 16:5 / 2 Tim. 2:19); can such a sample be taken as indicative of anything? Ironically, the quotation that the UBS does not index is from a synoptic gospel (Luke 10:7 / 1 Tim. 5:18). So, should one conclude that Paul (or the pseudonymous writer) had no acquaintance with Matthew's gospel, because out of three quotations he did not include one from Matthew? Or should we conclude that this argument from silence is almost worthless?

---

[1] *Epistle of Barnabas*, 25 (4:14).

Looking at the positive evidence for dating Matthew's gospel, it is worth reiterating the observation that the evangelist seems to imply that the temple is still standing, that the temple cult is still in operation, and that the parting of ways with Judaism has yet to occur (Matt. 5:23–24, 12:5–7; 17:24–27). J. A. T. Robinson writes,

> Matthew's gospel shows all the signs of being produced for a community (and by a community) that needed to formulate, over against the main body of Pharisaic and Sadduceeic Judaism, its own line on such issues.[2]

Moreover, Robinson notes that this most Jewish of gospels lacks any echo of the martyrdom of James (c. 62) or any prominence given to his successor Simeon.[3] John Wenham draws attention to Matthew's apologetic regarding the report that the disciples stole the body, which, the evangelist says, is still commonly told by the Jews "until this day" (Matt. 28:15). While it is true that this report was told and mythologized by the Jews for centuries afterwards, the only reason for Matthew to defend against such a report is if it was detracting from the evidence of the empty tomb. Wenham observes,

> As serious apologetic this extra evidence would have had limited value outside Jerusalem, but in Jerusalem itself in the early days the story would have been known to almost everyone, and the true version of the story would carry weight.[4]

These indicators would place Matthew's gospel more naturally in the 50s or early 60s.

It is worth noting, though it has not been widely accepted, the proposal of Carsten Peter Thiede that the Magdalen Papyrus, which preserves fragments of Matt. 26, should be dated no later than c. 66.[5] If his

---

[2] Robinson, *Redating*, 103.
[3] Robinson, *Redating*, 106.
[4] Wenham, *Redating*, 243.
[5] Thiede and D'Ancona, *The Jesus Papyrus*.

paleographic analysis is accepted, then the composition of Matthew's gospel must be dated to the early 60s at the latest.

One's answer to the question of the literary relationship between the synoptic gospels is also a factor in dating those gospels. If, as is generally supposed, Mark was written first and the other synoptics depended on this gospel, then Matthew's gospel must post-date Mark (generally dated c. 70). Yet this proposal is not universally accepted. John Rist, for example, has argued for the independence of Matthew and Mark; he proposes a date for both between 60 and 70. [6] Wenham has proposed that the three synoptics draw separately from a shared tradition and has defended the priority of Matthew, as was universally affirmed before the modern era. He argues that Luke was already well-known by the mid-50s,[7] that Mark was written following Peter's first visit to Rome in the early 40s, and so dates Matthew to c.40.[8] Robinson, though accepting a more conventional solution to the synoptic question, still dates the composition of Matthew to around 40–60.[9]

Therefore, while nodding politely at the typically assumed c. 80 date of composition, it seems more probable that Matthew's gospel dates to several decades earlier. Let us then, for sake of argument, date Matthew's gospel to c. 60 (though I see no strong reason why it could not be earlier).

DATING LUKE'S GOSPEL

When we come to date Luke's gospel, much of the argumentation is similar. We nod politely at the scholarly consensus that would date the composition c. 80 and then proceed to reject the arguments upon which this consensus is based (see above).

There are two additional arguments to consider. Firstly, Luke ends Acts with Paul dwelling in prison for "two whole years" (Acts 28:30). Two whole years till when? Not his death (c. 66); Luke makes no mention of that, nor of his appearance before Caesar, though that would be the

[6] Rist, *Independence*, 106.
[7] One piece of evidence for this is 1 Tim. 5:18, which appears to quote Luke 10:7.
[8] Wenham, *Redating*, 243.
[9] Robinson, *Redating*, 352.

natural terminus for his narrative arc. So why end there? The conclusion that seems so obvious to many scholars (and yet is strangely considered insignificant to many others) is that Luke ends there because the rest hadn't happened yet. And if that is the case then that provides a (relatively) small window in which Acts could have been composed (Robinson gives 57–62).[10] And given that Acts is a sequel to Luke (cf. Acts 1:1) then Luke must pre-date Acts (though perhaps not by much).

The second consideration is the quotation of Luke's gospel in 1 Tim. 5:18. If 1 Timothy is authentic, then it dates from sometime between 55 and Paul's martyrdom c. 66. If 1 Timothy is pseudonymous, then it dates no later than its earliest citation (c. 110).[11]

Therefore, once again we nod politely at the c.80 date of composition, but judge that c. 60 is more likely and, for sake of this argument, accept that date.

GOSPEL SOURCES

We must not suppose that by dating Matthew and Luke we have thereby dated the origin of belief in the virgin birth. These contain not one virgin birth narrative but two, and laying aside the staggering coincidence that two evangelists invented the same conception, we must conclude that the idea did not originate with them both individually. There must be some interrelationship between the two narratives.

The relationship between Matthew and Luke is disputed (the synoptic question) and I do not propose to settle the question here. Rather I will explore what each of the major alternatives would mean for the virgin birth narrative.

---

[10] *Redating,* 352.

[11] Polycarp, *Letter to the Philippians,* 337–39, 351 (4.1, 12.3). See also Gaston, "When Did the New Testament."

THE FARRER THEORY

The theory that postulates the greatest level of dependence between Matthew and Luke is the Farrer theory, more recently defended by Michael Goulder and Mark Goodacre. According to this theory, Mark is the earliest gospel; Matthew depends on Mark and Luke depends on these two.[12] The implication for the infancy narratives is that Luke was aware of Matthew's account when he penned his own. Goulder proposed that both Matthew and Luke simply invented incidents, like the infancy narratives. However, Rist responds arguing that even had Matthew invented his infancy narrative, it is unlikely that Luke, depending on Matthew, would have done so.[13] Knight claims that "Luke writes with a knowledge of Matthew's Gospel" as the source of the virginal conception, though he makes no visible attempt to show how the one account could be derived from the other.[14] Given the differences between the two narratives, this would mean that either Luke chose to edit out Matthew's account in favor of another source, or else to deliberately alter Matthew's account for narrative purposes.

There is very little that is similar between Matthew's and Luke's accounts, which suggests it is unlikely that Luke is using Matthew's as a base. Parrinder writes "Luke writes blithely in ignorance or disregard of Matthew."[15] It would be odd for Luke to ignore Matthew's infancy narrative, given Luke follows (on the Farrer theory) Matthew nearly word-for-word in places. It is not obvious that Luke's theological purposes would lead him to so utterly reject Matthew's account. The possibility that Luke is using another source for his infancy narrative looks more promising but still does not explain why Luke chose to reject all of Matthew's account, except perhaps that he found this approach easier than trying to integrate the two accounts. Perhaps then we have reason to be skeptical about the Farrer approach.

---

[12] Goodacre, *Case against Q*, 152–69.

[13] Rist, *On the Independence*, 110.

[14] Knight, *Luke's Gospel*, 73.

[15] Parrinder, *Son of Joseph*, 27.

At any rate, on the Farrer theory, Luke, writing with knowledge of Matthew's account, chose to change every part of the narrative except the central core. Both accounts record that Mary was a virgin,[16] that Jesus was conceived by the Holy Spirit,[17] the angelic prescription of the name "Jesus,"[18] his birth in Bethlehem,[19] the fact that Mary was betrothed (not married),[20] and the name of her fiancée ("Joseph").[21] If Luke felt so free as to change every other part of Matthew's account then we must provide some reason why Luke felt compelled to preserve this core. And the most straightforward explanation is that he knew this core from some other tradition in addition to Matthew's account.

Drawing out the implications, if we date Luke to c. 60 (see above) then, on the Farrer theory, Matthew must be dated earlier. Let us assign a gap of five years and date Matthew c. 55. If, as I have argued above, there must also have been another tradition or source known to Luke, this would be of unknown date and provenance; let us assign the same date of c. 55 to this tradition. Since Matthew and this other tradition have a shared core, the belief in the virgin birth could not have originated with either, if they are truly independent. Therefore, belief in the virgin birth must pre-date both. Let us assign a gap of five years, and say that this belief dates to c.50.

TWO-SOURCE THEORY

The majority view regarding the synoptic question is that Matthew and Luke are independent of each other but draw on two shared sources: Mark and (the hypothetical) Q. This theory derives from the observation that both Matthew and Luke replicate much that is in Mark and that they also parallel each other in passages not present in Mark. This non-Markan overlap is thought to be derived from a hypothesized source dubbed "Q"

---

[16] Matt. 1:23–25; Luke 1:27, 34.

[17] Matt. 1:18, 20; Luke 1:35.

[18] Matt. 1:21; Luke 1:31.

[19] Matt. 2:1, Luke 2:4.

[20] Matt. 1:18; Luke 1:27, 2:5.

[21] Matt. 1:19; Luke 1:27, 2:4.

by modern scholars. Grand claims have been made for *Q*; it has been called the "lost gospel,"[22] the "first gospel,"[23] and the authentic teaching of Jesus.[24] For some scholars *Q*, or its earliest redaction, is their core for reconstructing the historical Jesus.[25] Yet it always must be remembered that *Q* is a *postulated* source, not a discovered one, and anything said about *Q* is conjecture based purely upon textual overlap between two gospels. As Craig Evans writes, "scholars say far too much about the hypothetical source."[26]

Mark does not include an infancy narrative, but might *Q* have included one? The simple answer: is we cannot know. We are not able to determine the true extent of *Q*, assuming that it existed at all. As Evans has argued, if we attempted to reconstruct Mark based upon overlap between Matthew and Luke we would recover only around 60% of the gospel, even though 80% is attested, and important sections would be lost.[27] If, say, Matthew depended on *Q* for his infancy narrative and Luke did not (for whatever reason), then there would be no overlap, and hence no evidence for the presence of this narrative in *Q*.

It is sometimes argued that *Q* was a sayings gospel, based upon comparison with the *Gospel of Thomas*[28] and the common scholarly assumption that the earliest records of Jesus would be a collection of sayings. However, the overlap between Matthew and Luke is not purely sayings (e.g. Luke 4:13), so we cannot rule out the possibility that *Q* included narrative passages. (It is not clear why one would think that *Thomas* is representative of the earliest gospel form when it evidently was *not* earlier than canonical gospels).[29] So we cannot rule out the possibility that *Q* (if such a source existed) contained an infancy narrative. And if (for

---

[22] Mack, *Lost Gospel.*

[23] Jacobson, *First Gospel.*

[24] For a synopsis of the claims made for *Q* see Goodacre, *Case Against Q*, 1–7.

[25] Crossan, *Historical Jesus.*

[26] Evans, "Authenticating," 6.

[27] Evans, "Authenticating," 7–10.

[28] For the remaining fragments of the *Gospel of Thomas* see Elliot, Apocryphal New Testament, 135–47.

[29] The general scholarly consensus is that the *Gospel of Thomas* dates to the mid-2nd century (Elliott, *Apocryphal New Testament*, 124).

some reason unfathomable to me) we judge that Q must be earlier than Mark, then the possibility that it included an infancy narrative is highly significant. But as I have said, anything we say about Q is at best reasonable conjecture, and at worst, groundless speculation.

Let us suppose that neither Mark nor Q contained an infancy narrative; whence came Matthew and Luke's infancy narratives? It might be proposed that neither evangelist had a source for what they wrote, despite the fact that according to the two-source theory they both depended heavily on sources for the majority of their respective gospels. Yet this proposal is immediately rendered untenable by the shared core between the two narratives. However creative the two evangelists might have been, it is necessary to suppose that they shared a source according to which Jesus was conceived by the Holy Spirit in the womb of the virgin Mary, who was betrothed to Joseph, and that his birth took place in Bethlehem and that his name was given by an angel. And if that source is not Mark (evidently) or Q then it is some third source/tradition.[30]

However, if this third source was a written source upon which both Matthew and Luke depended, then we once again encounter the problem that their two accounts are so different. We might speculate that, say, Matthew followed the source closely and that Luke only followed the source loosely, but then once again it is left inexplicable why Luke should depend upon a source and yet deviate so widely from it. The more promising alternative is that there was more than one source.

A rival to the two-source solution to the synoptic question is the four-source solution that posits that there were two other sources, in addition to Mark and Q, that the evangelists used. Thus, Matthew depended on another hypothesized source "M" for the material unique to his gospel, and Luke depended on yet another hypothesized source "L" for the material unique to his gospel. It is generally supposed that M, if it existed, contained a number of parables, and that L, if it existed, contained narrative sections and some sayings. Yet, in fact, we can only guess at the full extent of these hypothetical sources. If they were, in any sense, cohesive gospels (that is, something analogous to the synoptics) then it is

---

[30] Evans, *Commentary: Luke*, 22.

entirely plausible that they might have included an infancy narrative. Or, if it is judged their style and form make it unlikely that they contained infancy narratives (and I don't know how one reliably makes those judgments) then we are left to speculate about some other sources or traditions that formed the basis of these narratives.

Again, drawing out the implications, if we date both Luke and Matthew to c. 60 (see above) then the source(s) on which they depend for their infancy narratives must be earlier. Following the procedure above, let us guess a gap of five years, and so date Q, M, L or any other written source for the infancy narratives to c. 55. As we have argued above, it is unlikely that Matthew and Luke can have used the same source for their narratives (given their clear differences), yet given the shared core between these narratives the belief in the virgin birth must pre-date both sources (whatever they were). Again, assigning a notional gap of five years, let us say that the belief must date, at least, to c. 50.

ORAL TRADITION

A third form of solution to the synoptic question is the proposal that, rather than depending one upon another, the evangelists wrote independently, using an oral tradition. It should not be assumed that "oral" means vague. Indeed, for this proposal to work requires that the tradition is stable and consistent. (How else would it explain the close similarity between the synoptics?)

There are various approaches to this theory. For example, Rist proposes that Matthew and Mark are independent, working from the same oral tradition(s), but that Luke depended on these prior gospels, whereas Wenham proposes that all three evangelists worked independently from the same tradition. Yet the point of significance is that according to these theories, there was a body of oral tradition predating the synoptic gospels upon which these gospels drew, and that oral tradition would include the infancy narratives.

Attempting to date something as amorphous as a hypothetical oral tradition is impossible. Suffice to say that it must pre-date Matthew (say, pre-60), and at least some of that tradition must pre-date Mark. Whether the infancy narrative was an oral tradition prior to Mark's composition is impossible to determine, but it would be arbitrary to rule it out.

MATTHEAN PRIORITY

We can briefly mention those theories by Augustine and by Griesbach that posit Matthew as the earliest gospel on which the other two depend.[31] Because Matthew contains an infancy narrative, on these theories the virgin birth forms part of the earliest known gospel tradition.

HEBREW GOSPEL

Finally, it is important to mention here the theory of James Edwards, referred to elsewhere in this book, that a gospel written in Hebrew, known through citations by early Christian writers, is the basis of *Special Luke* (i.e. the content unique to Luke's gospel). This theory is significant for the present question because of the likelihood that the *Hebrew Gospel* contained a virgin birth narrative, though Edwards himself does not comment on this. My reasons for thinking that the *Hebrew Gospel* contained a virgin birth narrative are threefold.

Firstly, if, as per Edwards's proposal, Luke's dependence on the *Hebrew Gospel* explains the high level of Semitisms[32] in *Special Luke* then it seems likely that the *Hebrew Gospel* must be the source of Luke's infancy narrative, which contains a high concentration of Semitisms.[33] None of the patristic citations of the *Hebrew Gospel* contain part of an infancy narrative, but one does include reference to John the Baptist being "of the lineage of Aaron the priest, the son of Zacharias and Elizabeth."[34] These

---

[31] For a summary of the history of proposed solutions to the "synoptic problem" see Goodacre, *Synoptic Problem*, 13–32.

[32] That is, peculiarities of Luke's Greek which suggest having been translated from a Semitic language such as Hebrew or Aramaic.

[33] See Edwards, *Hebrew Gospel*, 294–99.

[34] Epiphanius, *Medicine Chest*, 142 (30.13.6).

are not details contained within any canonical gospel except Luke's infancy narrative,[35] suggesting dependence in one direction or other. Edwards also notes that one citation repeats verbatim the words of Luke 1:5 ("It came to pass in the days of Herod, King of Judaea"),[36] again implying dependence.

Secondly, Epiphanius says that the Ebionites had altered the *Hebrew Gospel* and specifically altered its beginning;[37] he says that

> They falsify the genealogical tables in Matthew's Gospel and make its opening... "It came to pass in the days of Herod, king of Judaea, in the high-priesthood of Caiaphas, that a certain man, John by name, came baptizing.. ." This is because they maintain that Jesus is really a man ... but that the Christ, who descended in the form of a dove, has entered him ... <and> been united with him.[38]

One possibility might be that Epiphanius is mistakenly comparing the canonical Matthew with the *Hebrew Gospel*, and assumes that the differences must be due to alteration. However, Epiphanius does seem to be aware of the *Hebrew Gospel* from others than the Ebionites, so he would be in a position to make comparisons between the *Hebrew Gospel* and the altered version of the Ebionites.[39] Therefore Edwards argues that when Epiphanius claims that the Ebionites removed the beginning of the *Hebrew Gospel* he does so on the basis of comparison with a version that contained that beginning.[40] This is another indication that the *Hebrew Gospel* contained an infancy narrative.

Thirdly, we do have some indications from the patristic citations of the *Hebrew Gospel* which, while not from an infancy narrative, would be consistent with the idea that the *Hebrew Gospel* contained such a narrative. Specifically, in his commentary on the passage, Jerome interprets Isaiah

[35] Edwards, *Hebrew Gospel*, 69.
[36] Epiphanius, *Medicine Chest*, 142 (30.14.3); Edwards, *Hebrew Gospel*, 72.
[37] *Medicine Chest*, 141–42 (30.13.2–3, 30.13.4–6).
[38] *Medicine Chest*, 142 (30.14.3–4).
[39] *Medicine Chest*, 133 (30.3.8–9).
[40] Edwards, *Hebrew Gospel*, 27.

11:1–2 as referring to the virgin birth, seeing Mary as the root of Jesse. In this context he cites a passage from *Hebrew Gospel*, where the Holy Spirit, descending on Jesus at his baptism, refers to him as her "firstborn son"; Jerome sees this as fulfilling Isaiah 11:2.[41] Unlike us, Jerome had the full text of the *Hebrew Gospel* in front of him; the fact that he cites it in connection with the virgin birth may indicate this gospel supported this idea. Elsewhere in that gospel, the Spirit is presented as Jesus' mother,[42] which to modern readers might seem inconsistent with the idea that Mary was Jesus' mother; Jerome did not see this as an issue. In Hebrew, the word spirit is feminine.

Now if the *Hebrew Gospel* contained a virgin birth narrative, and if Luke is dependent on this gospel for his virgin birth narrative, then the *Hebrew Gospel* must be dated earlier than Luke's gospel. If we date Luke's gospel to c. 60, then assigning our estimated gap of 5 years, we would date the *Hebrew Gospel* to c. 55. Since the virgin birth narratives contained in canonical Matthew and the *Hebrew Gospel*, we are supposing, are different but have a shared core, there must be some shared source between them, which we can date, with our presumed gap, to c. 50.

However, we may be able to go further than that. There are repeated patristic statements that the first gospel was written by Matthew in Hebrew.[43] This claim has often been rejected on the assumption that it refers to the canonical Matthew, which is considered by many scholars to be dependent on Mark's gospel. Yet if these statements refer to the *Hebrew Gospel*, and not canonical Matthew, then the supposed difficulty disappears. If these statements are correct, then the *Hebrew Gospel* must predate Mark's.[44]

[41] Edwards, *Hebrew Gospel*, 90–91.

[42] In his commentary on the gospel according to John, Origen mentions "the Gospel according to the Hebrews, where the Savior himself says, 'My mother, the Holy Spirit, took me just now by one of my hairs and carried me off to the great mountain Thabor.' " (Origen, *Commentary on John*, 116 [2.87]).

[43] Eusebius, *Ecclesiastical History*, 114, 130, 226, (3.24, 3.39, 6.25); Jerome, *On Illustrious Men*, 10 (3.1–2); *Commentary on Matthew*, 53 (Preface, 2).

[44] Irenaeus gives a different testimony: "Matthew . . . produced a writing of the Gospel among the Hebrews in their own language, whereas Peter and Paul evangelized at Rome

DATING MARK

What can we conclude from all of this? I have sought to explain the shared core between the Lukan and Matthaean infancy narratives based upon the different proposed solutions to the synoptic question. We cannot rule out the possibility that Matthew simply made up his infancy narrative and Luke took only the core of Matthew's infancy narrative when he made up his own, but it does not seem particularly likely (for reasons explained above). The more likely alternative is that both Matthew and Luke drew on other written sources (whether gospels or separate narratives). Yet if Matthew and Luke had separate sources, then we still need to explain the shared core between these sources, and that (on most theories) requires a two-stage process.

I have, for sake of argument, dated Luke c. 60. I have then assigned a notional gap of five years between sources and, on that basis, argued that belief in the virgin birth must date to at least c. 50. These figures are all notional but take on special significance for the question of the absence of the infancy narrative in Mark. If Luke (and/or Matthew) depends on Mark, then given the goose/gander sauce equivalency, we should assign the same notional five year gap and date Mark c. 55, that is, we should date the composition of Mark after the origin of the belief in the virgin birth. It may be felt that the five-year gap is too meager, and that Mark should be dated earlier but, given this criterion alone, we should also date Matthew and Luke's sources earlier. Only based on indications independent of our present considerations would it be justified to date Mark earlier. Indeed, some scholars think there are such indicators and have dated Mark as early as c. 45.[45] Yet if we date Mark earlier, then we have no strong reason to date Matthew as late as c. 60, so the conclusion persists. Similarly, if we reject the early date for Matthew and Luke proposed above and choose to follow conventional dates (i.e. c. 80) then

---

and founded the Church [there]." (Irenaeus, *Against the Heresies (Book 3)*, 30 [3.1.1]). If Peter and Paul preached in Rome, this is more likely to have occurred in the late 50s or early 60s.

[45] See Crossley, *Date of Mark's Gospel*.

we do not destroy the conclusion, because given a two stage source process, belief in the virgin birth can be dated as early as the conventional date for Mark's gospel (i.e. c. 70).

The only way to escape the conclusion that belief in the virgin birth pre-dates the composition of Mark's gospel is to suppose that Matthew and Luke, or their immediate sources, fabricated their infancy narratives without prior traditions. We cannot rule out the possibility that Matthew fabricated his infancy narrative and then Luke changed all but the bare bones for his own (on the Farrer theory). Nor can we rule out the possibility that one author invented the virgin birth, that it was then incorporated into two separate narratives and that these narratives were copied by Matthew and Luke (on the Two/Four-Source theory). But the fact that we cannot rule it out does not make it likely, because either proposal imagines at least two stages of fabrication.

Nor does this hypothesized fabrication have significant explanatory power when trying to explain the origin of belief in the virgin birth. As Davies argued, it is difficult to explain the origin of this belief if it was not common amongst the early Christians, since it does not derive from either pagan or Jewish sources. Matthew's text does not draw on Hellenistic biographical form of the semi-divine Greek heroes as is sometimes naively proposed.[46] Nor does Matthew base the virginal conception solely on the Hebrew scriptures; "the Isaiah prophecies themselves, read in their own context, could hardly have given rise to an expectation of a miraculous conception."[47] Though Matthew certainly uses the Old Testament to justify his story to a Jewish audience,[48] this is certainly not the origin of his account of Jesus' miraculous conception. France goes further, stating that the Old Testament passages are so far from prompting the Matthean narrative that "it is hard to see why they should ever have been introduced

---

[46] Davies, *Matthew*, 31. Another commenter observes that "Suggestions that the tradition derives from pagan stories of gods having intercourse with women ignore both the quite different tone of such stories, and the impossibility of their being accepted in a Palestinian Jewish setting; yet the Gospel accounts are both intensely Jewish in their context and expression" (France, *Matthew*, 76).

[47] Davies, *Matthew*, 34.

[48] "the aim of the formula-quotations in chapter 2 seems to be primarily apologetic" (France, *Matthew*, 71).

into a Christian account of Jesus' origins"[49] unless the story was already circulating that Jesus was born of a virgin. Therefore, we can provide no explanation as to why Matthew would choose to fabricate the virgin birth, nor why Luke should choose to fabricate a similar story (either in ignorance of Matthew's account or in disregard of it).

If we conclude that it is too unlikely that both Matthew and Luke composed their infancy narratives without prior sources, then we are forced to conclude that belief in the virgin birth pre-dates Mark's gospel, and it follows that the absence of an infancy narrative in Mark's gospel cannot be taken as evidence that belief in the virgin birth is a late invention.

ABSENCE IN MARK'S GOSPEL

Why then is there no infancy narrative in Mark's gospel? One possibility we must consider is that belief in the virgin birth was not universal. After all, we have insufficient evidence from this period to guarantee the universality of all Christian doctrine in this period. Perhaps some Christians believed in the virgin birth while others did not; perhaps Mark was one of the ones who didn't. Yet he gives no hint that he is arguing against this belief, nor does he present any opposing infancy or genealogical information. He does not, as later the Ebionites would do, claim that Jesus was the son of Joseph, as we might expect were he seeking to contradict the virgin birth.

Another possibility might be that though belief in the virgin birth was extant, Mark was simply unaware of it. Perhaps he had received no tradition, either way, as to Jesus' origins and so did not comment on this issue. Yet there is evidence within Mark's gospel that he presupposed the virgin birth when he wrote. Had Mark received no tradition about Jesus' origins, he would have assumed that Jesus would have had a human father (like other humans). But Mark never mentions Joseph or any other earthly father; instead God is presented as Jesus' father (Mark 1:11, 9:7). Further, Mark records that Jesus was called "the son of Mary" (Mark 6:3),

---

[49] France, *Matthew*, 71.

something he is unlikely to have done had he assumed that Jesus had a human father. Parrinder comments that "Apart from the birth narratives of Matthew and Luke . . . there would seem to be no reason to reverse the normal Semitic usage and refer to Jesus as his mother's son instead of his father's."[50] Evans goes further, asserting that "among Jews a man was not denoted the son of his mother unless illegitimate."[51] Although Parrinder objects that there are instances of the mother being named, he cannot provide any examples earlier than Muhammad.[52] The other explanation, that Joseph was not referred to because he was dead by this time[53] is nullified by the numerous examples of individuals being denoted by the name of their dead father or ancestor (e.g. 1 Sam. 23:6).

One further piece of evidence is Jesus' use of Ps. 110 to confound his critics, recorded in Mark 12:35–37. He asks if David calls the Messiah "Lord," how he can be David's son (i.e. descendant). Now, Mark believed that Jesus was the "son of David" (Mark 10:47-48) and it would be a great departure from Jewish ideas if he did not understand that genealogically. Yet the implication of Jesus' recorded teaching is that the Messiah is more than just a son of David.[54] At very least, Mark is claiming that Jesus was more than just the heir to the throne of David, and for Mark, that something more is bound up in the central claim of his gospel that Jesus is the Son of God (Mark 1:1; 15:39).[55] This falls short of requiring a virgin birth, but is certainly suggestive.

But if Mark presupposed belief in the virgin birth when he wrote his gospel, why does he not include an infancy narrative? Firstly, we should

---

[50] Parrinder, *Son of Joseph*, 56.

[51] C. F. Evans, quoted in Parrinder, *Son of Joseph*, 57.

[52] Parrinder, *Son of Joseph*, 57.

[53] Parrinder, *Son of Joseph*, 58.

[54] Hooker, *Mark*, 292.

[55] Hurtado suggests that Jesus is only saying that the "model" of David is inadequate for the Messiah, because Jesus views (or Mark views) the work of Messiah as being far greater than that of David (Hurtado, *Mark*, 203–4). While this interpretation is not ruled out by the passage, we should remember that these remarks by Jesus are set in the context of the Pharisees, Sadducees, and scribes questioning Jesus' authority. The natural response, then, would be for Jesus to justify his authority from the scriptures, rather than proposing a new model for the understanding of the concept of Messiah.

question the expectation that Mark would include an infancy narrative. Though we might expect modern biographers to give a full life story from childhood to death, there doesn't seem to be any strong reason to expect Mark to follow this form. In fact, it is evident that Mark didn't feel compelled to include details about Jesus' infancy (miraculous or otherwise) or indeed any details about Jesus' life prior to his baptism. From the gospel itself it is clear that Mark's purpose is to give an account of Jesus' ministry. So, we have no reason to expect an infancy narrative in Mark's gospel. Instead, we should be more intrigued by the fact that both Matthew and Luke choose to include an infancy narrative, and that, presumably, tells us something interesting about their purposes.

Secondly, if we take it as given that Mark presupposed belief in the virgin birth when he wrote his gospel, then presumably he presupposed that belief in his audience too. After all, Mark is not writing apologetic literature, seeking to defend Christianity from criticism, nor is he writing evangelistic literature, seeking to convince others of the truth of Christianity. Mark's primary audience for his gospel is his fellow Christians, so he has no need to persuade them that Jesus was born of a virgin, as though that was something they did not already know.

Thirdly, we should free ourselves from the false assumption that Mark had no constraints about what he could write about. Mark did not have the freedom of a novelist because Mark was writing about (what he believed to be) real events. He could not just make stuff up; he would depend upon (direct or indirect) testimony. Rist writes:

> The disciples were not eyewitnesses of the events of Jesus' childhood . . . As has often been observed, this fact may be one of the reasons governing Mark's choice of a starting point: he wanted a point where his eyewitnesses had first-hand evidence.[56]

Here it is important to note the work of Richard Bauckham, who proposes that the naming of individuals within Mark's gospel, such as Bartimaeus and Simon of Cyrene, was an intentional device to link

---

[56] Rist, *Independence,* 101.

testimonies to living witnesses.[57] More significant is his analysis of the *inclusio* device[58] in biographies such as Lucian's *Alexander* and Porphyry's *Life of Plotinus,* and the argument for similar devices in Mark (relating to Peter) and Luke (relating to the women).[59] Using both internal evidence and the testimony of Papias, [60] Bauckham can thus defend the position that the testimony of Peter stands behind the main part of Mark's gospel. We do not need to retrace all his arguments here. We may simply note that (1) there is nothing implausible about Papias's testimony, and (2) Peter stands large within the Marcan narrative. Further, Bauckham's thesis has *a priori* plausibility, since the early Christian message was centered on the testimony of the apostles (cf. 1 Cor. 15:1–6; Gal. 1:18–19). If Mark's gospel was largely based on the testimony of Peter, then it is understandable that it doesn't include an infancy narrative, because Peter wasn't there at the birth of Jesus. This doesn't mean that Mark (or Peter for that matter) didn't believe in the virgin birth; it only means that the story of Jesus' birth wasn't part of the testimony that Mark had access to.

Lastly, we cannot rule out the possibility that Mark, while aware of the virgin birth claim, judged it too controversial to include in gospel. If the counter-story that Jesus was illegitimate (see below) was already circulating by this point, perhaps Mark viewed the question of the birth of Jesus as a "can of worms" and thought it better not to start his gospel with controversary.

ABSENCE IN PAUL

The other consideration that leads some scholars to date belief in the virgin birth late is that, as well as not appearing explicitly in Mark's gospel, the virgin birth is not explicitly mentioned in other early Christian writings, such as the letters of Paul. Yet the relevance of this absence is

---

[57] Bauckham, *Jesus and the Eyewitnesses,* 39–66.

[58] An *inclusio* is a literary device that creates a frame by placing similar material at the beginning and end.

[59] Bauckham, *Jesus and the Eyewitnesses,* 114–54.

[60] *Jesus and the Eyewitnesses,* 155–82 and 202–39.

much the same as the relevance of the absence in Mark's gospel, that is to say, not great. The majority of Paul's letters date from 55 or later, by which time belief in Jesus' miraculous conception was already widespread. Even the earliest letters, 1 & 2 Thessalonians, do not date before 50, which is within the window identified above. Thus, the absence of explicit reference to the virgin birth in the letters of Paul cannot be taken as evidence that this belief was not extant. Nevertheless, there is still an important question as to why Paul does not mention it. The situation with Paul is slightly different than with Mark. With Mark, who is writing narrative, the question was why does Mark's narrative not include Jesus' infancy. With Paul, who is not primarily writing narrative and refers to only a few events in Jesus' life, there is no expectation that Paul's letters would include an infancy narrative. Instead the question is why Paul, in known of his Christological passages, does not choose to mention and draw significance from Jesus' virgin birth.

G. H. P. Thompson urges that absence of explicit mention "must be carefully interpreted." He writes, "for example, the silence of the speeches of Acts points only to the conclusion that the early preaching of the Gospel concentrated on the end of Jesus' life rather than the beginning."[61] This is significant, because Luke did believe in the virgin birth but resists the temptation to write that belief into those early speeches. Thompson takes this as evidence that Luke was a faithful historian. More to the point, it demonstrates that those writing early on Christology need not have felt compelled to discuss the virgin birth.

Indeed, it can be argued that there is no passage in the Pauline literature that would naturally feature a mention of the virgin birth. Since Paul believes that Jesus is the Son of God and since, as argued above, it is likely that the idea of a virgin birth was already current when Paul wrote, it may be that Paul simply presupposes that his audience would have the same understanding of the sonship of Jesus as his own. However, though this is possible, probable even, it is not in itself positive evidence that Paul did believe in the virgin birth.

[61] Thompson, *Luke*, 41.

In this regard Galatians 4:4 has been the key text in contention. Broadly speaking, Catholic scholars have seen here an allusion to the virgin birth, while Protestant scholars have not. Alfred Norris argues that for Paul to conjoin the concepts of Jesus' filial relationship with God and of Jesus' being born of a woman is a clear statement from Paul that Jesus had a human mother and a divine father (and there aren't so many options to make that statement explicable). He comments, "There is a breath-taking completeness about this evidence which makes one wonder, once composure has been regained, how its teaching could ever have been overlooked."[62] Yet the scholarly consensus seems to be that *genomenon ek gunaikos* ("born of a woman") is a Jewish idiom for a human person.[63] As evidence for this idiom Bligh cites Job 14:1–2, 15:14–15, 25:4–5; Sir. 10:6; Matt. 11:11 (parallel: Luke 7:28);[64] Dunn adds some passages in the *Dead Sea Scrolls*;[65] Williams[66] also cites passages in Josephus's, *Antiquities*,[67] though I think he is mistaken about the appearance of the idiom in these passages.

It is noticeable that in all the Greek sources cited the word for "born" in the phrase "born of woman" is a cognate of *gennao,* the common word for birth:

- Job 14:1–2, LXX   – *gennetos gunaikos*
- Job 15:14–15, LXX   – *gennetos gunaikos*
- Job 25:4–5, LXX   – *gennetos gunaikos*
- Sir. 10:6   – *gennemasi gunaikon*
- Matt. 11:11   – *gennetois gunaikon*
- Luke 7:28   – *gennetois gunaikon*

Paul, however, does not use this word. In Galatians 4:4 he says *genomenon ek gunaikos,* using a cognate of the root word *ginomai* ("to become").

---

[62] Norris, *Virgin Birth*, 13.

[63] Dunn, *Galatians*, 215.

[64] Bligh, *Galatians*, 347.

[65] 1QS 11.21, 1QH 13.14, 18.12, 13, 16; SB 3:570 (Dunn, *Galatians,* 215).

[66] Williams, *Galatians*, 111.

[67] Josephus, *Antiquities*, 3:368–69, 8:360–61 (7.21, 16.382).

Literally Paul says Jesus "came in existence out of a woman" (cf. Darby: "come of a woman," KJV: "made of a woman," Young's Literal Translation: "come of a woman"). The issue is not whether *ginomai* and its cognates can refer to human birth; they can. The issue is whether Paul's choice of words shows him deviating from the common idiom because he wants to say something different.

Usually idioms use the same words whenever they occur; it is the consistency of language that makes them idiomatic. "Born of woman" is a Hebrew/Aramaic idiom so, I suppose, it is possible that some may have translated it into Greek in different ways. The evidence from the examples cited, though, is that consistently cognates of *gennao* are used. It seems reasonable to suppose Paul would have used those words were he using them idiomatically.

Also, though it would be acceptable for a Greek writer to use a cognate of *ginomai* to refer to a birth, it is not usual. Norris writes that "since [Paul] makes no categorical statement of the circumstance of Jesus's conception, he is scrupulous that no misconception shall arise through a misconstruction of words carelessly used."[68] He contrasts Paul's use of a cognate of *gennao* when referring to the births of Isaac and Ishmael in Galatians 4:23.[69] Paul's deviation both from the idiom and from his own practice suggests that he is using his words purposefully. And if Paul means to distinguish Jesus' origins from usual human birth then this may indicate that he knows something special about Jesus' birth.[70]

Elsewhere in Paul's letters there are possible allusions to the virgin birth. Bligh suggests that 1 Cor. 7:36–39 contains an allusion to the situation of Mary and Joseph,[71] though this seems weak. Norris also argues

---

[68] Norris, *Virgin Birth*, 13.

[69] Norris, *Virgin Birth*, 14.

[70] It is worth mentioning, in passing, that *ginomai* is far too common a word to read much into its usage here. For example, it can be used both of an origin and of a change of state. We cannot from Gal. 4:4 alone determine that Paul believed that Jesus came into existence (i.e. "was made") when his mother became pregnant, any more than we can, on the basis of this verse alone, rule out that Paul believed that Jesus was incarnated at his birth. This word alone will not help us in regard to this question.

[71] Bligh, *Galatians*, 348.

that Rom. 1:3–4 hints at the virgin birth with its presentation of the dual descent of Jesus from David and from the Spirit.[72]

WIDE ACCEPTANCE OF THE MIRACULOUS CONCEPTION

One strong argument in favor of the idea that the belief in the miraculous conception was primitive is the relative ease with which it was accepted so widely. We have seen how the miraculous conception narrative existed before the gospels of Matthew and Luke, and it is likely that this belief found acceptance amongst the circles that produced these gospels. But we know that Matthew's and Luke's gospels were accepted widely throughout the first century churches, and there is no evidence of them being rejected or treated as suspect until we come to the Gnostics and the Ebionites of the second century. The community that produced the *Didache* accepted Matthew's gospel, so although the *Didache* does not mention the virgin birth, it is likely that they accepted it. The Johannine phrase "only-begotten" also implies a belief in the virgin birth,[73] especially since John connects it with the phrase "made flesh."[74] The derisive tale that Jesus was an illegitimate child that arose amongst Jews in the latter half of the first century[75] is strong evidence that the miraculous conception was being preached by Christians at this time. The (almost creedal) statements of Ignatius[76] and Aristides (2nd c.)[77] show that by the early second century the belief in the miraculous conception was widely accepted amongst Christians. The second-century, apocryphal *Protoevangelium of James* also demonstrate that this belief was common.[78]

---

[72] Norris, *Virgin Birth*, 13.

[73] John 1:14, 1:18, 3:16, 3:18; 1 John 4:9; also see Heb. 11:17.

[74] John 1:14.

[75] Rabbi Eliezer (c.40–120 CE) recounts a tale that when in Sepphoris, in Galilee, he heard someone teaching "in the name of Jesus the son of Panteri." Some have thought that the name "Panteri" may be "an abusive deformation of *parthenos*, the Greek word for 'virgin'" (Smith, *Jesus the Magician*, 46). Also see John 8:41.

[76] Ignatius, *Ephesians*, 239 (19:1), Ignatius *Smyrneans*, 297 (1:1).

[77] Aristedes, *Apology of Aristides*, 265 (2).

[78] *Protoevangelium of James*, 48 (11.1).

Given the wide acceptance of this belief in the latter first and early second centuries, it is reasonable to suppose that this belief was primitive—or, at very least, any prior belief about Jesus' origins was ambiguous, understated or not positively opposed to the virgin birth. The fact that both Mark and Paul seem to presuppose this belief is a strong indication of its primacy.

HOW EARLY IS BELIEF IN THE VIRGIN BIRTH?

So far in this chapter I have been arguing conservatively from the broadly accepted evidence (i.e. the gospels of Matthew and Luke) against a broadly accepted conclusion (i.e. that belief in the virgin birth is late). On this basis I have, rather coyly, concluded that belief in the virgin birth must pre-date 50. Yet I don't for a moment suppose that belief in the virgin birth originated in the late 40s. Despite the relative silence of Mark and of Paul, I think we can be confident (as argued above) that belief in the virgin birth pre-dated both these writers and so we have no particular reason to doubt that it dates back to the earliest days of Christianity. I argued above that the birth narratives of both Matthew and Luke are best explained by their dependence on sources. Elsewhere I have argued that these sources were the testimonies of Mary (for Luke's narrative) and of Joseph (for Matthew's narrative), perhaps mediated through others to the evangelists.[79] If this is the case then belief in the virgin birth predates the virgin birth.

Jesus seems to have understood his own intimacy with God as transcending even that of the radical intimacy he teaches to his followers. This is most clearly displayed in the *abba* (father) prayers of Jesus, as explained by the New Testament scholar Jeremias. Though the Aramaic word *abba* is only found once in the gospels (cf. Mark 14:36), it probably underlies the vocative case word *pater* (father) in the other prayers of Jesus. There is some evidence that God was previously addressed as *'abi*, but *abba* seems unique to Jesus and the early Christians (cf. Rom. 8:14; Gal.

---

[79] Gaston, "Eyewitnesses."

4:6).[80] The fact that followers of Jesus used *abba* to address God in prayer demonstrates of itself *abba* has "no exclusively Christological weight."[81] It does, however, when used by Jesus, indicate a special intimate relationship between him and God, which led him to address only one person as "father" (*abba*) (Matt. 23:9; cf. Mark 3:31-35). Also, as many commentators have noted, Jesus says, "my father" and "your father" but never "our father."[82]

The filial consciousness of Jesus is demonstrated elsewhere in the gospel traditions. The parable of the vinedressers portrays Jesus as the son and heir of the vineyard (Israel). This parable is multiply attested (Mark 12:1–9; Matt. 21:33–41; Luke 20:9–16).[83] Even the notoriously skeptical and revisionary Jesus Seminar proposed that some form of the parable goes back to Jesus, and Patterson's reconstruction of the parable includes a contrast between the servants and the son.[84] Perhaps more significant is the saying of Jesus recorded in Matt. 11:27 / Luke 10:22: "All things have been handed over to me by my Father, and no one knows who the Son is except the Father, or who the Father is except the Son and anyone to whom the Son chooses to reveal him."

The authenticity of this saying (which scholars would include in the hypothesized *Q*-source) has been questioned because of the radical claims it makes. Some have objected that the self-ascription of "Son" by Jesus is uncharacteristic, though for our purposes this argument is circular. The major objection is that this saying "has a distinctively Johannine ring."[85] Witherington has argued that since this passage is unlikely to derive from Johannine material, parallel passages in John can be taken as independent witness of this tradition (cf. John 5:19–20, 7:27–29).[86] The idea that this verse is an early Christian expansion or commentary on the preceding

[80] Cf. Dunn, *Jesus Remembered*, 716; Witherington, *Christology of Jesus*, 220.

[81] Witherington, *Christology of Jesus*, 220.

[82] Cf. Dunn, *Jesus Remembered*, 717–18; Witherington, *The Christology of Jesus*, 220.

[83] A version of this parable is also in the Coptic, mid-second-century, gnostic *Gospel of Thomas*, 143–44 (65).

[84] Patterson, *God of Jesus*, 138–39.

[85] Dunn, *Jesus Remembered*, 718; cf. Vermes, *Religion of Jesus*, 162.

[86] Witherington, *Christology of Jesus*, 225.

verse[87] does not account for these Johannine parallels, and it is not clear what textual cues could have led to such an expansion. In favor of the authenticity of this saying is the probability that it derives from an Aramaic original, and that it contains the potentially embarrassing implication that the Son is unknowable. Accepting it as authentic, Jesus is claiming not only to be heir of "all things" but also to stand in a unique relationship with God whereby he alone can truly reveal God to mankind. "In short, Jesus saw himself as the unique mediator of the final revelation of God, and thus God's unique Son."[88]

All this falls short of an explicit statement from Jesus that he believed that he was the "Son of God" because of a miraculous birth. We have sufficient evidence in the gospels that Jesus deliberately sought to minimize public proclamations about his identity (Mark 7:36, 8:30, 9:9), as well as Luke's statement that Mary concealed her testimony about the events of Jesus' birth until much later (Luke 2:19, 2:51.) Nevertheless, Jesus does claim to stand in a unique filial relationship with God, from which he derives significant knowledge and authority. Such a self-understanding is compatible with one more than one understanding of the sonship of Jesus—one might be a "special" son without being miraculously born—but since Jesus' followers believed his birth was miraculous, we have reason to conclude Jesus believed this too.

SUMMARY

A common approach to dating belief in the virgin birth has been to observe that Mark, conventionally posited as the earliest canonical gospel, does not contain an infancy narrative and therefore belief in the virgin birth must be a later development. However, playing out the various scenarios and source theories by which two gospels, Matthew and Luke, could publish two very different infancy narratives yet with such significant agreement, it is difficult to escape the conclusion that they depended on some earlier source(s). Also, we cannot date Mark earlier

---

[87] Boring, *Sayings of the Risen Jesus*, 150
[88] Witherington, *Christology of Jesus*, 228.

than this source without arbitrariness. While neither Mark nor Paul explicitly refers to the virgin birth, the idea does seem implicit in both. Dating (for sake of argument) Matthew and Luke to c.60, their sources to c.55, and thus belief in the virgin birth to c.50, the absence of an explicit mention in Paul, writing in the mid-50s, becomes irrelevant.

Yet the point is not about dates or source theories, but about Christology; in what sense is Jesus the Son of God? For the Logos theorists of the late second and third century, sonship referred to the procession of the Logos from the Father. For an Adoptionist, sonship was something bestowed on the good man Jesus by God. For the evangelists, sonship was a consequence of a special birth (cf. Luke 1:35). It is this same view of the sonship of Jesus held by the Dynamic Monarchians: neither a pre-existent Son, nor an adopted Son, but a born Son.

Jesus himself, while stopping short of describing his origins, had a unique filial consciousness. He was more than the heir to the Davidic throne; he stood in special relation to God, with unique authority and status. Yet nothing in his teaching would lead us to believe that he existed before he was born (even, I have argued, within the Gospel of John.) The Christology of Jesus—the earliest Christology—describes a unique filial relationship, without either pre-existence or adoption.

So, I conclude this book with a controversial, but nonetheless plausible, idea: that the Dynamic Monarchian Christology dates from the early first century, that this was the view of Jesus himself.

Conclusion

"DYNAMIC MONARCHIANISM" is a modern term used to categorize a number of Christians from the second and third centuries, who denied the literal pre-existence (and thus the deity) of Jesus. I have sought to distinguish these Dynamic Monarchians from Adoptionist Christians by a second Christological affirmation, a belief in the virgin birth. While these two claims are not the sum total of Dynamic Monarchian Christology, together they form a set of criteria by which to distinguish this Christology from that of other Christians.

Typically, Dynamic Monarchianism has been associated with a handful of individuals, namely: Paul of Samosata, Beryllus of Bostra, Artemon, and Theodotus of Byzantium. The standard narrative has been that Dynamic Monarchianism was deviation from an established orthodoxy, proposed by a small number of Christian "heretics." This has sometimes been explained as motivated by a Judaizing tendency amongst these individuals, or by other individual factors. That is to say, Dynamic Monarchianism has typically been viewed as being a relatively late innovation, as being not very widespread, and as not closely associated with the views of the earliest Christians. In this book I have sought to dismantle this typical narrative and to present a narrative which better explains the facts.

In the first part of this book, I have argued that there is more evidence than is usually adduced for the extent of Dynamic Monarchian belief. In addition to the individuals mentioned, I have considered the evidence from the "other" Ebionites (i.e. Jewish Christians who affirmed the virgin birth) and the presence of textual variants in the New Testament manuscripts responding to Dynamic Monarchian tendencies. Taken together, the evidence is that in the late second and third centuries, Dynamic Monarchianism was spread across the Roman Empire.

However, the fact that these different examples of Dynamic Monarchianism are not from a single group, argues against the proposition that this phenomenon only arose in the late second century. Instead, the geographical spread and lack of direct connection between these examples is indicative of a wider shared tradition within Christianity.

It is likely that this Dynamic Monarchian tradition existed within "mainstream" Christianity and co-existed with other viewpoints until it was first condemned as heretical with the excommunication of Theodotus by Victor, bishop of Rome. Dynamic Monarchianism was not rejected because it was a late innovation, but because it came into conflict with an emerging Christology, the Logos Christology of Justin and his successors, that was quickly gaining acceptance in late second century Christianity. This, coupled with the changing ecclesiastical situation, led to the excommunication of Theodotus and led prominent Christian thinkers who endorsed the Logos Christology, such as Hippolytus and Origen, to condemn Dynamic Monarchians as heretics.

While it is more difficult to detect the presence of Dynamic Monarchianism at a time when it was not explicitly distinguished from other forms of Christianity (i.e. by being condemned as heretical), I have adduced some evidence for the presence of this Christology in the early second and late first centuries. The proof-text dossier used by both Theodotus and Tertullian may be the product of an early Dynamic Monarchian. By projecting backwards from the views of the Gnostics and other "heretics," we can hypothesize what form of Christianity they deviated from; in most cases, a Dynamic Monarchian form of Christianity seems the mostly likely precursor to these "heresies." Both Ignatius of Antioch and John the evangelist, though often seen as proto-orthodox writers, are, I have argued, consistent with Dynamic Monarchianism in their teachings.

In fact, the Dynamic Monarchian tradition stretches right back to the earliest Christians. Despite efforts by some scholars to argue to the contrary, neither the synoptic gospels nor the letters of Paul provide evidence that the earliest Christians affirmed the pre-existence of Jesus. The evidence proposed is meager, particularly when compared with the evidence we would expect had these writers believed that Jesus existed before his human career. Messiahs and prophets were not typically thought to pre-exist—first century Jews did not believe in reincarnation or the transmigration of the soul—so one would have had expected far more frequent and explicit references to the pre-existence of Jesus were it being affirmed.

Though the earliest Christians did not affirm the pre-existence of Jesus (let alone, his deity), they were not Adoptionists. Once again, the evidence claimed for this proposal is meager and open to more satisfying explanations. While it is true that only two of the biblical gospels include an infancy narrative, I have argued that belief in the virgin birth both pre-dates Mark's gospel and is presupposed by him. There is also evidence that Paul presupposes the miraculous conception of Jesus. It is not unreasonable to suppose that this belief was part of Jesus' own self-understanding. We find that the earliest Christology matches the two criteria of Dynamic Monarchianism: affirming the virgin birth while not affirming the pre-existence of Jesus. Therefore, contrary to the standard narrative, Dynamic Monarchianism represents a Christological tradition that was present within Christianity through the first and second centuries and can lay claim to be the earliest Christology.

APPENDIX A:

Cast of Characters

A

Alcinous (fl. late 2nd c.) – Platonist philosopher, author of *The Handbook of Platonism* (*Didaskalikos*); scholars disagree about whether or not he is one and the same as the philosopher Albinus.

Alexander of Alexandria (d. 328) – Bishop of Alexandria in Egypt, most remembered for his dispute with the presbyter Arius which initiated the long "Arian" controversy, c. 317–381.

The Alogi, a.k.a. The Alogoi, The Alogians (2nd–3rd c.?) – A group who denied the apostolic authorship and authority of the Gospel of John and thus rejected the Logos of its first chapter. The name "Alogi" was coined by the heresiologist Epiphanius as word–play, meaning both against the Logos and illogical. While we know from other sources that there were those denied the apostolicity of the Gospel of John, whether the Alogi as such ever existed is debatable.

Ambrose of Alexandria (d. c. 250) – Friend and wealthy supporter of Origen whom Origen had converted to orthodoxy from Valentinian Gnosticism; many of Origen's works are dedicated to him.

Ammonius Saccas (c. 175–242) – Platonic and Neo–Pythagorean philosopher in Alexandria, Egypt, believed to be the teacher both of Plotinus and of Origen.

Anicetus (fl. mid-2nd c.) – bishop at Rome (r. 155–66) who opposed Marcionism and Valentinianism.

Apelles (fl. mid-2nd c.) – A disciple of Marcion in Rome who either left or was expelled from the Marcionite churches and taught for a time in Alexandria, Egypt, later returning to Rome, the author of a now mostly lost book called *Syllogisms* in which he tried to prove the general unreliability of the Old Testament.

Apuleius (c. 124–70 CE) – Writer, speaker, and Platonic philosopher, most famous for his Latin novel *The Golden Ass.*

Aristedes (2nd c.) – Athenian Christian philosopher, author of an *Apology* which may be the earliest public defense of Christianity addressed to an emperor (ancient reports differ on which emperor and when).

Aristo, a.k.a. Ariston (fl. c. 135–78) – Early Christian apologist from Pella in Jordan reported to be the author of *The Dialogue between Jason and Papiscus*, which features an argument between a Jewish Christian and a non-Christian Jew, respectively.

Aristotle of Stagira (384–22 BCE) – Influential philosopher and polymath whom his teacher Plato called the "Mind" of Plato's Academy in Athens, the author of extant works on ethics, metaphysics, logic, and other subjects.

Arius (c. 250–336) – Presbyter in Alexandria whose dispute with his bishop Alexander over the status of the Logos instigated the long 4th c. "Arian" controversy.

Arius Didymus (fl. 1st c. BCE) – Stoic philosopher and author of philosophical handbooks, he was the teacher of Caesar Augustus (63 BCE–14 CE).

Artemon, a.k.a. Artemas, Artemidorus (fl. c. 235–50) – Dynamic Monarchian teacher at Rome; see Chapter Three.

Asclepiodotus (fl. c. 199–217) – Dynamic Monarchian and follower of Theodotus, named in the *Little Labyrinth* and accused of inappropriate emendations to Scripture.

Athanasius (295–373) – Theologian and powerful Bishop of Alexandria (r. 328–73), most known for his untiring defense of the new language of the 325 Nicene Creed, and the author of many polemical works during the so-called "Arian" controversy (c. 317–81).

Athenagoras (c. 133–c. 190) – Athenian Christian apologist, philosopher, and Logos theologian, author of *Embassy for the Christians* (a.k.a. *A Plea for the Christians, Plea on Behalf of Christians*).

Aurelian (214–75) – Roman emperor (r. 270–75), a supporter of the Sun god *Sol Invictus* and persecutor of Christians; he was murdered by officers of his army.

Axionicus, a.k.a. Axionikos (fl. late 2nd c. – early 3rd c.) – Valentinian teacher reported to be of the "eastern" school or faction which held that Jesus had a spiritual body.

B

Bardesianes, a.k.a. Bardaisan (154–222) – Valentinian teacher reported to be of the "eastern" school or faction which held that Jesus had a spiritual body.

Basil, a.k.a. Basil the Great, Basil of Caesarea (330–79) – Bishop of Caesarea in Cappadocia, ascetic, author, and leader of "the Cappadocian Fathers," at first in the Homoiousian party during the long "Arian" controversy, but later on a leader of the pro–Nicene party (i.e. those in favor of the new language of the 325 Nicene Creed), the side made the victor by emperor Theodosius I in 380–81.

Basilides, a.k.a. Basileides (fl. mid-2nd c.) – Earliest known gnostic teacher in Alexandria, Egypt, whose views are hard to reconstruct because of apparent conflicts between the ancient hostile reports of his teachings (but as to Christology he seems to be been a docetist), he is reported to have written his own gospel and a commentary on it, both of which are now lost.

Beryllus of Bostra, a.k.a. Beryl Apuleius (fl. c. 222–35, d. after 244) – Learned Dynamic Monarchian bishop of Bostra in Arabia, called to a synod c. 238–44 to be refuted by Origen of Alexandria, and according to Eusebius Origen persuaded him to change his views.

Blastus, a.k.a. Vlasto (fl. late 2nd c.) – Leader of a faction in Rome which opposed the Roman bishop Victor, taking the eastern side in the Quartodecimanism controversy about the date of Easter.

C

Callistus (d. 222) – Bishop of Rome (r. c. 217–22) after Zephyrinus, accused by Hippolytus of being a Modalistic Monarchian, some speculate that he may be the "Praxeas" (Busybody) refuted by Tertullian.

Caracalla, a.k.a. Marcus Aurelius Antoninus (188–217) – Emperor of Rome from 198 till his death in 217, aged 29.

Carpocrates, a.k.a. Karpokrates (2nd c.) – Either a gnostic teacher in Alexandria, Egypt, or a merely hypothesized founder of a sect known as

"Carpocratians" or "Harpocratians" which survived into the 4th century and was remembered particularly for teaching the pre–existence of human souls and an antinomian approach to morality.

Celsus (late 2nd c.) – Cultured pagan critic of Christianity, author of the *True Account* (or: *The True Word*) (c. 177–80), which expresses his eclectic Middle Platonist views and is known mainly through extensive quotations in Origen's critique *Against Celsus*.

Celsus Africanus, a.k.a. Celsus the African (late 3rd c.) – Obscure author so-called by scholars in order to differentiate him from the earlier anti-Christian polemicist named "Celsus"; he is known only for translating *The Dialogue between Jason and Papiscus* from Greek into Latin and for his brief summary of it.

Cerdo, a.k.a. Kerdon (fl. c. 136–40) – A gnostic teacher in Rome who according to Irenaeus taught that the god of the Jews is different from the god of Jesus (the Father), the former being just and the latter being benevolent but unknowable.

Cerinthus, a.k.a. Kerinthos (fl. end of the 1st c.) – Early Christian heretic who denied that God created the physical world. He seems to have believed that "Christ" was a spirit who descended upon Jesus for a time.

Cicero (106–43 BCE) – Roman statesman, lawyer, and philosopher. His extant writings make him an important source for the period.

Clement of Alexandria (c. 150–215) – Christian philosopher and head of a school in Alexandria, he tried to steer a course between the Gnostics and the Greek philosophical schools, authoring an *Exhortation to the Greeks*, *Christ the Educator*, and a wide–ranging *Miscellanies (Stromata)*.

Clement of Rome (fl. late 1st c.) – A leader of the Roman church believed to be the author or the primary author of *First Clement* (or *1 Clement*), a letter from the Roman Christians to those at Corinth, written around the end of the first century.

Cyprian of Carthage (c. 200–58) – Latin author and bishop of Carthage (r. c. 248–58) who was beheaded by the Romans for his faith.

D

Demetrianus, a.k.a. Demetrian, Demetrius (fl. mid-3rd c.) – Bishop of Antioch until 253 when he was captured by the Persian king Shapur I, who took him to Persia where he served as bishop of Gundeshapur.

Diodore (d. c. 390) – Nicene theologian, head of monastery near Antioch, and then bishop of Tarsus from 378, whose works were later largely dismissed as proto–Nestorian.

Dionysius Bar Salibi, a.k.a. Jacob Bar Salibi (d. 1171) – Syrian Jacobite (Miaphysite) scholar and prolific author who at the end of his career served as the Metropolitan of Amid (Diyarbakır).

Dionysius of Alexandria (d. 264) – Student of Origen, head of the catechetical school in Alexandria (c. 233–48) and then bishop of Alexandria from 248, Logos theologian and opponent of Dynamic and Modalistic Monarchianism.

Dionysius of Corinth (fl. c. 171) – Bishop in Corinth and author of several letters to various churches, though only a portion of one of these has been preserved.

Dionysius of Rome (fl. mid-3rd c.) – Roman priest and then bishop (c. 260–68), who wrote against Modalistic Monarchianism and denounced talk of three *hypostases* in God.

Domnus (fl. mid-3rd c.) – Son of the bishop of Antioch Demetrianus, he served as the bishop of Antioch in Syria (r. 268–73), having been appointed by the synod which deposed Paul of Samosata.

E

The Ebionites (2nd–3rd centuries) – Little-understood law-keeping Jewish-Christian groups condemned by heresiologists starting with Irenaeus, supposed by later authors to have been founded by a certain "Ebion," their name is from an Aramaic word meaning "the poor ones."

Eleutherus (d. 189) – 2nd c. bishop of Rome numbered as the twelfth in a list given by Irenaeus.

Eliezer, a.k.a. Rabbi Eliezer ben Hyrcanus, Rabbi Eliezer the Great (c. 40–120 CE) – Prominent Jewish teacher, one of the Tannaim (rabbinic sages whose views are recorded in the Mishnah) and teacher of the famous Rabbi Akiba.

Epiphanius of Salamis (c. 315–403) – Ascetic and Nicene bishop of Constantia in Cyprus and heresiologist, author of *Medicine Chest* (*Panarion*), also called the *Refutation of All Heresies*.

Euclid (fl. c. 300 BCE) – Prominent Alexandrian mathematician, author of *Elements*, the influential treatise on geometry.

Eusebius of Caesarea (c. 260–340) – Bishop of Caesarea in Palestine and subordinationist theologian, most remembered for his important *Ecclesiastical History* and his role as court propagandist for the emperor Constantine.

Eusebius Hieronymus – see Jerome.

F

Fabian (d. 250) – Bishop of Rome (r. 236–50) who was martyred during the persecution of the Roman emperor Decius.

Firmilian, a.k.a. Firmilianus (d. c. 269) – Bishop of Caesarea in Cappadocia, disciple of Origen, who presided over the second council discussing Paul of Samosata.

Filaster – see Philastrius.

Flavius Josephus – see Josephus.

Florinus (fl. late 2nd c.) – Roman presbyter and follower of the gnostic Valentinus who seemed to fellowship in mainstream churches until he was repeatedly called out as a heretic by Irenaeus.

G

Gaius (fl. early 3rd c.) – A now obscure Roman presbyter and scholar, author of a lost Greek anti–Montanist dialogue, the *Dialogue Against Proclus*, he is reported to have rejected the Gospel according to John.

Galen (129–c. 200) – An influential doctor and prolific author of works on medicine and philosophy, he served as the court physician to the Roman emperors Marcus Aurelius (r. 161–80), Commodus (r. 180–92), and Septimius Severus.

Gnostics (1st–3rd c.) – a controversial term which in a narrow sense has been used to describe particular Christian groups whose elaborate mythologies, cosmologies, and interpretations of Scripture (and differing scriptures) competed with those of mainstream (or catholic) Christianity. In a broad sense, the term has also been used to describe a fluid category of religions developing in the first and second centuries CE which also includes non-Christian traditions. While some scholars have argued for the abandonment of this term in light of the wide diversity of movements and ideas which it attempts to corral, others have argued for its usefulness as a comparative category.

Gordian III (225–44) – Emperor of Rome from 238 till his death in 244, aged 19.

H

Hadrian (76–138) – Roman emperor (r. 117–38), famous for building Hadrian's wall in England. In his edict preserved by Justin Martyr (*First Apology* [68.6–10]) he ruled that accusers of Christians bore the burden of proof.

Hegesippus (c. 110–80) – Author of a mostly lost book of church history in Greek called *Memoirs* (*Hypomnemata*) who is most remembered for traveling to Rome and compiling a list of what he believed was the sequence of orthodox Roman bishops up to his time.

Heracleon (fl. 145–80) – Disciple of the gnostic Valentinus, the author of a now-lost early commentary on the Gospel according to John which later helped to stimulate Origen to write his own *Commentary on John*. He is thought by some scholars to be the author of *The Tripartite Tractate* in the Nag Hammadi texts.

Heraclides (fl. mid-3rd c.) – Monarchian bishop known only through the *Dialogue with Heraclides* (discovered in 1941), meeting minutes of a synod where he was confronted by the Logos theologian Origen and urged to confess "two gods," the Father and the Logos.

Hermas (fl. early to mid-2nd c.) – Roman author of the moralistic, quasi-prophetic book *The Shepherd of Hermas*, which was widely read in the second and third centuries, described in one ancient source as the brother of the Roman bishop Pius (r. c. 140–54).

Hilary of Poitiers (c. 315–67) – Nicene polemical writer and bishop of Poitiers (r. 350–67) in present–day France, author of *On the Trinity* (*De Trinitate*).

Hippocrates (c. 460–375 BCE) – Famous ancient Greek physician considered by them to be the founder of medicine, to whom many medical writings were later falsely attributed.

Hippolytus of Rome, a.k.a. Hippolytos (c. 170–236) – Presbyter at Rome, possible rival bishop of Rome, Logos theologian and anti–Monarchian writer, author of *Against Noetus* (*Contra Noetum*) and believed by some scholars to be the author of *Refutation of All Heresies*.

I

Ignatius of Antioch (c. 35–107) – Bishop of Antioch, believed to be the author of seven short letters to churches in various cities, composed on his trip to Rome where he was executed.

Irenaeus of Lyons (c. 130–c. 202) – Bishop of Lyons from 177 and important anti–Gnostic writer, Logos theologian, and one–bishop system proponent, the author of *Against the Heresies* (a.k.a. *Against Heresies, Adversus Haereses*).

J

Jacob Bar Salibi – see Dionysius Bar Salibi.

James, a.k.a. James the Just (d. c. 62 CE) – Half-brother of Jesus, traditionally believed to be the author of the letter from James in the New Testament. Even though he was not one of the twelve apostles, he was an influential early leader of the Christians in Jerusalem.

Jason (fl. mid-2nd c.) – Hebrew Christian known only from the *Dialogue of Jason and Papiscus*, a work which survives only in few fragments quoted by later authors.

Jerome, a.k.a. Eusebius Hieronymus (c. 347–419) – Prolific author, Bible translator, controversialist, and sometime secretary to the Roman bishop Damascus, most remembered for his long–used Latin Vulgate translation of the Bible.

John of Scythopolis (early 6th c.) – Learned lawyer and Bishop of Scythopolis in Palestine and author of "neo-Chalcedonian" works against Monophysite views about Christ and a commentary on the pseudepigraphic, Neoplatonic works misattributed to Dionysius the Areopagite (who is mentioned in Acts 17:34).

Josephus, a.k.a. Flavius Josephus, Joseph Ben Mattias (37–c. 100) – Jewish Pharisee and military leader in the first Jewish-Roman war who surrendered and found favor with emperor Vespasian, most remembered for his historical works *History of the Jewish War* (75–79 CE) and *The Antiquities of the Jews* (93 CE).

Julius Cassianus (fl. c. 170) – Obscure Egyptian teacher who is said in ancient sources to have been an Encratite ascetic and the originator of Docetism.

Justin Martyr (c. 100–65) – Christian philosopher and apologist at Rome and influential Logos theologian, author of two short apologies and the *Dialogue with Trypho* (c. 155), a Jewish teacher.

K

Karpokrates – see Carpocrates.

Kerdon – see Cerdo.

Kerinthos – see Cerinthus.

L

Linus – Purported to the first bishop of Rome, conventionally dated 64–76.

Lucian (fl. mid-2nd c.) – Hellenized Syrian satirist and rhetorician.

M

Malchion (fl. mid-3rd c.) – Presbyter and rhetor at Antioch in Syria, and head of a school of Greek literature there, he disputed with Paul of Samosata at the synod which condemned him and then wrote a public letter on behalf of the synod.

Mani (c. 216–76) – Syncretistic Persian religious teacher and prophet, founder of the ancient Manichean religion, considered as a heresy by many patristic authors, which eventually spread as far as Rome, North Africa, and China.

Marcellus of Ancyra (c. 280–374) – Bishop of Ancyra in Galatia, theologian, sometime ally of Athanasius, and early Nicene opponent of "Arianism," who was eventually disowned by most Nicenes because of his Modalist Monarchian views, after having been condemned and vindicated by various councils.

Marcion, a.k.a. Markion (d. c. 154) – Excommunicated by the mainstream Roman church in 144, he founded a sect of "Marcionite" churches who taught that that only Paul correctly understood the message of Jesus and that the god of the Old Testament is someone other than the God and Father of Jesus, the former being an incompetent and vengeful maker of the world whose bungling left the world mired in sin, while the latter is a god of love.

Marcus, a.k.a. Marcos (fl. mid-2nd century) – Valentinian teacher from Lyons in present-day France.

Marcus Aurelius Antoninus – see Caracalla.

Maximus of Alexandria (d. 282) – Bishop of Alexandria 265–82 who took part in a synod which condemned Paul of Samosata.

Maximus of Bostra (fl. mid 3rd c.) – Bishop of Bostra (successor of Beryllus) who took part in the synod which condemned Paul of Samosata; he is probably the "Maximus" in Origen's *Dialogue with Heraclides*.

Maximus the Confessor (c. 580–662) – Byzantine theologian and monk, remembered particularly for his opposition to the doctrine that the incarnate Christ has only one will (Monotheletism).

N

Natalius (fl. c. 199–217) – Dynamic Monarchian who was persuaded to be the bishop of a Theodotian church in Rome. He later returned to the "orthodox" church.

Nero, a.k.a. Nero Claudius Caesar Augustus Germanicus (37–68) – Fifth Roman emperor (r. 54–68), most remembered for his erratic personality and for blaming the Christians for the large fire which levelled portions of Rome in 64 CE, initiating official imperial persecution.

Nestorius (c. 381–452) – Antiochene monk and student of Theodore of Mopsuestia and archbishop of Constantinople (r. 428–31) who was condemned by the council at Ephesus in 431 and consequently deposed and exiled because of his Christology which seemed to present two persons in Christ, the divine nature (i.e. the Logos) and the human nature (i.e. the man Jesus), which was later labeled "Nestorianism."

Nicephorus Callistus, a.k.a. Nikephoros Kallistos Xanthopoulos (c. 1256–c. 1335) – Church historian, author of the eighteen volume *History of the Church* (*Historia Ecclesiastica*) which depends heavily on early works of the same nature.

Noetus (fl. 230) – A presbyter of a church in Asia Minor who was excommunicated for his Modalistic Monarchian Christology, known mostly through Hippolytus's book *Against Noetus*.

Numenius of Apamea (fl. mid-2nd c.) – Neopythagorean and Platonist Greek philosopher influential both on later Platonists and Christian triadic speculations, he who taught a system of three gods, the highest being The Good (a.k.a. Being, the First Mind), followed by the Demiurge (Craftsman) who contains all the Forms, and the World Soul.

O

Origen of Alexandria (c. 185–c. 253) – Leading Greek–speaking Logos theologian, ascetic, and scholar, author of numerous works and head of Christian schools at Alexandria and then at Caesarea, posthumously condemned at the second council at Constantinople in 553.

P

Pamphilus (c. 240–310) – Teacher of Eusebius of Caesarea, author of the *Defense of Origen*, priest and scholar who helped to preserve the library of Origen at Caesarea, who was tortured and then beheaded by the Romans in 310 for refusing to sacrifice to the emperor.

Papias of Hierapolis (fl. early-2nd c.) – bishop in Asia Minor classified by modern scholars as an "apostolic father," known only through fragmentary quotations, most remembered for his lost book *Expositions* *of the Sayings of the Lord* which influenced later authors on the order and composition of the New Testament gospels.

Papiscus (fl. mid-2nd c.) – Alexandrian Jew known only from the fragmentary second-century *Dialogue of Jason and Papiscus*, which states that Papiscus was converted and baptized.

Paul of Samosata (fl. mid-third century) – Dynamic Monarchian bishop of Antioch in Syria (r. 260–68), investigated by a succession of three synods in Antioch; the first exonerated him, the second made him promise to change his teachings, and the third condemned his christological teachings, which led to his being forcibly deposed about four years later (272) when the emperor Aurelian regained control of Antioch from the Syrian queen Zenobia.

Philastrius, a.k.a. Philaster, Filaster (fl. late 4th c.) – Ascetic and itinerant preacher, later the Pro–Nicene Bishop of Brescia in northern Italy from c. 377, author of the *Book of Various Heresies (Diversarum Hereseon Liber)*.

Philo of Alexandria (c. 20 BCE–50 CE) – Jewish philosopher and Bible commenter strongly influenced by Platonic philosophy who seems to have influenced Platonism–sympathetic Christian theologians in the 2nd–4th centuries, he allegorized the Jewish scriptures and theorized about God interacting with his creation through his "Logos" and his other "powers."

Photinus of Sirmium (d. c. 376) – Learned rhetorician and Dynamic Monarchian bishop of Sirmium, deposed because of his christology by a council at Sirmium in 351.

Photius (c. 810–895) – Learned aristocrat, monk, and patriarch of Constantinople who was involved in the filioque controversy with western Christians and authored the important historical source *A Thousand Books (Myrobiblion)*, a.k.a. *The Library (Bibliotheca)*.

Plato (c. 429–347 BCE) – Massively influential Athenian Greek philosopher, author of about forty extant philosophical dialogues, teacher of Aristotle.

Pliny, a.k.a. Pliny the Younger (61–c. 113) – Roman lawyer, author, and governor of Bithynia, famous for his letters. His letter to the Emperor Trajan regarding trials against Christians is an important historical witness to the persecution of Christians in the Roman Empire.

Plotinus (c. 204–70) – Influential Egyptian Platonic philosopher considered by historians to be the founder of Neoplatonism, author of the *Enneads.*

Plutarch (c. 45–120) – Platonist philosopher, historian, and prolific author.

Polycarp (c. 69–156 CE) – Bishop in Smyrna and author of two short extant letters, known for assisting the bishop of Antioch Ignatius during his transportation as a prisoner through Asia Minor.

Polycrates (c. 130–96) – Bishop of Ephesus most remembered for his participation in the Quartodecimanism controversy about the date of Easter, which included presiding over a meeting of eastern bishops and writing a letter to Victor, bishop of Rome.

Porphyry (c. 234–c. 305) – Neoplatonist philosopher and student of Plotinus; a prolific author who integrated the thought of Aristotle into Neoplatonic thought, he was interested in traditional Greco-Roman religion and authored a book *Against the Christians.*

Proclus, a.k.a. Proklos, Proculus (fl. late-2nd–early-3rd c.) Montanist teacher in Rome. Not to be confused with the influential pagan Platonist Proclus of Athens (d. 485 CE).

Ptolemy (fl. mid-2nd c.) – Disciple of the Gnostic teacher Valentinus and author of the *Letter to Flora.*

Rashi, a.k.a. Rabbi Shlomo Yitzḥaqi, Rabbi Solomon ben Isaac of Troyes (1040–1105) – Influential medieval Jewish scholar and author of commentaries on the Jewish Bible and the Talmud.

Rufinus of Aquileia, a.k.a. Tyrannius Rufinus (c. 345–410) – Monk, priest, theologian, and translator, best known for his quarrel with Jerome and his Latin translations of the Greek works of Origen, some of which he "improved" in a Nicene direction, believing that heretics must have corrupted some passages in them.

S

Sabellius (fl. early 3rd c.) – Obscure North African Christian priest and theologian believed to be a Modalistic Monarchian, after whom later writers coined the term "Sabellianism."

Saturninus, a.k.a. Satorneilos, Satorninus, Satornilus (fl. early 2nd c.) – Gnostic teacher in Antioch, Syria, who according Irenaeus taught, among others things, that the world was created by seven angels (one of whom is the god of the Jews), that Christ only appeared to be a human being, and that Christ came to destroy the god of the Jews.

Serapion (fl. late 2nd–early 3rd centuries) – Bishop of Antioch in Syria (r. 191–211), the author of *The So-Called Gospel of Peter*, a lost polemical work directed against a second-century gospel with a docetic Christology.

Severus, Septimius, a.k.a. Lucius Septimius Severus Pertinax (c. 145–211) – Roman emperor (r. 193–211) most remembered for his militarization of the government and his military campaigns which expanded the empire to its greatest size.

Simeon, a.k.a. Symeon (d. c. 108) – Second leader of the church in Jerusalem after the martyrdom of James c. 62 CE; according to Eusebius,

Simeon was the son of the Clopas mentioned in John 19:5, he was a cousin of Jesus, and he was martyred c. 108.

Socinus, a.k.a. Faustus Socinus, Fausto Paolo Socini (Sozini, Sozzini) (1539–1604) – Italian Reformer and unitarian Christian theologian, author of *De Jesu Christo Servatore* [*On Jesus Christ, the Savior*] (written in 1578), he eventually settled in Poland, where he was the leading theologian of the Minor Reformed Church, a.k.a. The Polish Brethren.

Socrates, a.k.a. Socrates Scholasticus (c. 380–450) – Not to be confused with the earlier philosopher Socrates (469–399 BCE), this Socrates was a lawyer and historian in Constantinople and the author of *Ecclesiastical History* (438–43), intended to be a continuation of Eusebius's work, covering the years 306–439.

Sophronius (c. 560–638) – Teacher of rhetoric, monk, and then patriarch of Jerusalem (r. 634–38). He was the author of works denouncing the view that Christ had only a single (divine) will (Monothelitism). He died not long after Jerusalem was conquered by the Muslim caliph Umar I in 637.

Soter (d. c. 175) – bishop at Rome (r. c. 166–75), who is reported to have opposed Montanism.

Stesichorus, a.k.a. Teisias (c. 632–c. 553 BCE) – Early Greek poet from what is now southern Italy.

T

Tatian (d. c. 185) – Syrian apologist, rhetorician, ascetic, and student of Justin Martyr, author of *Address to the Greeks* (c. 155–65) and a harmony of the New Testament gospels called the *Diatessaron*.

Tertullian, a.k.a. Quintus Septimus Florens Tertullianus (c. 160–c. 225) – Influential Roman North African Logos theologian and author of many Latin apologetic works, a champion of orthodoxy who in the first decade of the third century was at least sympathetic to the controversial Montanist movement.

Theodore of Mopsuestia (350–428) – Student of Diodore of Tarsus, leading Antiochene theologian and author, and from 392 bishop of Mopsuestia, whose works were condemned by the Council at Constantinople in 553.

Theodoret (c. 393–460) – Bishop of Cyrrhus (Cyrus) in Syria, bishop and theologian, author of a *The Ecclesiastical History* covering the years 323–428; an advocate of "two natures" in Christ, he was posthumously condemned as a "Nestorian" at the second Council at Constantinople in 553.

Theodotus of Byzantium, a.k.a. Theodotus the Byzantian, Theodotus the Tanner (Fuller, Shoemaker, Cobbler) (fl. 189–99) – Dynamic Monarchian teacher at Rome; see Chapter Five.

Theodotus the Banker (fl. early 3rd c.) – A disciple of Theodotus of Byzantium who is reported to have founded a "Melchizedekian" sect.

Theophilus of Antioch (d. c. 185) – Bishop of Antioch, apologist, and Logos theologian, author of the apologetic work *To Autolycus* (*Ad Autolycum*).

Theophrastus (c. 371–287 BCE) – Colleague of and successor to the philosopher Aristotle, he is reported to have written over 200 books on many subjects, most of which have been lost to history.

Tiberius, a.k.a. Tiberius Claudius Nero, Tiberius Julius Caesar Augustus (42 BCE–37 CE) – The second Roman emperor (r. 14–37 CE), who was murdered on his sickbed by his guards after they chose to support his successor Caligula.

Trajan (53–117) – Roman Emperor (r. 98–117) who presided over a period of territorial expansion of the empire. In his response to Pliny, he advised that Christians should be executed if they refused to recant.

Trypho (fl. early-mid 2nd c.) – A learned Jew known only from Justin's *Dialogue with Trypho*, which says (1.3) he is a refugee from the recent war, presumably the one instigated in Palestine by Bar Kochba (132–35).

V

Valentinus (c. 100–c. 160) – Influential and prolific Gnostic teacher, believed by some to be the author of the *Gospel of Truth*; Valentinian communities founded by his disciples rivalled the mainstream churches in the late 2nd and early 3rd centuries.

Victor (d. 199) – Bishop of Rome (r. 189–99), reckoned by some ancient authors to be the thirteenth bishop of Rome after Peter.

Vlasto – see Blastus.

X

Xenophanes (late 6th–early 5th centuries BCE) – Greek philosophical poet most remembered for his critique of anthropomorphism in religion.

Z

Zenobia (c. 240–c. 274) – Queen–consort of the Palmyrene Empire from 260, becoming empress in 272. While herself a pagan, she accommodated Judaism and Christianity. Some have claimed she was a supporter of Paul of Samosata and that she appointed him to a political office.

Zephyrinus (d. 217) – Modalistic Monarchian bishop of Rome (r. 199–217).

APPENDIX B:

Fragments of Theodotus of Byzantium

Fragment 1: Epiphanius, *Medicine Chest* 54.1.9[1]	John 8:40[2]
ὅτι, φησίν, ὁ Χριστὸς ἔφη· νῦν δέ με ζητεῖτε ἀποκτεῖναι ἄνθρωπον, ὃς τὴν ἀλήθειαν ὑμῖν λελάληκα. ὁρᾷς, φησίν, ὅτι ἄνθρωπός ἐστιν.	νῦν δὲ ζητεῖτε με ἀποκτεῖναι ἄνθρωπον, ὃς τὴν ἀλήθειαν ὑμῖν λελάληκα
"He asserted that 'Christ said "But now you seek to kill me a man, one who has told you the truth." You see,' he asserted, 'that Christ is a man.' "	"but now you are trying to kill me, a man who has told you the truth"

[1] The Greek text for the fragments is from Holl and Dummer, *Epiphanius*. Translations are my own.

[2] New Testament Greek texts are from Aland, *Greek* [UBS 5]. Old Testament Septuagint Greek quotations are from Rahlfs and Hanhart, *Septuaginta*. Unless otherwise noted, translations are from the New Revised Standard Version, Updated Edition.

Fragment 2: Epiphanius, *Medicine Chest* 54.2.3	Matthew 12:31–32
αὐτοῦ, φησί, τοῦ Χριστοῦ εἰπόντος· πᾶσα βλασφημία ἀφεθήσεται τοῖς ἀνθρώποις, καὶ ὁ λέγων λόγον εἰς τὸν υἱὸν τοῦ ἀνθρώπου ἀφεθήσεται αὐτῷ· τῷ δὲ βλασφημοῦντι εἰς τὸ ἅγιον πνεῦμα, οὐκ ἀφεθήσεται αὐτῷ. "He asserted Christ himself said, 'All blasphemy shall be forgiven men,' and 'Whoever speaks a word against the Son of Man, it shall be forgiven him, but he who blasphemes the Holy Spirit, it shall not be forgiven.' "	πᾶσα ἁμαρτία καὶ βλασφημία ἀφεθήσεται τοῖς ἀνθρώποις, ἡ δὲ τοῦ πνεύματος βλασφημία οὐκ ἀφεθήσεται. καὶ ὃς ἐὰν εἴπῃ λόγον κατὰ τοῦ υἱοῦ τοῦ ἀνθρώπου, ἀφεθήσεται αὐτῷ· ὃς δ' ἂν εἴπῃ κατὰ τοῦ πνεύματος τοῦ ἁγίου, οὐκ ἀφεθήσεται αὐτῷ "people will be forgiven for every sin and blasphemy, but blasphemy against the Spirit will not be forgiven. Whoever speaks a word against the Son of Man will be forgiven, but whoever speaks against the Holy Spirit will not be forgiven."
Fragment 3: Epiphanius, *Medicine Chest* 54.3.1	Deuteronomy 18:15 [LXX]
καί ὁ νόμος περὶ αὐτοῦ ἔφη· προφήτην ἐκ τῶν ἀδελφῶν ὑμῶν ἐγερεῖ ὑμῖν κύριος ὡς ἐμέ· αὐτοῦ ἀκούσατε. Μωυσῆς δὲ ἄνθρωπος ἦν· ὁ οὖν ἐκ θεοῦ ἐγειρόμενος Χριστὸς οὗτος, φησίν, ἦν, ἀλλὰ ἄνθρωπος, ἐπειδὴ ἐξ αὐτῶν ἦν, ὡς καί ὁ Μωυσῆς ἄνθρωπος ἦν. " 'The Law also said of him, "The Lord will raise up to you a prophet of your brothers who is like me; listen to him." But Moses was a man. Therefore the Christ whom God raised up,' he asserts, 'was also a man, for he was descended from them. As Moses, he was also a man.' "	προφήτην ἐκ τῶν ἀδελφῶν σου ὡς ἐμέ ἀναστήσει σοι κύριος ὁ Θεός σου, αὐτοῦ ἀκούσεσθε "The Lord your God will raise up for you a prophet like me from among your brothers; you shall hear him." (Deut. 18:15, NETS)

Fragment 4: Epiphanius, *Medicine Chest* 54.3.5	Luke 1:35
καί αὐτὸ τὸ εὐαγγέλιον ἔφη τῇ Μαρίᾳ· πνεῦμα κυρίου ἐπελεύσεται ἐπὶ σέ, καί οὐκ εἶπε· πνεῦμα κυρίου γενήσεται ἐν σοί. " 'The Gospel itself said to Mary, "The Spirit of the Lord shall come upon you," and it did not say, "The Spirit of the Lord shall come to be in you." ' "	καί ἀποκριθεὶς ὁ ἄγγελος εἶπεν αὐτῇ, Πνεῦμα ἅγιον ἐπελεύσεται ἐπὶ σέ "The angel said to her, 'The Holy Spirit will come upon you' "
Fragment 5: Epiphanius, *Medicine Chest* 54.4.1	Jeremiah 17:9 [LXX]
ὅτι καί ὁ Ἰερεμίας περὶ αὐτοῦ ἔφη ὅτι ἄνθρωπός ἐστιν, καί τίς γνώσεται αὐτόν " 'Jeremiah also said about him, "He is a man, and who will know him?" ' "	ἄνθρωπός ἐστιν· καί τίς γνώσεται αὐτόν "man, and who shall understand him." (Jer. 17:9, NETS)
Fragment 6: Epiphanius, *Medicine Chest* 54.5.1	Isaiah 53:3 [LXX]
καί Ἡσαΐας περὶ αὐτοῦ ἔφη ὅτι ἄνθρωπός ἐστιν, οὕως εἰπών· ὅτι ἄνθρωπος εἰδὼς φέρειν μαλακίαν·καί εἴδομεν αὐτὸν ἐν πληγῇ καί ἐν κακώσει καί ἠτιμάσθη καί οὐκ ἐλογίσθη. " 'Isaiah also said about him he is a man, because he said, "A man acquainted with bearing infirmity; and we knew him afflicted and abused and despised and not esteemed." ' "	ἄνθρωπος ἐν πληγῇ ὢν καί εἰδὼς φέρειν μαλακίαν, ὅτι ἀπέστραπται τὸ πρόσωπον αὐτοῦ, ἠτιμάσθη καί οὐκ ἐλογίσθη. "a man being in calamity and knowing how to bear sickness; because his face is turned away, he was dishonored and not esteemed." (Is. 53:3, NETS)

Fragment 7: Epiphanius, *Medicine Chest* 54.5.9	Acts 2:22
εἶπαν οἱ ἀπόστολοι ἄνδρα ἀποδεδειγμένον εἰς ὑμᾶς σημείοις καὶ τέρασι, καὶ οὐκ εἶπαν· θεόν ἀποδεδειγμένον.	ἄνδρα ἀποδεδειγμένον ἀπὸ τοῦ θεοῦ εἰς ὑμᾶς δυνάμεσιν καὶ τέρασιν καὶ σημείοις
" 'The apostles said, "a male approved among you by signs and wonders," and did not said, "a God approved." ' "	"a man attested to you by God with deeds of power, wonders, and signs"
Fragment 8: Epiphanius, *Medicine Chest* 54.6.1	1 Timothy 2:5
ἔφη περὶ αὐτοῦ ὁ ἀπόστολος ὅτι μεσίτης θεοῦ καὶ ἀνθρώπων, ἄνθρωπος Χριστὸς Ἰησοῦς	μεσίτης θεοῦ καὶ ἀνθρώπων, ἄνθρωπος Χριστὸς Ἰησοῦς
" 'The apostle said about him, "the mediator between God and men, the man Christ Jesus." ' "	"mediator between God and men, the man Christ Jesus." (1 Tim. 2:5, RSV)

BIBLIOGRAPHY

Against All Heresies. Translated by S. Thelwall. In *The Ante-Nicene Fathers: Volume 3 – The Writings of Tertullian.* Edited by Alexander Roberts, James Donaldson, and Arthur Cleveland Coxe. Edinburgh, 1885 [early 3rd century].[1]

Aland, Barbara et. al. *The Greek New Testament.* 5th Rev. ed. [UBS 5] Stuttgart: Deutsche Bibelgesellschaft, 2014.

Alcinous. *The Handbook of Platonism [Didaskalikos].* Translated by John Dillon. In *Alcinous: The Handbook of Platonism.* New York: Oxford University Press, 1993 [late 2nd c.].

Altendorf, Hans-Dietrich. "Zum Stichwort: Rechtgläubigkeit und Ketzerei im ältesten Christentum." *Zeitschrift für Kirchengeschichte* 80 (1969).

Anderson, Bernhard W. "The Messiah as Son of God: Peter's Confession in Tradito-Historical Perspective." In *Christological Perspectives: Essays in Honor of Harvey K. McArthur,* edited by Robert F. Berkes and Sarah A. Edwards. New York: The Pilgrim Press, 1982.

Anderson, Paul N. *The Riddles of the Fourth Gospel.* Minneapolis: Fortress, 2011.

Aristedes. *The Apology of Aristedes.* Translated by D.M. Kay. In *The Ante-Nicene Fathers: Volume 9 – Recently Discovered Additions to Early Christian Literature,* edited by Allan Menzies. Edinburgh, 1897 [mid-2nd century].

Ashton, John. *Understanding the Fourth Gospel.* Oxford: Oxford University Press, 1991.

---

[1] As this book has been traditionally mis-attributed to Tertullian, some scholars refer to the author as "Pseudo-Tertullian."

Ashwin-Siejkowski, Piotr. *Clement of Alexandria on Trial: The Evidence of 'Heresy' from Photius' Bibliotheca.* Boston: Brill, 2010.

Athanasius. *Councils of Ariminum and Seleucia [De Synodis] (a.k.a. Concerning the Synods).* Translated by J. H. Newman and A. Robertson. In *A Select Library of Nicene and Post-Nicene Fathers of the Christian Church, Second Series: Volume 4 – St. Athanasius: Select Works and Letters.* Edited by Philip Schaff and Henry Wace. London, 1891 [c. 359–62]

———. *History of the Arians [Historia Arianorum].* Translated by J. H. Newman and A. Robertson. In *A Select Library of Nicene and Post-Nicene Fathers of the Christian* Church, Second Series: Volume 4 – St. Athanasius: Select Works and Letters. Edited by Philip Schaff and Henry Wace. London, 1891 [358].

———. *On the Incarnation of Our Lord Jesus Christ, Against Apollinaris.* Translated by members of the English Church. In *Later Treatises of S. Athanasius, Archbishop of Alexandria, with Notes, and an Appendix on S. Cyril of Alexandria and Theodoret.* London, 1881 (372).

Athenagoras. *Embassy for the Christians [A Plea for the Christians].* Translated by Joseph Hugh Crehan. In *Athenagoras: Embassy for the Christians, The Resurrection of the Dead.* Westminster: The Newman Press, 1956 [c. 176–80].

Ball, David M. *'I am' in John's Gospel: Literary Function, Background and Theological Implications.* Sheffield: Sheffield Academic Press, 1996.

Balz, H. and G. Schneider, eds., *Exegetical Dictionary of the New Testament.* Grand Rapids: Eerdmans, 1994.

Bardy, Gustave. *Paul de Samosate.* Louvain: Spicilegium Sacrum Lovaniense, 1929.

Barnard, L. W. "The Background of St Ignatius of Antioch." *Vigiliae Christianae* 17 (1963).

———. "God, the Logos, the Spirit and the Trinity in the Theology of Athenagoras." *Studia Theologica* 24:1 (1970).

———. *Justin Martyr: His Life and Thought.* Cambridge: Cambridge University Press, 1967.

Barnes, Jonathan, ed. *Early Greek Philosophy*. London: Penguin Books, 1987.

Barnes, T. D. "The Date of Ignatius." *The Expository Times* 120:3 (2008).

Barrett, Charles Kingsley. *Essays on John*. London: SPCK, 1982.

Basil. *Letter 52: To the Canonicae*. Translated by Blomfield Jackson. In *Nicene and Post-Nicene Fathers, Second Series, Volume 8: Basil: Letters and Select Works*. Edited by Philip Schaff and Henry Wace. 1894 [c. 370].

Bauckham, Richard. "The Origin of the Ebionites." In *The Image of the Judaeo-Christians in Ancient Jewish and Christian Literature*, edited by P. J. Tomson and D. Lambers-Petry. Tübingen: Mohr-Siebeck, 2003.

———. *Jesus and the Eyewitnesses: The Gospels as Eyewitness Testimony*. Cambridge: Eerdmans, 2006.

———. *Jesus and the God of Israel: God Crucified and Other Studies on the New Testament's Christology of Divine Identity*. Grand Rapids: Eerdmans, 2008.

———. *The Testimony of the Beloved Disciple: Narrative, History, and Theology in the Gospel of John*. Grand Rapids: Baker Academic, 2007.

Behr, John. *The Way to Nicaea*. 2 vols. Crestwood: St Vladimir's Seminary Press, 2001.

Bertrand, D. A. "L'argumentation scripturaire de Théodote le Corroyeur." *Cahiers de Biblia Patristica* 1 (1987).

Bligh, John. *Galatians: A Discussion of St Paul's Epistle*. London: St. Paul Publications, 1969.

Book of Elijah [a.k.a. *Sefer Elijah, Sefer Eliahu, Sefer Elias*]. Translated by John C. Reeves. In *Trajectories in Near Eastern Apocalyptic: A Postrabbinic Jewish Apocalypse Reader*, edited by John C. Reeves. Boston: Brill, 2006 [3rd–7th centuries CE].

Boring, M. Eugene. *Sayings of the Risen Jesus: Christian Prophecy in the Synoptic Tradition*. Cambridge: Cambridge University Press, 1982.

Bovon, François and John M. Duffy. "A New Greek Fragment from Ariston of Pella's *Dialogue of Jason and Papiscus*." *Harvard Theological Review* 105:4 (2012).

Boyarin, Daniel. *Border Lines: The Partition of Judaeo-Christianity.* Philadelphia: University of Pennsylvania Press, 2004.

————. "Logos, a Jewish Word: John's Prologue as Midrash." In *The Jewish Annotated New Testament,* 2nd ed, edited by Amy-Jill Levine and Marc Zvi Brettler. New York: Oxford University Press, 2017.

Brent, A. "Was Hippolytus a Schismatic?" *Vigiliae Christianae* 49:3 (1995).

Broadhead, Edwin K. *Jewish Ways of Following Jesus: Redrawing the Religious Map of Antiquity.* Tübingen: Mohr Siebeck, 2010.

Brodie, Thomas L. *The Gospel according to John.* New York: Oxford University Press, 1997.

Brown, Raymond. *The Birth of the Messiah: A Commentary on the Infancy Narratives in the Gospels of Matthew and Luke.* Updated Edition. New York: Doubleday, 1993 [1977].

————. *The Epistles of John: Translated, with Introduction, Notes, and Commentary.* Garden City: Doubleday 1982.

————. *The Gospel According to John.* London: Geoffrey Chapman, 1982.

Bultmann, Rudolph. *The Gospel of John: A Commentary.* Oxford: Basil Blackwell, 1971.

Burney, Charles Fox. *The Aramaic Origin of the Fourth Gospel.* Oxford: Clarendon Press, 1922.

Burrus, Virginia. "Rhetorical Stereotypes in the Portrait of Paul of Samosata." *Vigiliae Christianae* 43:3 (1989).

Buzzard, Anthony F. and Charles F. Hunting. *The Doctrine of the Trinity: Christianity's Self-Inflicted Wound.* San Francisco: Christian Universities Press, 1998.

Carrington, Philip. *The Early Christian Church.* 2 vols. Cambridge: Cambridge University Press, 1957.

Charlesworth, James H. "Did the Fourth Evangelist Know the Enoch Tradition?" In *Testimony and Interpretation: Early Christology in its Judeo-Hellenistic milieu,* edited by J. Roskovec, J. Mrazek and P. Pokorny. Edinburgh: T&T Clark, 2005.

Clarke, E. G. *The Wisdom of Solomon.* Cambridge: Cambridge University Press, 1973.

Clement. *First Letter of Clement to the Corinthians*. Translated by Bart D. Ehrman. In *The Apostolic Fathers, Vol. 1*. Cambridge: Harvard University Press, 2003. [late 1st c.].

Collins, Adela Y. and John J. Collins. *King and Messiah as Son of God: Divine, Human and Angelic Messianic Figures in Biblical and Related Literature*. Grand Rapids: Eerdmans, 2008.

Coloe, Mary L. "Like Father – Like Son: The Role of Abraham in Tabernacles, Jn 8:31–59." *Pacifica* 12 (1999).

Conzelmann, Hans. *1 Corinthians: A Commentary on the First Epistle to the Corinthians*. Translated by James W. Leitch. Philadelphia: Fortress Press, 1975.

Corwin, Virginia. *St Ignatius and Christianity in Antioch*. New Haven: Yale University Press, 1960.

Crossan, John Dominic. *The Historical Jesus: The Life of a Mediterranean Jewish Peasant*. San Franciso: HarperSanFranciso, 1992.

Crossley, James G. *The Date of Mark's Gospel*. London: T&T Clark, 2004.

Cullmann, Oscar. *The Johannine Circle*. London: SCM Press, 1976.

Curry, Carl. "The Theogony of Theophilus," *Vigiliae Christianae* 42:4 (1988).

Danielou, Jean. *The Theology of Jewish Christianity: A History of Early Christian Doctrine Before the Council of Nicaea*. Westminster Press, 1977.

Davies, Margaret. *Matthew*. Sheffield: JSOT Press, 1993.

Dillon, John. *The Middle Platonists: 80 B.C. to A.D. 220*. Rev. ed. Ithaca: Cornell University Press, 1996.

Dodd, C. H. *The Interpretation of the Fourth Gospel*. Cambridge: Cambridge University Press, 1968.

Donfried, Karl P. "The Theology of Second Clement." *The Harvard Theological Review* 66:4 (1973).

———. *The Setting of Second Clement in Early Christianity*. Supplement to *Novum Testamentum* vol. 38. Leiden: Brill, 1974.

Dorner, I. A. *History of the Development of the Doctrine of the Person of Christ.* Translated by W. L. Alexander and D. W. Simon. Edinburgh: T&T Clark, 1868–70.

Dunn, James D. G. *Christology in the Making,* 2nd ed. London: SCM Press, 1989.

———. *A Commentary on the Epistle to the Galatians.* London: A&C Black, 1993.

———. *Did the First Christians Worship Jesus?* London: SPCK, 2010.

———. *The Epistles to the Colossians and to Philemon.* NIGTC; Grand Rapids: Eerdmans, 1996.

———. *Jesus Remembered.* Grand Rapids: Eerdmans, 2003.

———. *The Theology of Paul the Apostle.* London: T&T Clark, 2003.

Edwards, James R. *The Hebrew Gospel and The Development of the Synoptic Tradition.* Grand Rapids: Eerdmans, 2009.

Edwards, Mark J. "Justin's Logos and the Word of God." *Journal of Early Christian Studies* 3:3 (1995).

Ehrman, Bart D, ed. *The Apostolic Fathers.* 2 vols. Translated by Bart D. Ehrman. Cambridge: Harvard University Press, 2003.

———. *Forged: Writing in the Name of God—Why the Bible's Authors Are Not Who We Think They Are.* New York: HarperCollins, 2011.

———. *How Jesus Became God: The Exaltation of the Jewish Preacher from Galilee.* New York: HarperOne, 2014.

———. *Lost Christianities: The Battles for Scripture and the Faiths We Never Knew.* Oxford: Oxford University Press, 2005.

———. *The Orthodox Corruption of Scripture.* Updated Edition. Oxford: Oxford University Press, 2011.

Elliott, J. K, ed. *The Apocryphal New Testament.* Oxford: Clarendon Press, 1993.

Emlyn, Thomas. *An Humble Inquiry into the Scripture-Account of Jesus Christ.* Updated Edition. Edited by Kegan Chandler and Dale Tuggy. Nashville: Theophilus Press, 2021 [1702].

Epiphanius. *Panarion [Medicine Chest].* In *The Panarion of Epiphanius of Salamis.* 2 Vols. 2nd, revised ed. Translated by Frank Williams. Atlanta: SBL Press, 2009, 2013 [374–76].

Epistle of Barnabas. Translated by Bart D. Ehrman. In *The Apostolic Fathers,* Vol. 2. Cambridge: Harvard University Press, 2003. [c. 125].

Epistle of Barnabas. Translated by James A. Kleist. In *The Didache: the Epistle of Barnabas, the Epistles and the Martyrdom of St. Polycarp, the Fragments of Papias, the Epistle to Diognetus.* New York: Newman Press, 1948 [c. 125].

Eusebius. *Ecclesiastical History.* Translated by Paul Maier. In *Eusebius: The Church History.* Grand Rapids: Kregel, 1999 [c. 324–25].

——. *On Ecclesiastical Theology.* In *Eusebius of Caesarea: Against Marcellus and On Ecclesiastical Theology.* Translated by Kelley McCarthy Spoerl and Markus Vinzent. Washington, D.C.: The Catholic University of America Press, 2017 [c. 338].

——. *Prophetic Extracts.* In *Patrologiae Cursus Completus. Series Graeca* 22: 1021–1262.

Evans, Craig A. *New International Biblical Commentary: Luke.* Peabody: Hendrickson Publishers, 1990.

——. "Authenticating the Words of Jesus" in *Authenticating the Words of Jesus,* edited by B. Chilton and C. A. Evans. Leiden: Brill, 1999.

Evans, C. Stephen, ed. *Exploring Kenotic Christology: The Self-Emptying of God.* Vancouver: Regent College Publishing, 2006.

Fee, Gordon D. *Paul's Letter to the Philippians.* Grand Rapids: Eerdmans, 1995.

——. *Pauline Christology: An Exegetical-Theological Study.* Peabody: Hendrickson, 2007.

Finley, Gregory C. "The Ebionites and 'Jewish Christianity': Examining Heresy and the Attitudes of Church Fathers." PhD diss., Catholic University of America, 2009.

1 (Ethiopic Apocalypse of) Enoch [a.k.a. *1 Enoch, First Enoch*]. Translated by E. Isaac. In *The Old Testament Pseudepigrapha: Volume 1: Apocalyptic Literature and Testaments.* Edited by James H. Charlesworth. Peabody: Hendrickson, 1983 [2nd c. BCE–1st c. CE].

Fisher, George Park. "Some Remarks on the Alogi." *Papers of the American Society of Church History* 2 (1890).

Fitzgerald, J. T. "Eusebius and *The Little Labyrinth*" in *The Early Church in Its Context: Essays in Honor of Everett Ferguson*, edited by A. J. Malherbe, F. W. Norris and J. W. Thompson. Leiden: Brill, 1998.

Foster, Paul. "The Epistles of Ignatius of Antioch (Part 1)." *The Expository Times* 117:12 (2006).

———. "The Epistles of Ignatius of Antioch (Part 2)." *The Expository Times* 118:1 (2006).

The Fourth Book of Ezra. Translated by Bruce M. Metzger. In *The Old Testament Pseudepigrapha: Volume 1: Apocalyptic Literature and Testaments*, edited by James H. Charlesworth. Peabody: Hendrickson, 1983 [late 1st c. CE].

France, R. T. *The Gospel According to Matthew.* Leicester: Inter-Varsity Press, 1985.

Galen. *The Doctrines of Hippocrates and Plato* [*De Placitis Hippocratis et Platonis*]. Edited and translated by Philip De Lacy. 3 vols. Berlin: Akademie Verlag, 1978–84 [late 2nd c. CE].

Gaston, Thomas E. "Does the Gospel of John Have a High Christology?" *Horizons in Biblical Theology* 36:2 (2014).

———. "The Eyewitnesses to the Birth of Jesus." *Christadelphian eJournal of Biblical Interpretation* 8:1 (2014).

———. "The Influence of Platonism on the Early Apologists." *The Heythrop Journal* 50:4 (2009).

———. "When Did the New Testament become Scripture?" *Christadelphian eJournal of Biblical Interpretation* 7:1 (2013).

———. "Wisdom and the Goddess." *Christadelphian eJournal of Biblical Interpretation* 2:1 (2008).

———. "Why Three? An Exploration of the Origins of the Doctrine of the Trinity with Reference to Platonism and Gnosticism." DPhil thesis. University of Oxford, 2014.

———. "Wisdom and the Goddess." *Christadelphian eJournal of Biblical Interpretation* 2:1 (2008).

Gaston, Thomas E. and Perry, Andrew. "Christological Monotheism" *Horizons in Biblical Theology*, 39:2 (2017).

Gathercole, Simon J. *The Pre-existent Son: Recovering the Christologies of Matthew, Mark, and Luke.* Grand Rapids: Eerdmans, 2006.

———. "What Did the First Christians Think about Jesus?" In *How God Became Jesus: The Real Origins of Belief in Jesus' Divine Nature,* edited by Michael F. Bird. Grand Rapids: Zondervan, 2014.

Gilliam, Paul R. *Ignatius of Antioch and the Arian Controversy.* Leiden: Brill, 2017.

Givens, Terryl. *When Souls Had Wings: Pre-Mortal Existence in Western Thought.* Oxford: Oxford University Press, 2009.

Goldstein, R. and G. G. Stroumsa. "The Greek and Jewish Origins of Docetism: A New Proposal." *Zeitschrift für antikes Christentum* 10 (2006).

Goodacre, Mark S. *The Synoptic Problem: A Way Through the Maze.* London: T&T Clark, 2001.

———. *The Case against Q.* Harrisburg: Trinity Press, 2002.

Goodenough, Erwin Ramsdell. *The Theology of Justin.* Amsterdam: Philo Press, 1968 [1923].

Gordon, R. P. *Hebrews.* Sheffield: Sheffield Academic Press, 2000.

The Gospel of Peter. Translated by J.K. Elliot. In *The Apocryphal New Testament.* New York: Oxford University Press, 1993 [mid to late 2nd c.].

The Gospel of Thomas. Translated by J.K. Elliot. In *The Apocryphal New Testament.* New York: Oxford University Press, 1993 [mid-2nd c.].

Goulder, Michael. "Ignatius' 'Docetists'." *Vigiliae Christianae* 53:1 (1999).

———. "A Poor Man's Christology." *New Testament Studies* 45:3 (1999).

———. "The Pre-Marcan Gospel." *Scottish Journal of Theology* 47:4 (1994).

———. *A Tale of Two Missions.* London: SCM Press, 1994.

Grant, Robert M. *The Early Christian Doctrine of God.* Charlottesville: University Press of Virginia, 1966.

———. "Gnostic Origins and the Basilidians of Irenaeus." *Vigiliae Christianae* 13 (1959).

———. *Heresy and Criticism: The Search for Authenticity in Early Christian Literature.* Louisville: Westminster John Knox Press, 1993.

———. *Second Century Christianity: A Collection of Fragments.* Louisville: Westminster John Knox Press, 2003.

Green, Bernard. *Christianity in Ancient Rome: The First Three Centuries.* London: T&T Clark, 2010.

Guthrie, Donald. *The Letter to the Hebrews: An Introduction and Commentary.* Leicester: Inter-Varsity Press, 1983.

Guthrie, Kennenth Sylvan. *Numenius of Apamea, the Father of Neo-Platonism: Works, Biography, Message, Sources, and Influence.* London: George Bell and Sons, 1917.

Häkkinen, Sakari. "Ebionites." In *A Companion to Second Century Christian "Heretics,"* edited by A. Marjanen and P. Luomanen. Leiden: Brill, 2005.

Hamerton-Kelly, R. G. *Pre-Existence, Wisdom, and the Son of Man: A Study of the Idea of Pre-existence in the New Testament.* Cambridge: Cambridge University Press, 1973.

Harnack, Adolf von. *History of Dogma [Lehrbuch der Dogmengeschichte].* 7 vols. Translated by N. Buchanan et. al. London, 1894–99 [1885–87].

Hellerman, Joseph. "*Morphe Theou* as a Signifier of Social Status in Philippians 2." *Journal of the Evangelical Theological Society* 52:4 (2009) 784–86.

Hengel, Martin. "The Prologue of the Gospel of John as the Gateway to Christological Truth." In *The Gospel of John and Christian Theology,* edited by Richard Bauckham and Carl Mosser. Cambridge: Eerdmans, 2008.

Hermas. *The Shepherd of Hermas.* Translated by Bart D. Ehrman. In *The Apostolic Fathers,* Vol. 2. Cambridge: Harvard University Press, 2003 [c. 100].

———. *The Shepherd of Hermas.* Translated by Graydon F. Snyder. In *The Apostolic Fathers: A New Translation and Commentary, Volume 6: The Shepherd of Hermas.* London: Thomas Nelson and Sons, 1968 [c. 100].

Hilary. *On the Councils [De Synodis]* (a.k.a. *The Faith of the Easterns*). Translated by L. Pullan. In *Nicene and Post-Nicene Fathers, Second Series, Volume 9: St. Hilary of Poitiers: Select Works,* edited by W. Sanday, 1893 [359].

Hildebrand, Stephen M. "The Trinity in the Ante-Nicene Fathers." In *The Oxford Handbook of The Trinity*, edited by Gilles Emery and Matthew Levering. New York: Oxford University Press, 2011.

Hippolytus. *Against Noetus 1–11 and 14–17.* Translated by Andrew Radde-Gallwitz. In *The Cambridge Edition of Early Christian Writings: Volume 1: God*, edited by Andrew Radde-Gallwitz. New York: Cambridge University Press, 2017 [early 3rd c.].

Holl, Karl and Jürgen Dummer, eds. *Epiphanius II: Panarion Haer. 34–46.* 2nd ed. Berlin: De Gruyter, 1980 [374–76].

The Holy Book of the Great Invisible Spirit [a.k.a. *The Gospel of the Egyptians*]. Translated by John D. Turner. In *The Nag Hammadi Scriptures: The Revised and Updated Translation of Sacred Gnostic Texts*, edited by Marvin Meyer. New York: HarperOne, 2007 [c. 200–350].

Hooker, Morna D. *A Commentary on the Gospel According to St Mark.* London: A&C Black, 1991.

Hoover, Roy W. "The *Harpagmos* Enigma: A Philological Solution." *Harvard Theologica Review* 64 (1971): 95–119.

Horton, Fred L. *The Melchizedek Tradition: A Critical Examination of the Sources of the Fifth Century AD and in the Epistle to the Hebrews.* Cambridge: Cambridge University Press, 1976.

Hultgren, Arland J. *The Rise of Normative Christianity.* Minneapolis: Fortress, 1994.

Hurtado, Larry. W. *New International Biblical Commentary: Mark.* Peabody: Hendrickson, 1998.

———. *Lord Jesus Christ: Devotion to Jesus in Earliest Christianity.* Grand Rapids: Eerdmans, 2003.

Hymenaeus, et. al. *The Letter of Six Bishops [a.k.a. The Letter of Hymenaeus].* Translated by Michael Emadi. In Forman, Matt and Doug Van Dorn, *The Angel of the Lord: A Biblical, Historical, and Theological Study.* Dacono: Waters of Creation Publishing, 2020 [268].

Ignatius. *To the Ephesians.* Translated by Bart D. Ehrman. In *The Apostolic Fathers*, Vol. 1. Cambridge: Harvard University Press, 2003. [early 2nd c.].

————. *To the Romans.* Translated by Bart D. Ehrman. In *The Apostolic Fathers,* Vol. 1. Cambridge: Harvard University Press, 2003. [early 2nd c.].

————. *To the Smyrneans.* Translated by Bart D. Ehrman. In *The Apostolic Fathers,* Vol. 1. Cambridge: Harvard University Press, 2003. [early 2nd c.].

————. *To the Trallians.* Translated by Bart D. Ehrman. In *The Apostolic Fathers,* Vol. 1. Cambridge: Harvard University Press, 2003. [early 2nd c.].

Irenaeus. *Against Heresies.* Translated by Alexander Roberts, James Donaldson, and Arthur Cleveland Coxe. In *Ante-Nicene Fathers, Volume 1: The Apostolic Fathers with Justin Martyr and Irenaeus.* New York: Christian Literature Publishing Co., 1885 [c. 180].

————. *Against the Heresies (Book 1).* Translated by Dominic J. Unger and John J. Dillon. In *St. Irenaeus of Lyons: Against the Heresies,* Vol. 1. New York: The Newman Press, 1992 [c. 180].

————. *Against the Heresies (Book 2).* Translated by Dominic J. Unger and John J. Dillon. In *St. Irenaeus of Lyons: Against the Heresies,* Vol. 2. New York: The Newman Press, 2012 [c. 180].

————. *Against the Heresies (Book 3).* Translated by Dominic J. Unger and M.C. Steenberg. In *St. Irenaeus of Lyons: Against the Heresies,* Vol. 3. New York: The Newman Press, 2012 [c. 180].

————. *The Demonstration of the Apostolic Preaching.* Translated by John Behr. In *St. Irenaeus of Lyons: On the Apostolic Preaching.* Crestwood: St. Vladimir's Seminary Press, 1997 [c. 175–89].

————. *Fragments.* Translated by Alexander Roberts, James Donaldson, and Arthur Cleveland Coxe. In *Ante-Nicene Fathers, Volume 1: The Apostolic Fathers with Justin Martyr and Irenaeus.* New York: Christian Literature Publishing Co., 1885 [late 2nd c.].

The Isaiah Targum. Translated by Bruce D. Chilton. In *The Isaiah Targum: Introduction, Translation, Apparatus and Notes.* Wilmington: Michael Glazier, Inc., 1987 [c. 150 BCE–c. 350 CE].

Jacobson, Arland Dean. *The First Gospel: An Introduction to Q.* Sonoma: Polebridge Press, 1992.

Jefford, Clayton N. "Ignatius and the Apostolic Fathers." In *The Routledge Companion to Early Christian Thought*, edited by D. Jeffrey. Bingham. London: Routledge, 2010.

Jerome. *Commentary on Galatians*. Translated by Andrew Cain. In *St. Jerome: Commentary on Galatians*. Washington, D.C.: The Catholic University of America Press, 2010 [386].

―――. *Commentary on Isaiah*. Translated by Thomas P. Scheck. In *St. Jerome: Commentary on Isaiah; Origen: Homilies 1–9 on Isaiah*. New York: The Newman Press, 2015 [410].

―――. *Commentary on Matthew*. Translated by Thomas P. Scheck. In *St. Jerome: Commentary on Matthew*. Washington, D.C.: The Catholic University of America Press, 2014 [398].

―――. *The Dialogue Against the Pelagians*. Translated by John N. Hritzu. In *St. Jerome: Dogmatical and Polemical Works*. Washington, D.C.: The Catholic University of America Press, 1965 [415].

―――. *Hebrew Questions on Genesis*. Translated by C.T.R. Hayward. In *Saint Jerome's Hebrew Questions on Genesis*. New York: Oxford University Press, 1995 [c. 391–93].

―――. "Jerome Letter 73 to Evangelus verses Ambrosiaster's Question 109 on Melchizedek." Translated by John Litteral. https://sites.google.com/site/aquinasstudybible/home/jerome-letter-73-to-evangelus [398].

―――. *On Illustrious Men*. Translated by Thomas P. Halton. In *Saint Jerome: On Illustrious Men*. Washington, D.C.: The Catholic University of America Press, 1999 [c. 392].

―――. *Tractate on the Psalms [Tractatus Sive Homiliae in Psalmos]*. In *Sancti Hieronymi Presbyteri: Tractactus Sive Homiliae in Psalmos,* in *Marci Evangelium Alique Varia Argumenta*, edited by Germain Morin, 1897 [c. 402].

"John 6:62 Commentary." Revised English Version. https://www.revisedenglishversion.com/John/chapter6/62.

Josephus. *Jewish Antiquities*. In *Josephus*, Vols. 4–9. Cambridge: Harvard University Press, 1930–65 [93 CE].

Jubilees [a.k.a. *The Book of Jubilees, The Little Genesis*] Translated by O.S. Wintermute. In *The Old Testament Pseudepigrapha: Volume 2: Expansions of the "Old Testament" and Legends, Wisdom and Philosophical Literature, Prayers, Psalms, and Odes, Fragments of Lost Judeo-Hellenistic Works*, edited by James H. Charlesworth. Peabody: Hendricksen, 1983 [c. 161–140 BCE].

Justin Martyr. *The First Apology.* Translated by Leslie William Barnard. In *St. Justin Martyr: The First and Second Apologies.* New York: Paulist Press, 1997 [c. 151–55].

———. *The Second Apology.* Translated by Leslie William Barnard. In *St. Justin Martyr: The First and Second Apologies.* New York: Paulist Press, 1997 [c. 155].

———. *Dialogue with Trypho.* Translated by Thomas Wells, revised by Thomas Halton. *In St. Justin Martyr: Dialogue with Trypho,* edited by Michael Slusser. Washington, DC: The Catholic University of America Press, 2003 [c. 155–61].

Keener, Craig, ed. *The IVP Bible Background Commentary—New Testament.* Downers Grove, InterVarsity Press, 1993.

Keown, Mark. *Philippians 1:1–2:18.* Bellingham: Lexham Press, 2017.

Kelly, J. N. D. *Early Christian Doctrines.* 5th ed. London: A&C Black, 1977.

Kittel, Gerhard, ed. *Theological Dictionary of the New Testament* [*Theologisches Wörterbuch zum Neuen Testament*] Translated and edited by Geoffrey W. Bromiley. Michigan: Eerdmans, 1986 [1933–79].

Kleist, J. A., trans. *Ancient Christian Writers,* vol.6. New York: The Newman Press, 1948.

Klijn, A. F. J. *Jewish-Christian Gospel Tradition.* Leiden: Brill, 1992.

Klijn, A. F. J. and G. J. Reinink. *Patristic Evidence for Jewish-Christian Sects.* Leiden: Brill, 1973.

Knight, Jonathan. *Luke's Gospel.* London: Routledge, 1998.

Knox, John. *The Humanity and Divinity of Christ: A Study of Patterns in Christology.* Cambridge: Cambridge University Press, 1967.

Lampe, G. W. H. *A Patristic Greek Lexicon.* Oxford: Clarendon Press, 1976.

Lampe, Peter. *From Paul to Valentinus: Christians at Rome in the First Two Centuries.* Translated by Michael Steinhauser. Edited by Marshall D. Johnson. Fortress Press: Minneapolis, 2003 [1989].

Lang, U. M. "The Christological Controversy at the Synod of Antioch in 268/9." *Journal of Theological Studies* 51:1 (2000).

Lawlor, Hugh Jackson. "The Sayings of Paul of Samosata." *The Journal of Theological Studies* 19: 73 (1917).

Lichtenberger, Hermann. "Syncretistic Features in Jewish and Jewish-Christian Baptism Movements." In *Jews and Christians: The Parting of Ways AD 70 to 135,* edited by J. D. G. Dunn. Grand Rapids: Eerdmans, 1992.

Lightfoot, J. B. *The Apostolic Fathers.* London, 1890.

———. *Saint Paul's Epistle to the Philippians.* London: Macmillan, 1908.

Lindars, Barnabas. *The Gospel of John.* Grand Rapids: Eerdmans, 1972.

Lindars, Barnabas. *The Theology of the Letters to the Hebrews.* Cambridge: Cambridge University Press, 1991.

Löhr, W. "Theodotus der Lederarbeiter und Theodotus der Bankier – ein Beitrag zur römischen Theologiegeschichte des zweiten und dritten Jahrhunderts." *Zeitschrift für die neutestamentliche Wissenschaft und die Kunde der älteren Kirche* 87:1/2 (1996).

Longenecker, Richard N. *The Christology of Early Jewish Christianity.* London: SCM Press, 1970.

Lucian. *Alexander or the False Prophet.* In *Lucian: Alexander or the False Prophet.* Translated by Peter Thonemann. Oxford: Oxford University Press, 2021 [c. 180 CE].

———. *A Professor of Public Speaking.* Translated by A.M. Harmon. In *Lucian: In Eight Volumes,* Volume 4. New York: G. P. Putnam's Sons, 1925 [c. 180].

Luomanen, Petri. "On the Fringes of Canon: Eusebius' View of the 'Gospel of the Hebrews.'" In *The Formation of the Early Church,* edited by Jostein Adna. Tübingen: Mohr Siebeck, 2005.

———. *Recovering Jewish-Christian Sects and Gospels.* Leiden: Brill, 2011.

Machen, J. Gresham. *The Virgin Birth of Christ.* James Clarke, 1987 [1930].

Mack, Burton L. *The Lost Gospel: The Book of Q and Christian Origins.* San Francisco: HarperSanFrancisco, 1994.

Mackay, Ian D. *John's Relationship with Mark.* Tübingen: Mohr Siebeck, 2004.

Malone, Andrew S. "God the Illeist: Third-Person Self-References and Trinitarian Hints in the Old Testament." *Journal of the Evangelical Theological Society* 52 (2009): 499–518.

Manor, Scott T. "Epiphanius' Alogi and the Question of Early Ecclesiastical Opposition to the Johannine Corpus." PhD Thesis. University of Edinburgh, 2012.

Manson, William. *The Epistle to the Hebrews.* London: Hodder & Stoughton, 1951.

Martens, Peter. "Origen's Christology in the Context of the Second and Third Centuries." In *The Oxford Handbook of Origen*, edited by Ronald E. Heine and Karen Jo Torjesen. New York: Oxford University Press, 2022.

McGrath, Alister E. *Christian Theology: An Introduction.* 4th ed; Oxford: Blackwell, 2007 [1993].

McGuckin, John A. "Christ: The Apostolic Fathers to the Third Century." In *The Routledge Companion to Early Christian* Thought, edited by D. J. Bingham. London: Routledge, 2010.

Migne, J. P., ed. *Patrologia Graeca.* 162 vols. Paris, 1857–86.

Millar, F. "Paul of Samosata, Zenobia and Aurelian: The Church, Local Culture and Political Allegiance in Third Century Syria." *Journal of Roman Studies* 61 (1971).

Minns, Denis. "Justin Martyr." In *The Cambridge History of Philosophy in Late Antiquity*, edited by L. P. Gerson. Cambridge: Cambridge University Press, 2010.

Minns, Denis. and P. Parvis. *Justin, Philosopher and Martyr: Apologies.* Oxford: Oxford University Press, 2009.

Morris, Thomas V. *The Logic of God Incarnate.* Ithaca: Cornell University Press, 1986.

Neander, Johann August Wilhelm. *Lectures on the History of Christian Dogmas* [*Allgemeine Geschichte Der Christlichen Religion Und*

Kirche]. 2 vols. Translated by J.E. Ryland. Edited by J.L. Jacobi. London: Henry G. Bohn, 1858 [1825–52].

Norris, Alfred D. *Acts and Epistles*. London: Aletheia Books, 1989.

———. *The Virgin Birth of the Son of God*. Birmingham: The Christadelphian, 1960.

Norris, Frederick W. "Paul of Samosata: *Procurator Ducenarius*." *Journal of Theological Studies* 35:1 (1984).

Norris, Richard A. "Articulating Identity." In *The Cambridge History of Early Christian Literature*, edited by Frances Young, Lewis Ayres and Andrew Louth. Cambridge: Cambridge University Press, 2004.

Novatian. *The Trinity*. Translated by Russell J. DeSimone. In *Novatian: The Trinity, The Spectacles, Jewish Foods, In Praise of Purity, Letters*. Washington, D.C.: The Catholic University of America Press, 1974 [c. 240–50].

Numenius. *Fragments. In Platonist Philosophy 80 BC to AD 250: An Introduction and Collection of Sources in Translation*. Edited and translated by George Boys-Stones. New York: Cambridge University Press, 2018.

Odes of Solomon. Translated by James H. Charlesworth. In *The Old Testament Pseudepigrapha. Vol. 2*. Edited by James H. Charlesworth. Peabody: Hendrickson Publishers, 1981 [late 1st–early 2nd c.].

O'Neill, J. C. *Who Did Jesus Think He Was?* Leiden: Brill, 1995.

Origen. *Against Celsus*. Translated by Henry Chadwick. In *Origen: Contra Celsum [Against Celsus]*. New York: Cambridge University Press, 1953 [c. 246–48 CE].

———. *Commentary on John*. Translated by Ronald E. Heine. In *Origen: Commentary on the Gospel According to John Books 1–10*. Washington, D.C.: The Catholic University of America Press, 1989 [c. 248].

———. *Commentary on Matthew*. Translated by Ronald E. Heine. In *The Commentary of Origen on the Gospel of St. Matthew*. 2 Vols. New York: Oxford University Press, 2018 [c. 249].

———. *Dialogue with Heraclides*. Translated and annotated by Robert J. Daly. In *Origen: Treatise on the Passover and Dialogue with*

Heraclides and his Fellow Bishops on the Father, the Son, and the Soul.
New York: Paulist Press, 1992. [c. 244–49].

———. *Genesis Homily III.* Translated by Ronald E. Heine. In *Origen: Homilies on Genesis and Exodus.* Washington, D.C.: The Catholic University of America Press, 1981 [c. 238–44].

———. *Homilies on Jeremiah.* Translated by John Clark Smith. In *Origen: Homilies on Jeremiah and 1 Kings 28.* Washington, D.C.: The Catholic University of America Press, 1998 [c. 241].

———. *Homily 6: Luke 1:24–32.* Translated by Joseph T. Lienhard. In *Origen: Homilies on Luke, Fragments on Luke.* Washington, D.C.: The Catholic University of America Press, 1996 [c. 231–44].

———. *Homily 10.* Translated by Gary Wayne Barkley. In *Origen: Homilies on Leviticus 1–16.* Washington, D.C.: The Catholic University of America Press, 1990 [c. 238–44].

———. *On Prayer.* Translated by John Ernest Leonard Oulton. In *Alexandrian Christianity: Selected Translations of Clement and Origen,* edited by John Ernest Leonard Oulton and Henry Chadwick. Philadelphia: The Westminster Press, 1954 [c. 233–34].

Osborn, E. F. *Justin Martyr.* Tübingen: J. C. B. Mohr, 1973.

Osiek, Carolyn. *The Shepherd of Hermas.* Minneapolis: Fortress Press, 1999.

Paget, James Carleton. *Jews, Christians and Jewish Christians in Antiquity.* Tübingen: Mohr-Siebeck, 2010.

Pamphilus, *Apology for Origen* [a.k.a. *Defense of Origen*]. Translated by Thomas P. Scheck. In *St. Pamphilus: Apology for Origen, with The Letter of Rufinus on the Falsification of the Books of Origen.* Washington, D.C.: The Catholic University of America Press, 2010 [c. 308–10].

Parrinder, Geoffrey. *Son of Joseph: The Parentage of Jesus.* Edinburgh: T&T Clark, 1992.

Pászton-Kupán, I. *Theodoret of Cyrus.* London: Routledge, 2006.

Patterson, Stephen J. *The God of Jesus: The Historical Jesus and The Search for Meaning.* Harrisburg: Trinity Press International, 1998.

Pawl, Timothy J. *The Incarnation.* New York: Cambridge University Press, 2020.

Pearson, Birger A. "Melchizedek in Early Judaism, Christianity, and Gnosticism." In *Biblical Figures Outside the Bible,* edited by Michael E. Stone and Theodore A. Bergren. Harrisburg: Trinity Press International, 1998.

———. *Gnosticism and Christianity in Roman and Coptic Egypt.* London: T&T Clark, 2004.

Peppard, Michael *The Son of God in the Roman World: Divine Sonship in Its Social and Political Context.* New York: Oxford University Press, 2011.

Perry, Andrew. *Before He Was Born.* 6th ed. Tyne & Wear: Willow, 2017 [1995–95].

———. "The Text of John 1:18." https://www.academia.edu/en/42679566/The_Original_Text_of_John_1_18_Examined.

Petrement, Simone. *A Separate God: The Christian Origins of Gnosticism.* Translated by C. Harrison. London: Darton, Longman and Todd, 1991.

Phan, Peter C. "Developments of the Doctrine of the Trinity." In *The Cambridge Companion to the Trinity*, edited by Peter C. Phan. Cambridge: Cambridge University Press, 2011.

Philastrius. *Diversarum Hereseon Liber [Book of Various Heresies].* Edited by F. Heylen, G. Banterle. *Scriptores circa Abrosium 2,* Milano-Roma: Biblioteca Ambrosiana–Città Nuova Editrice, 1991.

Philo. *Allegorical Interpretation of Genesis II, III.* Translated by F.H. Colson and G.H. Whitaker. In *Philo: Volume I.* Cambridge: Harvard University Press, 1935 [mid-1st c.].

———. *On Drunkenness.* Translated by F.H. Colson and G.H. Whitaker. In *Philo: Volume III.* Cambridge: Harvard University Press, 1930 [mid-1st c.].

———. *On the Confusion of Tongues.* Translated by F.H. Colson and G.H. Whitaker. In *Philo: Volume IV.* Cambridge: Harvard University Press, 1935 [mid-1st c.].

———. *Questions and Answers on Exodus.* Translated by Ralph Marcus. In *Philo: Supplement II – Questions and Answers on Exodus.* Cambridge: Harvard University Press, 1953 [mid-1st c.].

————. *Questions and Answers on Genesis*. Translated by Ralph Marcus. In *Philo: Supplement I - Questions and Answers on Genesis*. Cambridge: Harvard University Press, 1953 [mid-1st c.].

————. *That the Worse is Wont to Attack the Better*. Translated by F.H. Colson and G.H. Whitaker. In *Philo: Volume II*. Cambridge: Harvard University Press, 1929 [mid-1st c.].

Photius. *The Library* [*Bibliotheca, Myriobiblion*]. Translated by J.H. Freese. In *The Library of Photius, Volume 1*. New York: Macmillan, 1921 [mid to late 9th c.].

Pietersma, Albert and Benjamin G. Wright, editors. *A New English Translation of the Septuagint and the Other Greek Translations Traditionally Included Under that Title*. New York: Oxford University Press, 2007.

Plato. *Meno*. Translated by G.M.A. Grube. In *Plato: Complete Works*, edited by John M. Cooper. Indianapolis: Hackett Publishing Company, 1997 [c. 385 BCE].

————. *Republic*. Translated by G.M.A. Grube and C.D.C. Reeve. In *Plato: Complete Works*, edited by John M. Cooper. Indianapolis: Hackett Publishing Company, 1997 [c. 380–75 BCE].

Plutarch. *Isis and Osiris*. In *Plutarch: Moralia, Volume V*. Translated by Frank Cole Babbitt. Cambridge: Harvard University Press, 1936 [late 1st c. CE].

————. *Moralia* [Morals]. In *Plutarch's Moralia in Fifteen Volumes, Volume X, 771E–854D*. Translated by Harold North Fowler. Cambridge: Harvard University Press, 1936 [late 1st c. CE].

Pollard, T. E. *Johannine Christology and the Early Church*. Cambridge: Cambridge University Press, 2005.

Polycarp, *Letter to the Philippians*. Translated by Bart D. Ehrman. In *The Apostolic Fathers*, Vol. 1. Cambridge: Harvard University Press, 2003 [mid-2nd c.].

Pratscher, W. *Der zweite Clemensbrief*, KAV 3. Gottingen: Vandenhoeck & Ruprecht, 2007.

Pritz, Ray. *Nazarene Jewish Christianity*. Leiden: Brill, 1988.

Protoevangelium of James. Translated by J.K. Elliot. In *The Apocryphal New Testament*. New York: Oxford University Press, 1993 [late 2nd c.].

Rahlfs, Alfred and Robert Hanhart, eds. *Septuaginta.* Editio altera. Stuttgart: Deutsche Bibelgesellschaft, 2006 [1935].

Rankin, David. *Athenagoras: Philosopher and Theologian.* Farnham: Ashgate, 2009.

Refutation of All Heresies [Philosophoumenua]. Translated by M. David Litwa. Atlanta: SBL Press, 2016 [c. 222].[1]

The Revelation of Adam [a.k.a. The Apocalypse of Adam]. Translated by Marvin Meyer. In *The Nag Hammadi Scriptures: The Revised and Updated Translation of Sacred Gnostic Texts*, edited by Marvin Meyer. New York: HarperOne, 2007 [late 1st c.–early 2nd c.].

Richardson, Cyril Charles. *The Christianity of Ignatius of Antioch.* New York: Columbia University Press, 1935.

Ridderbos, Herman. *The Gospel of John: A Theological Commentary* [*Het Evangelie naar Johannes. Proeve van een theologische Exegese*]. Translated by John Vriend. Grand Rapids: Eerdmans, 1997 [1987, 1992].

Rist, John. *On the Independence of Matthew and Mark.* Cambridge: Cambridge University Press, 1978.

Roberts, Colin H. *Manuscripts, Society, and Belief in Early Christian Egypt.* London: Oxford University Press 1977.

Robinson, J. A. T. *The Priority of John.* London: SCM Press, 1985.

———. *Redating the New Testament.* London: SCM Press, 1976.

Robinson, Thomas A. *The Bauer Thesis Examined: The Geography of Heresy in the Early Christian Church.* Lewiston: Edwin Mellen, 1988.

Rogers, Rick. *Theophilus of Antioch: The Life and Thought of a Second-Century Bishop.* Lanham: Lexington Books, 2000.

Rudolph, K. *Gnosis: The Nature and History of Gnosticism.* Edinburgh: T&T Clark, 1983.

Rutherford, Will. "*Altercatio Jasonis et Papisci* as a Testimony Source for Justin's 'Second God' Argument?" In *Justin Martyr and his Worlds,*

---

[1] Some modern scholars have attributed this book to Hippolytus (Hippolytos), but recent scholarship is conflicted and doubtful about the author of this book, and no ancient author attributes it to Hippolytus, so it is listed here as a work by an unknown author.

edited by Sara Parvis and Paul Foster. Minneapolis: Fortress Press, 2007.

Sample, Robert Lynn. "The Christology of the Council of Antioch (268 CE) Reconsidered." *Church History* 48:1 (1979).

Sanders, J. N. *A Commentary on the Gospel According to Saint John.* Edited and completed by B. A. Mastin. London: Adam & Charles Black, 1968.

Schleiermacher, Friedrich. "On the Discrepancy Between the Sabellian and Athanasian Method of Representing the Doctrine of the Trinity." Translated by Moses Stuart. *The Biblical Repository and Quarterly Observer*, Nos. 18 & 19, April & July 1835. Reprinted as: *On the Discrepancy Between the Sabellian and Athanasian Method of Representing the Doctrine of the Trinity.* Morrisville: Lulu.com, 2010 [1822].

Schnabel, Eckhard J. "Paul, Timothy, and Titus: The Assumption of a Pseudonymous Author and of Pseudonymous Recipients in the Light of Literary, Theological, and Historical Evidence." In *Do Historical Matters Matter To Faith?*, edited by James K. Hoffmeier and Dennis R. Magary. Wheaton: Crossway, 2012.

Schneemelcher, Wilhelm, ed. *New Testament Apocrypha*, 2 vols. Louisville: Westminster John Knox Press, 2003.

Schoedel, W. R. *Ignatius of Antioch: A Commentary on the Letters of Ignatius of Antioch.* Philadelphia: Fortress Press, 1985.

Schweizer, Eduard. *The Letter to the Colossians.* Translated by Andrew Chester. London: SPCK, 1982 [1976].

2 Baruch. Translated by A. F. G. Klijn. In *The Old Testament Pseudepigrapha: Volume 1: Apocalyptic Literature and Testaments*, edited by James H. Charlesworth. Peabody: Hendrickson, 1983 [early 2nd c. CE].

2 Baruch. Translated by Michael E. Stone and Matthias Henze. In *4 Ezra and 2 Baruch: Translations, Introductions, and Notes.* Minneapolis: Fortress Press, 2013 [late 1st c.].

Second Letter of Clement to the Corinthians. Translated by Bart D. Ehrman. In *The Apostolic Fathers*, Vol. 1. Cambridge: Harvard University Press, 2003 [mid-2nd c.].

Skarsaune, Oskar. *The Proof from Prophecy: A Study in Justin Martyr's Proof-Text Tradition: Text-Type, Provenance, Theological Profile.* Supplement to *Novum Testamentum* 56. Leiden, Brill, 1987.

Skinner, Christopher W. "Misunderstanding, Christology, and Johannine Characterization: Reading John's Characters Through the Lens of the Prologue." In *Characters and Characterization in the Gospel of John,* edited by Christopher W. Skinner. London: Bloomsbury T&T Clark, 2013.

Slusser, Michael. "How much did Irenaeus learn from Justin?" In *Studia Patristica* XL, edited by F. Young, M. Edwards & P. Parvis; Leuven: Peeters, 2006.

Smith, Morton. *Jesus the Magician.* San Francisco: Harper and Row, 1978.

Socrates. *Ecclesiastical History.* Translated by A.C. Zenos. In *Nicene and Post-Nicene Fathers, Second Series, Volume 2: Socrates, Sozomenus: Church Histories.* Edited by Philip Schaff and Henry Wace. 1890 [c. 440].

Steenborg, M. C. "God." In *The Routledge Companion to Early Christian Thought.* Edited by D. J. Bingham. London: Routledge, 2010.

Stevenson, J. A. *New Eusebius.* Revised by W. H. C. Frend. London: SPCK, 1987 [1957].

Stökl Ben Ezra, Daniel. " 'Christians' observing 'Jewish' festivals of Autumn." In *The Image of the Judaeo-Christians in Ancient Jewish and Christian Literature.* Edited by Peter J. Tomson and Doris Lambers-Petry. Mohr Siebeck, 2003.

Stroumsa, G. A. G. "Christ's Laughter: Docetic Origins Reconsidered." *Journal of Early Christian Studies* 12:3 (2004).

Stuhlmacher, Peter. *Paul's Letter to the Romans: A Commentary.* John Knox, 1994.

Swanson, Reuben J. *New Testament Greek Manuscripts: John.* Sheffield: Sheffield Academic Press, 1995.

Tatian. *Address to the Greeks.* Translated by Molly Whittaker. In *Tatian: Oratio ad Graecos and Fragments.* New York: Oxford University Press, 1982 [c. 155–65].

———. *Diatesseron.* Translated by Hope W. Hogg. In *The Ante-Nicene Fathers Volume 9: Recently Discovered Additions to Christian*

Literature. Edited by A. Cleveland Coxe and Allan Menzies. New York: Christian Literature Publishing Co., 1896–97. [c. 170–75].

Teixidor, Javier. "Palmyra in the Third Century" in *A Journey to Palmyra: Collected Essays to Remember Delbert R. Hillers.* Edited by Eleonora Cussini. Leiden: Brill, 2005.

Tertullian. *Against Marcion.* Translated by S. Thelwall. In *The Ante-Nicene Fathers: Volume 3 - The Writings of Tertullian,* edited by Alexander Roberts, James Donaldson, and Arthur Cleveland Coxe. New York: Christian Literature Publishing Co., 1885 [early 3rd century].

Tertullian. *On the Flesh of Christ.* Translated by Ernest Evans. In *Tertullian's Treatise on the Incarnation: The Text Edited with an Introduction, Translation, and Commentary.* London: SPCK, 1956 [c. 206].

———. *Prescription Against Heretics.* Translated by Peter Holmes. In *The Ante-Nicene Fathers: Volume 3 - The Writings of Tertullian,* edited by Alexander Roberts, James Donaldson, and Arthur Cleveland Coxe. New York: Christian Literature Publishing Co., 1885 [early 3rd century].

Testament of Isaac. Translated by F.W. Spinespring. In *The Old Testament Pseudepigrapha: Volume 1: Apocalyptic Literature and Testaments,* edited by James H. Charlesworth. Peabody: Hendrickson, 1983 [2nd c. CE].

Testament of Job. Translated by R.P. Spittler. In *The Old Testament Pseudepigrapha: Volume 1: Apocalyptic Literature and Testaments.* Edited by James H. Charlesworth. Peabody: Hendrickson, 1983 [1st c. BCE–1st c. CE].

Thatcher, Tom. "Anatomies of the Fourth Gospel: Past, Present, and Future Probes." In *Anatomies of Narrative Criticism: The Past, Present, and Futures of the Fourth Gospel as Literature,* edited by Tom Thatcher and Stephen D Moore. Atlanta: Society of Biblical Literature, 2008.

Theodoret. *A Compendium of Heretical Mythification* [a.k.a. *The Discernment of Falsehood and Truth*] [selections]. Translated by

István Pásztori-Kupán. In *Theodoret of Cyrus*. New York: Routledge, 2006 [c. 452–53].

———. *The Ecclesiastical History*. Translated by Blomfield Jackson. In *A Select Library of Nicene and Post-Nicene Fathers, Second Series, Volume 3: Theodoret, Jerome, Gennadius, Rufinus: Historical Writings, Etc*, edited by Philip Schaff and Henry Wace. New York: The Christian Literature Co., 1892 [mid-5th c.].

Theophilus of Antioch. *To Autolycus*. Edited and translated by Robert M. Grant. In *Theophilus of Antioch: Ad Autolycum*. New York: Oxford University Press, 1970 [c. 180].

Thiede, Carsten Peter and Matthew D'Ancona. *The Jesus Papyrus*. London: Weidenfeld & Nicolson, 1996.

Thompson, G. H. P. *The Gospel according to Luke*. Oxford: Clarendon Press, 1972.

Thompson, Marianne Meye. *The God of the Gospel of John*. Grand Rapids: Eerdmans, 2001.

Thompson, Thomas R. "Nineteenth-Century Kenotic Christology: The Waxing, Waning, and Weighing of a Quest for a Coherent Orthodoxy." In *Exploring Kenotic Christology*, edited by C. Stephen Evans. Vancouver: Regent College Publishing, 2006.

The Tripartite Tractate. Translated by Geoffrey S. Smith. In *Valentinian Christianity: Texts and Translations*. Oakland: University of California Press, 2020 [3rd c.].

Tuckett, Christopher. *2 Clement: Introduction, Text and Commentary*. Oxford: Oxford University Press, 2012.

Tuggy, Dale. "On Bauckham's Bargain." *Theology Today* 70:2 (2013).

———. "What John 1 Meant (UCA Conference 2021)." YouTube. November 12, 2121. https://youtu.be/nb4TogqyTrw

van Brussen, Jakob. *Jesus the Son of God; The Gospel Narratives as Message* [*Het evangelie van Gods zoon: Persoon en leer van Jezus volgens de vier evangeliën*]. Translated by Nancy Forest-Flier. Grand Rapids: Baker Books, 1999 [1996].

van der Watt, J. *An Introduction to the Johannine Gospel and Letters*. London: T & T Clark, 2007.

Van Nuffelen, P. "Two Fragments from the *Apology for Origen* in the *Church History* of Socrates Scholasticus." *Journal of Theological Studies* 56:1 (2005).

Varner, William. "On the trail of Trypho: Two fragmentary Jewish-Christian dialogues from the ancient church." In *Christians Origins and Hellenistic Judaism: Social and Literary Contexts for the New Testament,* edited by Stanley E. Porter and Andrew W. Pitts. Leiden: Brill, 2013.

Vermes, Geza. *The Religion of Jesus the Jew.* London: SCM Press, 1993.

Vinzent, Markus. "From Zephyrinus to Damasus—What did Roman Bishops Believe?" In *Studia Patristica Vol. LXIII: Papers Presented at the Sixteenth International Conference on Patristic Studies held in Oxford 2011, Volume 11: Biblica, Philosophica, Ethica,* edited by Markus Vinzent. Walpole: Peeters, 2013.

Walzer, Richard. *Galen on Jews and Christians.* Oxford: Oxford University Press, 1949.

Warns, R. 'Untersuchungen zum 2. Clemensbrief.' PhD diss. University of Marburg, 1989.

Wenham, John. *Redating Matthew, Mark and Luke: A Fresh Assault on the Synoptic Problem.* London: Hodder & Stoughton, 1991.

Werner, Martin. *The Formation of Christian Dogma: An Historical Study of Its Problem.* London: Adam & Charles Black, 1957.

Westcott, B. F. *The Gospel According to Saint John.* 2 vols. London: John Murray, 1908.

White, Percy E. *The Doctrine of the Trinity: Analytically Examined and Refuted,* 2nd ed. London: Dawn Book Supply, 1937 [1913].

Whiteley, D. G. H. *The Theology of St Paul.* Oxford: Basil Blackwell, 1964.

Wickings, H. F. "The Nativity Stories and Docetism." *New Testament Studies* 23:4 (1977).

Williams, A. Lukyn. *Adversus Judaeos: A Bird's-eye View of Christian Apologiae until the Renaissance.* Cambridge: Cambridge University Press, 1935.

Williams, C. H. " 'I am' or 'I am he'?: Self-Declaratory Pronouncements in the Fourth Gospel and Rabbinic Tradition." In *Jesus in Johannine*

Tradition, edited by Robert T. Fortna and Tom Thatcher. London: Westminster John Knox Press, 2001.

Williams, Sam K. *Galatians.* Nashville: Abingdon Press, 1997.

Wingren, Gustaf. *Man and the Incarnation: A Study in the Biblical Theology of Irenaeus* [*Människan och Inkarnationen enligt Irenaeus*]. Translated by Ross Mackenzie. Edinburgh: Oliver & Boyd, 1959 [1947].

Witherington III, Ben. *The Christology of Jesus.* Philadelphia: Fortress Press, 1990.

Wrede, William. *The Messianic Secret* [*Das Messiasgeheimnis in den Evangelien*]. Translated by J. C. G. Greig. London: James Clarke & Co., 1971 [1901].

Xenophanes. *Fragments.* Translated by Jonathan Barnes. In *Early Greek Philosophy,* edited by Jonathan Barnes. London: Penguin Books, 1987 [late-6th–early-5th c. BCE].

Young, Frances M. "Monotheism and Christology." In *The Cambridge History of Christianity: Volume 1 Origins to Constantin,* edited by Margaret M. Mitchell and Frances M. Young. Cambridge: Cambridge University Press, 2006.

Ziesler, J. A. *Pauline Christianity.* Oxford: Oxford University Press, 1983.

INDEX

A

Aaron 289

abba 302–3

Abraham 20, 27–28, 132, 164, 223–24, 229–30

Acta/Acta Disputationis (from the synod at Antioch) 37–52

Acts of the Apostles 72, 90, 173, 255, 266, 269, 271, 282, 298

date 283

relationship to Luke 283

1:1 283

2 266

2:14 269

2:22 75, 81, 172–73, 175, 177, 336

2:30–33 65, 269

2:33–36 265, 268–70, 273

4:24–27 265, 268

4:27 277–78

5:30–31 265, 270

10:42 155

13:13 268

13:23–41 265, 270–72

17:34 321

24:5 93

28:30 282

Adam 26–27, 53, 106, 176, 210, 245–48

type of Jesus 246–48

Adoptionism 2–3, 6, 8, 81, 83, 86–87, 91, 115, 117, 132–35, 145, 164, 168, 193, 210, 236–37, 256, 263–78, 279, 305, 307, 309

Adoptionism (*cont'd.*)

vs. Dynamic Monarchianism 3–4, 6, 8

Aelia 61

aeons 28, 156–58, 185–93, 212

Artificer/Creator/Most High 189

Christ 185–87, 189, 191

Church/*Ecclesia* 156–57, 185, 189–90

Desired 189

Jerusalem 158

Jesus 185

Holy Spirit 188–89

Life/*Zoe* 185, 189

Light 188–89, 192

Man/Human/*Anthropos* 156, 185, 189–91

Mind/*Nous* 28, 185

Power of the Highest 188–89

pleroma of 189

primal Ogdoad of 156, 188–89

Wisdom/*Sophia* 186, 189

Word/*Logos* 185–86, 189, 191

Against All Heresies 68, 70, 80, 83–84, 182–83, 186, 189–91

author 68, 182

1 182–83

3 186

4 189–90

5 190

6 182–83

8 68, 70, 72, 79, 84

Akhmim 180

Alcinous 23–24, 311

B

Ball, David M. 222
Bardaisan. *See* Bardesianes
Bardesianes 189, 313
Barnabas, Epistle of 82, 149–53, 166,
 168
 author 148
 date 148–49
 4:14 149, 280
 5:5 149
 5:10 149
 7:3 150
 11:9 150
 16:3–4 149
 19–20 149
 25 149
Barnard, L. W. 21, 199–200, 203
Barrett, Charles Kingsley 220–21
Bartimaeus 296
Basil of Caesarea 49, 314
 Letter 52
 1 49
Basilides 183–85, 188, 191–92, 314
Bauckham, Richard 223, 236, 252,
 296–97
Bauer, Walter 125–27
Baur, Ferdinand Christian 63
Behr, John 30, 37, 40, 45, 50
bereishit 162
Bertrand, D. A. 68, 78
Beryl Apuleius. *See* Beryllus of Bostra
Beryllus of Bostra 6, 39, 61–66, 90, 105,
 110, 117, 119, 307, 314, 323
Bethlehem 285, 287
bishops 37–43, 47, 55–57, 62, 69–72,
 105–6, 120, 137–38, 206–7, 311–
 14, 316–31
Blastus 142, 314
Bligh, John 299–300
Book of Elijah 158
"born again" 227, 229
"born from above" 227

Bostra 61–62, 66, 119, 314, 323
 synod at 62–63
Bovon, François 161
Brown, Raymond 222
Bultmann, Rudolf 222, 224
Buchanan, George Wesley 217
Burney, Charles Fox 217
Burrus, Virginia 43–44
Byzantium 69–70, 89–90

C

Callistus 57, 314
Caracalla 61, 314
Carpocrates 64–65, 91, 133, 186–88,
 314–15
 on Jesus' human soul 64–65, 186
Carrington, Philip 69, 87, 89, 145
Celsus 101, 159, 315
 True Account 159, 315
Celsus Africanus 160, 315
Cerdo 182, 315
Cerinthus 67, 73, 80–82, 86–87, 91, 98,
 111–12, 133, 153, 181, 186–88, 315
Christ. *See* Jesus
Christ (someone other than Jesus)
 180–81, 186–90, 290
 impassibility of 186
Church, the 39, 46, 51–52, 63, 71, 91,
 101, 106, 141, 143–44, 156, 205
 aeon 157
 pre-existence 154–59, 166–67
Cicero 17, 315
Clement of Alexandria 115, 159, 315
Clement of Rome 138, 154, 315
 1 Clement 138, 154
 44.1–6 138
Collins, Adela 268, 273, 275, 277
Coloe, Mary L. 223
Colossians 58, 200, 244, 256
 1:15–20 58, 76, 107, 201, 256–61
 2:3 15

G

K

L

Printed in Great Britain
by Amazon

44100670R00228